# The Matter With Us:

# A Materialistic Account of the Human Predicament

## John Rawles

Pen Press

First published in Great Britain by Pen Press

All paper used in the printing of this book has been made from wood
grown in managed, sustainable forests.

ISBN13: 978-1-907499-63-0

Printed and bound in the UK
Pen Press is an imprint of Indepenpress Publishing Limited
25 Eastern Place
Brighton
BN2 1GJ

A catalogue record of this book is available from
the British Library

Cover design by Jacqueline Abromeit
Based on a sculpture by Cyd Jupe

*For our grandchildren*

Alistair, Anna, Cydonie, Daisy, Felix and Harvey,

whose predicament this is

# Acknowledgements

Family, friends and acquaintances have all contributed much to this book in their conversations and discussions and in their support and encouragement. I am especially grateful to my good friends Jane Bateman, Corinne Carr, David Dearlove, Kevan Rudling and Joan Smith, and my daughter Kate, for their careful reading and constructive criticisms of the whole manuscript, and their exhorting me to find a publisher. In this respect the kind review by Peter Forbes of The Literary Consultancy was most helpful. Most of all I owe an enormous debt of gratitude to my wife, Katharine Mair, who endured book-widowhood and my exposition of the arguments morning, noon and night during the five years it took me to write *The Matter with Us*. Naturally, she was the first to read each chapter, and she was the fairest and firmest of critics. I can't thank her enough.

# About the Author

John Rawles was born in 1938 and took a degree in physiology before training as a doctor. He practised as a consultant physician until 1989 when he relinquished clinical work to concentrate on research. This ranged from computer modelling of the heartbeat to the delivery of immediate care in the community for victims of heart attack. This book was written in retirement and is an extension of his work as a doctor, diagnosing the ills, not of individuals, but of humankind and contemporary society. He lives in Cornwall with his second wife, and between them they have five children and six grandchildren.

The bridge of spaceship Earth is deserted; nobody is in charge. Down below, the passengers are fighting amongst themselves, damaging the craft, looting the stores, and squandering the reserves. As a fellow passenger it gives me no pleasure to report what I see. What's the matter with us that we should behave like this? Surely, we would all prefer that many future generations should continue to enjoy the cruise of a lifetime in safety, comfort and good health; but that seems unlikely. And it was such a beautiful ship.

# Contents

# Introduction

Dust thou art, and unto dust shalt thou return.
*Genesis 3:19*

This is the story of matter. It starts with a bang; the biggest bang imaginable; *the* Big Bang – yet one which was small, silent and went unheard.

It continues with the formation of the sun, by far the heaviest object in the solar system, yet made from hydrogen gas, the lightest of elements.

Then comes planet Earth which, to begin with, was without form and void.

But in an exciting twist, the story then becomes our story, the story of our matter, matter which comes to life. For life, microscopic at first, colonises planet Earth from subterranean depths to the tops of mountains, and fills the skies with breathable air.

Many pages later matter becomes us, and we inherit its amazing properties of unpredictability and creativity. Our species of matter, *Homo sapiens*, differs from other species in walking upright, and having a big brain.

A story within the story explains how, by using our big brain, we have been able to rewrite our history, so that we can now tell it roughly how it is, which is not always how we would like it to be. But in facing up to our challenging human situation we have the chance to be the heroes of this thrilling saga, which is one of amazing coincidences, dreadful setbacks, lucky breaks and fantastic opportunities for happiness and enjoyment. But then, towards the end of the tale, a whole heap of stuff just happens to us.

Which is where we are now, in a predicament. The end of this epic is a cliff-hanger – nobody knows how it's going to end, and it's touch and go. This is where we, inhabitants of planet Earth, can turn storyteller and do our bit to change the ending from *Epilogue* to *New chapter*.


**How to Use This Book**

The story of matter, from the Big Bang to the election of Barack Obama, is told in the following chapters. It is a materialistic account which rejects any religious or spiritual 'top-down' explanation for our being here. However, every culture needs to have a creation myth – an account of how we and our home on this planet came into existence, and one which fits the current state of knowledge and our contemporary world view. In this book a modern creation myth is developed in parallel with the main story in 21 boxes interspersed through 10 chapters. It is a 'bottom-up' account based on systems theory, chaos and emergent properties. Each box makes one or two simple points, and is complete in itself.

The human predicament is sketched in the Frontispiece, which shows some of the complicated interactions between nine major problems selected for consideration. A detailed account of these problems is given in the final *Epilogue, or New Chapter?* together with some suggestions for action.

Throughout the text numbered superscripts refer to sources listed at the end of each chapter. A superscript in bold refers to an additional explanatory note.

There is a comprehensive index enabling readers to trace the development of various themes through the book.

# Chapter 1

# The Big Bang

In the beginning God created the heaven and the earth. And the earth was without form, and void; and darkness was upon the face of the deep. And the Spirit of God moved upon the face of the waters. And God said, Let there be light: and there was light. And God saw the light, that it was good: and God divided the light from the darkness. And God called the light Day, and the darkness he called Night. And the evening and the morning were the first day.[1]

## Big Bang Basics

In the beginning was the Big Bang. The Big Bang is, of course, a metaphor. It is a metaphor for the moment when the whole mass of the universe exploded from an infinitesimally small point, whose density was infinitely great, and temperature unimaginably hot. The 'Big' of Big Bang is therefore symbolic, representing not size but importance: the Big Bang was certainly a momentous event, since had it not occurred there would now be nothing: no space, no time, no matter, nothing. The Bang, too, is metaphorical, because a bang is a sound, a pressure wave transmissible through a gas, which can be heard at a distance as a sudden noise. But there was nothing and nobody outwith the Big Bang itself to appreciate the magnificence of the awesome event which marked the origin of space, time and matter. The Big Bang was small, silent and went unheard.

The initial explosive expansion of the universe started about 14 billion years ago. About one hundredth of a second after its commencement the temperature was 100,000,000,000°C.[2] This raw energy gave rise to a number of elementary particles such as electrons and positrons, some of which, having been generated from energy, proceeded to annihilate each other yielding up their energy again. Also created at this time were photons, or particles of light. The universe then was expanding rapidly in all directions, but was still a dense, hot, cosmic soup of energy and elementary particles that materialised, collided with each other, and vanished. It was far too hot for the formation of atoms, although there were some protons and neutrons from which atomic nuclei of hydrogen and helium began to be formed some three minutes later when the temperature had cooled to a mere 1,000,000,000°C.

It was not until 300,000 years later that surplus electrons that had not been annihilated combined with nuclei to form atoms of hydrogen and helium in proportions of about 10:1. At this time, when its temperature had fallen to 6000°C and photons of light were no longer colliding with electrons and other charged particles, the universe became transparent, and light travelled unhindered in all directions. The distribution of matter and light in this early universe was not quite homogeneous, and over the next billion years, because of their increased gravitational pull, the denser areas attracted more matter to themselves to become the first stars, clustered together in protogalaxies. The matter in the universe now consisted almost entirely of hydrogen and helium, with none of the heavier elements of which the most important from our point of view is carbon, an essential component of all things living. Chemical elements were, and still continue to be, created by nuclear reactions in stars. Hydrogen is converted to helium, and helium to carbon, in nuclear fusion reactions releasing energy which we appreciate as starlight, or sunlight in the case of our local star. As a star starts to die from lack of fuel, it collapses in on itself and may burn more brightly for a while. Increased pressure and temperature in its interior create conditions in which are formed the heavier elements of the periodic table. Finally, it may implode and then disintegrate into cosmic debris which is scattered throughout the universe, to condense later by mutual gravitational attraction to form new stars. In this way light elements may be alchemised into heavy elements by repeated passage through various nuclear solar furnaces.[3]

The formation of our solar system within the galaxy we know as the Milky Way is relatively recent cosmic history, occurring less than 5 billion years ago.[4] The first life-forms materialised on earth quite soon after, some 3-4 billion years ago, but *Homo sapiens* did not put in an appearance until about 100 thousand years ago. So recent is our arrival compared with the immense period of time since the Big Bang, that if the entire history of the universe is represented as the distance between the fingertips of two outstretched arms, then human existence could be eliminated with a single stroke of a nail file.[5]

Baldly stated, the Big Bang story seems literally incredible. For a start, how could we possibly know what happened in the far reaches of space and time? How could the immensity of the universe be contracted to a single point? How could it have originated from nothing? How can we believe such an astonishing tale?

For a wonderfully readable account of the development of the Big Bang model, the reader is referred to *Big Bang* by Simon Singh, from which many of the cosmological facts in this chapter have been taken. The project of this book, however, is not simply to recount the history of the universe, a history which tells of our advent, and, from our perspective, will perhaps culminate in our self-destruction, but rather to reach an understanding of our human situation. To this end we need an insight into the way in which we reason and how we acquire knowledge of the world

# Box 1

## Systems

A recurring theme throughout this book will be that of systems and their emergent properties. A system is a collection of items, many of which will be the same sort of thing, and which interact with each other. The first system to be considered is that of the universe soon after the big bang, consisting simply of hydrogen and helium atoms. Hydrogen is the simplest of elements, with helium second, two gases that are so much lighter than air that a balloon filled with either floats upwards into the sky and out of sight, apparently weightless. In fact, both gases are so light that let free they escape from the earth's atmosphere and disappear into space. Hydrogen and helium atoms in the early universe interacted with each other by means of gravity. The gravitational attraction between two bodies is proportional to the product of their masses, divided by the square of the distance between them (Newton's law of gravity). We are familiar with the gravitational pull of the immense mass of the earth acting on objects on the earth's surface. Compared with the earth's gravitational pull, that between individual atoms of hydrogen and helium acting over the huge distances present even in the early universe was unimaginably slight. Nevertheless, this exceedingly weak interaction of atoms with each other across great distances had enormous consequences. Hydrogen and helium were distributed throughout the young universe, but the distribution of gas was not quite homogeneous, and over billions of years regions with greater density attracted more atoms to themselves, increasing the concentration there, and accelerating the attraction of yet more gas, resulting ultimately in the formation of thick clouds of hydrogen and helium in protogalaxies. The continuation of the same process of gravitational attraction led to dense accumulations of hydrogen in stars, at the centres of which the gravitational pressure was so high that hydrogen atoms were fused into helium and other elements, with the release of immense amounts of heat and light energy. Thus it was that a universe with a whole array of new classes of objects with distinctive properties, from atomic elements to galaxies, emerged as a consequence of the infinitesimal gravitational interaction of atoms of the simplest elements.

In a system with emergent properties, the whole is greater than the sum of the parts: new properties arise that are not present in the components of the system, but derive from, and can be explained in terms of, interactions between the components. Emergent properties arising from complex natural systems are often wonderfully unexpected. Manmade systems may have emergent properties that are unintended and unwelcome.

we live in. In this regard, the early history of the universe provides us with an epic case study of how we come by knowledge and understanding, a method of knowing that some people might call scientific, but which I would suggest, is the only way we can hope to attain a simulacrum of truth.

## How Do We Know About the Big Bang?

Cosmological knowledge has been accumulating since before the beginning of history. By the third century BCE the Greeks knew that the earth was a sphere, and had made remarkably good measurements of the circumference of the earth and its distance from the sun and the moon.[6] The 16th century saw the Copernican revolution, when the earth-centred model of our solar system was challenged and eventually overturned; the planets, including Earth, were thereafter considered to orbit the sun. Hitherto, the only orbits thought fitting for heavenly bodies were perfect circles, but Kepler redefined planetary orbits as elliptical, basing his choice of axes on careful observations made by astronomer Tycho Brahe. Galileo, using a x60 telescope of his own design, was the first to observe that the phases of the planet Venus were just as predicted by Copernicus, providing confirmation of the Copernican sun-centred model.[7] As is well known, Galileo was subsequently found guilty by the Inquisition, his heresy being to refute the geocentric Ptolemaic system that had been adopted by the Church. This system was apparently supported by the Biblical statement that 'the world also shall be stable, that it be not moved', and the account of God causing the sun to stand still in the sky, so as to give Joshua light and time to complete the slaughter of Israel's enemies.[8,9] Galileo died in 1642 while still under house-arrest.

In the same year that Galileo died, Newton was born, of whom Alexander Pope wrote:

> Nature, and Nature's laws lay hid in night.
> God said, let Newton be! and all was light.

6

Newton's laws of motion and his law of gravity provided a unifying account of physics and the solar system that went unchallenged for more than two centuries.

Knowledge of the cosmos at that time was acquired largely through direct sensory experience of distant light from the night sky: as the old proverb has it, 'seeing is believing'. The development of bigger and better telescopes increased astronomers' visual acuity manyfold, resulting in major advances in cosmology. As they looked beyond our solar system, astronomers discovered that the sun is but one star among millions in the galaxy of the Milky Way, and our galaxy is but one among countless others scattered throughout space. But how quickly did light from distant objects reach us? Is its speed infinite, so that we can observe distant events as they happen, or is it finite, so that we are seeing what happened some time in the past? This question was settled in the 17th century when the speed of light was shown to be finite; its present accepted value is 300,000 km/s, or 186,000 miles per second.[10] Using this value, distances in the universe came to be measured by how far light would travel in a year, a light year being equivalent to $9.5 \times 10^{12}$ km or nearly 6,000,000,000,000 miles. The Hubble space telescope is now able to penetrate several billion light years into the far distant universe, showing us what the universe used to be like billions of years ago.[11] The appreciation of the immense dimensions of the universe, the innumerability of its galaxies and stars, and the enormous lapse of time since its origin, has led to a drastic reappraisal of our position within it: from being inhabitants of the most important object at its very centre, we earthlings find ourselves relegated to being inconsequential latecomers occupying an insignificant peripheral position in a universe of unimaginable immensity.

Until the early years of the 20th century, cosmology was largely an observational science with little theoretical underpinning. But Einstein's theory of relativity on the one hand, and the development of quantum theory on the other, resulted in a sea

Box 2

Gravity

Under the influence of gravity, 99% of the matter in the solar system came to be in the sun, with the remainder spinning around it as a disc of gas and dust from which the planets formed by accretion. Newton's laws of motion and of gravity describe how the matter of the solar system now behaves in an orderly fashion such that the movements round the sun of the earth and the other planets are accurately calculable to the second. Newton's law of gravitation is written as $F = G\ (m_1 m_2/d^2)$ where F is the force of gravity between masses $m_1$ and $m_2$, d is the distance between the centres of both masses, and G is a universal constant. The force, F, being proportional to the product of $m_1$ and $m_2$, is indicative of the mutual attraction of gravity, which is always a two-way affair, though in the case of ourselves and the earth it is a lopsided relationship: the earth's attraction of us to itself is very much stronger than our attraction of it to ourselves. The force of gravity appears also to act instantaneously at a distance, though it becomes exponentially weaker as the distance increases. Newton's first law, known also as the law of inertia, states that in the absence of outside forces, the momentum of a body remains constant: a body which is still will stay in place until acted on by a force, and one which is moving will continue to move in a straight line until forced to change its speed or direction. This inertia is also a gravitational effect, being due to the mutual attraction between the mass of the body and that of the rest of the universe distributed in all directions around it.

The orbit of any single planet is an ellipse, being the merger of the trajectory imparted to the planet when it was first formed (law of inertia), and its course towards the sun, to which it is drawn by the sun's gravitational pull (law of gravity). Small perturbations of this orbit are caused by gravitational interactions with other orbiting planets. Indeed, anomalies in the orbit of Uranus led to the prediction of an as yet unseen planet, Neptune, whose visual discovery in the predicted position was a confirmation of Newtonian theory. Thus, the mutual gravitational attraction described by very simple laws, and operating to begin with at an atomic level, and later at a planetary level, has resulted in the self-organisation of matter and the imposition of order on chaos. The regular occurrence on earth of day and night, summer and winter, is an emergent property of the matter of the solar system.

change in physics and cosmology. Just as simple geometry had enabled the Greeks to extrapolate from their terrestrial measurements and extend them to the sun, so relativity extended our perception to the outer reaches of space and time, while quantum theory expanded our insight in the opposite direction, into invisibly small atoms of matter.

The special theory of relativity (1905) specifies that the speed of light in a vacuum is the same for all observers, overturning as a consequence the commonsense notion that time is the same for all observers. The theory correctly predicts that the time shown by a clock on a high speed spacecraft is slow relative to that shown by a clock on earth. The faster the spacecraft goes, the slower the clock, until at the speed of light the clock is stationary. If you could hitch a lift on a photon, you could travel anywhere in the universe instantaneously, or so it would seem to you. Einstein's general theory of relativity (1915) showed that energy and mass were related by the famous $E=mc^2$ equation, and that the force of gravity results from a warp in space-time, revolutionary ideas that are still difficult to grasp.

At the other end of the scale of things, quantum theory confirmed the long-postulated existence of atoms, and elucidated their fine structure of a nucleus and encircling shells of electrons. The theory has extensive ramifications, explaining as it does the properties of chemical elements and their position in the periodic table, as well as the spectrum of emitted light which characterises each element when it is heated.[12] Quantum theory and relativity have something very significant in common: light. It is light that links these theories of the very small with the very large. Light, whose constant velocity is at the heart of relativity, is an elementary particle emitted as a result of sub-atomic events, for which quantum theory provides an explanation.

Spectroscopy, the study of light spectra, had been established in the latter half of the 19th century before its basis in quantum theory was understood. Applied to the light from the sun and from other stars, the spectroscope had revealed the same characteristic patterns which are produced by chemical elements on earth; it was therefore concluded that earth and stars are all made of the same basic elements.

In 1929, at a time when theoretical physics was in turmoil, the astronomer Edwin Hubble published, in a paper entitled *A Relation Between Distance and Radial Velocity Among Extragalactic Nebulae*, the observation which is the cornerstone of the Big Bang theory.[13] He and his assistant reported that spectra from distant galaxies show a so-called 'red shift' – a displacement of spectral lines towards the red end of the spectrum where the wavelength of light is longer. This implies that the galaxies showing this effect are receding away from observers on earth, going deeper into space. Moreover, every galactic velocity is proportional to the distance from our own galaxy, the Milky Way. Assuming that recession velocities have always been the same, the implication of this correlation between velocity away from us, and distance away from us, is that at some time in the past all the galaxies were in close proximity to each other.

To understand this better, consider four walkers of differing fitness, N, S, E and W, all setting off at the same time from the same spot towards the four points of the compass, and walking at 1, 2, 3 and 4 km/h respectively. At any time thereafter their distances from the start would be proportional to their speeds. Thus, after 5 hours, they would be 5, 10, 15 and 20 kilometres from their point of departure, and all four walkers would be increasingly distant from each other. Assuming speed and direction to have been constant, we could deduce from their locations and speeds when and where they had commenced walking. In the case of the receding galaxies, the red shift of their light is due, not to their flight through space, but rather to the expansion of space itself. Nevertheless, the implication is the same, that at some time in the past the universe began to expand in all directions from a single point in time and space – the singular event known as the Big Bang.

Box 3

Light

Emergent properties of a system arise from interactions between the system's components. In the
system that is the universe, besides gravity, another
means by which matter interacts with itself is light.
According to the little-known 'transactional interpretation' of quantum mechanics, the transmission of
light is also a two-way process, somewhat like the
mutual effect of gravity. Although it appears strange
at first encounter, the theory goes a long way to de-
mystify quantum mechanics, eliminating any necessity for the involvement of consciousness in quantum events as some physicists have proposed.

An atom in a distant sun is energised and ready to
give off a photon of light. It transmits an offer wave in
all directions. Entering your eye, the offer wave finds
a receptive atom in your retina, which returns an acceptance wave, the receipt of which by the transmit-
ting atom confirms the transaction – the transfer of
a photon. The energy of the photon is passed from
transmitter to receiver and triggers a nerve impulse
which travels from your eye to your brain: you see
a twinkling star. From the point of view of the photon, the two-way transaction is instantaneous because at the speed of light, time stands still. From
our standpoint, the offer wave travels forward in
time and space from transmitter to receiver, while
the acceptance wave travels backwards in time and
space, to arrive back at the transmitter at the same
moment that the offer wave is transmitted. We might
think of this transaction as the simultaneous trans

-fer of positive energy forwards and negative energy backwards. Thus, when we gaze in wonder at the myriad stars in the night sky, in a very real sense we are communing and at one with the universe.

When physicists speak of light they mean electromagnetic radiation, which besides visible light includes ultraviolet, infrared, microwaves and radio waves. All of these varieties of electromagnetic energy are transferred from atom to atom as photons or quanta, involving similar transactional quantum mechanics as just described for visible light. Electromagnetic energy is never transmitted into a void, but is only transferred when its destination has been established. Matter is thus hugely interactive, all the matter in the universe being united in a web of electromagnetic as well as gravitational transactions. This entanglement of matter is an emergent property and is responsible for what Einstein called 'spooky action at a distance', where a change in the quantum state of a particle in one location causes simultaneously a change of state in a related particle at a distance. He did not believe it could occur because it implies there being something which travels faster than light, but such action at a distance has been confirmed experimentally.

Thus, an emergent property has three characteristics: first, it cannot exist in some mystical way independently of the lower level from which it arises. Second, the new property is not just the predictable result of summing the constituent parts of the system. Third, an emergent property is not simply an epiphenomenon or by-product, but it has causal effects on lower level components of the system.

Reference: John Gribbin. *Schrödinger's Kittens*.[14]

Einstein, who had himself constructed a steady state mathematical model of the universe, was sufficiently impressed by Hubble's results to change his mind and support the Big Bang model. In spite of this authoritative endorsement, most astronomers were unconvinced and continued to back a static model, which was assumed to have always existed. And there the matter rested for 30 years or so.

Meanwhile, a group of Big Bang believers, who delighted in the names of Alpher, Bethe and Gamow, showed that conditions prevailing in the first few minutes of the expanding universe could account for the formation of hydrogen and helium in the 10:1 proportions present today.[15] They also calculated that a flood of light, that should still be detectable now, was created at the same time.

The tipping point for general acceptance of Big Bang theory came in 1964 with the serendipitous detection by means of a radio telescope of cosmic microwave background (CMB). This was the 'light' which was formed soon after the Big Bang, whose existence had been predicted by Alpher, Bethe and Gamow nearly 20 years previously. When identified by Penzias and Wilson, billions of years after its formation, CMB was no longer visible light, but a radio signal in the microwave region of the electromagnetic spectrum, exactly as had been predicted.

One final piece of evidence clinched the Big Bang theory. In order to explain the existence of protogalaxies in the young universe, it was necessary to postulate some unevenness in the distribution of light and matter shortly after the Big Bang. This lack of homogeneity should have been imprinted on the light emitted at that time, and should be perceptible now as a variation in the wavelength of CMB received from different parts of the sky. Accordingly, a Cosmic Background Explorer satellite known as COBE was launched in 1989, and three years later the results of its survey of the sky were announced. The predicted fluctuations in CMB were present, providing a strong endorsement of the Big Bang model, which is now generally accepted to be the best account of the formation of the universe.

Altogether this is such a fantastic tale, why on earth should we believe it? And what makes the account given above better than the creation story recorded in Genesis?

Firstly, modern cosmology results from the experience of countless observers over many centuries. By 'experience' is meant direct sensory experience: seeing. Visual acuity has been augmented by the use of the telescope, microscope, camera and computer, but it is still seeing. More recently our vision has been extended by the radio telescope into other sectors of the electromagnetic spectrum. However indirectly, all observations are thus grounded on reality.

Secondly, almost all the observations made by astronomers are repeatable. We can see for ourselves newly discovered asteroids, supernovae and nebulae. We can observe the phases of Venus that convinced Galileo that the earth is not the centre of the solar system. Hubble's red shift is a fact for all to see, and no doubt the results from COBE will be confirmed and extended.

Thirdly, the theories used to explain observations are falsifiable. Such a theory entails predictions which, if confirmed support the theory, and if not constitute a challenge to it.

Fourthly, a theory is also judged on its scope, the extent to which it explains disparate phenomena. Inasmuch as present cosmological theory explains the predominance of hydrogen in the universe, the formation of other chemical elements, the heat and light of the sun, the origin of the moon, the colour of the red planet, the distribution of stars in the milky way, and the presence of background hiss on the radio, it is a good theory. Moreover, it is not the diktat of some unapproachable authority, but it is negotiable. If you have a better theory, put it to the test, it will be considered on its merits.

Using these criteria of a good theory, how does the creation story in Genesis fare? Apart from its incomparable prose-poetry, and its rich patina of history and custom, not well. The six day creation of heaven and earth was not observed, but is given on scriptural authority, which is not negotiable; moreover, there is much evidence against it, unless God has been amazingly devious. The scope of the theory is extremely limited, but it is, however, falsifiable. For 'God saw that it was good'. But it is not good that the earth was made in such a way that there should be droughts or floods or hurricanes. It is not good that there should occur earthquakes, such as the one in 2010 which caused devastation in Haiti, or which destroyed Lisbon in 1755, stimulating Voltaire to write *Candide*, a satirical protest against the evil in the world. The biblical account of the Creation and Fall, however, was never meant to be taken literally, but is a myth whose purpose is to help us understand the human predicament – why human life is filled with suffering, hard labour, agonising childbirth and death. The creation story is a metaphor, and as such, it is a means of explaining something outside of our experience, and therefore difficult to understand, in terms of something familiar. Abstract and complicated concepts are easier to grasp when likened to things and ideas with which we are familiar, familiarity giving us a feeling of understanding. The origin of the earth is quite outside our experience, though we do have knowledge of building homes and gardens. How better to explain creation than as the handiwork of a larger-than-life God? But the Big Bang theory, and not just its epithet, is also metaphoric, the metaphor being mathematics with which astrophysicists, at least, feel quite at home. But whatever the metaphor used, no explanation of creation, whether religious or scientific, should be exempt from critical scrutiny directed at finding the truth, insofar as that is possible.

To recap, the most reliable knowledge is based on reproducible evidence incorporated into a theory which has wide scope and is falsifiable, and which has survived all attempts at its falsification. We now need to look at how we reason, and how our reasoning is to a large extent based on the use of metaphor.

## Metaphor in the Service of Reason

The results obtained by the COBE satellite attest to the veracity of the Big Bang theory, and the extensive media attention following their presentation could be described as a topping out ceremony. For the Big Bang explanation of the origin of the universe constitutes the pinnacle of a great cathedral, an edifice that has been under construction for centuries, a temple dedicated to knowledge of the cosmos. The foundations of the building were laid by the Greeks, and in the ensuing centuries layer after layer of observations were added. The superstructure is buttressed by well-grounded theory, and observation and theory are cemented together so solidly that it is inconceivable that the building could now be toppled, strengthened as it is by the overarching theories of quantum mechanics and relativity. The existence today of cosmic background radiation provides a central plank in the argument for the Big Bang, for which Hubbles' discovery of galactic recession provides the corner stone.

The foregoing passage of purple prose illustrates some of the virtues and vices of using metaphor in the service of reason.

Far from being just a poetical or rhetorical device, metaphor permeates our everyday language and thought to such an extent that we are often unaware of it. The very word 'permeate' is associated with an image of a fluid diffusing between the interstices of words as if they were crumbs of soil (! = metaphor).

As indicated above, there are many widely used expressions that relate to the extended metaphor *Knowledge as a Building*. The metaphor works for us all because we have the experience in common of having seen a building under construction. Using metaphor, we describe something abstract and unfamiliar in terms of something concrete and commonplace. A metaphor brings new understanding to a purely factual narration, sometimes carrying inferences that are not present in the raw (!) statement of facts. The metaphor *Cosmology as a Cathedral* draws out a sense of history, tradition and conservatism. Correspondingly, in cosmology there is, indeed, more than a nod (!) in the direction of past masters such as Copernicus or Galileo. In building a cathedral there is upward progress, each stage being built on the preceding one. When we view the completed masterpiece we are awed at the scale of its conception (!), and at its unity, how all its myriad component parts join to form a single, elegant whole. A cathedral, too, is a sanctuary, a place where we are sheltered from the winds of change (!), and where we might expect to find eternal truths.

In this manner, the use of metaphor may evoke an emotional response in a way that the domain targeted (!) by the metaphor does not. Thus, the idea that light is the link between quantum theory and relativity may leave us cold (!), whereas we can enthuse at the sight of the overarching vault of a cathedral. Metaphor breathes passion into reason and brings it alive (!).

The metaphor *Cosmology as a Cathedral* implies another metaphor, that of *Scientific Method as Constructing a Building*, which misses an important point (!), for building is essentially a linear activity, extending upwards by placing layer upon layer, whereas the scientific method, as well as being linear, is also iterative, moving repeatedly between observation and theory. Observation gives rise (!) to theory; theory gives rise to prediction; predictions are confirmed or refuted by observation; refutation results in partial or complete reconstruction of the theory, and so the cycle continues. A scientific theory is therefore judged by its ability to withstand a deliberate attempt to destroy it, which is not the main criterion for judging the merits of a wall put up by a builder. Another important feature of a good scientific theory is its scope, its ability to provide an explanation for a wide range of disparate phenomena.

We see then that some key features of the scientific method are lacking in the metaphor *Scientific Method as Constructing a Building*, and metaphoric reasoning, because of its imprecision may be incoherent or even contradictory. Yet the splattering (!) of exclamation marks in the preceding paragraphs indicates that metaphors are extensively used in ordinary discourse, and they are often used in science, in spite of their limitations. Newton, after studying the refraction of light, concluded that light was propagated as a wave. The use of this metaphor carries the implication that even in a vacuum there is an invisible substance, the luminiferous ether, in which waves occur: it is obvious, is it not, that there cannot be an undulation of just empty space. Now the earth, in its rotation round the sun, is travelling at 100,000 km/h through ether-filled space, causing a sort of ether draught. It follows that the speed of light through the ether measured across the direction of travel should differ from that measured along the direction of travel. This prediction, however, was shown to be false in a famous experiment by the Michelson-Morley duo.[16] The use of the metaphor *Light Propagating as a Wave* had given rise to a serious flaw in the concept of space. The metaphor, however, has been retained, but its inference, that space is filled with luminiferous ether, has been abandoned.

Another example of a misleading metaphor is that of *Atoms as Solar Systems*: the forces at work in the atom and its metaphorical equivalent are totally different, gravity having no part to play at atomic level. As science writer John Gribbin writes:

> The point is that not only do we not know what an atom is 'really', we cannot ever know what an atom is 'really'. We can only know what an atom is like. By probing it in certain ways, we find that, under some circumstances, it is 'like' a billiard ball. Probe it another way, and we find that it is 'like' the solar system. Ask a third set of questions, and the answer we get is that it is 'like' a positively charged nucleus surrounded by a fuzzy cloud of electrons. These are all images that we carry over from our everyday world to build up a picture of what the atom 'is'. We construct a model, or an image; but then, all too often, we forget what we have done, and we confuse the image with reality.[17]

In physics, verbal metaphors of the sort just mentioned are used to convey difficult and unfamiliar concepts, particularly to lay people. Physicists themselves communicate using the language of mathematics, which, as well as being precise, is considered to be objective and universal, even to be part of the structure of reality. Mathematician and writer Martin Gardner asks:

> If a photon or quark or superstring isn't made of mathematics, pray tell me what it is made of?[18]

In this brief survey of our mental toolkit, we need now to examine more closely one of the most powerful reasoning tools we possess, that of mathematics.

## Mathematics as Metaphor

The idea that the cosmos can be interpreted in terms of number goes back at least as far as Pythagoras, who is credited with discovering the numerical ratios underlying the musical scale and the mathematics of harmony. Numbers were thought to permeate the physical world and some, such as 10, had deep mystical significance. Plato endorsed Pythagorean notions and promulgated the idea that abstract concepts, such as those of mathematics, goodness, or justice, had an objective, independent, timeless existence as 'forms'. The natural world was a manifestation of concordant mathematical relationships waiting to be discovered.

The idea of underlying mathematical order in nature persists to this day. Galileo wrote that the 'Book of Nature is…written in mathematical characters',[19] while Kepler described God as a geometer,[20] and Newton believed in a Designer who was both mathematician and engineer.[21] More recently, Paul Dirac, renowned for his contribution to quantum mechanics, declared that 'God is a mathematician.'[22] The advertising copy for a book by the Astronomer Royal answered in the affirmative the question 'Could everything around us be explained by just six numbers?'[23] According to Deep Thought, in *The Hitch-hiker's Guide to the Galaxy*, the answer to the great question of Life, the Universe, and Everything is encapsulated more economically in just one number, 42.[24]

Plato believed that idealised 'forms' of mathematical objects had an independent extra-mental existence which is more real than the world in which we live. An ardent present-day

Platonist is Roger Penrose who denies absolutely that mathematics is an invention of the human mind, and describes advances in mathematics as being like discovery, as of Mount Everest.[25]

This claim by scientists and mathematicians that mathematics is transcendental and exists independently of human minds is directly challenged by cognitive psychologists Lakoff and Núñez in *Where Mathematics Comes From*:

> Mathematics as we know it is human mathematics, a product of the human mind. Where does mathematics come from? It comes from us! We create it, but it is not arbitrary – not a mere historically contingent social construction. What makes mathematics nonarbitrary is that it uses the basic conceptual mechanisms of the embodied human mind as it has evolved in the real world. Mathematics is a product of the neural capacities of our brains, the nature of our bodies, our evolution, our environment, and our long social and cultural history.[26]

These authors relate how babies are born with a rudimentary arithmetical ability, and are able when only a few days old to differentiate collections of two, three or sometimes four items; humans share this innate, elementary capability with many animal species.[27] We develop the concept of number in infancy as we make collections of similar things, pile bricks on top of each other, use a measuring stick, or count steps along a line. In 'playing' in these various ways, we develop conceptual metaphors by which numbers become 'things', things which these different activities have in common. Learned also at this time are fundamental rules of arithmetic, grounded on reality and experienced by means of our human nervous system. We absorb the basics of mathematics as infants, when we are literally in touch with reality.

Conceptual metaphors acquired early in life are so deeply embedded in our thinking that we may have difficulty in recognising them as anything other than truisms. Nine is said to be bigger than one, although the qualities of nineness or oneness do not have magnitude, any more than colours do. Red light has a longer wavelength than blue light, but red is not longer than blue, neither is *n* bigger than *m*.

Children are taught to extend the concept of number far beyond the inborn limit of four or five, and also in the other direction, to include zero. Another important advance is the conception of numbers as points on a line, which then makes possible the notion of negative numbers placed to the left of a point designated zero. Descartes had the idea of mapping space with two number lines at right angles, zero of each line being located at the intersection or origin. In two-dimensional Cartesian space, positive numbers to the right of the origin are mirrored by negative numbers to the left of the origin. Rotation of a number line through 180° around the origin is equivalent to multiplying by -1, changing positive numbers to negative, and vice versa. So here we have at least four nested metaphors: *Oneness, Twoness, Threeness, etc as Numbers*; *Numbers as Points on a Line*; *Space as a System of Coordinates*; *Rotation in Cartesian Space as Multiplication by -1*.

Algebra is a part of mathematics in which the rules of arithmetic are applied, not to numbers, but to letters which represent any number, $x$ being conventionally an unknown quantity, and $n$ being any positive integer. Algebraic functions may be plotted in Cartesian space, with some remarkable consequences. For example, if the paired values of $x$ and $y$ that satisfy the equation $x^2 + y^2 = 1$ are plotted on squared graph paper, $x$ on the horizontal axis, $y$ on vertical, we have – a circle, radius 1! In this metaphorical nest the merger of the three main divisions of mathematics – arithmetic, algebra and geometry

– gives rise to an equation that represents that most perfect of Platonic forms, the circle.[28]

But can this elegant equation $x^2 + y^2 = 1$ be said in any sense to be present in naturally occurring circles? It is certainly not in the profiles of a full moon, or a water droplet, both of which are two-dimensional representations of spheres. Nor is it in the cross-section of the bole of a tree, or the lesion of ringworm, both of which result from equal outward growth in all directions from a point on a plane. Nor is the equation used in the construction of most man-made circles, from ancient rings of stone, to crop circles or school book geometry. These involve the rotation of a radius around a centre point, the radius being a rope or a pair of compasses, and not necessarily involving any numbers at all.

So the book of nature is not written in mathematical characters, at least, not in any literal sense, which is what it would need to be for this claim to be more than a charming metaphor. Mathematics, rather than being woven into the stuff of reality, is just a man-made language used in an attempt to describe reality. The close fit of mathematics to reality is made in the minds of physicists, who comprehend both mathematics and the regularities of nature. Regular planetary movements are not determined by mathematics but merely described by it. But even here mathematics has its limitations. Newton's laws of motion accurately describe the relative motion of the sun and a planet such as Earth, which each revolve around a point which represents the common centre of mass of the system consisting of just these two bodies. But with a more complicated system with three or more substantial bodies of sufficient size for them all to be mutually attracted, the equations of motion are insoluble – even in theory – and their orbits cannot be calculated. This is known as the n-body problem.

There are other arguments which counter the grandiose claims of mathematicians for their subject.[29] If mathematics is woven into reality and is waiting to be discovered, there should be just one true mathematics. But in fact, there are many versions of different branches of mathematics, for example, many different geometries with any number of dimensions. There are different theories of number, which are mutually inconsistent; with Grassmann numbers, for example, $AxB$ yields $-BxA$ rather than $BxA$ which is what we obtain with real numbers.[30] Moreover, most of the mathematics that has been done in the history of the discipline has no physical correlates at all, so it cannot be said to be external to human beings. Mathematics, far from being transcendental, has a human face.

## Summing Up

The project of this book is to reach an understanding of how we humans have come to be where we are. The only tools in this quest are knowledge and reason, and both need to be examined for flaws which might lead to false conclusions about the universe we live in, and our relationship with it. The adversarial nature of the scientific method means that new knowledge based on evidence is subject to the critical scrutiny of other scientists who are intent on destroying theories that rival their own; this is the best guarantee we have that such knowledge is reliable.

As for reasoning itself, much of our thinking involves metaphor, and the powerful reasoning instrument of mathematics has a metaphorical structure. Over the millennia much knowledge of the universe we inhabit has been accumulated, and with the latest optical and radio telescopes located in space, observations of the universe as it was billions of years in the past have been made. By means of mathematics it is possible to extrapolate from these observations to within a fraction of a second of the Big Bang. Big Bang theory predicts the existence of cosmic microwave background (CMB) whose discovery provided a powerful endorsement of the theory.

Commencing from a naturalist position, with no presupposition of a deity, we find no grounds in cosmology for invoking one. On the other hand, those who presuppose the existence of a Creator find support for their beliefs in Big Bang theory. It is important that their arguments are examined further because we need to know whether we can look to resources outside ourselves for assistance in solving our many problems. Certain Hellenic and Enlightenment philosophies will also be briefly considered, not because ancient philosophy necessarily has any virtue by being ancient, but because ideas that are still being discussed centuries after they were first propounded may throw light on the direction of thought, not necessarily correct, which we humans find congenial.

# Notes

## Chapter 1: The Big Bang

1. Genesis 1:1-5.
2. Steven Weinberg. *The First Three Minutes: A Modern View of the Origin of the Universe.* Updated edition. New York: Basic Books, 1993, p5.
3. Simon Singh. *Big Bang: The Most Important Discovery of all Time and Why you Need to Know About It.* London: Harper Perennial, 2005: p389.
4. Stephen Hawking. *The Universe in a Nutshell.* London: Bantam Press, 2001, p169.
5. Simon Singh. *Big Bang: The Most Important Discovery of all Time and Why you Need to Know About It.* London: Harper Perennial, 2005: p476.
6. Ibid, p11-18.
7. Ibid, p66.
8. 1 Chronicles 16:30.
9. Joshua 10:13.
10. Simon Singh. *Big Bang: The Most Important Discovery of all Time and Why you Need to Know About It.* London: Harper Perennial, 2005: p90-92.
11. Stephen Hawking. *The Universe in a Nutshell.* London: Bantam Press, 2001, p168.
12. J P McEvoy, Oscar Zarate. *Introducing Quantum Theory.* Cambridge: Icon Books Ltd, 1999.
13. Simon Singh. *The Most Important Discovery of all Time and Why you Need to Know About It.* London: Harper Perennial, 2005: p254.
14. John Gribbin. *Schrödinger's Kittens.* London: Weidenfeld & Nicolson, 1995: p223-247.
15. Simon Singh. *Big Bang: The Most Important Discovery of all Time and Why you Need to Know About It.* London: Harper Perennial, 2005: p306-22.
16. Ibid, p94-98.
17. John Gribben. *Schrödinger's Kittens and the Search for Reality.* London: Weidenfeld & Nicolson, 1995: p186.
18. Martin Gardner. *Are Universes Thicker than Blackberries?* New York: W W Norton & Company, 2003, p63
19. *Galileo.* Britannica CD 99 Multimedia Edition 1994-1999 Encyclopaedia Britannica, Inc.

20. Paul Davies. *The Mind of God*. London: Penguin Books, 1993: p95.
21. Ibid, p76.
22. Stewart I. *Nature's Numbers: Discovering Order and Pattern in the Universe*. London: Weidenfeld & Nicolson, 1995: p55.
23. Martin Rees. *Just Six Numbers: The Deep Forces that Shape the Universe*. London: Weidenfeld & Nicolson, 1999.
24. Douglas Adams. *The Hitch-hiker's Guide to the Galaxy*. London: Pan Books, 1979.
25. Roger Penrose. *The Emperor's New Mind*. Oxford University Press, 1999: p125.
26. George Lakoff, Rafael E Núñez. *Where Mathematics Comes From: How the Embodied Mind Brings Mathematics into Being*. New York: Basic Books, 2000: p9.
27. Ibid, p15-22.
28. Imagine a radius of length 1 rotating around the origin and describing a circle. For any position of the radius a right angled triangle may be constructed of which the radius is the hypotenuse and $x$ and $y$ are the other two sides. By Pythagoras' theorem $x^2 + y^2 = 1^2 = 1$.
29. George Lakoff, Rafael E Núñez. *Where Mathematics Comes From: How the Embodied Mind Brings Mathematics into Being*. New York: Basic Books, 2000: p342-363.
30. Stephen Hawking. *The Universe in a Nutshell*. London: Bantam Press, 2001, p49.

# Chapter 2

# God and the Cosmos

'It would seem that present-day science...has succeeded in bearing witness to that primordial *Fiat lux* uttered at the moment when, along with matter, there burst forth from nothing a sea of light and radiation... Therefore there is a Creator. Therefore God exists!'
*Pope Pius XII*[1]

Knowledge and reason are the only tools at our disposal for reaching an understanding of our human predicament. The most reliable knowledge is based on evidence which is reproducible and which constitutes part of a falsifiable theory which has survived critical attack. Much of the reasoning we employ in constructing theories makes use of metaphor, explaining unfamiliar ideas in terms of the familiar; this use of metaphor, however, carries the risk of confusing the likeness with the reality. Knowledge, like the universe, is ever expanding, and every advance generates new questions. Two questions are commonly asked of the Big Bang: *'What caused it?'* and *'What was there beforehand?'* For many people, including Pope Pius XII, these questions seem to require a supernatural answer, but to some extent these questions arise from the particular metaphors used to describe the event, namely, those of mathematics.

## The Singular Nature of the Big Bang

Earlier, an illustration of Big Bang theory was provided by walkers N, S, E and W setting off at 1, 2, 3 and 4 km/h towards the four points of the compass. From a knowledge of their speed and direction, we can calculate when and where they started walking. Let us imagine that our walkers are the only objects in their flat little universe, whose boundary is a circle centred on the point of departure, and which is being extended by the quickest walker. After an hour, the radius of the universe is 4 km, and its area about 50 sq km. Assuming that our walkers are of average weight, the average downward pressure they exert on their universe is very slight, at about 280 (4 x 70) kg per 50 sq km, equivalent to $5.6 \times 10^{-6}$ kg/m². If we run the mathematical model backwards, the walkers' universe shrinks and the average pressure exerted by the combined mass of their heavenly bodies rises. At 1 minute it has increased to $2.0 \times 10^{-2}$ kg/m², and by 1 second it is 72 kg/m². As we approach time zero, the calculated pressure soars, so that at 1/1,000,000 of a second the pressure is 72,000 tonnes per sq mm. A pressure this high concentrated at a point would needle through the earth's crust to its very centre. We cannot calculate the pressure at exactly time zero because that would involve dividing by nought, which is disallowed by the rules of arithmetic, this point being known as a singularity.

If we now run the mathematical model forwards again, after a fraction of a millisecond our space travellers pop up through the ground with a little bang, and then start moving off in different directions. Observing this event we would ask what caused the little bang, and what happened before it. The mathematical singularity has imposed a discontinuity and an information gap on a process that might well be continuous if described differently. Thus, alternatively, we might imagine that at some time previously, N, S, E and W were converging on the start point to pass close to each other at time zero, with an *'excuse me'* or a *'good day'*, but with no appreciable change of speed or direction. We would not ask of this chance crossing of paths *'What caused that?'* or *'What happened before?'*, because the event would have been largely deprived of all significance. We know, too, that the little bang scenario is impossible because the weight of a body cannot be concentrated at a single point, let alone the weight of all the bodies in the little universe. Nevertheless, if our knowledge of this 'event' was strictly limited to that contained in the mathematical model we might be tempted to consider the model to be the real thing, and to conclude that the present situation had evolved from a little bang.

In the case of the Big Bang, I am not suggesting that it is just a mathematical construct and never really happened. The theory has much circumstantial evidence in its favour, tremendous explanatory scope, and inescapable logic. There is no doubt that 14 billion BCE was a turning point in the history of the universe, a point that is marked in standard Big Bang cosmology by a singularity. But the singularity is not a breakdown of the laws of physics, but rather a breakdown of the language of mathematics that is used to model the physical world – in fact, the breakdown results from the prohibition of division by zero. The information gap imposed by the singularity ensures that we can never know what happened beforehand, not that there was nothing beforehand to know about. Indeed, the claim has been made that time, at least, existed (if that is the right word) before the Big Bang.[2] Another possibility, postulated by string theory – the leading candidate today for a quantum theory of gravity, is that there is a minimum quantum of length, which gets round the singularity and the moment of infinite density. If this is the case, the Big Bang becomes a landmark rather than a *de novo* event, and the question of what caused it becomes inappropriate.

The Big Bang model incorporates a number of constants which determine the way in which the model of the universe evolves. One of these constants represents the force of gravity. If gravity is increased above its actual value, the model universe is predicted to collapse in a Big Crunch after too short a time for stars to form. On the other hand, if it is assigned a weaker value, there is insufficient attraction between matter for it to condense into protogalaxies and stars. Either way, the absence of stars would result in there being none of the chemical elements necessary for life. Similarly with other constants: if they are slightly altered from their measured values, the model predicts that the universe would be lifeless. One view – the so-called weak anthropic principle – is that there is nothing surprising in this: had the universe not been able to support life we would not be here to observe it and ask about its origins. From our *post hoc* position the probability of there being a universe that supports life is 1 – it is a certainty – we inhabit one such. To calculate the prospective probability of such an outcome is much more difficult however.

Six mathematically independent 'constants of nature' have been identified, and, it is claimed, they all show evidence of 'fine tuning', with the result that the universe does furnish the necessary conditions for the evolution of life. The likelihood of all the constants just happening to have the values they do, thus allowing the evolution of life, is infinitesimally small, and has been compared with that of surviving a firing squad of 50 sharpshooters.[3] It is asserted on the basis of this calculation that there must be a Fine-Tuner, and it is the Fine-Tuner's purpose that we should be here. This is the strong anthropic principle.

There are problems with this line of argument, the first being that the constants are described as being 'constants of nature'.[4] As argued above, they are nothing of the sort, but constants in a Big Bang model, or metaphor. It is granted that the model is in some respects a good fit to reality, but that is because it was constructed by humans to be that way, to fit the observed facts. But the book of nature is not written in mathematical characters but in a language to which we have no direct access, and of which we have little understanding. And the sensitivity of the model to changes of its constants may bear no relationship whatsoever to the sensitivity of the real universe to changes in its fundamental forces, if, indeed, it is possible for them to be otherwise than they are. Moreover, because the universe is unique there is no way of finding out whether a universe with different 'constants' would support life. Furthermore, the model on which these suppositions are based is far from being complete and co-herent. Quantum theory has a fudge factor at its heart,[5] and is incompatible with general relativity.[6] Quantum theory does not encompass gravity, which is a central concern of relativity, and much effort is currently being expended on a complete Theory of Everything (TOE) that will resolve the inconsistency between the two theories, an inconsistency which assumes great importance in the early moments of the Big Bang when strong gravitational effects encounter subatomic dimensions.

There is another deficiency of Big Bang theory which must surely have a bearing on the calculation of the likelihood of our being here: the theory only accounts for a small propor-tion of the matter in the universe. The shortfall is known as dark matter, whose nature is quite unknown; its recognition is owed to its gravitational effect within galaxies.[7] There is also dark energy, which is equally mysterious but provides a repulsive force causing the universe to expand at an ever-increasing rate.[8] According to a recent estimate, the composi-tion of the universe is 23% dark matter, 73% dark energy and just 4% ordinary matter.

Box 4

Chaos Out of Order

Few naturally occurring systems are as orderly and predictable in their working as that of the solar system. Most systems are chaotic and seemingly capricious in their operation. Erratic behaviour may, however, arise from simple underlying laws. Imagine a mountain stream flowing smoothly and silently towards a cliff edge where it drops 100 feet in a spectacular waterfall. In the stream all is orderly: the rate of the smooth laminar flow is the same from hour to hour, and there is not a ripple on the water's dark surface. Its speed is greatest in the centre, and under the influence of friction it smoothly tapers down to near stagnation at the water's edge on either side.

What a contrast with the waterfall! There, we see ceaseless turbulence, an ever changing cascade of tumbling white water and spray; the exact trajectory of any water droplet is impossible to predict. Yet the water there is flowing at the same rate (litres per minute) as in the stream above, and the driving force of gravity is unvarying: at a critical speed of flow order gives way to chaos and unpredictability. A similar transition is seen when we turn on the tap at the kitchen sink. To begin with water flows steadily in a clear column, but open the tap a little further and flow becomes turbulent.

Another familiar example of a chaotic system is the weather, notoriously unpredictable in spite of the conformity of atmospheric gases to simple physical laws, and the regularity of the input of solar energy into the system. Another term for a chaotic system is 'non-linear' meaning that when such a system is perturbed, cause and effect are not proportional one to the other, so that once in a while the flutter of an apocryphal butterfly in Peking is said to result in a storm in New York. The way such a system behaves is critically dependent on the starting conditions, and a small difference there may have a disproportionate effect later.

A system may thus be subject to the deterministic laws of physics and yet manifest unexpected and erratic behaviour apparently spontaneously, or following an event that seems too trivial to trigger such a response. Such was the case when large sections of the electricity grid in North America crashed in the summer of 1996 and again in 2003 following minor local breakdowns. Because of the connectivity and non-linear nature of the network a small perturbation became amplified as it passed through neighbouring structures to involve a large swath of the system.

Behaviour that is capricious, unpredictable and sometimes lifelike may arise as an emergent property of inanimate matter in a deterministic system operating by simple laws. Conversely, simple laws operating in a chaotic system may result in matter becoming organised into elaborate and sometimes beautiful structures which have the deceptive appearance of having been designed.

# Arguing from Big Bang to God Almighty

The Big Bang is a godsend to the Church because it appears to be a scientific endorsement of the act of creation, reconciling science and the creation myth found in Genesis. But the Big Bang singularity is factitious, and the questions *'What caused it?'* and *'What came before it?'*, which seem to point to the existence of God, arise in fact from the mathematical metaphors used to model the event. But even if it were not inappropriate to ask what caused the Big Bang, as the philosopher David Hume pointed out in the 18th century, by attributing the creation of the universe to a Creator we do not advance the argument for the existence of God one whit.[9] Nor does giving the Creator an alternative title of First Mover, First Cause or Prime Necessary Being add anything to the explanation of how the universe was created; nor can it be inferred that the Creator has any qualities that might explain why the universe was created. The only knowledge about how the universe came to exist is gleaned from the universe itself. From the fact of the existence of the universe, we cannot make any inferences about the existence of a Creator, nor about his or her nature or intentions, particularly with regard to ourselves.

We need not linger on this point: it follows from the nature of explanation that at the end of every explanatory road there are some fundamental truths about the way things are that simply have to be accepted.[10] The universe just exists, and probably always has. Sometimes, though, a deity is invoked to explain the even more fundamental question of why there is something rather than nothing. This enquiry will be discussed later.

                    *

Prior to Darwin, the most powerful argument for God's existence was the appearance of design in the natural world. The

36

topic of evolution will be considered in the next chapter, but to anticipate a little, we note that Darwin himself wrote:

> The old argument of design in nature... fails now that the law of natural selection has been discovered. We can no longer argue that, for instance, the beautiful hinge of a bivalve shell must have been made by an intelligent being, like the hinge of a door by man.[11]

However, the argument from design now has a new lease of life, applied, not just to the natural world, but to the universe, and to the fine-tuning of the so-called constants of nature. Setting aside for a moment the previous criticisms, that the constants appertain, not to nature but to an incomplete mathematical model, let us take the argument head-on. It is asserted that it is very improbable that the constants would have the values they do if the universe had been left, so to speak, to its own devices. The universe had to be tweaked by the Fine-Tuner to ensure that it would support life. But how do the fine-tunists know what is probable and what is not in an un-tuned universe? The probability of an event is the frequency of that event when the circumstances causing it recur.[12] The probability of tossing heads or tails is the frequency of obtaining heads or tails in a series of coin tosses. In a large enough sample the probability of either is 0.5. Or, with a biased coin, the propensity for throwing heads, a property of the coin rather than the act of tossing it, might be 0.9, but knowledge of its value is only obtained by a series of throws. In the case of the universe, we have only the outcome of a single throw to contemplate; we are therefore in no position to say that this outcome is improbable.

Some cosmological constants are known to an extraordinary degree of precision, for example, Dirac's number, a constant of central importance in quantum theory, is obtained experimentally to the 11th decimal place, and the precision of agree-

37

ment between theory and experiment is spectacular.[13] But this may tell us more about mathematics than about nature: the agreement between measured and calculated values of pi is no less precise.[14] More remarkable is the balance between the nuclear weak force and gravity, which is related to the rate of expansion of the universe, and is critical for the formation of stars and the evolution of life.

> [A] deity wishing to bring about life-permitting conditions would seemingly need to have made two components of an expansion-driving 'cosmological constant' cancel each other with an accuracy better than of one part in $10^{50}$. A change by one part in $10^{100}$ in the present strengths either of the nuclear weak force or of gravity might end this cancellation, disastrously.[15]

This type of remark, ascribed here to philosopher John Leslie, gives an impression of fine-tuning of extraordinary precision, but, in fact, has absolutely no bearing on the likelihood of constants with the same values recurring with multiple reruns of the Big Bang.

There are a great many other examples of harmony and orderliness in the universe, ranging from Newton's laws of motion to the structured formation of a hurricane, or the spontaneous appearance of the elaborate pattern of a snowflake. But just as the fact of the existence of the universe tells us nothing about a Creator, the appearance of order within the universe tells us nothing about an Orderer.[16]

*

There are two further arguments used by religious apologists in support of their belief in the existence of God: revelation, and the evidence of history.

For a person who already believes in the existence of God, a religious experience in which God reveals himself to the believer vindicates his belief. But an account of such an experience to a third party, however intense the encounter may have been, is not acceptable proof of God's existence, being entirely self-authenticated. The claim that the subject encounters an object, that the experience is not purely subjective, is weakened by the fact that Roman Catholics do not report visions of Shiva, nor do Hindus encounter the Virgin Mary.

Also, a state of altered consciousness, in which the subject experiences a dissolution of the subject/object divide and has an intense feeling of being at one with the universe, may be induced by meditation. Such states are associated with characteristic brain scan appearances which suggest possible neurological mechanisms.[17] Also, some patients with temporal lobe epilepsy experience a nearby personal 'presence' during attacks. The 'presence' is usually benign but sometimes evil; similar experiences may be provoked by external electromagnetic stimulation of the temporal lobes. These empirical findings weaken the claims made by mystics that their encounters with the divine are anything of the sort.

Notwithstanding these objections, Christian believers may claim that their daily, personal, religious experience convinces them overwhelmingly of the truth of their beliefs. Theologian John Hick goes further, claiming that the God hypothesis is capable of being verified or falsified.[18] But like other large-scale theories, such as the expanding universe or the theory of evolution, it is not open to confirmation by a single observation, but rather by an accumulation of evidence. Thus, after living their lives according to their respective views of the universe, theists and atheists alike would reach what Hick delicately calls 'the eschatological state', aka death. Then, their respective experiences of heaven or hell would confirm beyond reasonable doubt the reality of God to the erstwhile atheist as much as to the theist. Hick does not say how a negative result would be communicated to participants in this experiential study.

There seems little doubt that the past existence of Jesus of Nazareth is a fact of history. But from this distance in time we can be sure of very little of his life, particularly since the earliest of the Gospels to be included in the canon of the New Testament was not written until three decades after his death.[19] The present form of the New Testament dates from 400 CE, when scores of disputed and theologically incorrect works were rejected for inclusion in it.[20] Besides, even if it were possible to agree criteria for miraculous events, which it is not, the historical grounds for believing in the miracles of the virgin birth and the resurrection are totally inadequate.[21]

The world-wide spread of Christianity is cited as evidence of its truth, but it probably owes as much to the Pax Romana and the conversion of the emperor Constantine as it does to any divine effect. Be that as it may, the life and influence of a man who claimed to be the son of God has no logical bearing on the basic question considered here, of whether or not God's existence can be proved. Jesus' claim to be divine is self-referential, and his undoubtedly powerful effect on his followers in no way constitutes an independent validation of that claim.

The concept of God as a Creator, then, is superfluous, supported neither by reason nor by empirical evidence. We may therefore apply the celebrated razor of William of Ockham (c 1285-1349) who declared that *entia non sunt multiplicanda praeter necessitatem*: entities are not to be multiplied beyond necessity. It is not necessary to invoke a Creator because the origin of the universe can be explained in other ways.

But although the concept of a supernatural providence, being explanatorily redundant, may be excised, there is still a need to explain the origin of the *idea* of the supernatural and the fact of its universal appeal in all cultures and throughout history. Darwin considered that both religion and morality had evolved, and he maintained that the question of the origin of religion was quite distinct from that of whether there exists a Creator and Ruler of the universe.[22] He thought that religion had evolved progressively from fetishism and animism by way of polytheism to monotheism; anthropologists such as James Frazer later took a similar view and anticipated that religion would progress to agnosticism.[23] Others considered that the evolution of religion was driven by its function, which is to provide an explanation for otherwise inexplicable things like death, and also to give meaning to our existence. Sigmund Freud proposed that religion meets the psychological need for a father figure who is not mortal. Karl Marx took the view that religion was a bourgeois device to oppress the lower classes and preserve the status quo in society. Emile Durkeim, the father of modern sociology, considered that religion's function was to promote social cohesion, while another sociological explanation was that religion provided exemplary figures like Jesus who inspire and motivate people to live up to an ideal. According to Max Weber, protestantism inspired hard work – the protestant work ethic – which greatly contributed to the success of capitalism.

Thus, the phenomenon of religion has given rise to a host of theories and remains an important, live topic of research and debate. Although most religious dogmas are intellectually untenable, religious belief is ubiquitous and is intricately bound up with many aspects of our problematic plight. In our endeavour to discover what is the matter with us, we must now consider the nature and origin of religious belief.

# The Origins of Religion

The conclusion reached above is that the concept of the supernatural is redundant, being supported neither by evidence nor reason; and of the various explanations for the existence of religion just mentioned, none is convincing. In a scientific age, however, the ubiquity and persistence of religious beliefs demands an explanation. Although most religious beliefs are intellectually indefensible, religion has been an integral part of all cultures throughout history, and still has wide prevalence today, even among intellectuals. How is it that people can believe that three separate invisible beings are also one and the same? Or that a woman can have a baby without having had sex, and a male baby at that? Or that a carved wooden statuette of the same young woman can heal the sick? Or that a mountain will make the fields fertile if it is fed on the flesh of a sacrificial animal? Or that an ebony tree can overhear what is said nearby, and reveal what it has heard to a shaman?[24]

We need to understand how it is that beliefs of this sort may be held by intelligent, sane and otherwise sensible people. We need to know whether there is a pattern to these beliefs, whether they have a common structure. And we need to know how it is that fanciful religious beliefs have come to be associated with, and give authority to, standards of morality. These are not trivial questions, but neither are they deep mysteries only to be understood by religious people themselves. Rather, they are problems amenable to scientific study.

The most promising approach to these questions comes from cognitive psychology, where research leads to the conclusion that religious beliefs are held, not because they are true, nor because they serve any particular function, but because of the way the brain has evolved and the way it now works.

By virtue of the latter, to believe in the supernatural is not perverse, but it is a perfectly normal thing to do; on the other hand, it is scientific reasoning that is difficult and unnatural, and for many people it is scientific knowledge which is truly incredible.[25] Let us see how psychologists, anthropologists, archaeologists and sociologists propose that religious beliefs have come about. The following synthesis draws particularly on *Religion Explained: The Human Instincts that Fashion Gods, Spirits and Ancestors* by anthropologist Pascal Boyer,[26] *Theological Incorrectness: Why Religious People Believe What They Shouldn't* by D Jason Slone, a professor of religious studies,[27] and *The Prehistory of the Mind: The Cognitive Origins of Art, Religion and Science* by Steven Mithen, archaeologist.[28]

There are three aspects of brain function which working together make it natural and easy for us to hold religious beliefs: the way we think about causality; our tendency, known as anthropomorphism, to attribute human characteristics to non-human things; and the 'stickiness' of religious ideas – how religious notions are fashioned in such a way that they are unforgettable and spread from person to person and from generation to generation.

*Causality:* One of the first concepts that infants learn is that of *Causation as an action to achieve a purpose*. It is put to use, for instance, in repeatedly dropping a spoon from a high chair – the causal association is soon made between the desire to hear the spoon clatter to the floor, and to see his mother pick it up, and the action necessary to cause this pleasing effect. A closely related metaphoric notion is that of *Causes as reasons.* When children are just a little older they are said to be 'teleologically promiscuous', the word 'teleology' being derived from the Greek word *telos* meaning 'end' or 'purpose'. Research psychologists asked children to give an explanation for rocks being 'pointy', and for drawings of imaginary animals having particular features. The children frequently resorted to the notion that things are arranged the way they are, and happen the way they do, 'for a reason'.[29] But it is not just children who are teleologically promiscuous: the idea that there must be a reason for there being something rather than nothing, or that we are put on the earth for a purpose, or that Gaia's purpose is to make the earth habitable, are commonplace.

According to anthropologists Shweder et al, to make sense of suffering from 'acts of God' such as accidents, illness or death, we have recourse to another layer of causes over and above the immediate material ones.[30] In the West these ultimate causes of suffering are said to be psychological (eg repressed wishes), socio-political (oppression), environmental (stress), astrophysical (inauspicious conjunctions of stars and planets) and, importantly, moral (having done wrong). In traditional societies an explanation for suffering may be found in bad interpersonal relationships, taking the form of sorcery or bewitchment. In the East, the moral causation of suffering is expressed as karma, in which the sum of a person's actions in this and previous lives decides their fate in a future existence. Cross-cultural studies indicate that world-wide the three main explanations for suffering are, in order of importance, interpersonal, moral and biomedical.[31] In the first, blame for suffering is attributed to others, but in the second, to the sufferer himself. In the case of biomedical attribution of suffering, the responsibility is outside the realm of human action, and the victim is said to be blameless. These putative causes of suffering due to illness are not mutually exclusive, and the victim of a cancer may feel shame and guilt and believe that he is being punished 'for a reason', such as a misspent youth. Moreover, attributing an illness to a misdeed does not inhibit the sufferer from seeking a biomedical treatment. It is therefore quite possible for a person to entertain two levels of causation at the same time, and by accepting some responsibility for an illness, the victim seems to gain a degree of control over it.

*Anthropomorphism:* It appears that there are five main categories we use to classify things: inanimate natural objects, inanimate man-made objects, plants, animals and humans.[32] Typical examples of these categories might be a rock, a chair, a flower, a dog and a man. A newly encountered object is rapidly put in one of these categories, not by careful consideration of its essential nature, but by seeing that it is more or less like a typical example of its class. Assignment of an object to a category triggers in our minds a host of inferences about it: Inanimate things do not die, whereas plants, animals and humans have a life cycle in which they start from a seed, grow, mature, reproduce and then die and perish. Plants stay put, but animals are capable of moving by themselves. Animals and humans have agency, that is, they have interests in pursuit of which they can will things to happen. And, of course, humans have minds, and they can understand other minds. All these inferences, and many others, are tacitly assumed to apply when something is classified as being in one or other of the five categories above.

We seldom make errors in assigning things to one of these categories, but when we do, most commonly it is to attribute agency to an object which does not have it, for example, in poor light we may mistake a bush for a person. We almost never make the mistake of thinking that a person is a bush. Thus, we have what has been called a 'hyperactive agency detection device'.[33] Going downstairs in the dark we are menaced by intruders lurking in every black corner, and the creak of a floorboard makes our hair stand on end. This hyperactive reflex would have been important during our evolution: better to mistake a rock for a bear than to be mauled by a bear mistaken for a rock. When we lived by hunting, a heightened awareness of the presence of prey, as well as of predator, would also have been evolutionarily advantageous. Projecting a human mind onto a cornered animal would be helpful in anticipating what its next move might be. This evolutionary trick, beneficial in the past, now results in anthropomorphism, in which human attributes are attributed to a non-human creature, or to an inanimate object, or applied just to a situation. Thus, animal behaviour, especially that of primates, is interpreted as if it were human. And we laugh at Basil Fawlty giving his errant car a thorough hiding, knowing that we ourselves have sometimes felt like doing the same, imputing a villainous nature onto something lifeless. But when would we be inclined to invoke a human mind to make sense of a situation? It is under just those circumstances when a straightforward biophysical explanation seems totally inadequate: as after a narrow escape from certain death, when we say 'Whew, thank God, that was close,' with more or less emphasis on the word 'God'. Or when our world is shattered by the sudden death of a partner or the serious illness of a child. At such times the need to find meaning in these devastating events is overwhelming. It is then that we think that these events must have happened for a reason, there is a purpose behind this loss and suffering. And if there is reason and purpose there must be a Mind: we detect the working of a supernatural agent.

***The Stickiness of Religious Ideas:*** In prehistoric times small communities of our distant ancestors, with their well tuned hyperactive agency detection devices, cooperated to make a living for themselves. With similar bodies and bodily development to our own, their embodied minds developed the same concepts of causation as ourselves, endeavouring always to discern the reasons and purposes underlying natural phenomena, drawing on their moral intuitions to do so. Why did my house burn down? Why has my cow aborted? Why has my wife died? Who caused these bad things to happen? What have I done to deserve this? Human imagination has never been lacking, and there must have been an immense range and variety of people's stories to account for these calamities. Most were private musings and never told, or told but once and then quickly forgotten. But amongst all the tales, some were so striking and unlikely that they were unforgettable. They became legends in their communities, and were told and retold from generation to generation, often changing in subtle ways which enhanced their 'stickiness' still further. The apocryphal stories that survive feature objects in the categories described above: a mountain, or a totem pole, or a tree, or a monkey, or a human. But what makes these objects special, and causes them to be revered, is that they all have at least one trait which is counter-intuitive, that would not be expected of an object in its category. So a mountain feeds on the meat of sacrificed animals; the totem pole speaks; the tree listens; the monkey vanishes; and a human ancestor has the remarkable property of surviving his own death and being invisible.

According to anthropologist Pascal Boyer, all supernatural objects from whatever religion fall into one of the five categories mentioned above, and all possess one or more features not typical of its class. It is possession of such unusual characteristics which gives them 'stickiness', ensuring their legendary survival through the ages. The tales that were most widely and repeatedly told had enough counter-intuitive features to be attention grabbing, but were not so far-fetched as to be totally incredible. Another factor influencing the stickiness of these tales is the richness and relevance of the entailed inferences.

One feature that is universally present in all supernatural objects is a mind. Moreover, it is a mind that can read the minds of those who approach it, and it possesses what Boyer calls 'full strategic knowledge'. Strategic knowledge is information relevant to our dealings with other people: who was, is, or might be whose sexual partner; who stole what from whom; to whom and of whom did I speak slanderously. Our own strategic knowledge is always incomplete, and we never know how much other people know that we know about them. But we do not have to explain to the supernatural agent the uncertainties and complexities of our moral dilemmas because the agent, spirit, ancestor, saint, god or whatever, knows all relevant aspects of our moral history and, in addition, has the same moral intuitions as ourselves! The possession by the supernatural agent of full strategic knowledge – its ability to read people's minds including our own – thus has a great many implications, not all of them welcome; nothing is secret. What's more, the possession of a mind implies agency, an agent being able to make things happen to fulfil its desires and bring about its intentions, which may include our adherence to its moral principles, which, happily, coincide with our own. In this account, morality is not owed to religion, but rather, religious beliefs are parasitic on pre-existing moral intuitions, whose authority is enhanced by their being projected onto a supernatural agent.

Religious legends, then, were local and practical, serving the needs of a community to make sense of misfortune and famine, and to celebrate good fortune and plenty. In most communities there would be a story teller who claimed to have a special relationship with the supernatural, and was able to act as an intermediary between the agent and the community. From time to time the deity acted on and through the intermediary in emotionally charged events of great pageantry in which the foundational legend was re-enacted in a prescribed ritual of noise, music and dance. The Christian mass, in which communicants symbolically eat the body and drink the blood of their god, is a good contemporary example. In many religions, Christianity included, a line of priesthood is traceable back to the deity of the foundational legend, the authority to initiate new recruits to the priesthood being henceforth restricted to accredited priests.

While the supernatural agent makes its intentions and desires known only infrequently, and in rituals of great moment, supplicants may make their aspirations known repeatedly, and with little formality. Communication with the supernatural may be made by silent thought or by spoken prayer, often at a local or household shrine where small placatory offerings may be left. Supplicants may plead for pardon for actual wrong-doing, or for an unspecified act which is presumed by the supplicant to have offended the deity and resulted in retribution in the shape of some new adversity. With access to full strategic knowledge, the agent's role in moral issues is predominantly that of an interested party, though the deity may also be credited with moral rules or commandments, or with an exemplary moral character.

*The Branding of Religion:* Some religions, Christianity being a good example, have long been institutionalised, the foundational legend, the doctrine and the practices having been laid down in a holy book and enshrined in rituals administered by an accredited priesthood. Boyer argues that this development was brought about by market forces similar to those that resulted in the setting up of medieval trade guilds. The market for religious services is particularly fragile because the intermediary brokerage of the priesthood, not requiring any great expertise nor any scarce raw materials, is liable to be undercut by unlicensed competitors. One way of dealing with this is to acquire political influence aimed at strengthening a monopoly position and suppressing the competition.

The success of this policy results in the religious product being 'branded' as the one true religion, of uniformly high quality, obtainable at every outlet in its enlarging domain. But while the deity and his proxies become more widely available, they become more abstract and remote, and less responsive to local needs. A rash of theologically incorrect versions of the faith may then emerge as a consequence. This is exemplified in the numerous representations of the Madonna found in Catholic countries. Although the official doctrine is that the Blessed Virgin Mary now lives in heaven, and entreaties may be made to her from anywhere on earth, many supplicants choose rather to undertake a long pilgrimage to be within speaking distance of a particular representation of her, especially if the local Madonna is reputed to have wrought miracles.

Thus, the way religions are practised, rather than preached, supports the claim that the essential feature of a living religion is the possibility of communicating with a superhuman being with access to full strategic information. The most serious challenge to this claim comes from Buddhism, particularly from the variety practised in the West, where it is said to be, not a religion, but an ethical system and a way of life, Buddha having been a philosopher and not a deity. In his book *Theological Incorrectness*, Slone devotes a chapter to summarising the evidence that practitioners of Theravada Buddhism, the more conservative of the two major traditions, conceptualise Buddha as a superhuman agent, and they worship him in hopes of achieving practical benefits.[34] Buddhism is therefore the exception that proves the rule. That communication with the supernatural seems a perfectly natural thing to do is evidenced by the fact that many young children have imaginary companions with whom they converse and have durable and complex relationships, which may well provide training in social and moral skills.[35]

In various ways, then, the perpetuation of the legend, doctrine and practices of a religion is ensured. Most importantly, young children are indoctrinated by their parents, and begin to follow their religious observances including regular communication with the deity, for example, in bedtime prayers, or daily readings from the holy book. The periodic high tension public enactments of the foundational legend reinforce the theologically correct version, while daily personal and informal supplications refresh the myth and make it readily available as an explanation for the vagaries of daily life. Thus a fine day for the Sunday school outing is taken to be an answer to prayer, as is a thunderstorm which washes out the picnic but brings much-needed rain. This is a natural way of thinking, in which there is a strong bias in favour of noticing events that confirm the religious myth, ignoring those that might represent a challenge to it. It is the reverse of the scientific method, where the non-fulfilment of a prediction – that the end of the world is nigh, perhaps – could represent the ugly little fact that slays a beautiful hypothesis. Rather, a myriad of successive life-events, good and bad, all serve to confirm the God hypothesis, which is almost indestructible.

In Western Europe at least, the influence of religion is waning, and a secular humanism is on the rise. Much of our thought, though, is still encumbered with metaphysical baggage dating from a time when the Church held the keys to heaven and hell, and also had a monopoly of learning. In our quest to discover flaws in the way we think, we will now re-examine some venerable ideas that still hold sway.

# Misplaced Concreteness, or the Reification of Essence

We humans have a universal propensity to classify things and people into categories: living/non-living, black/white, Jew/gentile, straight/gay, introvert/extrovert and so on. The collection of properties that an entity possesses that puts it in a particular category is known as its 'essence', in other words, its essential nature.[36] Placing something or somebody in a particular category implies its possession of qualities not possessed by members of an alternative category. The paradigm for a category of things with an essence in common is that of a plant or animal species.

This is one of those ideas which permeates our thinking and has a perennial appeal, and we must pause for a moment to examine it a little further. It is easy to define unambiguously the essence of geometrical figures such as circles or polygons. But when it comes to describing the essence of naturally occurring objects, such as trees, it is more difficult. Trees have a characteristic form, with a trunk and branches which sprout leaves. But how do trees differ from bushes? And is it still a tree when it is dead and leafless, or after it has been felled? The paradigm category, the species, that of *Canis familiaris* for example, also poses problems since it may include members with such a wide range of appearances – from Chihuahua to Afghan hound – that we are hard put to say what exactly they have in common. But the trouble really starts when we try to define the essence of being human. Is it merely membership of the species *Homo sapiens*? Or does that need qualifying, by excluding those who are anencephalic, brain dead or demented? Does being human start at conception, or at quickening, when the mother first notices foetal movement, or at birth, or later still, when rational thought is possible? A lot may hinge on the answer.

Plato expounded these notions of essences and categories and maintained that when we have an idea of a circle that idea approximates to the form of a circle. For Plato, however, the form of an entity such as a circle is not just a typical example, but it is the most perfect specimen that there could ever be. Moreover, it has a transcendental existence which is more real than that of any example that might be found in the world. The notion of essence has been reified and turned into something concrete. A worldly instance of a circle would be but an imperfect representation of the form of a circle, and on a scale of reality it would be at the bottom, with the form of the circle at the top and the mind's idea of a circle somewhere in-between. By the same counter-intuitive argument, Platonic love would be considered more real and more desirable than the imperfect earthy sort!

The form or essence of a circle is something real, and there are many such things: essences of triangles, squares and pentagons, and also of all sorts of animals and plants, as well as of inorganic objects like mountains, plains and rivers. According to Plato, the essences of all these different sorts of things are themselves things; there is a category of things called essences. Plato now arbitrarily decrees that what characterises essences, and what they all have in common, is existence: the essence of essences is existence, or being. Moreover, as we learnt above, the essence of, for example, the category of husbands, is not just a typical husband, but something very different, namely, a perfect husband. So the essence of essences is not only existence but it is also perfection, the Ultimate Good. Note that it is not existence and perfection of any particular thing, just the abstraction. Plato, then, was an idealist, one who believes that ultimate reality lies in the world of ideas. But enough has been said about the concept of essence to put a question mark over it as a basis for a philosophical system.

Aristotle, on the other hand, was a realist. For him the essence of an entity resides not in the world of ideas but in the material world, in the entity itself. When we contemplate an imperfectly drawn circle the essence of it becomes our idea of a circle. In both philosophies the idea in the mind is connected to reality because it grasps the essence, which is transcendental for Plato, but a material property for Aristotle. Direct knowledge of reality is therefore possible in both philosophies, and another feature in common is that the highest and all inclusive category is that of existence or being.

Plato and Aristotle were not the first to pay their respects to the awesome state of Existence or Being. Scholars of ancient religions consider that some of the oldest religious monuments in the world celebrate, not a particular being or god, but Being as an abstraction. [37] The most fundamental religious idea is to be awestruck at the fact of the existence of the world, and to marvel that there is something rather than nothing. How better to express such an idea than to mark out a sculpted tor or a subterranean cavern as being a sacred place in which to enact religious rituals? What could symbolise the durability of existence better than a mountain top or a rocky outcrop in the wilderness? Thus is Existence, the essence of essences, reified. It was an anonymous prophet known as second Isaiah who took the religious idea a further step and personified, or rather deified, Existence or Being as Yahweh, the One and only God.[38]

In this lightning tour of early western thought we pass on quickly to the arrival of Christianity. The opening words of the Gospel according to St John (which is unlikely to have appeared before 125 CE, long after the events to which it relates)[39] are: 'In the beginning was the Word'. The use here of the Greek word *Logos*, meaning the Word of God, or divine reason, marks the beginning of a fusion of Judeo-Christian theology with Hellenic philosophy, in which Platonic and

54

Neoplatonic principles acquired new significance in a Christian context.[40] The specific Christian contributions to this new synthesis were Incarnation and Resurrection, while the Hellenic components were the existence of transcendental eternal perfection, cosmic wisdom, primacy of the spiritual over the material, and the notion of an immortal soul. It is interesting to note just how many ideas in Christianity are owed, not to Jesus, nor to Judaism, but to the Greek philosophers. But there is a tension between the Christian Incarnation, where Jesus was the fleshly vehicle for the Divine, and the Platonic idea of the immortal soul temporarily enfleshed in a profane body. Resolution was largely achieved by St Augustine (354-430 CE), who taught that corruption came not from the flesh *per se*, but from the sin of Adam.[41] This original sin is transmitted from generation to generation through the sexual act, this belief necessitating not only the doctrine of the Virgin Birth of Jesus, but also that of the Immaculate Conception of Mary, his mother. Body and soul as two feuding components of a divided self was henceforth a fundamental western idea.

The Middle Ages saw the joining of faith with reason in an attempt to support revealed truths with rational analysis. Perhaps the best example of this enterprise is given by Anselm (1033-1109) and his notorious 'ontological' argument for the existence of God.[42] Passing over the tortuous logic itself – which has puzzled philosophers for a thousand years and has generally been found wanting – the underlying idea is pure Plato: the mind, by having the idea of God is in touch with the ultimate reality of God's existence, God being the Essence of essences and the Ultimate Good. Stated simply: being able to conceive of God is proof of God's existence.

Here we have a conflation of the stern, jealous, tribal God of the Jews, who is, however, engaged with the world of mankind, and Plato's abstract essence of essences. The latter, though, is no more than the end point of a series of metaphoric transformations based on the dodgy concept of the essential nature shared by members of a category. Essences, and the essence of essences, have been talked into existence and are now taken to be real; their insubstantial origins having been forgotten. The notion of essence has been reified and turned into a concrete object, and the notion of essence of essences has been deified and transformed into God. Notwithstanding their shaky foundations, these antique modes of thought still form the basis of much of our reasoning.

## The Intelligent Universe

For Plato, divine Reason was the king of heaven and earth, the universe being ruled by a wondrous regulating intelligence. In fact, the notion that a transcendent intelligence rules and orders all things goes back at least to the time of Pythagoras and the presocratic philosophers.[43] We have already encountered Pythagoras' belief that there are mathematical forms in nature; he thought that these were evidence of divine intelligence. Anaxagoras proposed that *Nous* or Mind was the transcendent source of cosmic order, while Heraclitus used the term *Logos* to signify the same principle.

Aristotle believed in an Unmoved Mover that caused the ordered movement of the heavens, and he developed new concepts of causation that promoted the role of reason. Objects in the material world do not just happen, but are caused. Aristotle recognised four types of causation: material, formal, efficient and final. Take a knife: its material cause is the metal of which it is made; its formal cause is the form the material takes – that of a knife; the efficient cause is the craftsman who made it; and the final cause is the purpose for which the knife was made, namely, cutting. These four types of cause contribute to the essence of a knife. For an artefact, the final cause is the use to which it is put; which purpose, together with its form or design, is present in the mind of the craftsman even before the thing exists. Its essence therefore precedes its existence. For living things, too, essence is said to precede existence. But what is the purpose, the final cause, of an oak for example? For Aristotle it is to fulfil its potential, to achieve its natural end or *telos*. Essence itself now becomes a cause. We say that an acorn grows into an oak because that is its nature. Never mind that this argument is circular, – that we know its nature by the way it behaves, and it behaves the way it does because of its nature – the link is made between causation and reason. For we say also that the *reason* an acorn grows into an oak is because that is its nature; it grows into a tree *in order* to fulfil its potential.

We should note here Aristotle's use of two metaphors which are still very much alive in our daily discourse. First, a metaphor we acquire early in life, ***Causation as Action to Achieve a Purpose.*** An infant's first understanding of causation comes from experiencing its own actions in pursuit of a purpose. More generally, caused actions are interpreted teleologically, as having a purpose: what is the end towards which an action strives? Why does he, she or it do that? Implicit in the infantile question *'Why?'* is the presupposition that every action has a purpose. Implicit in the question of why there is something rather than nothing is the idea that nothing happens or exists without a purpose, a pervasive notion, but fallacious.

Aristotle's second metaphor is ***Causes as Reasons.*** This indispensable metaphor is expressed in the dictionary definition of the word 'because':

because of = by reason of

The inference is that causation, wherever it is found, is an expression of reason.

Box 5

Feedback

In speaking of systems, the terms negative or positive feedback are often used. Examples of negative feedback abound in man-made mechanical and electrical systems, and in living organisms, where their function – *telos* – is to restore and maintain a steady state. A simple example of a negative feedback system is a room with a thermostatically controlled heater. The heater is turned off or on by the thermostat according to whether room temperature is above or below the temperature selected. The *purpose* of the thermostat is to counteract any deviation of the temperature from that desired; in a more sophisticated system the amount of heating or cooling would be proportionate to the deviation.

In our bodies the equivalent of the thermostat is the thermoregulatory centre in the brainstem. If we are exposed to cold the centre closes down the blood supply to the skin to reduce heat loss; should our core body temperature start to fall, we shiver to generate body heat and restore the status quo ante. If we become overheated the blood supply to the skin is increased and we perspire, losing heat by radiation and by evaporation of sweat.

We also have an exquisitely sensitive negative feedback mechanism for disposing of carbon dioxide, the product of our own internal combustion. When we break into a run, our muscles, fuelled by the controlled combustion of glucose, yield carbon dioxide whose rising concentration is detected by sensors in the blood stream. Within seconds we are breathing faster and getting rid of excess carbon dioxide, at the same time as we take in lungfuls of oxygen.

Positive feedback is generally *purposeless* and *dysfunctional*. It occurs if the room thermostat is wired up incorrectly so that the heater only comes on when the set temperature is exceeded: the room then gets hotter and hotter. Conversely, if room temperature falls below the set value, the heater is turned off and room temperature continues to fall.

In inanimate, naturally occurring systems, positive feedback is a frequent cause of instability and runaway behaviour, while negative feedback is rare. An example of positive feedback concerns global warming due to accumulation of greenhouse gases. The rising temperature causes snow fields to melt, exposing the darker earth beneath. Less of the sun's energy is reflected back into space, and global warming is accentuated. Another twist is that greenhouse gases methane and carbon dioxide locked in frozen arctic tundra will be released into the atmosphere if the tundra melts. In this global system, stabilising negative feedback is not much in evidence. The main inorganic mechanism for reducing the atmospheric concentration of carbon dioxide is the weathering of rocks by rain made acid by dissolved carbon dioxide. Aeons of this slow erosion of mountain ranges has resulted in huge quantities of carbon dioxide being locked away in limestone strata. However, this mechanism is much too slow and is ill adapted to counteract the present sharp increase in atmospheric carbon dioxide.

This presumption, that reasoning intelligence in some form underlies the workings of the physical world was explicitly enunciated by Plotinus, a third century philosopher who was the founder and leading exponent of Neoplatonism, which later became assimilated into Christian theology. According to him, the first creative act of the One was the issuing forth of Nous, the pervasive wisdom of the universe, within which are contained the archetypal Forms that cause and order the world.[44]

These ancient assertions of the existence of God and of an ordered universe of forms and free-floating ideas, assertions that are only occasionally supported by any argument, however dubious, have gone largely unrepudiated to this day.

*

Enlightenment luminaries such as Voltaire and Kant, while disavowing the God of Christianity, professed a distant unknowable deity. Thoroughgoing atheism, however, was a rarity. The contemporary philosopher Daniel Dennett puts this down to the impossibility in the 18th century, before Darwin, of conceiving that Mind could have originated from matter. He cites John Locke (1632-1704) as saying that just as matter cannot arise from nothing, thought cannot arise from matter.[45] Here we have another venerable but mistaken belief that is still prevalent. In the beginning was not the Big Bang, but Mind. Dennett goes on to quote from Hume's *Dialogues Concerning Natural Religion* where Philo, representing Hume himself, having roundly demolished the argument from design – that the appearance of design in nature must have resulted from the work of a Designer – in the end concedes that, if not God, then Mind or Thought must have come first.

Another reason for being diffident about atheism in earlier centuries was that to profess it was considered socially unacceptable, even scandalous. Hume willed that his *Dialogues Concerning Natural Religion* should not be published until after his death for fear of the offence it would cause, and Darwin deferred publication of *The Origin of Species* because he did not wish to hurt the religious feelings of his wife.

In 1945, Jean-Paul Sartre fearlessly promoted the vigorously atheistic philosophy of existentialism. This had little to do with intelligent order in the universe at large, but was concerned with man's responsibility for himself. If there is no God, man's essence does not pre-exist in God's mind; man is therefore the exception: his existence precedes his essence. Man is condemned to be free: once cast into the world he alone is responsible for everything he is and does; he determines his own essence.[46] There is no such thing as human nature because we have shaken off any pre-existing final cause for our existence, Sartre referring here to Aristotle's concept of causation. He has overlooked, however, that there are material, formal, efficient and final causes of our being here that are natural: our biological substance, human form, developmental history and biological destiny; we may not be quite so free as he thinks.

In Western Europe atheism is now on the increase and is no longer stigmatised,[47] but the prevalence of the idea of intelligent order in the universe is undiminished. We have already seen how some mathematicians claim to discover new territories in a Platonic world of number. The idea also underlies the claim that some new development is wrong 'because it interferes with Nature'. The implicit assumption here is that there is a Natural Order where all is for the best. But there is no such order to interfere with; nature does not know best, insentient nature knows, sees, hears, feels, and understands nothing. Giving nature a capital N personifies the all-too-human concepts of *Causes as Reasons*, and *Causation as Action to achieve a Purpose*.

61

Box 6

The Earth as a system

Planet Earth constitutes a system which is much more complicated than anything we have considered so far. It consists of physical, chemical, biological and human components, and known as Gaia, it is said to behave as a single, self-regulating system with the goal, *telos*, of sustaining habitability, though this is highly disputed. Of great current concern is the temperature of the planet and the role of greenhouse gases in determining it. Now negative, rather than positive, feedback loops characterise systems designed or evolved for the maintenance of the state of equability required by living things. So if Gaia has as one of its aims the maintenance of an equable temperature so as to support life, we might expect to find evidence of negative feedback mechanisms which would bring down the planet's fever. No direct mechanism for losing surplus heat is known to exist. Alternatively, perhaps there is some self-regulatory mechanism for reducing the level of greenhouse gases.

Carbon dioxide in the atmosphere is in equilibrium with carbon dioxide dissolved in seawater, where it forms carbonic acid; carbonic acid reacts with calcium to form chalk which precipitates down to the seabed. This huge inorganic system has a tremendous buffering capacity which resists change. Thus the effect on global temperature of a given quantity of emitted carbon dioxide is reduced because a proportion of it will end up on the seabed as chalk. If we now add plant life into this system it gains even greater stability as the biomass also constitutes a large reservoir of carbon, some of which may be fossilised in the fullness of time, to be taken out of the system, at least, until we dig it up and burn it. But although the increase of carbon dioxide may be buffered by these mechanisms, there is no large negative feedback which would counteract the greenhouse effect. On the contrary, the increasing temperature is detrimental to two important carbon dioxide sinks: ocean algae and tropical forests. As these die back they will decompose and release large quantities of greenhouse gases into the atmosphere. Only in polar regions will global heating result in a possible increase in forestation. Although this will pump down carbon dioxide, the boreal forest is dark and absorbs more of the sun's heat, so the overall effect on global warming is likely to be slight.

Thus, with regard to the control of temperature, the planet appears to be dominated by positive feedback mechanisms. Because of the great size and buffering capacity of the system there has been in the recent geological past a stable level of temperature congenial to life, the planet appearing to have functioned like a thermostatically controlled heating system. But the appearance is deceptive, for while we purposefully set the domestic thermostat for our own comfort, a stable global temperature results from the way things are and not from the way things need to be for the maintenance of life, let alone for human benefit.

The medieval idea of Order in Nature surely has its apogee in James Lovelock's Gaia hypothesis:

> We have...defined Gaia as a complex entity involving the Earth's biosphere, atmosphere, oceans, and soil; the totality constituting a feedback or cybernetic system which seeks an optimal physical and chemical environment for life on this planet. The maintenance of relatively constant conditions by active control may be conveniently described by the term 'homoeostasis'.... [The Gaia hypothesis] is an alternative to that pessimistic view which sees nature as a primitive force to be subdued and conquered. It is also an alternative to that equally depressing picture of our planet as a demented spaceship, forever travelling, driverless and purposeless, around an inner circle of the sun.[48]

Or perhaps the Gaia hypothesis is just wishful thinking.

Lovelock's huge contribution to our appreciation of the fragility of the global ecosystem of which we are a part is acknowledged. But his insistence on using the metaphor of planet Earth as a living organism is dangerously misleading. For if Gaia is truly a self-regulating, homoeostatic, system, then we have nothing to worry about since her negative feedback mechanisms will restore the planet's equilibrium. But paradoxically, in his later writings, Lovelock emphasises the positive feedback loops which are implicated in runaway global warming past the point of no return.[49] He cannot have it both ways.

## Descartes' Disembodied Reason

Descartes famously deduced that the only thing of which he could be absolutely certain was his own thought. '*Cogito, ergo sum*: I am thinking, therefore I am'. He went on to argue

64

that ideas which were seen by 'the light of reason' to be distinctly separate were different entities. From his introspective viewpoint, the body and the mind were such clearly separate things. The body had extension (*res extensa*), that is, occupied space, whereas the mind did not; the mind was a conscious, thinking thing (*res cogitans*). He convinced himself that his essence consisted solely in his being a thinking and unextended thing, which could exist independently of his body. This conscious, thinking faculty was the soul, the essential indivisible 'I'. And it was located, according to Descartes, in the pineal gland, a unitary structure situated in the midbrain. From its midline seat behind the eyes, the soul could drive the body by means of spirits coursing through nerves and blood. Descartes' ruminations were in line with the body-soul tradition that went back at least as far as Plato, and which was now a central doctrine of the Church. His powerful endorsement of the idea spared him Galileo's fate, and also ensured the perpetuation of the mind-matter distinction with its massive implications for philosophy, theology, morality and science. His clear formulation of dualism resonates with the notion that 'I' am located in my head, and 'I' am viewing my conscious experience on the stage of what Dennett calls 'the Cartesian theatre'.[50] This is an extraordinarily pervasive and persuasive idea, playing on the universal metaphor *Knowing as Seeing*, combined with the notion of a self which has an essence and is the locus of reason, seemingly independent of the body. Descartes' mind/body dualism has been widely discredited, but his influence lives on in what might be described as the reification of reason, by which is meant the projection of human reasoning onto the universe where it is taken to be universal, if not transcendental.

Besides seeing intuitively that body and mind were separate entities, Descartes could also see clearly that imagination and emotion were bodily functions, which therefore had no place in the mind, and contributed neither to his thought nor to his essential nature. As well as being a philosopher, Descartes was the founder of analytic geometry, in which mathematical operations are carried out using a formal, symbolic notation. Descartes saw his mathematics as a model for rational thought, in which true conclusions are attained by manipulation of symbols and expressions independent of their specific content, and untainted by emotion or imagination. Reason was therefore abstract, formal, cold and calculating and also transcendental, as mathematics was considered to be.

The irony of this remarkable and far-reaching conclusion is that, far from being the result of a cold calculation, it was reached making imaginative use of metaphors which engage the emotions. These included *Knowing as Seeing*, *Ideas as Objects* and *Reason as Illumination*, reason providing the light by which the ideas of mind and body were seen to be distinct objects, and imagination and emotion were viewed as bodily functions. These metaphors are part of the brain's conceptual apparatus acquired as the result of emotive learning experiences in early life. Descartes was also mistaken in his premise, *Cogito*. For his conscious cogitation, far from being purely rational, involved sensory experience, particularly of the visual sort, and also, emotion. After all, *'Cogito, ergo sum'* must have been quite a eureka moment.

We now turn to modern cognitive psychology for an up-to-date view of human reasoning.

## The Embodiment of Reason

We acquire basic mathematical concepts early in life through experience of the real material world. Thus, during the course of play with a collection of objects arranged, for example, like so, ::: , we see for ourselves the truth of the commutative property of numbers – that 2+4 is the same as 4+2, and 2x3 is the same as 3x2. At the same time as the concept of number is developed, another conceptual metaphor is reinforced until it becomes permanently wired into the brain's neural network: that of **Knowing as Seeing**, a metaphor whose use is ubiquitous: see what I mean? Other conceptual metaphors acquired in infancy are *Knowing as Grasping*, *Affection as Warmth* and *Important as Big*.

It is the structure of our bodies and brains that fashion the concepts that we deploy.[51] Our sensory modalities shape the ways we conceptualise knowing – by seeing, or grasping; that sounds right. Our method of locomotion structures other metaphors: we are moving towards a decision, but walking away from a problem. On the other hand, we flounder in a sea of uncertainty because water is not our natural medium.

Striking instances of metaphors shaped by peculiarities of neural anatomy occur in synaesthesia, a hereditary condition in which there is an association between different modalities of sensation, so that, for example, hearing a musical note would be linked with the experience of a particular colour.[52] However, we are all to some extent synaesthetes, in that we often describe one sensation in terms of another, for example, in saying that a taste is sharp, or a sound is sweet. Pathological synaesthesia has an incidence of 0.5%, but is much more common in artists, novelists and poets. The disorder is attributed to increased neural connectivity in a region of the cerebral cortex where nerve tracts for vision, hearing, touch and proprioception are in close proximity to each other. It has been suggested that artistic people may have a more generalised hyper-connectivity, explaining the increased incidence of synaesthia and their creative use of metaphor. In these various ways, then, our particular human anatomy and physiology determine the possibilities for conceptualisation and categorisation.

As for categorisation, new born babies can discriminate human faces and voices from other sights and sounds, and they prefer familiar ones.[53] Obviously, this innate ability is determined by possession of the sense of sight, and also by a neurological predilection for faces, which are then soon categorised as familiar or not. By 18 months, babies spontaneously sort objects into different groups, and by three years old have a deeper understanding about an object's essential nature, being able to look beneath the surface and classify things by their internal structure as well as by their appearance.[54] The grouping together of objects that are in the same category leads to the metaphor *Similarity as Closeness*: two colours may not be quite the same but they are close. This activity also gives rise to the commonplace but important metaphor *Categories as Containers*. An object can either be in a container or not; no intermediate position is possible. An object within a container which is itself inside a larger container is necessarily within the larger container. A container $p$ within a container $q$ represents a subcategory of a larger category. For example, dogs, $p$, are a subcategory of four-legged animals, $q$. From this conceptual metaphor derives the syllogism:

> All dogs have four legs; this is a dog; therefore this has four legs.
> If $p$ then $q$; $p$; therefore $q$.

> Or the alternative form:
> All dogs have four legs; this creature does not have four legs; therefore this is not a dog.
> If $p$ then $q$; not $q$; therefore not $p$.

This fundamental logical form is thus grounded on experience of the properties of groups of individual objects in the real world. Each of us learns the truth of the metaphor for ourselves in infancy, even though we may never come to appreciate the abstract notational representation of it shown above, and found in books on logic.

In the introduction to *Philosophy in the Flesh*, Lakoff and Johnson state that:

> The mind is inherently embodied.
> Thought is mostly unconscious.
> Abstract concepts are largely metaphorical.[55]

The implications of these three major findings of cognitive science for our understanding of ourselves and our powers of reasoning are profound and extensive:

- Because most thought is unconscious, the mind cannot be understood by intuition, but only by empirical scientific study from a third person point of view (this point will be developed in a later chapter).
- The structure of reason derives from the structure and size of our bodies, our anatomy and physiology, and our neural circuitry.
- Reason has evolved using perceptual and motor structures possessed by our evolutionary ancestors, with whom we are on a continuum.
- Reason, including mathematics, is largely metaphorical and imaginative, and engages the emotions.
- Human reason is universal only in the sense that our human concepts have been projected onto the universe wherever we have probed it. Where regularities are found these are not determined by transcendental reason such as mathematics, but at the best, imperfectly described by it.
- If there are intelligent beings elsewhere in the universe, it is unlikely that we would be able to communicate with them since their concepts would differ from ours, theirs having been shaped by bodies and an environment very different from our own.

- Some basic philosophical concepts, including self, causation, essence, and mind as distinct from matter, are now seen to be sources of error in our thinking.

Although knowledge and reason are the only instruments we have for solving our many problems, we must be heedful that reason is a human and fallible construct.

## Summing Up

We have come to the end of our brief survey of the universe. We have peered into the outer reaches of space and time as far back as the singular event of the Big Bang, which limits our view in that direction; we are unable to see far into the future. We have glimpsed the interior structure of atoms, from which come particles of light. Wherever we have looked, we have found matter or its equivalent, energy. We have no reason to believe that the universe does, or even could, consist of anything but matter and energy. It is as fatuous to ask who or what made matter, as it is to ask what matter is made of. The matter of the universe is a brute fact which neither has, nor requires, an explanation; it is probable that it has always existed, but we have no way of knowing that.

Much of our reasoning involves the creative use of metaphor, engaging both imagination and emotion. One of the ironic consequences of intuitive reasoning is that the metaphors used lead us to believe that reason is disembodied, objective and universal. But this belief is mistaken, and we are prone to serious error, in particular, by projecting our categories and concepts onto the external world where we accord them uncritical deference. The archetypal projection of a human concept is, of course, God, but other instances are nature, and nature's laws; also, reason itself, including mathematics.

70

Although reason is a fallible human construct, nevertheless, by systematically applying reason to evidence in the so-called scientific method we can obtain reliable, stable knowledge. This enables us to understand the human origin of the myths by which we live, and to realise that they are but myths. Reason and knowledge lead us to conclude that we are material creatures living in a material universe which is unmindful, purposeless and completely indifferent to us. To solve our many problems we have only human resources to draw upon. What we humans make of our life on planet Earth is up to us. It is of absolutely no concern to anybody or anything else. We are on our own.

# Notes

## Chapter 2: God and the Cosmos

1. Cited *in* Simon Singh. *Big Bang: The Most Important Discovery of All Time and Why You Need to Know About It.* London: Harper Perennial, 2005: p360.
2. Gabriele Veneziano. *The Myth of the Beginning of Time.* Scientific American 2004; 290: 30-39.
3. John Leslie. *Universes.* London: Routledge, 1996: p13.
4. John D Barrow. *From Alpha to Omega: The Constants of Nature.* London: Jonathan Cape, 2002.
5. Richard P Feynman. *QED: The Strange Theory of Light and Matter.* London: Penguin Books, 1985: p128.
6. Brian Greene. *The Elegant Universe: Superstrings, Hidden Dimensions, and the Quest for the Ultimate Theory.* London: Jonathan Cape, 1999: p117- 31.
7. Roger Penrose. *The Road to Reality: A Complete Guide to the Physical Universe.* London: BCA, 2004, p773.
8. Simon Singh. *Big Bang: The Most Important Discovery of All Time and Why You Need to Know About It.* London: Harper Perennial, 2005: p481-2.
9. David Hume. *Writings on Religion.* Ed Antony Flew. Chicago: Open Court, 1992: p100-102.
10. Antony Flew. *God and Philosophy.* New York: Prometheus Books, 2005: p93.
11. Charles Darwin. *Autobiography.* Cited in Ibid, p72.
12. Robin Le Poidevin. *Arguing for Atheism: An Introduction to the Philosophy of Religion.* London: Routledge, 1996: pp50-52.
13. Richard P Feynman. *QED: The Strange Theory of Light and Matter.* London: Penguin Books, 1985: p7.
14. The high degree of agreement between predicted and measured values of Dirac's number suggests that the theoretical result is not contingent but is somehow entailed mathematically; Feynman sought but did not find an explanation such as the following illustration. If we did not know that the earth is spherical, we would be amazed to find that comparing the distance

travelled in circumnavigating the world with that of the direct route to the antipode through the centre of the earth, a ratio remarkably close to the value of pi would be obtained, the latter being calculable to any number of decimal places as the sum of an infinite series. The result is not surprising, however, if we know that the earth is spherical. *See:* Lancelot Hogben. *Mathematics for the Million: How to Master the Magic of Numbers.* London: The Merlin Press, 1989: p104.

15. John Leslie. *Universes.* London: Routledge, 1996: p4.
16. Antony Flew. *God and Philosophy.* New York: Prometheus Books, 2005: p84.
17. Rita Carter. *Consciousness.* London: Weidenfeld & Nicolson, 2002: pp283-290.
18. John Hick. *An Interpretation of Religion: Human Responses to the Transcendent.* 2nd edition. Basingstoke: Palgrave Macmillan, 2004: p178-9.
19. Brian Moynahan. *The Faith: A History of Christianity.* London: Aurum Press Limited, 2002: p45.
20. Ibid, p50.
21. Antony Flew. *God and Philosophy.* New York: Prometheus Books, 2005: p150.
22. Charles Darwin. *The Descent of Man, and Selection in Relation to Sex.* London: Penguin Books, 2004: p116.
23. D Jason Slone. *Theological Incorrectness: Why Religious People Believe What They Shouldn't.* Oxford University Press, 2004: p20-3.
24. Pascal Boyer. *Religion Explained: The Human Instincts That Fashion Gods, Spirits and Ancestors.* London: William Heinnemann, 1991: pp75-80.
25. Lewis Wolpert. *The Unnatural Nature of Science.* London: Faber and Faber, 1992.
26. Pascal Boyer. *Religion Explained: The Human Instincts that Fashion Gods, Spirits and Ancestors.* London: William Heinnemann, 1991.
27. D Jason Slone. *Theological Incorrectness: Why Religious People Believe What They Shouldn't.* Oxford University Press, 2004.
28. Steven Mithen. *The Prehistory of the Mind: The Cognitive Origins of Art, Religion and Science.* London: Thames and Hudson Ltd, 1996.

29. D Jason Slone. *Theological Incorrectness: Why Religious People Believe What They Shouldn't.* Oxford University Press, 2004: p116.
30. Richard A Shweder, Nancy C Much, Manamohan Mahapatra, Lawrence Park. *The "Big Three" of Morality (Autonomy, Community, Divinity) and the "Big Three" Explanations of Suffering.* In Allan M Brandt, Paul Rozin (eds). *Morality and Health.* New York: Routledge, 1997: pp121-3.
31. Ibid, p128.
32. D Jason Slone. *Theological Incorrectness: Why Religious People Believe What They Shouldn't.* Oxford University Press, 2004: p60.
33. Ibid, p57.
34. Ibid, p72.
35. Pascal Boyer. *Religion Explained: The Human Instincts That Fashion Gods, Spirits and Ancestors.* London: William Heinnemann, 1991: pp169-71.
36. George Lakoff, Mark Johnson. *Philosophy in the Flesh: The Embodied Mind and its Challenge to Western Thought.* New York: Basic Books, 1999: p363.
37. Karen Armstrong. *The Case for God.* London: Vintage Books, 2010: p19-24.
38. Ibid, p52.
39. Brian Moynahan. *The Faith: A History of Christianity.* London: Aurum Press Limited, 2002: p46.
40. Richard Tarnas. *The Passion of the Western Mind: Understanding the Ideas that Have Shaped our World View.* London: Pimlico, 1996: p101.
41. Roy Porter. *Flesh in the Age of Reason: The Modern Foundations of Body and Soul.* New York: WW Norton & Company, Inc, 2004: p36.
42. Saint Anselm (1033-1109). Medieval philosopher and theologian, Archbishop of Canterbury from 1093. His 'ontological' argument for the existence of God runs as follows, where God is defined as '…Something than which nothing greater can be conceived'. God then exists in the understanding, since we understand this concept. But if He only existed in the understanding, something greater could be conceived, for a being that exists in reality is greater than one that exists only in the

understanding. But then we can conceive of something greater than that than which nothing greater can be conceived, which is contradictory. Hence, God cannot exist only in the understanding, but exists in reality. Simon Blackburn. *The Oxford Dictionary of Philosophy*. Oxford University Press, 1994: p269.

43. Richard Tarnas. *The Passion of the Western Mind: Understanding the Ideas that Have Shaped our World View*. London: Pimlico, 1996: pp44-45.
44. Ibid, p85.
45. Daniel C Dennett. *Darwin's Dangerous Idea: Evolution and the Meanings of Life*. London: Penguin Books, 1995: p27.
46. Jean-Paul Sartre. *L'existentialisme est un Humanisme*. Paris: Editions Gallimard, 1996: p39.
47. For example a series of programmes by Jonathan Miller on atheism broadcast on BBC television in 2005, and two programmes on Channel 4 television by Richard Dawkins denouncing religion in 2006. On the other hand it is said that the profession of atheism would be an absolute bar to election to the US Congress.
48. James Lovelock. *Gaia: A New Look at Life on Earth*. Oxford University Press, 1995: pp10-11.
49. James Lovelock. *The Revenge of Gaia: Why the Earth is Fighting Back – and How We Can Still Save Humanity*. London: Allen Lane, 2006: p34-35.
50. Daniel C Dennett. *Consciousness Explained*. London: Penguin Books, 1993: pp101-38.
51. George Lakoff, Mark Johnson. *Philosophy in the Flesh: The Embodied Mind and its Challenge to Western Thought*. New York: Basic Books, 1999: pp18-19.
52. Vilayanur S. Ramachandran. *The Emerging Brain, Lecture 4: Purple Numbers and Sharp Cheese*. BBC Radio 4 – Reith Lectures 2003. www.bbc.uk/radio4/reith2003
53. Alison Gopnik, Andrew Meltzoff, Patricia Kuhl. *How Babies Think: The Science of Childhood*. London: Weidenfeld & Nicolson, 1999: p27.
54. Ibid, pp82-83.
55. George Lakoff, Mark Johnson. *Philosophy in the Flesh: The Embodied Mind and its Challenge to Western Thought*. New York: Basic Books, 1999: pp3-6.

# Chapter 3

# The Evolution of Matter into Life

'Can we doubt (remembering that many more individuals are born than can possibly survive) that individuals having any advantage, however slight, over others, would have the best chance of surviving and of procreating their kind? On the other hand, we may feel sure that any variation in the least degree injurious would be rigidly destroyed. This preservation of favourable differences and variations, and the destruction of those which are injurious, I have called Natural Selection, or the Survival of the Fittest.' *Charles Darwin* [1]

It was concluded in the previous chapter that we are material creatures living in a material universe. Now matter has the remarkable property of organising itself so that it manifests regularities which make its behaviour predictable. One of the most marvellous ways in which it does this, is to form living organisms, including ourselves. Although what makes for order in the universe may be ultimately unknowable, we have an intimate relationship with the universe since we are made of exactly the same stuff as the rest of it, and the stuff of our bodies abides by the same universal principles, whatever they might be. During our evolutionary history we have developed a fine appreciation of reality through interacting with our immediate environment, and this process continues during our individual lifetimes, moulding not just our bodies, but the way we think. And it is the way we think and reason that is at the root of many of our problems.

We have seen how much of our reasoning involves the use of metaphor, and how vision and light feature strongly in our metaphors for acquiring knowledge. Hitherto, we have depended on insight to understand ourselves, but this approach is seriously deficient because most of our thought is subconscious and not accessible by intuition. We are especially prone to the error of projecting our categories and concepts onto the external world, including notions of God, nature, mathematics and reason itself.

In this chapter I consider the theory of evolution which, like that of the Big Bang, is a monumental achievement of the human intellect, and also an epic story which may be understood at several levels. The formation of the solar system and planet Earth, the appearance of life and its impact on the earth's geology and meteorology, the subsequent development of plants, animals, vertebrates, fish, reptiles, birds, mammals, primates and man – it is a marvellous saga, unrivalled in scope, complexity and splendour by any creation myth. There is space here, however, for only those parts of the story which have a direct bearing on our present predicament. Thus, the microbial production of our atmosphere, and the laying down of carbon in limestone and fossil fuels, is relevant to our concerns about climate change, while the evolution of *Homo sapiens* may give us some insight into why we think the way we do.

Box 7

Water

Water, $H_2O$, has a host of properties not possessed by its constituent gases, hydrogen and oxygen, and which make it essential for life. Each molecule of water consists of an atom of oxygen bonded to two atoms of hydrogen separated from each other by an angle of 105°. Liquid water is denser, more viscous and has a greater surface tension than would be expected of such a small, lightweight compound. In fact, its weight is effectively increased because in liquid form it assembles itself into loosely linked molecular chains (polymers). In pure water a small number of molecules dissociate into charged hydrogen and hydroxyl ions: $H_2O = H^+ + OH^-$. When there is an excess of hydrogen over hydroxyl ions in a solution it is said to be acidic, and when there is an excess of hydroxyl over hydrogen ions it is said to be alkaline. The degree of acidity in the interior of living things is tightly regulated.

A great many substances dissolve in water, including inorganic salts, which dissociate into their constituent ions. Common salt, sodium chloride, is a good example: $NaCl + H_2O = Na^+ + H^+ + Cl^- + OH^-$. This dissociative state facilitates many chemical reactions, such as the formation of salt from sodium hydroxide and hydrochloric acid: $NaOH + HCl = NaCl + H_2O$.

By virtue of these emergent properties, water is the universal medium in which all chemical reactions vital to life take place. Water comprises 60% of our bodyweight.

In liquid water the molecules are continually moving relative to each other, the energy of that movement being heat. As the temperature falls, and the movement lessens, a given amount of water takes up less room; the maximum density of water occurs when its temperature is 4°C. Below that temperature crystals of ice begin to form and these take up more space. At 0°C water freezes completely, and water molecules become fixed in a three-dimensional hexagonal lattice which has a greater volume and is therefore less dense than the liquid form: ice therefore floats on water. This has two consequences for life on earth. If water were to behave like most substances, where the solid form is denser than the liquid, water in a lake would freeze completely from the bottom upwards, and all living things would be trapped in the ice. As it is, water freezes from the top downwards and because ice is a poor conductor of heat, even at the poles in winter a diversity of life is supported by water at 4°C beneath the ice. On the other hand, if the oceans were to freeze over completely, the ice would block access of both sunlight and air, causing deoxygenation and extinction of many marine species. This appears to have happened between 750 and 600 million years ago in the so-called the Snowball Earth period.

Water thus possesses an array of emergent life-giving and life-enhancing properties which would not be predicted from a knowledge of its constituent gases. The self-organising propensity of this species of matter is wonderfully illustrated in ice crystals and the patterns of snowflakes.

# The Origin of Life on Earth

Our solar system was formed about 4500 million years ago when a swirl of interstellar gas and dust agglomerated into the sun and its encircling planets, amongst whose number was planet Earth. Almost all of the material, of which the predominant element was hydrogen, came to be in the sun, where kinetic energy and the intense pressure of gravity ignited the nuclear furnace that continues still to give us light and life. By contrast, the predominant elements that formed the earth were iron, oxygen, silicon and magnesium; molten iron formed the earth's heavy core, while light compounds of silicon made up the earth's rocky surface.[2] The first, dusty, hydrogenous atmosphere was blown away by the solar wind, but a secondary atmosphere was formed of gases driven out of the earth's hot interior. The first gases to be emitted had been equilibrated with metallic iron, which avidly combines with oxygen to form iron oxides – rust. Consequently oxygen was absent, but vented gases were rich in hydrogen and its compounds, hydrogen sulphide, methane and ammonia, as well as nitrogen and carbon monoxide.

Later, as exposure to iron lessened, the vented gases consisted predominantly of carbon dioxide, water vapour and nitrogen. Water vapour condensed to form the oceans, carbon dioxide dissolved in the water and combined with calcium in the earth's crust to form chalk, and nitrogen consequently became the predominant atmospheric constituent.

Although the sun's radiation then was substantially less than at present, there was a higher concentration of 'greenhouse' carbon dioxide which made for a moderate temperature, conducive to the origin and maintenance of life.[3]

Life is thought to have originated on earth about 4000 million years ago (MYA), less than a 1000 million years after the planet had first formed, and only a relatively short time before the first sedimentary rocks were laid down.[4] One theory has it that in the shallow waters of the first oceans there was a dilute 'primordial soup' of organic molecules derived from interactions between hydrogen, methane and ammonia energised by lightning strikes or by intense ultraviolet light as yet unfiltered by an oxygen or ozone layer. Another theory is that life started close to a volcanic vent, not necessarily in the sea, but perhaps in the hot, wet seams and fissures in rocks deep underground permeated with volcanic gases, hydrogen sulphide in particular.[5] But what did this early life consist of, and how do we define 'life'? According to the evolutionist, John Maynard Smith, any population of entities which has the properties of multiplication, heredity and variation may be regarded as being alive. The justification for this definition is that any population with these properties will evolve by natural selection so as to become better adapted to its environment.[6]

The details of how life originated are not known, but it seems likely that the earliest forms of life were simple lipid sacs containing a self replicating molecule for which RNA (ribonucleic acid) is the favoured candidate.[7] This nucleic acid was perhaps the first carrier of hereditary information, and errors in its replication would have been the source of variation on which natural selection could act. To begin with though, it would have carried little information except that of its own structure, which was such as to catalyse its multiplication by forming copies of itself. Later, DNA (deoxyribonucleic acid) became the vector of hereditary information, and RNA the go-between, translating instructions coded in DNA into those for the synthesis of different enzymatic proteins which would determine the development of the individual organism.

Single celled creatures known as archaea may today occupy the same ecological niches as the first living creatures, from which all life has descended. Their hardiness in resisting hot, acidic or salty conditions may be indicative of the earth's early environment. The archaean *Methanobacterium*, for example, is found in warm, wet and oxygen-free locations where it absorbs carbon dioxide and produces methane (marsh gas) as, waste. We have not heard the last of these methanogens.

In order to be fruitful and multiply, all living things have to have a source of carbon and energy for synthesis of their constituent parts. In the very first organisms this would have been carbon dioxide and simple inorganic compounds such as hydrogen sulphide, which yield chemical energy when split and recombined.[8]

A huge evolutionary advance was the development of photosynthesis in the cyanobacteria. In photosynthesis the green pigment chlorophyll captures energy from sunlight which is used to power the synthesis of sugar from carbon dioxide and water.

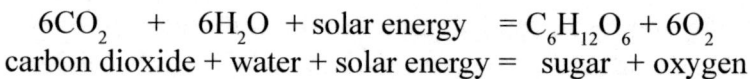

$$6CO_2 \ + \ 6H_2O + \text{solar energy} \ = C_6H_{12}O_6 + 6O_2$$
$$\text{carbon dioxide} + \text{water} + \text{solar energy} = \ \text{sugar} \ + \text{oxygen}$$

The waste product of this reaction is oxygen, which, like all biological waste products, is toxic to the organism that produces it. At that point in evolutionary history, however, the atmosphere contained no oxygen, so the excreta of cyanobacteria was readily dissipated.

After the development of photosynthesis, the appearance on the evolutionary scene of energy-rich organic matter derived from sugar opened up the possibility that an organism could take its nourishment ready-made rather than synthesising it anew. The first creatures to do this may have broken down sugar or other carbohydrates into alcohol and carbon dioxide (like present day yeasts), releasing just some of the energy stored during photosynthesis.

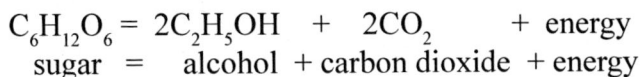

$$C_6H_{12}O_6 = 2C_2H_5OH \quad + \quad 2CO_2 \quad + \text{energy}$$
$$\text{sugar} \quad = \quad \text{alcohol} + \text{carbon dioxide} + \text{energy}$$

Another major evolutionary stage was reached when the metabolic pathways which enable sugar to be completely broken down to water and carbon dioxide were evolved. This oxidative process, known as respiration, is the complete reversal of photosynthesis, and releases all of the sugar's stored energy.

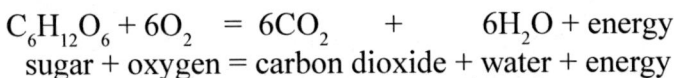

$$C_6H_{12}O_6 + 6O_2 \quad = \quad 6CO_2 \quad + \quad 6H_2O + \text{energy}$$
$$\text{sugar} + \text{oxygen} = \text{carbon dioxide} + \text{water} + \text{energy}$$

To begin with, this mode of living, dependent on ready availability of oxygen, would have been possible only close to photosynthesisers. Much later, when their excreta was ubiquitous, oxidative metabolism was practised world-wide.

Thus, living matter developed four broad strategies for obtaining energy from the environment: from simple inorganic or organic compounds, from sunlight, by fermentation or by oxidation of preformed organic matter. There is a supplementary tactic which must have appeared at an early stage: that of motility. The ability of an organism to propel itself towards a scarce source of its preferred nutrition would have given it substantial reproductive advantage.

# Box 8

## Order Out of Chaos

At the scale of the universe, matter organises itself to form galaxies and solar systems, including our own. On a terrestrial scale, this self-organising property of matter may be seen at work in weather systems, such as hurricanes and tornados. Hurricanes form unpredictably over the ocean when sea temperature is higher than 27°C, except within 5° of the equator, where the rotational force imparted by the turning earth (Coriolis effect) is weak. An area of low atmospheric pressure at sea level draws in warm moist air from surrounding high pressure areas. The pressure drop causes water vapour to condense and fall as rain, thereby releasing the heat that had been used in the water's evaporation. This further warms the air, and it begins to rise. In so doing it loses pressure and precipitates more rain, releasing more latent heat which accelerates its ascent. In this positive feedback loop, moist air from a greater area is drawn into the system at ever increasing, and increasingly destructive, speeds. Due to the Coriolis effect, the system rotates in a counterclockwise direction in the northern hemisphere and clockwise in the south. A hurricane may persist for a week or more, and its dynamic, spiral structure, with a funnel shaped vortex at its centre, may be seen from space. It represents the coherent behaviour of matter interacting in accordance with simple physical laws. The higher the temperature of the ocean, the greater the energy of the system and the more severe the hurricane, which is why global heating is expected to increase the frequency and strength of hurricanes. The flow of energy through the system is interrupted once the hurricane reaches land and the supply of moisture is cut off, causing the hurricane to collapse.

On a much smaller and more domestic scale, the self-organising property of matter in dynamic structures may be demonstrated in a saucepan containing, let's say, porridge. Heated gently from below, the porridge begins to erupt in a number of miniature volcanoes roughly equidistant from each other. The boundaries of each volcano-containing cell are approximately hexagonal, and form a regular pattern across the exposed surface of the semi-liquid. The heated porridge rises by convection from the bottom of the pan to the centre of each cell where it flows outwards on the upper surface, cooling as it goes, porridge from adjacent cells then sinking back down to the bottom in the boundary areas. With water or oil the convection cells (also known as Bénard cells) are much smaller, and their emergence to form an intricate honeycomb pattern in a homogenous medium is startling.
Hurricanes and Bénard convection cells are examples of dynamic structures, that require a throughput of energy for their continued existence. Matter in a chaotic state may also give rise to static structures that are in equilibrium with their environment and need no energy for their maintenance: a diamond, crystalline carbon, for instance.

In these, and many other examples which could be given, order arises spontaneously out of inanimate chaos, without the aid of any intelligence or consciousness within or without the system.

Motility in these simple unicellular organisms was achieved by the evolution of the flagellum, a slender whip-like appendage which enabled the organism possessing it to swim. Most remarkably, in some creatures a spiral flagellum terminates at a hub which rotates indefinitely, driven by a tiny molecular motor: not quite a wheel, but certainly the first rotary propeller.[9]

## Symbiotic Evolution

Today's descendants of these first unicellular organisms are known as prokaryotes, consisting of two major domains, the *Archaea* (previously *Archaebacteria*), which we have just met in the hot, sulphurous depths, and *Eubacteria*, familiarly known as just bacteria.[10] Prokaryotes are characterised by having neither a distinct nucleus, nor other specialised walled structures within the cell. The chromosomes containing DNA lie loose in the cytoplasm, together with chlorophyll in those which live by photosynthesis, or oxidative enzymes in those which live by respiration. Prokaryotes differ fundamentally from all other living things in not having a cell nucleus. The transition from prokaryote to eukaryote, from non-nucleated to nucleated cells, was perhaps the most important in all evolutionary history once life had commenced. For it was from the unicellular eukaryotes that three great kingdoms of life evolved: fungi, plants and animals. There is thus a continuous chain of life linking each one of us via the first unicellular eukaryotes to our furthest ancestors, the prokaryotic bacteria at the start of life some 4000 MYA. It is truly astonishing that we know so much about the remarkable evolutionary history of these microscopic creatures, a history which was enacted so many aeons ago.

The evolution of eukaryotes from prokaryotes involved symbiosis, defined as an interaction between two different organisms living in close physical association, typically to the advantage of both. That this theory is now mainstream is owed in large measure to the persistence of Lyn Margulis who describes her battle against orthodoxy in *The Symbiotic Planet: A New Look at Evolution.*[11]

Orthodox evolutionary theory has it that the origin of species results from division of existing species into separate populations, particularly by reason of geography. Gradually, the separated groups accumulate changes in structure and function as a result of genetic mutations, until, even if members of the groups are brought together, interbreeding between them no longer occurs, or the offspring are infertile: one species has now divided into two. The claims of Margulis are unorthodox because she maintains that new species, indeed, a new kingdom of creatures, arose from fusion rather than division of species. Underlying orthodox Darwinian evolution is also the idea of competition for resources between and within species, with survival of the fittest, and dying out of the unfit. Symbiotic evolution, on the other hand, conveys the idea of cooperation rather than competition, to the mutual advantage of the symbiont species. Opponents of Darwinian evolution have seized on symbiotic evolution and cite Margulis with approval as providing support for a softer view of nature, and a kinder model for society.[12]

The pullulating kingdom of unicellular eukaryotes known as *Protista* includes algae, seaweed, amoebae, ciliates and slime moulds, all descendants from the fusion of at least four bacterial lines. Between them they possess the characteristics of fermentation, respiration, photosynthesis and motility in every conceivable permutation and combination. In evidence of their separate bacterial origins, mitochondria and chloroplasts, comprising packets of enzymes for respiration and photosynthesis respectively, reproduce independently of the nucleated cells in which they live. Moreover, the DNA of these organelles more closely resembles that of the bacteria to which they are related rather than that of the nuclei of the cells in which it is found.

Margulis' account of the evolution of eukaryotes by serial symbiotic fusion is now generally accepted, certainly insofar as it explains the origin of mitochondria and chloroplasts. But as a mechanism of species formation, fusion of species, as in her account, is an exception, while fission is the norm. As for symbiotic fusion representing cooperative behaviour, this is not how Margulis herself views it.

> The central idea is that extra genes in the cytoplasm of animal, plant, and other nucleated cells...originated as bacterial genes. The genes are a palpable legacy of a violent, competitive, and truce-forming past. Bacteria, long ago, which were partially devoured and trapped inside the bodies of others, became organelles...Survivors of thwarted aggression formed uneasy truces.[13, 14]

But really, the use of the value-laden terms cooperation, competition or aggression to describe the mechanism of evolution is inappropriate, especially in connection with the behaviour of organisms as simple as bacteria. We should note, too, that it was a poet, Tennyson, rather than a scientist who described 'Nature, red in tooth and claw'. The appearance of eukaryotes was brought about, not by some innate, aggressive force of Nature, but by the blind and unconscious operation of natural selection, succinctly described by Darwin in the epigraph to this chapter as 'the procreating of their kind' by 'individuals having any advantage, however slight'. An organism enters into a living arrangement with another species because it thereby gains an immediate survival and reproductive advantage, by shelter, protection from predators, the provision of nutrition, or by some other means. In no way can this arrangement be construed as altruistic, though sometimes both parties do benefit. More often, perhaps, the arrangement benefits one species to the detriment of the other, when it is known as parasitism.

## The Prokaryote Prelude

In many accounts of evolution the passage from prokaryote to eukaryote receives hardly a mention, but in fact, this phase of evolution occupied some three quarters of the time since life on earth began, 4000 MYA. Although the oldest microscopic prokaryote fossils date from 3500 MYA, evidence of multicellular organisms did not appear until the Precambrian era about 700 MYA, and animals and plants as we would recognise them today have only appeared in the last 500 million years. There does seem to be a puzzle here: 3 billion years to evolve 'simple' creatures like amoebae and algae, but only half a billion thereafter to evolve the whole panoply of complex multicellular fungi, plants and animals, including ourselves. Why did this evolutionary prelude take so long, and does this period of evolution have any relevance for us today?

During the immense time that passed between the start of life and the appearance of plants and animals, the microscopic *Archaea* and *Eubacteria*, the simplest of living creatures, succeeded in colonising the whole of the globe from a rocky depth of 5-10 km up to the highest mountain summits. It is estimated that today the biomass of subterranean bacteria may exceed that of all the surface organisms owing their existence to the sun,[15] of which trees constitute more than 80%.[16]

Box 9

Living Systems

All living things are dynamic rather than static structures, more akin to hurricanes than to crystals, though crystalline DNA is a universal component. Like a hurricane, a living system is open allowing a throughput of energy necessary for the maintenance of its orderly configuration in a chaotic environment. Integration of an organism into its environment ensures the provision of the material constituents and the energy required for its sustenance, and is also necessary for shelter, and essential for a social life, even if that consists solely of procuring a mate.

Unlike hurricanes, which form de novo and leave no descendants, all creatures now living have a lineage and a potential succession. Every individual has an intimate link with its immediate and distant antecedents, and incorporates a programme for reproducing its kind. So besides being a focus of interchanges with its surroundings, an organism is also a relay station on an information highway that goes back without a break for 4 billion years. Like time, life is continuous, though conveniently measured out in days, years, or lifetimes. But unlike time, life can be suspended at some stages of the life cycle: we are now accustomed to the marvel of frozen sperm or embryos; some plant seeds may remain dormant for decades until the right conditions enable them to germinate, and desiccated bacterial spores may survive for centuries. Inherited DNA encodes only a small part of all the know-how an organism is bequeathed from the past, and which largely determines its future. DNA is a stable, relatively inactive molecule, which makes it suitable archive material. But it is no use without the biological apparatus needed to read the code and translate it into protein sequences, or the nurture provided by parents, community and ecosystem in which the young are reared. Besides its genome, an organism inherits the physical environment and the social and cultural structures which have evolved with the speciés and which will provide a congenial milieu for individual development. What use would be the frozen embryo, or even less the DNA, of an extinct blue whale? How would we recreate and raise a whale pup so that it could fend for itself in its natural environment?

In a different dimension, life is a continuous uphill struggle against the second law of thermodynamics, that which says that heat of itself always flows 'downhill', from a higher to a lower temperature; it never flows 'uphill'. Another formulation is that the amount of disorder in a closed system can only increase. Warm-blooded creatures are an apparent contradiction to this law, but that is because all living things are open systems in disequilibrium with their surroundings, life being an unstable state which is maintained by the continuous expenditure of energy extracted from the environment. Death, the dis-integration and de-composition of an organism's orderly processes and structures, comes with cessation of this flow of energy through the system, analogous to the collapse of a hurricane when its source of energy-containing moist warm air is cut off.

Life, then, arises at the intersection of two streams of information. Life is an emergent property of a material system which integrates inherited information being relayed from past to future generations with the rich energy-bearing communication occurring between organism and environment, here and now.

Meanwhile, on the surface, photosynthesising bacteria had been spewing out their waste oxygen until, from none at all, there was a concentration in the atmosphere equivalent to about one tenth of that found today, and sufficient to support respiring plants and animals. The further increase in atmospheric oxygen to the present concentration of 21% is owed to photosynthesis in plants, especially trees. Referring back to the equation for photosynthesis, we should note that for every molecule of oxygen in the air there is an equivalent quantity of carbon derived from sugar that is bound up in dead vegetation or fossil fuels. Were we to burn up completely the planet's fossil fuels we would not only roast from global warming, but also suffocate from lack of oxygen.

Photosynthesis altered the composition of the early atmosphere, substituting oxygen for carbon dioxide. The high initial level of the latter was also reduced by another mechanism. In the plankton layer of the oceans were simple creatures called coccolithophores which grew chalky shells of calcium carbonate; later in evolutionary history they were joined by crustaceans which performed the same function.[17] Calcium is an excretory product of these creatures which is put to good use as a protective shell by being combined with carbonic acid, itself formed by solution of atmospheric carbon dioxide in sea water. When these organisms died, their shells fell to the ocean bed and formed thick layers of chalk, later compressed into limestone. In this way huge quantities of carbon dioxide taken from the atmosphere have been locked away in the ocean bed and underground for millions of years. In our time an important use of limestone is for the manufacture of cement, in which lime and clay are calcined. In this process calcium carbonate is heated and converted to calcium oxide, or quicklime, and carbon dioxide is released into the atmosphere.

$$CaCO_3 \;=\; CaO \;+\; CO_2$$
$$Limestone = quicklime + carbon\ dioxide$$

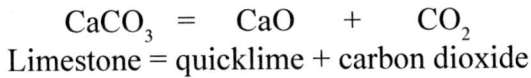

The manufacture of cement, for use in large quantities in the construction of nuclear power stations for example, thus delivers a double whammy of carbon dioxide: from limestone, by the above equation, and from the fossil fuels used in heating it and driving the process.

The huge underground mass of archaebacteria constitutes another menace. Over the aeons they have been producing methane, much of which is locked in polar icecaps and frozen tundra, to be released into the atmosphere should these melt. Like carbon dioxide, methane too is a greenhouse gas, but with a difference: it is some 20 times more potent than carbon dioxide in retaining the sun's heat.[18] Once the tundra and icecaps start to melt, global warming will therefore accelerate as a result of the positive feedback effect of methane release.

Methanogens today play yet another role in global warming. We recall that they require warm, wet and oxygen-free conditions, which are just those that are found inside the rumen of cattle and other ruminants, where symbiotic methane-producing bacteria assist in the digestion of cellulose from grass; methane waste is belched into the atmosphere. Methanogens play a similar role in the gut of termite ants, where they digest wood fibre. Other sources of bacterial methane are rice paddy fields and garbage landfills. Some methane is also produced by the combustion of fossil fuels; about 60% of methane emitted into the atmosphere is directly or indirectly of human origin.[19]

So the first reason for the long evolutionary prelude is that it took 3 billion years to create the atmospheric conditions in which animals and plants could flourish. Moreover, the primitive micro-organisms that created a world fit for us to live in still play a key role in keeping it that way.

We may surmise that a second reason for the long prokaryote prelude is the sheer complexity of the biochemical mechanisms that were developed during that time. Pathways were established for obtaining biochemical energy from a host of different organic and inorganic substrates, as well as from the sun. Structural materials made of carbohydrate, fat and protein were developed, as well as the innumerable enzymes and coenzymes necessary for catalysing every step of their synthesis. Each stage of development had to confer by itself a survival advantage, even though the mechanisms were incomplete when considered from a later point of view. It was all so improbable; no wonder it took so long! But once the eukaryotic (nucleated) cell – what Richard Dawkins calls 'the high-tech, miniature machine that is the microfoundation of all large-scale and complex life' – was up and running, the rest of evolutionary development was comparatively simple.

So what was so special about the nucleated cell that it took so long to evolve? And why was its eventual appearance on the evolutionary scene described by Dawkins as a 'cataclysmic event, arguably the most decisive event in the history of life'?[20] The answer is, in brief, sex.[21]

It will be recalled that bacteria, the most familiar representatives of prokaryotes, have no nuclei to their cells, their chromosomes lying loose in the cytoplasm. Reproduction of bacteria is usually by cell fission, each newly formed cell being a copy of the parent cell, including the chromosomes which contain genes for synthesis of all the cell's different proteins. If this sexless, vegetative reproduction were the only mechanism of passing on genetic information, all bacteria would be identical clones. But, according to Lyn Margulis:

> Bacteria pass their genes with abandon as one bac-
> terium donates its genes to another... Or gene uptake
> may be casual necrophilia; the recipient may just grab
> genes shed earlier when some dead donor left them in
> the water.[22]

Under optimum conditions bacteria may divide every 20 minutes. Coupled with the casual acquisition of DNA, this means
that they are extremely adaptable, for example, quickly adjusting to a new substrate or acquiring resistance to a toxic (to
them) antibiotic. While the free movement of genes between
different bacteria makes for adaptability, it does not support
a progressive increase in complexity because a gene may be
lost or corrupted just as quickly as it is gained. And with free
movement of genetic material even between different species, there is little likelihood of new species evolving because
for this to happen some obstacle to interbreeding is required.

The big breakthrough that allowed the evolution of organisms
more complicated than bacteria was the development of the
nucleated cell. This represents a division of labour between
the genotype and the phenotype.[23] The genotype is the genetic information for the development of the organism, which
is held in a linear molecule, the double helix of DNA, which
can be faithfully replicated. The phenotype is the whole life
cycle of the organism, on which natural selection operates.
The phenotype is now able to evolve multiple physiological
functions and a specialised three dimensional structure too
complicated to be replicated by simple division. In order to
reproduce it therefore has to revert to the recipe for its development coded in the genotype DNA. Being sequestered
within the nucleus, the genes, and the information which they
encode, are protected from corruption, to be faithfully copied
and passed on from generation to generation.

The genotype consists physically of two sets of chromosomes containing thousands of genes. But the germ cells, sperm or egg, contain only one set of chromosomes, the genes of which derive about 50-50 from each parent by a random process. When in sexual reproduction sperm fuses with egg, a double set of chromosomes is restored. About half the genes in the embryo will come from each parent, and about a quarter from each grandparent. In every offspring resulting from sexual reproduction the combination of many thousands of genes is unique, and it is this extensive reshuffling of the genes from one generation to the next which provides the variation of structure, function and behaviour of the organism on which natural selection can act.

The definition of life given earlier entailed multiplication, heredity and variation. These properties of living things arise from the replication of genes. According to Richard Dawkins in *The Selfish Gene*, the qualities of a successful replicator are longevity, fecundity and copying fidelity: qualities that characterise the operation of genes in organisms that reproduce sexually.[24] A successful gene is a length of chromosome which survives intact for many generations, during which time natural selection takes effect and increases its frequency in the population. The gene confers a survival and reproductive advantage on the individuals that possess it, thus causing more copies of itself to be made than would be the case with a less successful gene. In order that advantageous variations will be cumulative, copies of successful genes must be faithful replicas, which is ensured by mechanisms to correct copying errors.[25]

*

We have been considering the 3 billion year evolutionary prelude before multicellular animals and plants first appeared.

There are three explanations for its long duration: the slow colonisation of the planet by the bacteria which made it habitable for us; the sheer complexity of all the high-tech biochemical mechanisms that make up the microfoundations of all large-scale and complex life; and the evolution of nucleated cells which made sexual reproduction and the progressive accumulation of advantageous change possible. These propositions, however, are in each case interpretations of events in the light of our knowledge of how things turned out later. They answer the question of why the evolution of nucleated eukaryote cells, with all their advantages, took so long. But that question is misconceived, and results from what Dawkins calls 'the conceit of hindsight'. For when we look back over our evolutionary history we tend to think that the appearance of creatures of increasing complexity, culminating in *Homo sapiens*, was foreordained, and that this happy outcome could not have been otherwise. But natural selection, the driving force of evolution, has no foresight, and the only thing it does 'see' is an immediate survival and reproductive advantage of a phenotype. Because of this short-termism, natural selection has led many a species into an evolutionary blind alley in which it has become extinct.[26]

In the long prokaryote prelude there was no logical, biological or any other necessity for any evolutionary change at all. Indeed, rather than understanding what did happen, it is easier for us to imagine life never having started, or else quickly spluttering out and leaving the earth as barren as Mars. But once life was established, and, in particular, photosynthesis was underway, the accumulation of oxygen in the atmosphere created opportunities for new forms of life to thrive. But it would be wrong to think that the first photosynthesising cyanobacteria were purposefully selected in order to make the planet habitable for future occupation by respiring creatures such as ourselves. That would be to make the Aristotelian error of equating causation with purpose or reason, of attributing a final cause to bacteria. This erroneous way of thinking was encountered previously in the deep anthropic principle which says that the universe was fine-tuned in order to furnish the conditions which make the evolution of life, and humans, possible.

The appearance in the natural world of design for a purpose is deceptive, being rather the outcome of Darwin's natural selection, preserving favourable differences and variations, and destroying those which are injurious. Eukaryote evolution did not take place in order that we should ultimately evolve from our primordial origins, but rather, had it not taken place we would not be here to wonder why it took so long. When considering cosmology, earth science or evolution we tend so often to think teleologically, reverting to the metaphor we acquired in infancy, *Causation as Action to Achieve a Purpose.*

## From Slime to Sapience

It is now time to leave our aquatic, unicellular, eukaryote ancestor, swimming in the ocean a billion years ago, and fast-forward the tape of evolution to retrace our human lineage. Among our most distant cousins are photosynthesising plants, from whose ancestors we parted company at an early stage. That we are related is shown by the fact that, despite appearances, we have much in common: DNA is the replicator for transmission of genetic information; we have the same DNA code for specifying the 20 amino acids from which proteins are made; and there are sequences of DNA code which differ from the human genome according to how distantly we are related. In fact, these three statements are true, not just for plants, but for all living things on earth, proof indeed of our common origin in the primordial soup.

98

We have much to be grateful to plants for. As we have seen, they excreted, and continue to excrete, oxygen, which supports a raft of creatures that live by respiration. Plants were the first living things to leave the sea and colonise the land, which they started to do 420 million years ago (MYA), though it was not until 140 MYA that flowering plants first appeared.[27] Green photosynthesising plants now jostle, albeit in slow motion, to cover the earth's surface and thrust their leaves skyward so as to maximise their catch of photons arriving from the sun. Hence we find plants at the end of almost every food chain, the ultimate edible source of energy.

Somewhat more closely related to us than plants are fungi, a great kingdom of multicellular organisms which branched off about 1100 MYA.[28] We are dependent on fungi for their involvement in a great many natural processes, and we share 51% of our genes with the fungus we know as yeast.[29] Fungi live by fermenting or respiring ready-made organic matter which they liquefy and absorb. Fungi are often found as symbionts of plants, whose root hairs are augmented by fungal filaments that absorb minerals needed by their hosts. Lichens, too, are a symbiotic mix of fungi, algae and bacteria, and have a vital role in breaking down rock to form soil fit for plants to live in.[30]

The next major branching of our family tree took place about 590 MYA when the ancestors of a whole host of creatures went their separate ways. These included arthropods, comprising insects, spiders and crustaceans, molluscs, and various sorts of worms. All these variegated creatures are classified as protostomes, whose mouths develop from a primary embryonic opening. Their common ancestor was perhaps the first that was recognisably an animal – some sort of worm. The protostomes having left us, the creatures remaining on our branch of the family tree are known as deuterostomes.

Deuterostome means 'mouth second', the primary embryonic opening becoming the anus, the mouth forming later at the other end of the gut. Thus the animal kingdom can be divided into protostomes and deuterostomes on the basis of these differing pathways of embryological development, and this dichotomous classification is upheld by DNA analysis.[31] This is just one example of a remarkable convergence of evidence for evolution derived from quite different scientific disciplines: embryology on the one hand, and genetics on the other.

The ancestors of present day fish left our family tree in two main branches, first the cartilaginous fish, 460 MYA, followed by bony fish and lung fish 20-23 MYA later.[32]

Our nearest fishy ancestor would have looked like *Tiktaalik roseae*, the recently discovered fossil lungfish with four rudimentary limbs.[33] By breathing air, present day lungfish are able to live in stagnant oxygen-poor water, or survive a dry season by burrowing into mud, leaving a breathing hole to the surface. Their, and our, common ancestor with its primitive legs would have been able to travel on land in search of water.

At about 340 MYA we parted company from ancestral amphibians. Although many live on land, most amphibians reproduce in water, whereas the vertebrates remaining on our branch of the family tree – reptiles, birds and mammals – mostly reproduce on land, and are known as amniotes. In them, fertilisation takes place internally in a moist milieu in which sperm can swim, and then they either give birth to live young, or they lay large, tough-shelled, waterproof eggs; in either case the embryo is enclosed with its own pool of water in an amniotic sac in which it can prepare for the privations of life on dry land.

By 310 MYA reptiles had branched off, including the progenitors of the dinosaurs, which gave rise later to birds. At this time our common ancestor would have looked like a lizard, but between then and 65 MYA when the reign of the dinosaurs ended, our forebears evolved into recognisably mammalian, nocturnal, insectivorous shrews.[34] The great cretaceous catastrophe, which caused the mass extinction of a great many species besides the dinosaurs, resulted from a collision into the earth of a large meteorite. The sun was obscured in the ensuing nuclear winter, and the food chain failed, especially for large herbivores. Many ecological niches previously occupied by dinosaurs then became available for mammals to fill.

We now fast-forward to 14 MYA when, having parted company from New and Old World monkeys, we catch up with the human family *Hominidae*, which includes us and our fossil cousins, as well as orang-utans, gorillas and chimpanzees.

Until this time the fossil evidence of hominoids and Old World monkeys came from Africa. But there is then a gap in the African fossil record spanning several million years until the appearance there of *Australopithecus* 3-4 MYA.[35] There are, however, a number of fossils from Eurasia dating from this period that would plausibly fill the gap in the lineage of modern apes and *Homo*. The gap may be explained by postulating a migration 20 MYA from Africa to Asia of a population of apes from which gibbons branched off first, followed by the orang-utans. Later, our ancestral apes migrated back from Asia to Africa, and became today's African apes and us. Land bridges were in existence between Africa and Asia at the relevant times.[36]

Molecular and fossil evidence suggests that gorillas left our family tree about 7 MYA, the chimpanzees leaving a million years later. We share 98% of our genes with chimpanzees, who are our closest living cousins.[37]

## Walking Upright with a Big Brain

From the time of our separation from the chimpanzee line, the feature written into the fossil record that is most distinctive of human ancestry is upright, two-legged walking, evidence for which is found especially in hip and thigh bones, and in the knee joint.[38] Touching corroborative evidence of walking on two legs has been provided by two trails of bipedal footprints left side by side in fossilised volcanic ash dating from 3.5 MYA.[39] Bipedalism originated in the Rift Valley in north-east Africa, and is epitomised by the fossilised remains of *Australopithecus afarensis* discovered in the Afar region of Ethiopia, and familiarly known as Lucy. Although partially modified for upright walking, her skeleton is not yet fully adapted, her feet being relatively larger than ours, and her knees not yet having a locking mechanism for standing upright. Bipedalism thus came at a high cost.

> This is what the orthodox theory asks us to believe: that millions of years ago a population of apes on the savannah chose to walk on two limbs, instead of running rapidly and easily on four like a baboon or a chimpanzee. They stood up, with their unmodified pelves, their inappropriate single-arched spines, their absurdly under-muscled thighs and buttocks, and their heads stuck on at the wrong angle, and they doggedly shuffled along on the sides of their long-toed, ill-adapted feet...The incentive must have been immediate and powerful.[40]

Elaine Morgan, from whose book *The Scars of Evolution* that quotation comes, presents a persuasive case that the incentive was one that is as immediate and powerful as it is possible to imagine: survival from drowning. For about 7 million years ago the sea flooded into the northern Afar depression where it was later cut off from the ocean, evaporating over millions of years to become the desert salt plain it is today. At the time of the inundation the area would have been forested and was probably inhabited by apes. Morgan argues that these were the very conditions in which being able to wade upright through swampland would have given an immediate survival and therefore, reproductive, advantage, and it was this that triggered bipedalism. Her aquatic ape theory also accounts for our being the only naked ape, as well as some other human peculiarities. While we were living in a briny swampland we lost our useless furry coat and acquired instead a subcutaneous layer of blubber, which is a better insulator in water. We also lost the use of our sweat glands which were no longer needed, and developed salt excreting glands to cope with the excess of salt which we were inadvertently ingesting. When the swampland eventually dried out we emerged to be exposed without protection to the heat of the savannah, and our salt excreting glands were pressed into service as sweat glands. As a consequence, our cooling mechanism is rather inefficient in that a greater degree of cooling could be achieved with evaporation of a thin film of sweat applied sparingly to each hair of a furry pelt; in a hot climate, drenching the naked skin with sweat is a waste of precious water. Moreover, heavy sweating exposes us to the risk of salt loss and circulatory collapse. We are unusual amongst mammals in not developing an appetite for salt when we are deficient in it; perhaps this human peculiarity also dates from the time when an excess of salt rather than a deficit was a problem.

*

It was subsequent to our ancestors' adoption of bipedalism that there was a large increase in brain size, a big brain now being our most distinctive physical feature, associated with language and culture. Lucy's brain, at 4-500 cc, was not much larger than a modern chimpanzee's. A brain volume of 750 cc or more is necessary for a hominoid to qualify as a member of the genus *Homo*. The earliest of our fossilised ancestors to gain this distinction was *Homo habilis*, the first tool maker, dating from about 2 MYA.[41] Then *Homo erectus* (also known as *Homo ergaster*) appeared in the fossil record 1.8 MYA with a brain of 8-900 cc,[42] followed by *Archaic Homo sapiens* 160,000 years ago with one of 12-1300 cc.[43] Self-proclaimed *Homo sapiens sapiens* dates from about 100,000 years ago, and for much of our prehistory we coexisted with big-brained *Homo sapiens neanderthalensis*, which like us was probably descended from *Archaic Homo sapiens*;[44] we may well have been responsible for its extinction 30,000 years ago. The modern human brain has an average volume of 1350 cc, which is three times as large as the average for primates,[45] and six times larger than that of an average mammal, taking account of body size.[46] Our brain is about three times as big as cousin chimp's, and it ballooned to its present size in a remarkably short period, evolutionarily speaking.

A large brain comes at a cost: that of the nutrients needed for its construction, the energy expended in its metabolism, and the lives of mothers and babies dying in childbirth. Compared with many mammals human babies are born prematurely before the head is fully grown, necessitating a long period of dependency while the brain triples in volume to reach its adult size.[47] Even so, the baby's skull is sometimes too big for easy passage through the birth canal of a pelvis adapted for upright walking. In view of the costs incurred by possession of such a large brain, we would expect it to be associated with some overwhelming survival advantage. There is no consensus, however, as to what that might be, and it seems that a brain capable of philosophising, or doing higher mathematics, is greatly over endowed for subsistence survival in a hunter-gatherer society. And if development of a big brain is such a good evolutionary trick, with advantages enough to justify the heavy costs, it is to be expected that a big brain would have evolved in other mammals besides ourselves.

As with bipedalism, a very powerful selection pressure has to be invoked to explain such an extraordinary feature that comes at such a high cost. Many explanations for the explosive growth of the brain have been proposed: bipedalism required a larger brain for the control of balance and locomotion; bipedalism also freed the hands for toolmaking, for which fine motor control from an enlarged brain was advantageous; bipedalism reduced the amount of solar radiation experienced when the sun was overhead, opening up a niche for scavenging carcasses in the middle of the day when carnivores needed to find shade; meat is energy-rich compared with vegetable matter, so our intestines became smaller and we used less energy for digestion; within the same energy budget we were able to support a bigger brain; the advantages of increased meat intake were reinforced by the new found ability to conceive of and make tools for hunting and butchering carcasses; there was a need to keep tabs on the relationships in a social group of increasing size, particularly to detect free riders in a group of hunters; the development of language would have increased the complexity of social relationships, and contributed to a spiralling cognitive competitiveness.[48-50] But none of these concomitants of a big brain seems to offer a sufficient *immediate* survival advantage to compensate for the heavy costs incurred.

*

Darwin had outlined his theory of evolution by means of natural selection many years before its publication, which was hastened when he learned that a naturalist called Alfred Russel Wallace had developed a similar theory. To avoid an unseemly wrangle over priority they wrote a joint paper which appeared one year before *The Origin of Species*, which appeared with great acclaim in 1859. In *The Descent of Man, and Selection in Relation to Sex,* published in 1871, Darwin went on to reason that sexual selection through mate choice provided an explanation for the development of what he calls secondary sexual characters:

> …such as the weapons of offence and the means of defence of the males for fighting with and driving away their rivals – their courage and pugnacity – their various ornaments – their contrivances for producing vocal or instrumental music – and their glands for emitting odours, most of these latter structures serving only to allure or excite the female. It is clear that these characters are the result of sexual and not of ordinary selection, since unarmed, unornamented, or unattractive males would succeed equally well in the battle for life and in leaving a numerous progeny, but for the presence of better endowed males.[51]

The peacock's tail is a classic example of male ornamentation. A mutation gives rise to fancy tail feathers which prove attractive to the peahen. The bearer of the lucky feathers pulls more birds and has more offspring than those with a plain tail. The mutant tail-feather gene then spreads through the gene pool; further mutations result in a tail that becomes more and more elaborate. At the same time, any genes that make peahens prefer fancy-tailed peacocks, perhaps enhancing colour vision or the recognition of certain patterns, would also increase in frequency. In this way a spiralling competition for developing the most elaborate tail is set in train, only reaching a limit when the tail becomes disadvantageous for survival, perhaps by preventing its possessor from escaping a predator.

It should be noted that sexual selection results in so-called sexual dimorphism, the gaudy peacock being admired by the dowdy peahen. Although sexual selection by the female is the commonest form, selection may take place in the opposite direction, or be mutual.

Although *The Descent of Man, and Selection in Relation to Sex* sold well at the time of its publication, it created little notice and was largely neglected during the next century. Darwin's sexual selection hypothesis has been revitalised in *The Ant and the Peacock* by Helena Cronin,[52] and *The Mating Mind* by Geoffrey Miller.[53] In the latter, the author develops the theory to account for the evolution of the large human brain. Following Darwin, he distinguishes between natural selection and sexual selection. Natural selection is the mechanism that results in adaptations necessary for survival in a physical environment which includes prey and predators. Such adaptations are lungs, and an amniotic method of reproduction, both necessary for survival out of water; also, the teeth and claws of a predatory carnivore, and the fleetness of foot of its prey.

Sexual selection on the other hand presupposes survival to adulthood, and is a mechanism for the development of features that are largely neutral with regard to survival, but which enhance reproductive success. The adaptations brought about by sexual selection are in relation to the social environment in which reproduction takes place, the milieu comprising the opposite sex as well as same-sex rivals.

One of the sexes, usually the female is discriminating in her choice of mate, selecting perhaps the male with the brightest coloration or the largest tail. Or, the males may directly compete with each other for rights over a harem of admiring females. The alpha male would have a lot of offspring carrying the gene for alpha qualities, while his rivals would have fewer offspring or none at all. At the same time, a gene promoting female preference for alpha qualities will be replicated in greater numbers when the female mates with a male possessing those qualities. In this way there is runaway elaboration of male adornment of which the female can never have enough, and there develops a marked disparity of ornamentation between the sexes.

Without modification, sexual selection theory cannot account for the big human brain because the brain is not, of course, a visible, decorative feature. Moreover, there is no appreciable difference in brain volume between males and females as is required by the theory. But the size of the brain may make itself manifest by the complexity of behaviour that it supports. Thus in the first toolmakers, the manual dexterity shown in the ability to shape flint into axe heads might serve to advertise the possession of a big brain, and attract female admirers. It would not, however, explain the similar brain size in men and women. Now a quirky, extravagant oddity that evolves by sexual selection requires the co-evolution of female preference as well as the masculine feature. In the case of the peacock's tail, or an elaborate courtship ritual, completely different genes, controlling completely different bodily functions are implicated in the development of the secondary sexual character of the male, and its appreciation by the female. But a similar expansion of the brain in both sexes would be expected if the same mental faculty was involved in both the courtship behaviour of the male and its adjudication by the female. Such would be the case with sweet nothings murmured seductively into the ear of the beloved. In this account, language – the product of a big brain – confers a reproductive rather than a survival advantage, having evolved as an element of the courtship ritual of *Homo sapiens*. While a peahen does not herself need an elaborate tail to appreciate that of the peacock, the human female needs a profound knowledge of language – and therefore a big brain – to be able to judge the wit, charm and sincerity of her would-be seducer's patter.

Another reason for equality of brain size and intelligence between the sexes is that men may in fact be just as choosy as women when it comes to long-term relationships. Also, about half the genes of the human genome are expressed in the brain, and most of them are common to males and females.[54] Genes for a big brain, passed on from a big-brained man, will therefore be inherited by daughters as well as sons.

With sexual selection, the choice of a mate may be made on the basis of the display of some arbitrary, ornamental feature, but Miller proposes that it may also serve a more serious function as a screen for general fitness.[55] The peacock flaunting his magnificent tail is also proclaiming that he is strong, well-nourished and disease free, with no harmful mutations to pass on to the offspring he will have with his partner. The more costly the display, the more reliably it reflects the fitness of its possessor. Which is why a dazzling display of creative intelligence and wit, reflecting a high degree of general and genetic fitness, may win a maiden's heart. This is not to say that either the peahen or the maiden are consciously performing a health screen on their prospective mates, but rather that the offspring of many previous generations of females have thrived because of their mothers' genetic predilection for displays that reflect fitness.

*

Susan Blackmore in *The Meme Machine* suggests that an important stage in human evolution was the acquisition of the ability to imitate the actions of others, a talent that requires a good deal of brain power.[56] If an axe maker is admired for the shapely axe heads he produces, how much more so would he be if he could quickly learn by imitation to make the latest arrow head or spear shaft as well. Genes for imitating the behaviour of others would then spread quickly through the population, preparing the ground for cultural evolution. Culture evolves by the spread and accumulation of ideas, or memes, the units of cultural inheritance. Memes are gossip, jokes, stories, pictures, songs, catchy tunes, and the like, and also fads and fashions. Nowadays memes may spread like an epidemic, being passed from person to person by word of mouth, or by radio, television or internet. Many more memes are generated than can be propagated, and most die out. Some memes, however, are especially good at being copied, and they multiply and spread widely. A successful meme, then, like a successful gene, is one that causes many copies of itself to be replicated. It is by this Darwinian process of multiplication of memes, and their variation and selection that cultures evolve.

Susan Blackmore describes meme-gene co-evolution, arguing that somebody with good memes to pass on, somebody musical, poetic or artistic, is likely also to pass on his or her genes, including those for whatever talent is called upon to play a tune, paint a picture, tell a story, or sweet-talk a lover. In this way, the evolution of culture and the evolution of the brain structures that support it – such as those predisposing to synaesthesia and creativity that we met in the last chapter – are mutually reinforcing, amplifying the effect of sexual selection.

*

We have been considering our most distinctive bodily characteristic, that of walking upright with a big brain. While many factors have undoubtedly contributed to the ballooning of the human brain, it seems clear that the single most important trigger for its development was our ancestors' assumption of an upright gait, which freed the hands for tool-making. Although no big brain theory is totally convincing, it is probable that sexual selection, with its whimsical preferences, has played an important part. It can therefore be argued that we have played a major role in our own evolution for, as Darwin wrote at the end of *The Descent of Man*:

> He who admits the principle of sexual selection will be led to the remarkable conclusion that the nervous system not only regulates most of the existing functions of the body, but has indirectly influenced the progressive development of various bodily structures and of certain mental qualities. Courage, pugnacity, perseverance, strength and size of body, weapons of all kinds, musical organs, both vocal and instrumental, bright colours and ornamental appendages, have all been gained by the one sex or the other, through the exertion of choice, the influence of love and jealousy, and the appreciation of the beautiful in sound, colour or form; and these powers of the mind manifestly depend on the development of the brain.[57]

If the aquatic ape theory of bipedalism is also admitted, then we must acknowledge that the evolution of our most distinctive bodily characteristic, of walking upright with a big brain, resulted from the fortuitous flooding of the Rift Valley 7 million years ago.

*

What is striking in the 4 billion year epic of life on earth, is its *contingency,* and the role that chance has played in our being here, starting with the origin of life itself. Just as we cannot know the prospective likelihood of the formation of a universe and a solar system that supports life, neither can we

111

know the prospective likelihood of life developing in such a solar system. But in retrospect it does appear that the evolution of matter into life on planet Earth was serendipitous, and we have the example of the not dissimilar planet Mars, where life never got going or else soon petered out. Another lucky break was at the end of the prokaryote prelude when nucleated cells – eukaryotes – appeared, the result of several apparently unlikely symbioses. We are on firmer ground in attributing to chance the Cretaceous catastrophe resulting from a meteor strike 65 million years ago. By causing the extinction of many creatures, including the dinosaurs, this chance cataclysmic event opened up ecological niches in which our shrew-like distant ancestors thrived. Although there is no agreement on what caused our ancestors to become bipedal, there is a consensus that it was a necessary preliminary to the explosive growth of the brain; the chance flooding of the Rift Valley provides a plausible explanation. As for our big brain, if we accept that sexual selection may have played a part in its evolution, then we must acknowledge that we owe our existence today to the first women's somewhat quirky preferences for brainy men. Prospectively, taking all these contingencies into account, the cumulative odds were very much against our appearance on earth in our present form. Some would argue that this very unlikelihood of our being here is evidence of a purpose in creation; we were meant to be here. As a corrective to that idea it should be noted how very recent is our arrival on earth, 100,000 years ago, in relation to the immense period of time since the Big Bang, 14,000,000,000 years ago. If we were meant to be here why did we dally so long in coming?

## Summing Up

Life has been present on earth for all but the first quarter of the planet's immensely long existence. The exact circumstances in which it arose are not known, and probably never will be, but whether life started in a primeval soup or a volcanic vent, it is unnecessary to invoke any supernatural agency or mystical life-force to explain it. Life started as a self-replicating molecule, and entails multiplication, heredity and variation, properties that are conferred on all living things today by their constituent DNA. Bacteria, protozoa, algae, fungi, plants and animals, from the smallest to the largest, have this replicator in common. This can only mean that all living things are related and arose from a common ancestor, which originated 4 billion years ago.

The origin of life was inauspicious, and for many millions of years the only forms of life were microscopic in size. Nevertheless, they had a profound effect on the earth's geology and climate, creating opportunities for the later evolution of new life forms. Darwinian evolution is without foresight and operates by natural selection of variants which have an immediate survival and/or reproductive advantage. By this process organisms adapt to their environment, and cumulative, progressive complexity is made possible, but is not inevitable.

Our bodies are living museums of evolutionary history: Nucleated cells, mitochondria, vertebrate body plan, lungs, internal fertilisation, embryonic development within an amniotic sac, and a myriad other features attest to our oneness with all living things and affirm our animal nature. Walking upright with a big brain marks our exceptionalism, and also underscores the contingency of our evolution.

# Notes

## Chapter 3: The Evolution of Matter into Life

1. Charles Darwin. *The Origin of Species by Means of Natural Selection.* Sixth (final) edition. London: Watts & Co, 1948: p59. The phrase 'survival of the fittest' was coined by Herbert Spencer and only appeared in later editions of *The Origin of Species*.
2. Press F, Siever R. *Earth, 2nd ed.* San Francisco: WH Freeman and Company, 1978: p14.
3. James Lovelock. *Gaia: A New Look At Life On Earth.* Oxford University Press, 1995: p18.
4. John Maynard Smith. *The Theory of Evolution.* Cambridge University Press, 2000: p109.
5. Richard Dawkins. *The Ancestor's Tale: A Pilgrimage to the Dawn of Life.* London: Phoenix, 2005: pp594-6.
6. John Maynard Smith. *The Theory of evolution.* Cambridge University Press, 2000: p109-110.
7. Lynn Margulis. *The Symbiotic Planet: A New Look at Evolution.* London: Phoenix, 1999: p104.
8. Ibid, p106.
9. Richard Dawkins. *The Ancestor's Tale: A Pilgrimage to the Dawn of Life.* London: Phoenix, 2005: p561.
10. Ibid, p569.
11. Lynn Margulis. *The Symbiotic Planet: A New Look at Evolution.* London: Phoenix, 1999: pp17-42.
12. For example "Populist interpretations of evolution...have accustomed people to the idea of nature being 'red in tooth and claw', with all life forms engaged in endless titanic struggles to ensure 'the survival of the fittest'...[But] the work of scientists such as Lynn Margulis and Janine Benyus has revealed fascinating patterns of mutual interdependence and elegant symbiosis....[There is a] mismatch between how evolution really works and how the majority of people have come to think it works..." *From* Jonathon Porritt. *Capitalism as if the World Matters.* London: Earthscan, 2005: pp80-81.
13. Lynn Margulis. *The Symbiotic Planet: A New Look at Evolu-*

*tion*. London: Phoenix, 1999: p48.

14. Ibid, p82.
15. Richard Dawkins. *The Ancestor's Tale: A Pilgrimage to the Dawn of Life*. London: Phoenix, 2005: p595.
16. Lynn Margulis. *The Symbiotic Planet: A New Look at Evolution*. London: Phoenix, 1999: p137.
17. James Lovelock. *Gaia: A New Look at Life on Earth*. Oxford University Press, 1995: p88-89.
18. Reg Morrison. *The Spirit in the Gene: Humanity's Proud Illusion and the Laws of Nature*. New York: Cornell University Press, 1999: p23.
19. John McNeil. *Something New Under The Sun: An Environmental History of the Twentieth Century*. London: Allen Lane, 2000: p53.
20. Richard Dawkins. *The Ancestor's Tale: A Pilgrimage to the Dawn of Life*. London: Phoenix, 2005: p549
21. Matt Ridley. *The Red Queen: Sex and the Evolution of Human Nature*. New York: Harper Perennial, 2003: pp55-87
22. Lynn Margulis. *The Symbiotic Planet: A New Look at Evolution*. London: Phoenix, 1999: p110-111.
23. John Maynard Smith. *The Theory of Evolution*. Cambridge University Press, 2000: p115.
24. Richard Dawkins. *The Selfish Gene*. Oxford University Press, 1989: p18.
25. John Maynard Smith. *The Theory of Evolution*. Cambridge University Press, 2000: p118.
26. "Extinction is the eventual fate of nearly all species. Perhaps 99 per cent of all species that have ever existed have gone extinct." Richard Dawkins. *The Ancestor's Tale: A Pilgrimage to the Dawn of Life*. London: Phoenix, 2005: p255.
27. *The Development of Life*. Britannica CD 99 Multimedia Edition © 1994-1999 Encyclopædia Britannica, Inc.
28. Richard Dawkins. *The Ancestor's Tale: A Pilgrimage to the Dawn of Life*. London: Phoenix, 2005: p471.
29. "We share 51 per cent of our genes with yeast and 98 per cent with chimpanzees – it is not genetics that makes us human." Tom Shakespeare http://genome.wellcome.ac.uk/node30068.html
30. Lynn Margulis. *The Symbiotic Planet: A New Look at Evolu-*

115

*tion*. London: Phoenix, 1999: pp134-6.

31. Richard Dawkins. *The Ancestor's Tale: A Pilgrimage to the Dawn of Life*. London: Phoenix, 2005: p389.

32. Ibid, pp328-60.

33. Discovered: missing link that solves a mystery of evolution. *The Guardian* April 6, 2006.

34. Richard Dawkins. *The Ancestor's Tale: A Pilgrimage to the Dawn of Life*. London: Phoenix, 2005: p176.

35. Chris Stringer, Peter Andrews. *The Complete World of Human Evolution*. New York: Thames & Hudson Inc., 2005: p12.

36. Richard Dawkins. *The Ancestor's Tale: A Pilgrimage to the Dawn of Life*. London: Phoenix, 2005: p121.

37. "We share 51 per cent of our genes with yeast and 98 per cent with chimpanzees – it is not genetics that makes us human." Tom Shakespeare http://genome.wellcome.ac.uk/node30068.html

38. Chris Stringer, Peter Andrews. *The Complete World of Human Evolution*. New York: Thames & Hudson Inc., 2005: p114.

39. Ibid, p118.

40. Elaine Morgan. *The Scars of Evolution: What Our Bodies Tell Us About Human Origins*. London: Souvenir Press, 1990: p34.

41. Richard Dawkins. *The Ancestor's Tale: A Pilgrimage to the Dawn of Life*. London: Phoenix, 2005: p79.

42. Susan Blackmore. *The Meme Machine*. Oxford University Press, 1999: p69.

43. Richard Dawkins. *The Ancestor's Tale: A Pilgrimage to the Dawn of Life*. London: Phoenix, 2005: p65-6.

44. Steven Mithen. *The Prehistory of the Mind: The Cognitive Origins of Art and Science*. London: Thames and Hudson Ltd, 1996: p25.

45. Susan Blackmore. *The Meme Machine*. Oxford University Press, 1999: p68.

46. Richard Dawkins. *The Ancestor's Tale: A Pilgrimage to the Dawn of Life*. London: Phoenix, 2005: p86.

47. Susan Blackmore. *The Meme Machine*. Oxford University Press, 1999: p71.

48. Elaine Morgan. *The Scars of Evolution: What Our Bodies Tell Us About Human Origins.* London: Souvenir Press, 1990:

p37-45.

49. Steven Mithen. *The Prehistory of the Mind: The Cognitive Origins of Art and Science.* London: Thames and Hudson Ltd, 1996: p99.

50. Susan Blackmore. *The Meme Machine.* Oxford University Press, 1999: p74.

51. Charles Darwin. *The Descent of Man, and Selection in Relation to Sex.* London: Penguin Books, 2004: p245.

52. Helena Cronin. *The Ant and the Peacock: Altruism and Sexual Selection from Darwin to Today.* Cambridge University Press, 1991.

53. Geoffrey Miller. *The Mating Mind: How Sexual Choice Shaped the Evolution of Human Nature.* London, William Heinemann, 2000.

54. Ibid, p121.

55. Ibid, p99-137.

56. Susan Blackmore. *The Meme Machine.* Oxford University Press, 1999: pp3-4.

57. Charles Darwin. *The Descent of Man, and Selection in Relation to Sex.* London: Penguin Books, 2004: p687.

# Chapter 4

# Problems with the Theory of Evolution

'That many and serious objections may be advanced against the theory of descent with modification through variation and natural selection, I do not deny.'
*Charles Darwin*[1]

In the last chapter the history of our evolution was recounted: how life originated as a self-replicating molecule, and subsequently evolved into the bountiful panoply of living things that make up the biosphere. The fortuitous events that may have resulted in our walking upright with a big brain were also reviewed. And it is our exceptionally big brain that has enabled us to learn and reflect on the significance of this epic 4 billion year family history. But before considering the implications of the theory of evolution for the way we think and, in particular, the way we think about ourselves, we must first ask of the theory of evolution the same question that we asked of the Big Bang – why should we believe such an amazing tale?

## The Development of the Theory of Evolution

In Darwin's time the prevailing ideas about our origins were creationism and essentialism, two defunct notions that nevertheless persist to this day in more or less explicit forms; these ideas have already been encountered in an earlier chapter on the Big Bang. But even before these ideas were challenged head-on by the publication of *The Origin of Species*, there was much circumstantial evidence in favour of evolution. The findings of comparative anatomy indicative of a uniform plan in the mind of the Creator might indicate instead that creatures sharing a common anatomical plan were descendants of a common ancestor. Descent from a common ancestor was also suggested by the remarkably similar appearance and development of embryos of reptiles, birds and mammals; embryonic development was thought (erroneously) to re-enact the historical development of the species, a belief neatly summarised later as 'ontogeny recapitulates phylogeny'. Anatomists were also discovering useless rudimentary organs, such as the appendix and the coccyx in man, and vestigial limbs in certain snakes: these structures gave the lie to the argument from design, that each species was created anew to be perfectly adapted to its ecological niche. Rather, existing structures were modified in response to new environmental pressures. Geologists were recognising the natural processes that were continuing to slowly mould the earth, and presumably had been doing so since the beginning of creation. And if the natural environment had been changing, so too had living things. Evidence for this was found in fossils of extinct forms of life, and in fossil series in which extinct and extant species apparently merged one with the other. Tangible evidence against immutability of species was also provided by plant and animal breeders, who, by selective breeding, produced new strains which were relatively permanent. Darwin's theory of evolution by natural selection took on board all of this evidence, and also provided answers to two crucial questions: how to account for the appearance of design, and how to explain 'likeness in diversity'.[2]

Darwin had been impressed by Malthus' essay on the growth of populations. In all creatures, many more individuals are born than survive to procreate as adults. There is therefore a struggle for existence: individuals of the same or different species compete with each other for nutrition or shelter, or struggle against the elements of the physical environment. Darwin also observed the extent of variation, between individuals in a litter, or of the same species, or of species within a genus, and he remarked that many of these variations were inherited. He argued that variations that were in any way injurious would be eliminated in this struggle for existence, while creatures possessing variations that offered an advantage, however slight, would be likely to survive, to pass on their advantageous features to their offspring. He compared this process of natural selection to that exercised by plant and animal breeders who produce new and stable varieties within a few generations by selecting individuals with desirable features as breeding stock for the next generation. In the same way, over many generations, natural selection results in the progressive accumulation of tiny variations which adjust individuals to their organic and inorganic environment. This adaptation, often exquisite, has the appearance of intelligent design but is, so the theory goes, the result of a mindless algorithmic process.

As for the explanation of likeness in diversity, Darwin, rather than resorting to the Platonic notion of forms, summons up the potent metaphor of the tree of life, ***Phylogeny as a Tree***.

> It is a truly wonderful fact – the wonder of which we are apt to overlook from familiarity – that all animals and all plants throughout all time and space should be related to each other in groups... If species had been independently created, no explanation would have been possible of this kind of classification... The affinities of all the beings of the same class have sometimes been represented by a great tree. The green and budding twigs may represent existing species; and those produced during former years may represent the long succession of extinct species. At each period of growth all the growing twigs have tried to branch out

on all sides, and to overtop and kill the surrounding twigs and branches, in the same manner as species and groups of species have at all times overmastered other species in the great battle for life. The limbs divided into great branches, and these into lesser and lesser branches, were themselves once, when the tree was young, budding twigs.[3]

Likeness in diversity is thus explained by inheritance with modification.

Besides the expected censure from churchmen, there were scientific criticisms of Darwin's theory, particularly concerning the origin and evolution of adaptations. How does natural selection act on a trivial variation when it is too rudimentary to be advantageous to its owner? This remains a conceptual difficulty even today, to which the answer seems to be that given time, even a minimally useful adaptation will become established. Also, a structure evolved to serve one function may be modified to serve another. Thus, feathers are thought to have evolved for warmth but were then used for gliding, and later adapted for flight. In the country of the blind, the one-eyed man is king, and even an eighth of an eye is better than none.

Another problem was that the gradual evolutionary changes postulated by Darwin required a very long period of time for their enactment. But Lord Kelvin, the renowned physicist, had produced an estimate of the earth's age which was based on the earth's supposed rate of cooling, and which indicated that it was too young for evolution to have occurred; Kelvin did not know of the heat generated within the earth by radioactive decay, such as that of uranium to lead. By measurement of uranium/lead ratios in ancient rocks, the earth was later shown to be much older than even Darwin had supposed, and it had also undergone enormous change since its formation. Recent knowledge of the sequence in which continental plates separated from the single land mass that once existed has contributed greatly to our understanding of the distribution of species in different continents. Geographical separation of island continents at an early stage resulted in Africa, Laurasia, South America, Madagascar and Australia each having their own distinctive fauna and flora.[4]

Other objections to the theory arose because in Darwin's time the principles of genetics were not understood: it was argued that a favourable variation would be progressively 'diluted' by interbreeding with individuals lacking it. The prevailing theory was Lamarck's inheritance of acquired characteristics, which translated into the popular beliefs that the brawny muscles acquired by the blacksmith during his lifetime would be inherited by his sons, or that a dog whose tail had been docked would father puppies without tails. The German biologist Weismann, however, was unable to find a single case where an acquired characteristic was inherited by the next generation, and, notoriously, he cut off the tails of several generations of mice to no inherited effect, thus disproving the theory.[5] He pointed out that germ cells, those giving rise to ova and sperm, are segregated at any early stage from the soma, the cells of the body that undergo adaptive changes in an individual's lifetime. The soma perishes with the death of the individual, whereas the germ line is effectively immortal, passing from generation to generation unaffected by the lifetime changes in the rest of the body. Weismann's theory was vindicated in the following century with the discovery of DNA, which is replicated from generation to generation in the germ line. Furthermore, DNA, located in chromosomes sequestered in cell nuclei, is effectively insulated from events affecting the soma. There is a flow of information between DNA and somatic cells, but changes in those cells are not translated back into changes in DNA, thus blocking the inheritance of acquired characteristics.

122

Since Darwin's time, major advances in the theory of evolution have been mainly in the domain of genetics. Mendel's discovery of the particulate nature of inheritance in plants was not known to Darwin, but came to light early in the 20th century. Mendel showed that there were dominant or recessive factors, now identified as genes, for features such as the smooth or wrinkly skin of peas. It became evident later that this was a relatively unusual type of inheritance, and that most characteristics are not determined by a single gene but by many, and that most genes have multiple effects acting on different processes and at different stages in an organism's development. Elucidation of the double helix structure of DNA a century after publication of *The Origin of Species* put genetics at the heart of evolutionary theory, and a further half-century saw the structural analysis of the 25,000 genes that comprise the human genome. The most recent advances in genetics concern the mechanisms of embryonic development, how genotype is translated into phenotype, of which more will be said later.

\*

In sum, Darwin's theory of evolution has three separate but related strands: all living things are related, being descended from some sort of micro-organism in the distant past; the hierarchical taxonomic system used in classification of living things is indicative of evolutionary lineage; natural selection is the principal evolutionary mechanism.

Modern genetics has provided an astounding independent corroboration of all three of these elements of the theory. That all living things are related is shown by the fact that all creatures, from algae to ash trees, and from bacteria to baboons, have identical DNA codes for the 20 amino acids used in building proteins.

Secondly, independent genetic evidence of evolutionary lineage has largely confirmed the validity of the taxonomic system based on comparative morphology, and originally devised by Linnaeus in the 18th century. The number of differences between DNA of different species is inversely proportional to the degree to which they are related. Thus, in the 19th century it was appreciated that we are more closely related to chimpanzees and orang-utans than to other primates; this has been confirmed by genetic studies.[6] Moreover, the number of differences in DNA gives an indication of the duration of time that has passed since two species had a common ancestor. This 'molecular clock' is calibrated against fossil dates, and provides supplementary data concerning the timing of evolutionary events.[7]

Thirdly, natural selection is now understood to act by altering the frequency with which alternative genes, or alleles, are found in a breeding population. Thus, in moths there are alleles for dark or light pigmentation, dark being dominant. With increasing industrialisation and pollution, dark moths have had a survival advantage, and the proportion of moths with genes for dark pigmentation has increased.[8] More important from a theoretical point of view has been the elucidation of the mechanisms by which a steady proportion of genes detrimental to their owners, such as that for sickle cell anaemia, may persist in a breeding population.[9]

In these various ways, the synthesis of Darwinism and modern genetics has served to confirm and extend Darwin's theory so that now, 'nothing in biology makes sense except in the light of evolution.'[10] The fundamental hypothesis, that all living things are related, having evolved from a common ancestor, and that evolution has a naturalistic explanation, is as true as is the belief that the earth is a globe, or that the planets encircle the sun.

124

But although there is a consensus among biologists of almost every persuasion that all living things are related, having evolved from a common ancestor, and that evolution has a naturalistic explanation, that is probably as far as the consensus goes. For amongst scientists there are deep divisions about the scope and mechanisms of evolution, and among academics in the humanities there is a widespread belief that Darwinism has been seriously challenged, if not fatally wounded.[11] And, of course, amongst religious fundamentalists the theory is held to be just plain wrong, contradicting, as it does, scriptural authority. After a century and a half the theory of evolution thus remains highly contentious, in a way that Big Bang theory is not.

Philosophers, too, continue to have their say about Darwin's theory of evolution. A recent diatribe is the much-trailed *What Darwin Got Wrong* by philosopher Jerry Fodor and molecular biologist Massimo Piattelli-Palmarini.[12] While fully accepting that evolution has occurred, and that it has a naturalist explanation, the authors take exception to natural selection as a scientific theory to explain its mechanism. For a theory to be scientific, they say, it needs to incorporate a law of nature, as do Newton's theory of universal gravitation or Einstein's general theory of relativity. These theories enàble predictions to be made – of the return of Halley's comet, or that light will bend when passing close to a star. But the 'theory' of natural selection says nothing about how a species will make a living in a given environment, whether by flying in the air and catching insects, burrowing in the ground and eating worms, or simply by being a wallflower and basking in the sun. Just as there is no 'general theory of history' which could have predicted the direction of history in the past, and predicts the future, there is no 'general theory of evolution' incorporating deterministic laws of nature which would make possible the prediction of the direction of evolution. The only thing that can be said is that a species will fit its ecological niche; but this is merely a truism, since a species and its ecological niche are defined mutually. If neither fits the other, the niche vanishes and the creature that was occupying it, and therein making a living, dies. Rather than conforming to a general principle, every species has its particular history – the leopard getting its spots, and the camel its hump, but by a variety of mechanisms we can never be sure about. Evolution, like history, is just one damn thing after another. Whether Fodor correctly describes the logical structure of the theory of natural selection is hotly contested.[13] What is more certain is that he and Piattelli-Palmarini have been rather unfair to Darwin for whom natural selection was not the only mechanism of evolution, and who did pretty well considering he could have had no idea of how genetics and molecular biology would develop.

For the most part, though, objections to Darwinism are not to its status as scientific theory, but to its reliability as a historical account of the origin of species. We need now to consider various reasons given for disbelief in the occurrence of evolution. Firstly, there are gaps and anomalies in the history that may be legitimate reasons to be sceptical about the theory as a whole, or in part. Secondly, there are many people who, while accepting the Darwinian account of evolution of the human body, cannot accept a naturalistic explanation for consciousness, and what Wallace, the co-discoverer of natural selection, called 'the higher intellectual and spiritual nature of man'. Thirdly, the theory may be rejected, not because of any inherent weakness, but because the consequences of its acceptance are considered pernicious, being destructive of human dignity, morality and society. Of course, all combinations of these reasons may be given for rejection of all or part of evolutionary theory. In particular, scientific objections may be a pretext for other reasons for dissent.

This brings us to the question of *The Darwin Wars: The Scientific Battle for the Soul of Man*. In this aptly titled book, Andrew Brown discusses the controversies surrounding the theory of evolution, particularly the modern synthesis of Darwin's theory with genetics and molecular biology.[14] According to Brown, the protagonists in the Darwin wars may be broadly divided into two opposing camps, the right-liberals versus the left Marxists or Marxist sympathisers. The principals on the right are Edward O Wilson, Richard Dawkins and John Maynard Smith, and on the left Richard Lewontin, Stephen Jay Gould and Steven Rose. Philosophical support comes, amongst others, from Daniel Dennett and Helena Cronin for the Dawkinsians, and from Mary Midgley and Susan Oyama for the Gouldians. The positions taken by the two camps in various contentious topics in evolution will now be considered.

## Missing Links

An objection to human evolution favoured by the creationists is the non-existence of fossil forms intermediate between humans and apes, 'missing links', with whom we share a common ancestor. We now have knowledge of many such intermediate forms, such as Lucy, *Austrolopithecus afarensis*, reconstructed from fossil fragments; in Lucy's case no more than 20% of the complete skeleton and with most of the skull missing.[15] In other cases reconstruction has been based on as little as a single bone.[16] This illustrates the point that conditions leading to fossilisation occur very rarely, so the absence of a fossilised representative of a putative evolutionary intermediary can never be fatally damaging to the theory that such a creature once existed. It can always be argued that no fossilised remains were bequeathed, or if they were, they have yet to been found. Or, there may be another explanation. As we saw in the last chapter, there is a long gap in the hominoid fossil record in Africa which may perhaps be explained by a migration of apes from Africa into Asia, and then their later return.

While considering creationism, and its rebranded derivative, 'intelligent design', the tactic used by religious fundamentalists of imputing 'irreducible complexity' to a biological feature must be mentioned. The most notorious example of this concerns the rotating flagellum possessed by some bacteria, which enables them to swim; this device was encountered in the last chapter. It consists of a tubular 'motor' in which rotates the shaft of the propeller, the flagellum. It is argued that this mechanism is irreducibly complex since neither the motor nor the propeller would have any function on its own. Therefore, this mechanism could not have evolved so it must have been designed by the Creator. It turns out that there is a tubular structure passing through the cell wall of some bacteria, whose function is to secrete large protein molecules, utilising the same sort of mechanism that rotates the flagellum, which is of course, also made of protein. It seems likely that this secretory motor has been adapted for locomotion by incorporating a flagellum.[17]

Intelligent design is 'God of the gaps' in disguise. Where there is a gap in the evidence, as in the fossil record, or in the theory as to how a complicated structure or mechanism might have evolved, the Creator is invoked to explain it. The problem for intelligent design is that as our knowledge of evolution is extended by new evidence, the Creator's scope becomes more and more restricted. In any case, Intelligent Design is usually a cover for lack of imagination, and is no more of an explanation than First Cause, Unmoved Mover or Prime Necessary Being that we met in chapter 1 in connection with the Big Bang.

## The Cambrian Explosion

A quite different problem from that of missing links has been posed, not by a scarcity, but by an abundance of well-preserved fossils where, unusually, details of soft body parts are discernible. These remains are of early marine invertebrates in the Burgess Shale in British Columbia. The circumstances of their discovery, description and classification, and the alleged implications for evolutionary theory are expounded in Stephen Jay Gould's book *Wonderful Life*.[18] The fossils date from the Cambrian period about 540 MYA, and many of them had such outlandish body plans, unrelated to each other's or to those of existing creatures, that they were thought to be representative, not just of previously unrecognised species, but of new phyla even.[19] Of 24 uniquely different body designs, only four have modern representatives, the others having disappeared from the fossil record without trace.[20] The sudden appearance of new life forms in this 'Cambrian explosion', and their subsequent disappearance, was considered by Gould to represent a challenge to orthodox Darwinian evolution, which was thought to progress by gradual accretion of change, and not by sudden large-scale jumps, so-called saltation. Gould illustrated his thesis of saltation, presumed to be due to mutations with a large effect, by a redrawn tree of life in which some branches come off the main trunk horizontally rather than obliquely upwards.[21] This is presumably intended to show that these phyla started as major branches rather than as twigs, violating the metaphor of the tree of life, if nothing else. There is a vigorous rebuttal of these claims by Daniel Dennett in *Darwin's Dangerous Idea*.[22] He points out that the Burgess Shale was laid down tens of millions of years after the start of the Cambrian explosion, a brief period geologically speaking, but sufficient time for many thousands of life cycles in which extensive evolutionary change could have occurred, enough to account for the appearance of radically new species in this evolutionary big bang. Besides, Darwin, in stressing the gradualism of evolution was arguing against the catastrophic change wrought by the biblical flood in which the creationists believed. Darwinism does not necessarily entail a constant rate of evolutionary change, but is perfectly compatible with periods of stagnation alternating with periods of more rapid change, which Gould, in a famous article co-authored with Eldredge, called 'punctuated equilibrium'.[23] Neither does orthodox Darwinism deny the influence of contingency: it was the extinction of the dinosaurs following a chance meteor strike that opened up new opportunities for mammals to exploit. There have been a number of such mass extinctions in which an element of luck must have played a part in determining which species survived and which were eliminated. In stressing the contingency of evolution – a point touched on in the last chapter – one of Gould's aims was to attack the popular notion that the pinnacle of consciousness, higher intelligence and spirituality that we humans now occupy represents evolution's destiny. Gould illustrates how this false identification of evolution with the march of progress is perpetuated by the illustration of a sequence of hominoids from apes to man, successively rising from all fours to adopt a proud upright human stance, head held high, striding into a glorious future. There never was a destiny for evolution, and our appearance on earth was a chance event. To underline this point, Gould asserts that however many times the tape of evolution were to be replayed, we would never again feature in it.

Gould (1941-2002) was an American palaeontologist whose shortcoming, according to Brown, was that he overstated the novelty and importance of his own ideas.[24] He was a prolific science writer and his monthly column in *Natural History* had a large following. Particularly in the US, he became known for his attacks on orthodox Darwinism, and more than anybody else, he is responsible for the widespread notion in non-scientific circles that the theory is fatally flawed. He thus gave ammunition to the creationists, and his insistence on the extraordinary nature of the Cambrian explosion, and on the contingency of human evolution, opened the door to supernatural explanations for these events. Although he had no formal religious education, he was brought up in a Jewish family, and this background explains his sensitivity to any suggestion that evolutionary theory might support eugenic policies. His Marxist beliefs perhaps explain his predilection for change by revolution rather than evolution. Although agnostic, he had a great respect for religion, and in *Rock of Ages*, published shortly before his death, he developed the theme that science and religion need not be in conflict because they concern 'non-overlapping magisteria', NOMA.

> Science tries to document the factual character of the natural world, and to develop theories that coordinate and explain these facts. Religion, on the other hand, operates in the equally important, but utterly different, realm of human purposes, meanings, and values – subjects that the factual domain of science might illuminate, but can never resolve.[25]

Gould gives approval to Pope Pius XII's apparent respect for the principle of NOMA in his encyclical *Humani Generis* (1950) which, while conceding the possibility that evolution may have been responsible for the body, insists that it is God who creates human souls.[26] In not challenging this statement, Gould condones Cartesian dualism and thereby allows the ghost to re-enter the human machine. Whether or not there are supernatural beings, and whether or not bodies have souls, are factual questions that impinge on the material world we inhabit. They are important matters which are not the exclusive concern of religion, but quite properly also pertain to the magisterium of science. Neither can Gould's fact/value distinction be maintained. To give one example, facts and values intersect acutely in the question of the fate of redundant human embryos obtained by in vitro fertilisation. Their status, and hence their availability as a source of stem cells, is said to depend on whether or not they have souls. No, Gould's magisteria cannot be kept separate, and science is increasingly cultivating the territory previously left fallow by religion.

The philosopher John Dupré, who in most of his opinions is firmly in the Gouldian camp, is also critical of Gould's claim that science is no threat to religion. Dupré asserts that by providing an alternative explanation for the appearance of design in nature, Darwinism undermines the only remotely possible reason for believing in the existence of God.[27]

Gould's tolerance of religion in general, and Roman Catholicism in particular, may be contrasted with the attitude of the leader of the opposite camp, Richard Dawkins. In an open letter to his daughter, he urges her to seek the evidence for any authoritative statement made by the Pope or, indeed, anybody else.[28] He uses as an example the Assumption of the Blessed Virgin Mary. In 1950, nearly 2000 years after the event, Mary was declared by Pius XII – acting in his capacity as infallible Pope – to have been whisked directly up to Heaven and not to have died like an ordinary mortal. Dawkins advises his daughter not to accept this statement unquestioningly, but to seek the evidence on which it is based. Dawkins is surely right to challenge this encroachment of the magisterium of religion into that of the factual world of history and science.

\*

Bill Bryson in *A Short History of Nearly Everything* has written a racy account of the controversy surrounding Gould's *Wonderful Life*, together with a postscript to it.[29] It turns out that the Burgess fossils were not so different after all, and many of them have been re-assigned to living phyla. An alternative account of the Cambrian 'explosion' would be that sexual reproduction of multicellular eukaryotes with recently evolved segmented body plans resulted in 'adaptive radiation' into a profusion of new ecological niches not previously available to simpler creatures. But the process was not really explosive, having perhaps started way back in the Precambrian era when the ancestors of the Cambrian creatures were mostly too small or soft-bodied to leave a fossil record.[30]

# The Level of Natural Selection: Gene, Individual or Group

Natural selection works in two ways, negatively, by eliminating 'any variation in the least degree injurious', and positively, by increasing the population frequency of a gene for a feature that is advantageous, that is, where the benefits outweigh the costs. It is to be expected that any biological trait that does not serve a useful function but entails some costs to the organism would be eliminated by natural selection; most components of an organism will therefore have a functional, or, at least a historical explanation. Natural selection in this formulation has to include sexual selection. We have already seen that Darwin himself resorted to sexual selection to explain features, such as the peacock's tail, that could not easily be accounted for by natural selection in the sense of survival of the fittest. So in this context natural selection means selection that occurs naturally, by differential reproduction as well as by differential survival. For a Darwinist all adaptation is brought about by natural selection, either in the positive sense of being a creative solution to a problem posed by the environment, or in the negative sense of being a modification of an adverse trait bequeathed from the past, so that it is no longer disadvantageous. Thus, the eye is wonderfully adapted to the task of seeing, while the human appendix, a legacy of our more vegetarian ancestry, is diminished to such an extent that it is no longer a significant liability.

The question arises as to what, exactly, is selected, and to whose benefit? What, so to speak, is the unit of evolution?

The slender leg of a horse is an adaptation that is clearly advantageous to the individual, enabling it to outrun its predators; and what is good for the individual is surely good for the species. But has natural selection, in fashioning the equine leg, acted on the individual or the group? Another example: a bird instinctively gives a warning cry on the edge of a feeding flock; by drawing attention to itself it may be exposed to an increased risk of being caught by a predator. This behaviour, though disadvantageous to the individual, may be said to benefit the species or the group of which the individual is a member. But that behaviour has first to become established before the group, in competition with others, reaps the benefits of the unselfish behaviour of its members. Other behaviour that benefits the species at a cost to the individual includes limitation of population density in order to avoid over-exploitation of food resources. This might be achieved by migration away from the best feeding area, or even a cull to reduce population numbers. It has been suggested that the latter behaviour, exemplified legendarily by the lemming, is genetically encoded in humans. It is claimed that we are about to undergo a cull of our expanding population, which ultimately, however, will be for the benefit of *Homo sapiens.*[31]

Although a trait that is disadvantageous to the individual but beneficial for the species may be readily attributed to 'group selection', there are three serious objections to selection at this level. Firstly, any implication that evolution disregards immediate costs in anticipation of long-term benefits must be rejected; evolution is without foresight: we are not like the lemmings of legend. The second objection is that the precise mechanism of group selection is unclear. How could a gene that predisposes to self-sacrificial behaviour become widespread in a breeding population? Dead men don't bite – neither do they make love. The third objection is that cheats would prosper in a population of unselfish individuals. A gene predisposing a lemming to not leaping into the sea with its peers would be expected to spread rapidly through the population and replace the gene for self-sacrifice. Group selection therefore seems unlikely, a conclusion reached by Wilson after considering various mathematical models of group selection for altruistic behaviour.[32]

But there is also a problem with selection at the individual level. Natural selection acts by repetitive winnowing of individuals in successive generations. But as we saw in the last chapter, every individual is genetically unique. Although it is individual bodies from each generation that survive to adulthood or not, and if surviving, produce more or less offspring, those offspring are not replicas of their parents. Each offspring will have only some of the genes of each parent, and in different combinations from the parental ones. Rather than a particular combination of genes, it is particular genes themselves that are replicated and keep their identity in the long term. The phenotypical expression of individual genes, faithfully passed from one generation to the next, is the substrate for natural selection: the unit of evolution is the gene.

This was the gene-centred view promulgated by Richard Dawkins in his hugely influential book, *The Selfish Gene*.[33] But his metaphor of **Genes as Selfish Agents** has often been misunderstood, and the purple prose used in expounding his thesis – 'we are survival machines – robot vehicles blindly programmed to preserve the selfish molecules known as genes' – has provoked widespread hostility.[34] The philosopher Mary Midgely took Dawkins to task for suggesting that a gene – a sequence of DNA – could be selfish, which provoked in him a vigorous retort.[35,36] But Dawkins' usage of the word was obviously metaphorical, representing the notion that a gene's only 'interest' is in propagating copies of itself, which it does by influencing the behaviour of the vehicles carrying it. Neither was Dawkins suggesting that there is a gene for selfishness, nor that selfishness is a principle by which we should live. Nevertheless, as Dawkins himself observes, in the Thatcher/Reagan era, the notion of the selfish gene (and perhaps Dawkins himself) acquired a nastiness by association.[37]

So if the unit of evolution turns out to be the gene, and 'selfish gene' is just a colourful metaphor, what, exactly, underlies the acrimonious dispute regarding the level of selection? It concerns the origin of altruistic behaviour. How can unselfish behaviour have evolved if the unit of evolution is the gene, and a selfish one at that? And if altruistic behaviour results from the expression of selfish genes, is not altruism negated by this ulterior motivation? On the other hand, is it not more flattering to our view of ourselves to believe in group selection of altruism, behaviour which is genuinely self-denying, and for the greater good of the species? 'Greater love hath no man than this: that a man lay down his life for his friends.'[38]

## Sociobiology and the Origins of Altruism

In 1975, Edward O Wilson, a Harvard zoologist and world authority on social insects, published *Sociobiology: The New Synthesis*.[39] The subtitle echoed JS Huxley's *Evolution: The Modern Synthesis* (1942), which had so fruitfully integrated genetics and evolutionary theory. Wilson's endeavour was no less ambitious: to put sociology on a biological basis. Socio-biology is a massive tome giving a theoretical structure to the immensely wide spectrum of social behaviour across the animal kingdom, from colonial micro-organisms to humans.

'I think it fair to say,' writes Wilson, 'that the zoology in the book, making up all but the first and last of its 27 chapters, was favourably received', but '...the brief segment of *Socio-biology* that addresses human behaviour, comprising 30 out of the 575 total pages, was less well received.'[40]

On both counts this was a massive understatement since the book was rated the most important on animal behaviour of all time, while on the latter count the storm of protest reverberates to this day.[41]

One element of the outcry was the social scientists' shock at learning that their territory was about to be taken over by biologists. More importantly, Wilson's new synthesis proclaimed that human behaviour was the product of biological rather than societal forces, nature rather than nurture. Moreover, shaped over aeons by survival of the fittest, human nature was genetically and, therefore, intractably Machiavellian. This idea was anathema in the aftermath of the Holocaust which had led to a fierce reaction against evolutionary accounts of race and 'aggressive' human nature. From its publication in 1859, Darwin's theory of evolution by survival of the fittest had been used to justify not only a laissez-faire social policy, but also eugenic programmes directed at eradicating 'feebler varieties of mankind'. The Nazi atrocities were deemed to have had their origins in theories of biological determinism, and a UNESCO statement on race in 1952 effectively put a ban on biological research into human behaviour.[42] Wilson, in publishing *Sociobiology*, broke the taboo, though through naivety rather than by intentional support of any particular political ideology.[43]

The attack on *Sociobiology* was led by Wilson's Marxist colleague Lewontin, who in a letter to the *New York Review of Books* (Gould was another of the signatories) linked Wilson's determinist theories of human nature with the gas chambers of Nazi Germany.[44] Moreover, sociobiology, the book and the discipline, served to legitimise and perpetuate the social order with its privileges for certain groups according to class, race or sex; it had to be attacked.

Let us look now at one of these determinist theories: the origin of altruism. For a philosopher, altruism is a disinterested concern for the welfare of another as an end in itself; altruism is also the cornerstone of Christian ethics.[45] 'Love thy neighbour as thyself.' For a zoologist, altruism is behaviour of an animal that benefits another at its own expense. The difference between human and animal altruism is that human motivation is known, and known to be well-intentioned, whereas animal motivation

137

is inaccessible; we can be pretty sure, though, that altruistic behaviour in animals is not guided by any moral maxims.

Wilson cites many examples of altruism in the animal kingdom: giving warning of predators, feeding and caring for young, sharing food, ritualised combat, and so on.[46] But the most striking examples are found in the *Hymenoptera*, a group of social insects that includes ants, bees and wasps.[47] In some species, a caste of female, sterile workers will defend the colony to the death, forage for food, care for the young of others, but forego reproduction themselves. The origin of this altruistic behaviour poses a serious problem for selection at the level of the individual, but is elegantly solved by a gene-centred explanation known as kin selection. We have seen that with normal sexual reproduction, offspring carry just half the genes of either parent. The relatedness of a parent to a child is therefore said to be ½, which is the same as that between siblings. From the point of view solely of propagating one's genes, it would therefore be equally beneficial for one's parents to have another child as to have one oneself. But in sterile worker ants, by a chromosomal quirk which we will not go into, the relatedness of workers to their sisters – potential queens – is ¾, compared with ½ for their offspring were they to have any. Thus, for propagating their genes, it is better for them to bring up their younger sisters rather than have offspring of their own. No one would suggest that worker ants are remotely conscious of this reproductive strategy, nor that they have any warm big-sisterly feelings, nor, indeed, is it likely that they have any feelings at all. Their reproductive strategy has evolved as a consequence of the cost-benefit analysis carried out by natural selection over many generations. The cost of foregoing reproduction is more than offset by the benefit of having more sisters reaching adulthood. A gene which favours this seeming altruistic behaviour produces more copies of itself than genes for other reproductive strategies, and eventually comes to prevail.

138

A similar chromosomal quirk is the explanation for the notorious selfishness of drones – males with the potential for mating with a queen bee. All of their genes are transmitted to their daughters, that is, their relatedness is 1; their relatedness to their siblings, however, has the usual value, ½. From the point of view of propagating their genes, it therefore pays the drones to laze around the hive not lifting an antenna to help in the upbringing of their sibs, begging food from their sisters, and only exerting themselves to beat off their brothers in an attempt to mate with a queen. If ever there was a gene for selfishness, drones have it. But, of course, it is just as inappropriate to use value-laden language for this instinctive and unconscious behaviour as it is to talk of the co-operative behaviour of symbiotic micro-organisms. Both are winning living arrangements picked from the possible alternatives by a cost-benefit analysis blindly conducted by natural selection.

In the case of insects, with their minute nervous systems, and where so much behaviour is instinctive, it may be supposed that 'altruism' and 'selfishness' are largely programmed genetically. But in creatures with large brains, and flexible, intelligent behaviour, that supposition becomes weaker. Nevertheless, the spread of altruism in 'higher' animals may be explained using mathematical models that posit a gene for altruism. Kin selection is again the key. For a gene for altruism to be propagated and prevail in a population, the altruistic behaviour which results from its expression must be selectively targeted at those who already possess the gene. These are most likely to be blood relatives, especially offspring and siblings. The recipients of the altruistic behaviour flourish under this care, and propagate copies of the gene for altruism. In this way, kin selection is seen as the explanation for the evolution of caring behaviour in family groups, especially parental care of offspring.

Box 10

Social Systems

One of the marvels of the natural world is the syn-
chronised flight of a large flock of birds doing aerial
manoeuvres. In Britain it is probably starlings that
put on the best balletic displays. What is so amazing
is that there is no leader, no choreographer or flight
commander to launch the troupe, tell them when and
which way to wheel, or when and where to come to
rest. Each bird keeps an eye on its immediate neighbours and follows much the same course as they
do. Here is a dynamic structure that emerges from
a throng, reminiscent perhaps of a benign twister,
except that its constituents interact with each other
by virtue of being alive rather than by conforming to
physical laws pertaining to gases. The system is of
the simplest, there being only one type of component,
and the way in which the birds interact with each other is straightforward: each bird's speed and direction
is intermediate between that of its immediate neighbours. But because of the connectivity and non-linearity of the system, the effect of a small deviation of
a single bird – to avoid an upcoming obstacle, or due
to a gust of wind – is amplified as it spreads to all the
other birds in the flock. If the birds are conscious of
what they are doing, that consciousness plays no part
in the planning and execution of the event overall.

Another example of an orderly organic structure is
that of a colony of social insects such as a hive of
bees. Here too, in spite of the fact that there is no
central intelligence or command, and that the colony
outlasts the lives of its constituent members, it per-
petuates itself as a self-organised dynamic structure.

Efficient division of labour within the organisation – foraging, building and defending the nest, breeding and feeding the brood – results in the appearance of global behaviour that is adaptive and purposive, brought about by the collective interactions of the colony's incognisant parts. This is a much more complicated system, with several types of components – female workers, male drones and breeding queens – related to each other in different ways genetically. The hive also interacts crucially with its physical environment, the bees remaining inside and forming a compact ball to conserve heat in frosty conditions, while foraging far and wide on warm days that are not too windy. And then there is the ecological setting: the flowering plants that fuel the system; other insects competing for the same foodstuffs; and the predators ready to plunder the honey stored for the winter.

In order to understand the functioning of the system as a whole, it has first to be simplified and reduced to its elements; the many modes of interaction have to be deduced by careful observation and experiment in which organism and environment are teased apart. The environment, however, is not really a given to which living creatures have to adapt. Rather, a species selects and creates its environment, just as the environment moulds the species. Moreover, this relationship of mutual specification has a long evolutionary history.

Scientific explanations are sometimes criticised for being 'reductionist'. But it is not possible to understand a complex system and its emergent properties as a whole, without first reducing it to its component parts and working out how they relate to each other. Reductionism is a necessary prelude to holistic understanding.

A characteristic of humans is that their caring behaviour, as well as being lavished on children and other family members, is also frequently directed at strangers. At first sight this altruistic behaviour is difficult to explain genetically since it comes at a cost with no apparent recompense. But its evolution has been successfully modelled mathematically using game theory.[48] In dealing with strangers in a potentially competitive situation, the best strategy is tit for tat, cooperating on the first move and thereafter copying the stranger's previous move. A gene for this strategy of reciprocated altruism would endow the possessor with the qualities of being nice, provokable, and forgiving. Altruistic man would not be the first to act in an unfriendly way, but he would be provoked to retaliate by a hostile act of another; he would then forgive his enemy, thus avoiding an endless vendetta. To use game theory jargon, reciprocated altruism leads to a win-win rather than a zero-sum result. As an example of altruistic behaviour, Wilson cites a person who puts his own life at risk in rescuing a drowning man.[49] If such altruistic behaviour is reciprocated at some time, everyone's lifetime risk of drowning is reduced, which is a sufficient explanation for the evolution of the phenomenon if it has a genetic origin. Midgley objects to this account because it neglects motives and emotions.[50] Besides, nobody does a risk-benefit analysis before jumping into the water to save someone drowning. But this misses the point: the risk-benefit analysis has been carried out by natural selection and shown to be favourable for this behaviour; kindness to strangers is a Darwinian adaptation to living in human society. But where does that leave our moral code and our emotions? If our altruistic behaviour is an evolved adaptation, so too, perhaps, is our emotional apparatus. Our feeling that to rescue a drowning man at risk to oneself is a worthy, courageous act, and that to not go to his aid would be shameful, is evolution's way of reinforcing altruistic behaviour.

The attack by Lewontin and others on these theories of the origin of altruism was inspired by 'a commitment to the prospect of the creation of a more socially just – a socialist – society.'[51] Theories of genetic determinism of human nature had to be attacked, not so much in the quest for scientific truth, but rather because of the way they were being used to support the status quo in an unjust society.

> Sociobiology...even derives cooperation and altruism, which it recognises as overt characteristics of human social organisation, from an underlying competitive mechanism. Sociobiology, drawing its principles directly from Darwinian natural selection, claims that tribalism, entrepreneurial activity, xenophobia, male domination, and social stratification are dictated by the human genotype as moulded during the course of evolution.[52]

Sociobiology appears to be an enemy of socialism, and if its theoretical base is natural selection, it follows that one stratagem of attack is to minimise natural selection's contribution as a mechanism of evolution, stressing instead contingency, random fixation of genes, developmental noise and sudden evolutionary jumps (saltation) – which is what Gould does. While all adaptations are the result of natural selection, not all biological traits are adaptations, and many features could have arisen through these other evolutionary pathways. For Gouldians, adaptationism or even worse, hyper-adaptionism, is a derogatory term for the assumption that every element of an organism has a function which optimally contributes to survival and reproductive fitness. Some features, says Gould, are the way they are, not through natural selection, but for historical or architectural reasons, like the renowned spandrels of Saint Mark's cathedral.[53]

The human leg, for example, is well adapted for walking upright, with a locking knee that reduces the fatigue of standing. But what about the female buttock? Has it been adapted by natural selection to attract the male of the species, or is its alluring shape simply due to the form of the powerful muscles needed to extend the hip when walking upright? Hyper-adaptionists believe the former, Gouldians the latter: the rounded buttock is incidental to upright walking, just as the redness of blood is incidental to the carriage of oxygen by haemoglobin, the latter being the feature on which natural selection has acted.

In the last chapter we considered three 'adaptionist' accounts, of upright walking, our big brain, and the peacock's tail. All such 'explanations' say Gouldians, are so much make-believe, like Kipling's *Just So Stories* of how the leopard got his spots, or the camel his hump. With sufficient ingenuity a good story can be devised to explain any biological feature, or support any theory, and none is capable of either verification or falsification. The 'aquatic ape theory' for explaining our upright gait is one of the better adaptionist accounts, with a good deal of circumstantial evidence in its favour. But there are some discrepancies, and it is not generally accepted even by Dawkinsian evolutionists.[54-56]

We have seen how our big brain, the seat of consciousness, and with its seemingly superfluous potential for philosophising or playing sudoku, poses a problem for adaptionists, who have not come up with a fully convincing explanation for its evolution by natural selection. But when it comes to human behaviour they are really struggling because there is an obvious alternative explanation for the way we behave – culture. Perhaps the reason for our kindness to strangers is not the possession of a gene for altruism, let alone one for reciprocal altruism, but that we have been brought up to behave that way. 'Do unto others as you would be done by.' And perhaps the motivation for loving our children, and being kind to strangers lies, not in our genes, but in ourselves.

Human nature is not a property of individuals isolated in a laboratory, but is largely the interactive behaviour expressed by individuals embedded in their society. Neither can the rich web of social behaviour be partitioned neatly into its elements, like 'aggression' or 'altruism'. These are sophisticated abstract notions that have been reified and then taken to be 'constants' of human nature. That being so, it would be extraordinary if there were to be genes whose expression matched these abstractions: a gene, say, for reciprocal altruism that endowed its possessor with properties of niceness, provokability and forgiveness in just the right proportions. Such a gene has never been identified, nor is it likely to be. No, reciprocal altruism is not a constant of human nature, it is a constant of a mathematical model of human nature which has to be 'fine tuned' for the model to work. As in cosmology so in sociobiology, the model must not be mistaken for the real thing.

*

Edward O Wilson, notwithstanding the furore raised by *Sociobiology*, defended and advanced his thesis of genetic determinism of human behaviour in a sequel entitled *On Human Nature*. This was a direct challenge to the prevailing view in the social sciences that human behaviour is the product, not of natural selection acting on the human genome during thousands of generations, but of culture.

Wilson observed that broad features of our social life – living in groups of 10-100, males being larger than females, the young undergoing a long period of social training and play

145

– are common to the majority of great apes and monkeys.[57] He maintained that these characteristics are as distinctive of our taxonomic group as are any anatomical features, and are similarly genetically determined. It is inconceivable that we would be able to adopt the social pattern of other vertebrates, such as birds or fish; we would quickly die out. During our evolution our social structure has been as important to our survival as our upright gait. He went on to list alphabetically 67 human behaviours, ranging from age-grading, funeral rites and joking, to weather control, which have all been recorded in every culture known to history. These are 'as diagnostic of mankind...as wing tessellation is to a fritillary butterfly', with the implication that these behaviours too are genetically determined. However, as Wilson's critics have pointed out, a feature that is universally present is not necessarily genetically inherited, but could be transmitted from generation to generation in the nurturing environment of the family and social group in which all humans are reared. Some critics take to extremes the argument that 'universal' does not mean 'genetic', doubting even whether being born with four limbs, walking upright or speaking a language can be said to have biological origins.[58,59] One approach to resolving this nature/nurture dichotomy is to seek confirmation of predictions arising from evolutionary theories of behaviour.

One such prediction is that a population in which reciprocal altruism is the norm would be vulnerable to free riders who would take advantage of the generosity of others but not reciprocate. To counteract such behaviour, detection of cheating on social agreements would have to be well developed; a mental tally would be kept of favours granted but not returned. To test this hypothesis, problems of logical reasoning were presented to test subjects from many different backgrounds. The problems were framed in terms of social behaviour, or, in some other concrete way but not involving personal obligations. The subjects consistently performed better when the problems implicated unfairness and a breach of a social contract of some sort, rather than being simply logical.[60],[61] While this result is supportive, it does not definitively settle the issue in favour of an innate sense of fairness and a heightened awareness of cheating: children are generally taught to be fair, and to expect fairness, in their dealings with others; a sense of fairness imbibed with mother's milk is not ruled out.

## Sociobiology Becomes Evolutionary Psychology

The 1980s incomer to the field of study previously covered by sociobiology was evolutionary psychology.[62] But in spite of the name change it did not escape criticism from Hilary and Steven Rose as being 'transparently part of a right wing libertarian attack on collectivity, above all the welfare state.'[63]

Evolutionary psychology has much to say about courtship and reproduction, in particular from the point of view of parental investment. There is a basic asymmetry between the sexes, the egg contributed by the female being larger and using more resources than the sperm contributed by the male. In addition, in a great many species it is the female which provides most of the parental care of the offspring. In humans the minimum investment needed for producing a child is respectively nine months for a woman and a few moments for a man. It is the female's investment in bearing and caring for her offspring that constitutes the limiting resource, and for this reason the female of most species can almost always secure a mate. On the other hand, amongst males there is a competition for females, and the most successful may have numerous offspring from many partners, while the least successful have none. From a gene-centred viewpoint, the strategy with the best cost-benefit ratio for a male is for him to promiscuously inseminate as many females as possible but not to be involved in their upbringing. But for the female it is quality rather than quantity that counts, which means setting her sights on an alpha male. Not only will he be the healthiest and strongest of his peers, but he is most likely to sire alpha males who in their turn will propagate widely their mother's genes as well as those of their macho father. Dawkins describes this as the 'he-man' strategy, to which the alternative is the strategy of 'domestic bliss'.[64] Here the male is enticed into caring for the offspring, so that his investment in them may at times equal that of the female; he is then less likely to desert, and a larger brood can be brought to maturity than if the female had no help from her mate. But he must be satisfied that he will be supporting his own progeny and not those of a rival. This is ensured by his excluding rival males from his territory for a time before consummation of the relationship, an engagement period which is, in effect, a quarantine period for the detection of insemination by a rival.

If the parental care has been shared, there is a potential contest between the couple when the young are almost ready to fend for themselves and could be looked after by one parent. Either parent could then leave and start a new relationship knowing that the remaining parent is unlikely to leave the brood to perish, so wasting the heavy investment he or she has made to bring them to this stage. As Dawkins points out, whether or not a parent deserts will depend on the availability of new partners. Postulating genes for coy or fast behaviour in females, and faithful and philandering behaviour in males, a mathematical model may be constructed which shows that the proportions of each in a breeding population will come to reach an evolutionary steady state in which opportunities for this unfaithful behaviour will never be lacking.[65]

Incest taboo is another topic that yields to an evolutionary explanation. Recessive genes for lethal conditions are present in the gene pool, but do no harm if they occur singly. Offspring of random matings very rarely inherit the same harmful recessive gene from each parent, which is just as well for that would be lethal. But in about one in eight matings between close relatives – parent/child or siblings – both parents carry the same harmful recessive genes which, passed on to a child in a double dose, would cause it to be stillborn or to die young.[66] There is thus a very strong Darwinian disincentive to such inbreeding, which has been shown to be very uncommon between children who grow up together under the age of six.[67] The biological hypothesis is that a gene resulting in aversion to bonding with a sib or parent will be replicated in greater numbers than a gene that allows it, and bond exclusion will become the norm. Incest taboos provide a moral reinforcement which, like the injunction 'love thy neighbour', may itself have a biological basis.

Concerning reproductive strategies, Wilson writes of the 'unsentimental calculus of marital conflict and deceit' and suggests that 'social scientists might find such an interpretation rather too genetic or even amoral for their tastes, yet the implications for the study of human behaviour are potentially very great.'[68] The philosopher John Dupré, however, does not agree. 'Biology, and hence more specifically evolution, is of very limited use to us in understanding sexual difference.'[69] Concerning the suggestion that males are more inclined to promiscuity than females, he writes, 'An obvious difficulty with this hypothesis is that sexual activity requires two participants...males and females engage in about equal amounts of copulation.' Ironically, it is from biology that there comes support for this liberal view of female sexuality, with evidence that female promiscuity is widespread in the animal kingdom, the main evolutionary drive probably being increased fertility.[70] There is also biological evidence relevant to the lesser claim that men are by nature inclined to have more sexual partners than women. In many mamma-lian species, males are larger than females, and the extent of this disparity correlates with the average number of females consorting with a successful male.[71] In primates, the species with the greatest difference in body size is the gorilla, where the alpha male has access to a large harem of females. On the curve relating sexual size difference in mammals to number of female partners, the predicted number for *Homo sapiens* is between one and three, corresponding to the reality that while polyandry is very rare, polygamy is permitted in many human societies and is often the de facto position in societies where only monogamy is legalised: humans are moderately polyga-mous. In this instance it seems that evolutionary psychology, biology, and sociology are in broad agreement about human sexual behaviour.

Although the gene-centred view of sexuality – with genes for coyness or flirtation, fidelity or philandering – may be dis-missed as hyper-adaptionism, it is far from being irrelevant to human behaviour, highlighting as it does many potential conflicts of interest between siblings, between generations, and, particularly, between the sexes.

## Development

Until very recently there has been a large gap in evolutionary theory, where evolution is taken to mean a change of gene frequency in a population. How does evolution, so-defined, relate to the survival and reproductive success of individual organisms? How exactly does genotype translate into pheno-type? The answer lies in development – the development of a fertilised egg into a flesh and blood organism, a process which until recently was little more than a mysterious 'black box'. An up-to-date account of evolutionary development biology – dubbed Evo Devo – is given in *Endless Forms Most Beauti-*

*ful* by Sean Carroll.[72] According to Carroll, who is a professor of genetics and an active researcher in the field of evo devo, the number of genes in the human genome is 25,000, and our genome is 98.8% the same as that of our closest cousin, the chimpanzee. Under the banner *Not in Our Genes*, opponents of Darwinism have interpreted this fact as being a conclusive refutation of a genetic explanation for human nature, parodying Shakespeare:

> Men at some time are masters of their fates: The fault, dear Brutus, is not in our stars, but in ourselves.[73]

Another anti-Darwinian writes

> We share 51 per cent of our genes with yeast and 98 per cent with chimpanzees – it is not genetics that makes us human.[74]

How, then, do we account for the differences between ourselves and cousin chimp, *Pan troglodytes*? To answer this question we have to look a little more closely at the way in which genes work. Ordinary human somatic cells contain 46 chromosomes in all, 22 pairs plus two sex chromosomes, comprising in all two metres of DNA packed into every cell nucleus. Of this length of DNA making up the human genome, only a small amount, 1.5%, represents genes that encode the 25,000 different proteins from which our bodies are built or which partake in vital metabolic processes.[75] Examples of structural proteins are myosin in muscle, and collagen in tendon, while haemoglobin is the protein in blood, indispensable for the transport of oxygen from lungs to tissues. A further 3% of DNA is involved in the regulation of the genes encoding for these proteins. Although every nucleated cell in the body has a complete set of genes, only those that are needed are switched on in any particular tissue. So-called housekeeping genes encode for proteins that are necessary in all body cells, but genes encoding haemoglobin are active only in bone marrow where red blood cells are made; similarly for genes encoding for muscle, tendon or bone. A gene is switched on or off as necessary by a promoter or a repressor protein that binds to a short stretch of DNA near to the gene being regulated. The regulatory proteins themselves are genetically encoded, and the genes for regulatory proteins are regulated in their turn. There is thus a complicated cascade of gene switches in a multitude of combinations and permutations controlling the 25,000 genes that we largely share with chimpanzees. Whether a particular gene is switched on or off depends on its location and the stage of development of the organism, which starts at the moment of fertilisation of an egg by a sperm. The origin of spatial information in the embryo may be traced back to molecular asymmetry in the egg when formed in the ovary, or else the point of entry of the sperm may be the datum for the geography of the rapidly developing zygote as it undergoes successive cell divisions.[76] Either way, fertilisation sets in train the demarcation of future regions of the body which are outlined by intersecting areas of gene expression which become progressively more refined. Besides location, another factor that determines the operation of gene switches is the previous developmental history, and the current stage of development, all of which gives a degree of flexibility to the system which is responsive also to environmental influences.

Carroll describes a 'toolbox' of regulatory genes that are found across the animal kingdom, indicating that they evolved at an early stage, certainly before the Cambrian explosion. Amongst the first to be discovered were those responsible for segmentation of the body and the positioning of appendages – legs, wings, mouth parts, antennae and so on. Think of insects, spiders, crustaceans; and also vertebrates, with a variable number of vertebral segments from our thirty-three to several hundred in some snakes. This variety of body plans is under the control of regulatory genes that go by the name of *'Hox'*. *Hox* genes show remarkable similarities across the animal kingdom, and because of their role in regulating the number, size and shape of structures such as body segments or limbs, minor differences in coding may result in major differences in body plan. In the fruit fly, *Drosophila*, a mutation which alters the sequence of a few letters of the code of a regulatory gene may result in a fly with extra wings, or with legs instead of antennae.[77]

Although the body plans of crustaceans and insects differ greatly from our own, we share a high proportion of our genes with such creatures. The differences between us and them are not so much related to the genes for structural proteins, which are broadly similar, but to regulatory genes like *Hox* which determine the number of body segments and the number and variety of appendages.

Animals closer to us not only share the same basic body plan, but also have a very similar early development: embryos of mammals, birds and amphibia are hardly distinguishable from each other. It is therefore not too difficult to imagine that minor differences in regulatory genes, particularly those involving the growth of the brain, could account for the different outcomes for the embryos of closely related primates, such as *Pan troglodytes* and *Homo sapiens*. Recent research comparing chimp and human genomes has shown that the gene which has the greatest number of differences between chimp and human versions is, indeed, involved in the growth of the brain.[78] Thus the difference between us and chimpanzees is apparently owed, not so much to genes for structural proteins, but to regulatory genes responsible for the fine tuning of our embryonic development, and that of our brains in particular.

Box 11

A Developmental System Adapted to Life on Dry Land

Colonisation of the land was an important evolutionary step for creatures that reproduced sexually. Hitherto, fertilisation of ova by motile sperm had taken place in the sea, where the developing eggs with their store of nutrition were extremely vulnerable to predation and to the vagaries of a marine environment. Begetting very large numbers of young is the principle mechanism which was developed by natural selection to overcome the heavy losses, an approach exemplified by frogs with their profusion of spawn. On land, once a mechanism for internal fertilisation had evolved, the stage was set for a more efficient reproductive strategy in which fertilisation and early development took place internally in a secure environment that could be more tightly controlled, resulting in a higher reproductive success rate.

Development of a human baby takes place within the security of the uterus where the mother's control systems maintain a steady supply of nourishment and a near constant biochemical milieu. Given the almost unwavering uterine micro-environment, the outcome of the pregnancy is largely determined by the initial conditions, to which the inherited genome makes a major contribution, necessary but not sufficient for development to occur, for the information coded in DNA has to be transcribed by apparatus found in the cytoplasm of the ovum, though that too is genetically prescribed – by the mother's genes. Once underway, each developmental step is determined by the previous one in a long causal chain, such as that resulting in the baby being a boy or a girl. By default an embryo will develop female internal organs. But if fertilisation of the ovum is by a sperm bearing a Y chromosome, testes develop, which, assisted by a placental hormone, produce testosterone which stimulates the formation of male reproductive apparatus. At the same time the testes produce a protein that suppresses the development of uterus and ovaries.

If fertilisation is by a sperm bearing an X chromosome the embryo will be genetically and, if all goes well, anatomically female. But occasionally the baby's sex is ambiguous at birth because of exposure at a critical stage to male hormones, either from the baby's own defective adrenal glands or from the mother.

The baby's sex at birth is thus predetermined by events at its conception nine months previously. It makes no sense to speak of the baby choosing its own destiny, for it has little autonomy being completely dependent on its mother for the stability of its environment while its own control systems, with their sensors and negative feedback loops, are being assembled and set in train.

The management of the embryo's carbon dioxide illustrates this. Being immersed in its private pool of amniotic fluid, the embryo cannot breathe so is dependent on diffusing its waste carbon dioxide across the placenta from the embryo's circulation into that of the mother. This is made easier by a lowering of the maternal blood concentration of carbon dioxide during pregnancy, brought about by a resetting of her carbon dioxide sensors.

In this way a new life develops at the confluence of the nurturing waters of the womb with the flow of genes passing down the generations.

Carroll, writing of gene switches, recounts how:

> ...regulatory DNA is organised into fantastic little devices that integrate information about position in the embryo and the time of development. The output of these devices is ultimately transformed into pieces of anatomy that make up animal forms. This regulatory DNA contains the instructions for building anatomy, and evolutionary changes within this regulatory DNA lead to the diversity of form.[79]

Genes and their DNA are centre stage.

A review of Carroll's book by Steven Rose was generally complimentary, but Rose, a neuroscientist, chides the author for not stressing enough the importance of location in the developmental system.

> It is the positional information that ensures which switches are thrown when... Carroll knows this, but doesn't, I think, quite appreciate the extent to which it undermines a merely gene-based model of development. It is, to put it simply, not the genes, but the developing organism that at each moment of its history determines the next phase of its life.[80]

The newly fertilised zygote inherits, besides the genome from its parents, the cytoplasm of the ovum with its proteins for reading the instructions encoded in the nuclear DNA, and the potential that has for modulating gene expression. There is also the DNA of the mitochondria, the organelles responsible for cell respiration, inherited always on the maternal side. Development of the zygote is only possible within a restricted range of physical environments, which are implied but not specified in the genome. Gravity, day length, seasonality, temperature range, these are all factors that feed into the successful development of the young of each generation, and are

156

inherited epigenetically, outwith the genome. Development of the organism is not, therefore, the unfolding of its predetermined nature encoded in DNA, because the information there is incomplete and can only be interpreted in the light of complementary information provided by the environment and by the developing organism itself. Rather than an unfolding, development is a dialectical process, as Susan Oyama describes in *The Ontogeny of Information*:

> What we are moving towards is a conception of a developmental system, not as a reading off of a pre-existing code, but as a complex of interacting influences, some inside the organism's skin, some external to it, and including its ecological niche in all its spatial and temporal aspects, many of which are typically passed on in reproduction either because they are in some way tied to the organism's activities or characteristics or because they are stable features of the general environment. It is in this ontogenetic crucible that form appears and is transformed, not because it is immanent in some interactants and nourished by others, or because some interactants select from a range of forms present in others, but because any form is created by the precise activity of the system.[81]

This holistic account of development denies the autonomous contributions of nature and nurture, ascribing the orchestration of development to the life processes of the organism itself. It is a rejection of essentialism, in which our natures are preformed in our genes, and an espousal of existentialism, in which, declares Sartre, existence precedes essence. Developmental systems theory ousts DNA from its centre-stage position. The nature of an organism is determined not by its genes nor by its environment: the organism determines for itself what it shall be. Rose writes:

The cell, the embryo, the foetus, in a profound sense 'chooses' which genes to switch on at any moment during its development; it is, from the moment of fertilisation, but increasingly through that long trajectory to birth and beyond, an active player in its own destiny.[82]

It is instructive to compare the accounts of Carroll and Oyama quoted above. Both make use of the same scientific facts, and acknowledge the dual contribution of genes and environment to the development of form in an organism. But the emphasis is quite different. For Carroll, instructions for development originate in the genes. For Oyama, information does not reside at any particular location but is created in the process of development by the entire developmental system including the environment. The essential issue here is the location of agency and self-determination. From the Dawkinsian gene-centred standpoint exemplified by Carroll, development is largely directed by inanimate molecules of DNA. In the Gouldian camp, the position taken by Oyama and Rose is that self-determination resides in the developmental system centred on the living organism. The science is not in dispute, but these are philosophical positions with very different consequences for the way we view ourselves.

# Summing Up

Various objections to the theory of evolution have been considered. Those originating from creationists, concerning missing links and 'irreducible complexity', are easily dismissed and need not detain us further, except to note the frequency with which these Christian folk bear false witness by misrepresenting  the work of evolutionary scientists and quoting them out of context. A more general religious objection is that the evolutionary account of our origins, emphasising

158

contingency and a blind natural process, undermines human morality, dignity and purpose. This point will be dealt with in a later chapter.

In the Gouldian camp of evolutionists, Lewontin and Rose make no bones about the political agenda underlying their attacks on Darwinism. Gould himself has not expressed his political views quite so openly, but for a biologist he shows an unusual tolerance towards religion. Dawkins suggests that this may be a ploy to recruit the support of moderate Christians to combat creationists.[83] Dennett, however, surmises that Gould has a dislike of the mindless algorithm of natural selection as a mechanism for the appearance of design in nature, and that he has a hankering after skyhooks rather than cranes, mind before matter.[84] To the extent that the Gouldians' political views are so strongly held and expressed, their scientific opinions are a little suspect. Theirs is a multipronged attack on natural selection, adaptionism and genetic determinism with the aim of putting human behaviour out of bounds to evolutionary theory, hence preserving the Marxist dream of human perfectibility.

In the opposite camp, Richard Dawkins is notorious as an evangelical atheist who sometimes gets carried away with his own rhetoric ('robot vehicles, blindly programmed'). His professed ideology is the search for truth based on reason and evidence. The selfish gene approach that he has promulgated provides a theoretical solution to the problem of altruism, and throws light on reproductive strategies, and much more besides. Since *The Selfish Gene* was published 40 years ago, advances in molecular genetics and evolutionary development have increasingly pointed up the centrality of DNA in all areas of biology. As a reaction, development systems theory de-emphasises the role of DNA, giving greater prominence to the interplay between organism and environment, apparently in an attempt to escape from genetic determinism and to restore to the organism the possibility of determining its own destiny. The irony is that Darwin, in *The Descent of Man, and Selection in Relation to Sex,* had long ago proposed a role for choice, love and jealousy in 'the progressive development of various bodily structures and of certain mental qualities.'[85]

These attacks on Darwinism thus seem to be motivated by a fear of the perceived consequences of the theory if it turns out to be true. If human nature is the outcome of 4 billion years of evolution, and is inscribed in the human genome as in stone, then this may have far-reaching consequences for our ethical, social and political systems, indeed, for our survival as a species. On the other hand, if we have no innate human nature, and our behaviour is moulded by a few hundred years of culture, then the hope of human betterment is not extinguished, and our prospects may be very different.

# Notes

## Chapter 4: Problems with the theory of evolution

1. Charles Darwin. *The Origin of Species by Means of Natural Selection*. Sixth (final) edition. London: Watts & Co, 1948: 384
2. Helena Cronin. *The Ant and the Peacock: Altruism and Sexual Selection From Darwin to Today*. Cambridge University Press, 1991: p7.
3. Charles Darwin. *The Origin of Species by Means of Natural Selection*. Sixth (final) edition. London: Watts & Co, 1948: p99.
4. Richard Dawkins. *The Ancestor's Tale: A Pilgrimage to the Dawn of Life*. London: Phoenix, 2005: p238.
5. Maynard Smith *cited in* Helena Cronin. *The Ant and the Peacock: Altruism and Sexual Selection From Darwin to Today*. Cambridge University Press, 1991: p39.
6. Matt Ridley. *Nature Via Nurture: Genes, Experience, and What Makes Us Human*. London: Fourth Estate, 2003: p24-5.
7. Richard Dawkins. *The ancestor's Tale: A Pilgrimage to the Dawn of Life*. London: Phoenix, 2005: p462-71.
8. John Maynard Smith. *The Theory of Evolution*. Cambridge University Press, 2000: pp165-8.
9. Andrew Brown. *The Darwin Wars: The Scientific Battle for the Soul of Man*. London: Touchstone, 2000: p32-4.
10. Theodosius Dobzhansky. Nothing in biology makes sense except in the light of evolution. *American Biology Teacher* 1973; 35: 125-29.
11. Daniel C Dennett. *Darwin's Dangerous Idea: Evolution and the Meanings of Life*. London: Penguin Books, 1996: pp262-7.
12. Jerry Fodor, Massimo Piattelli-Palmarini. *What Darwin Got Wrong*. London: Profile Books Ltd, 2010.
13. Jerry Fodor. Why Pigs Don't Have Wings. *London Review of Books* Vol 29 No 20, 18 Oct 2007. Subsequent letters in Vol 29,

No 21 and 22, 1 and 15 Nov 2007, Vol 30, No 1, 3 Jan 2008.

14. Andrew Brown. *The Darwin Wars: The Scientific Battle for the Soul of Man.* London: Touchstone, 2000.

15. Chris Stringer, Peter Andrews. *The Complete World of Human Evolution.* New York: Thames & Hudson Inc., 2005: p122

16. Ibid: p118

17. Richard Dawkins. *The God Delusion.* London: The Bantam Press, 2006: pp125-34.

18. Stephen Jay Gould. *Wonderful Life: The Burgess Shale and the Nature of History.* London: Vintage, 2000.

19. Stuart Kauffman, *cited in* Richard Dawkins. Unweaving the Rainbow. London: Penguin Books, 1998: p203.

20. Stephen Jay Gould. *Wonderful Life: The Burgess Shale and the Nature of History.* London: Vintage, 2000: p209.

21. Ibid: p46.

22. Daniel C Dennett. *Darwin's Dangerous Idea: Evolution and the Meanings of Life.* London: Penguin Books, 1996: pp262-312.

23. Gould SJ, Eldredge N. Punctuated equilibrium comes of age. *Nature* 1993; 366:223-27.

24. Andrew Brown. *The Darwin Wars: The Scientific Battle for the Soul of Man.* London: Touchstone, 2000: p61.

25. Stephen Jay Gould. *Rock of Ages: Science and Religion in the Fullness of Life.* London: Vintage, 2002: p4.

26. Ibid: p78.

27. John Dupré. *Darwin's Legacy: What Evolution Means Today.* Oxford University Press, 2003: p56.

28. Richard Dawkins. *A Devil's Chaplain.* London: Weidenfeld & Nicolson, 2003: p242-8.

29. Bill Bryson. *A Short History of Nearly Everything.* London: Black Swan, 2004: pp390-406.

30. Richard Dawkins. *The Ancestor's Tale: A Pilgrimage to the Dawn of Life.* London: Phoenix, 2005: pp454-462.

31. Reg Morrison. Forward by Lynn Margulis. *The Spirit in the Gene: Humanity's Proud Illusion and the Laws of Nature.* New York: Cornell University Press, 1999: pp233-59.

32. Edward O Wilson. *Sociobiology: The New Synthesis.* 25th anniversary edition. Cambridge Mass: The Belknap Press of Harvard University Press, 2000: p113.

33. Richard Dawkins. *The Selfish Gene.* New Edition. Oxford University Press, 1989.
34. Ibid: v.
35. Mary Midgley. *Beast and Man: The Roots of Human Nature.* Revised edition. London: Routledge, 1995: xvii-xviii.
36. Richard Dawkins. *The Selfish Gene.* New Edition. Oxford University Press, 1989: p278.
37. Ibid: p268.
38. John 15:13                                    ·
39. Edward O Wilson. *Sociobiology: The New Synthesis.* 25th anniversary edition. Cambridge Mass: The Belknap Press of Harvard University Press, 2000.
40. Ibid: vi.
41. Robin Headlam Wells, Johnjoe McFadden (eds). *Human Nature: Fact and Fiction.* London: Continuum, 2006.
42. Ullica Segerstråle. *Defenders of the Truth: The Battle for Science in the Sociobiology Debate and Beyond.* Oxford University Press, 2000: p30.
43. Andrew Brown. *The Darwin Wars: The Scientific Battle for the Soul of Man.* London: Touchstone, 2000: pp15-16.
44. Ibid: p55-56.
45. Simon Blackburn. *The Oxford Dictionary of Philosophy.* Oxford University Press, 1994: p13.
46. Edward O Wilson. *Sociobiology: The New Synthesis.* 25th anniversary edition. Cambridge Mass: The Belknap Press of Harvard University Press, 2000: pp 121-29.
47. Ibid: pp397-437.
48. Richard Dawkins. *The Selfish Gene.* New Edition. Oxford University Press, 1989: pp202-33.
49. Edward O Wilson. *Sociobiology: The New Synthesis.* 25th anniversary edition. Cambridge Mass: The Belknap Press of Harvard University Press, 2000: p120.
50. Mary Midgley. *Beast and Man: The Roots of Human Nature.* Revised edition. London: Routledge, 1995: pp111-124.
51. RC Lewontin, Steven Rose, Leon J Kamin. *Not in our Genes: Biology, Ideology, and Human Nature.* New York: Pantheon Books, 1984: ix.
52. Ibid: p74.
53. The magnificent dome of the cathedral of San Marco in Ven-

ice is supported on four arches at right angles to each other. A spandrel is an architectural term applied by Gould to the tapering triangular spaces bounded by supporting arches on each side and the perimeter of the dome above. In St Mark's, each spandrel is filled with a beautiful design illustrating an aspect of Christian faith. Gould, in a lecture attacking adaptionism, famously argued that these spandrels have the appearance of being exquisitely adapted to the needs of the illustrators, when, in fact, they are incidental to the architectural design. 'Spandrel' has become a byword for a feature which, despite appearances, is not an adaptation, but has some other explanation. Incidentally, what Gould calls spandrels are, in fact, pendentives. Dennett deconstructs Gould's argument at length *in* Daniel C Dennett, *Darwin's Dangerous Idea: Evolution and the Meanings Of Life*. London: Penguin Books, 1996: pp267-282.

54. Richard Dawkins. *The Ancestor's Tale: A Pilgrimage to the Dawn of Life*. London: Phoenix, 2005: p96.
55. Andrew Brown. *The Darwin Wars: The Scientific Battle for the Soul of Man*. London: Touchstone, 2000: pp101-14.
56. Daniel C Dennett. *Darwin's Dangerous Idea: Evolution and the Meanings of Life*. London: Penguin Books, 1996: pp243-5. Dennett suggests that this might have something to do with the fact that its author, Elaine Morgan, is female and a science writer rather than a professional biologist. He also notes that Gouldians, too, spin adaptionist just-so stories when it suits them.
57. Edward O Wilson. *On Human Nature*. Cambridge Mass: Harvard University Press, 1978: p20-22.
58. John Dupré. *Darwin's Legacy: What Evolution Means Today*. Oxford University Press, 2003: p93.
59. Tim Ingold *in* Hilary Rose, Steven Rose. *Alas, Poor Darwin: Arguments Against Evolutionary Psychology*. London: Jonathan Cape, 2000: pp225-246.
60. A set of cards has letters on one side and numbers on the other. Which of the following four cards would you need to turn over to test the rule that if a card has a D on one side it has a 3 on the other? D F 3 7 Only 5-10% of people get the right answer which is D and 7. You are a bouncer at a bar and your job is to enforce the rule that if somebody is drinking beer he must be

eighteen or older. Which of the following would you check? A beer drinker; a Coke drinker; a 25 year-old; a 16 year-old. Most people now get the correct answer, checking the beer drinker's age, and the drink of the 16 year-old. The logical structure of the two problems is identical. Steven Pinker. *How the Mind Works*. The Softback Preview, 1998: 336-7.

61. Matt Ridley. *The Origins of Virtue*. London: Penguin Books, 1997: pp125-131.
62. Ullica Segerstråle. *Defenders of the Truth: The Battle for Science in the Sociobiology Debate and Beyond*. Oxford University Press, 2000: p316.
63. Hilary Rose, Steven Rose. *Alas, Poor Darwin: Arguments Against Evolutionary Psychology*. London: Jonathan Cape, 2000: p8.
64. Richard Dawkins. *The Selfish Gene*. New Edition. Oxford University Press, 1989: p149.
65. Ibid: pp150-53.
66. Ibid: p293.
67. Edward O Wilson. *On Human Nature*. Cambridge Mass: Harvard University Press, 1978: pp37-8.
68. Edward O Wilson. *Sociobiology: The New Synthesis*. 25th anniversary edition. Cambridge Mass: The Belknap Press of Harvard University Press, 2000: pp126-7.
69. John Dupré. *Darwin's Legacy: What Evolution Means Today*. Oxford University Press, 2003: p117-118.
70. Tim Birkhead. *Promiscuity: An Evolutionary History of sperm Competition and Sexual Conflict*. London: Faber and Faber, 2000: pp193-233.
71. Edward O Wilson. *On Human Nature*. Cambridge Mass: Harvard University Press, 1978: p20.
72. Sean B Carroll. *Endless Forms Most Beautiful: The New Science of Evo Devo and the Making of the Animal Kingdom*. London: Weidenfeld & Nicolson, 2006: p268.
73. William Shakespeare. *Julius Caesar* Act 1, scene 2, line 134 *cited in* RC Lewontin, Steven Rose, Leon J Kamin. *Not in our Genes: Biology, Ideology, and Human Nature*. New York: Pantheon Books, 1984: v.
74. Tom Shakespeare http://genome.wellcome.ac.uk/node30068.html

75. Sean B Carroll. *Endless Forms Most Beautiful: The New Science of Evo Devo and the Making of the Animal Kingdom.* London: Weidenfeld & Nicolson, 2006: p12.

76. Ibid: p92-3.

77. Ibid: pp50-1.

78. *A Gene That Makes Us Human?* World Science Aug. 16, 2006. www.world-science.net/othernews/060816_braingene.htm

79. Sean B Carroll. *Endless Forms Most Beautiful: The New Science of Evo Devo and the Making of the Animal Kingdom.* London: Weidenfeld & Nicolson, 2006: p12.

80. Steven Rose. Why I'm Not a Daffodil. *Guardian* 13 May 2006.

81. Susan Oyama. *The Ontogeny of Information: Developmental Systems and Evolution.* 2nd Edition. Durham NC: Duke University Press, 2002: p39.

82. Steven Rose. *The 21st Century Brain: Explaining, Mending and Manipulating the Mind.* London: Vintage Books, 2006: p62-3.

83. Richard Dawkins. *The God Delusion.* London: The Bantam Press, 2006: p66.

84. Daniel C Dennett. *Darwin's Dangerous Idea: Evolution and the Meanings of Life.* London: Penguin Books, 1996: pp309-12.

85. Charles Darwin. *The Descent of Man, and Selection in Relation to Sex.* London: Penguin Books, 2004: p687.

# Chapter 5

# The Evolution of Matter into Mind

'The Origin of Man as an Intellectual and Moral Being: On this great problem the belief and teaching of
Darwin was, that man's whole nature – physical, mental, intellectual, and moral – was developed from the
lower animals by means of the same laws of variation
and survival; and, as a consequence of this belief, that
there was no difference in *kind* between man's nature
and animal nature, but only one of degree. My view,
on the other hand, was, and is, that there is a difference in kind, intellectually and morally, between man
and other animals; and that while his body was undoubtedly developed by the continuous modification
of some ancestral animal form, some different agency,
analogous to that which first produced organic *life*,
and then originated *consciousness*, came into play in
order to develop the higher intellectual and spiritual
nature of man.' *Alfred Russel Wallace.*[1]

Our most distinctive anatomical feature is walking upright
with a big brain, and it is in the brain, if anywhere, that our
higher intellectual and spiritual nature has its seat. Although
there is a wide range of opinion as to what constitutes human
nature, and, indeed, as to whether there is any such thing,[2]
it is surely the case that our most distinctive mental feature
is intelligence, the ability to formulate and solve problems.
Our intelligence outstrips that of all other creatures, and must
have endowed us with survival and reproductive advantages,
such that genes for intelligence, or rather, for aspects of brain
size, structure and function, would have been incorporated

into the human genome. This a priori reasoning is supported by growing evidence of associations between IQ and genetically determined features of the brain.[3] Intelligence – cognitive ability – is the foundation of human nature, and it is its most researched aspect.

## Causality

Before proceeding further, a short digression is necessary. It is said that the Inuit have a great many words for snow. In English – I cannot speak for Eskimo languages – we have a different problem. We have only one word for the relationship between cause and effect: causation, and its close synonym causality. But causation has a great many shades of meaning, and confusion arises because we only have the one word for them all. We recall that Aristotle broached the tricky topic of causation with his four types of cause: material, formal, efficient and final. But there are many other degrees of meaning of the word 'cause', expressed in many different metaphors with their own logic, and which do not represent a single, unified phenomenon of causation existing out there in the world independently of us.[4] The philosopher Hume noted that causation cannot be perceived, it is only inferred from the regular association of cause and effect, which are not logically related one to the other. The concept of causation has been created by us, and as acquired in infancy it has at its centre the idea of a conscious human agency acting via direct physical force, which is why the metaphor **Genes as Selfish Agents** has such a powerful resonance. Some of the difficulty in accepting a gene-centred account of evolution and development arises because of a conflation of the rigid, instantaneous type of causation linking, for example, electricity and magnetism, with the more flexible and delayed relationship between genotype and phenotype, for which the closest word in our dictionary is 'correlation'. But as every statistician will tell you, correlation is not the same as causation. Nevertheless, a causal chain is envisaged linking a gene with its expression, but because the chain has many links, some of which are weak, the chain may be broken in some individuals, and the correlation between genotype and phenotype in a population is less than one.

Genetic determinism, then, is a derogatory term based on the misunderstanding that a given gene will inevitably result in a particular phenotypic feature; an electro-magnetic type of causation is implied when *Causation as a Causal Chain with Weak Links* would be a more appropriate metaphor.

In many situations, particularly involving biological systems, causation is said to be multifactorial, and is partitioned between several factors. A good illustration would be a road traffic accident involving one or more drivers interacting with each other, their vehicles, the roadway and its furniture. Responsibility for the accident can often only be approximately apportioned between these several components of a complex, dynamic, evolving situation where the outcome might so easily have been different. In a similar way, the development of an organism might have any number of outcomes arising from the interaction of many factors, of which the genotype is just one.

There is another common misunderstanding that needs to be cleared up here. We often talk of a gene 'for' something or other, brown or blue eyes, for example. The metaphor in this case is that of a volitional agent willing a particular outcome, like me saying 'I'm for Barack Obama'. This usage is a convenient shorthand for saying that the possession of one gene rather than another results in brown eyes rather than blue. There is no gene for brown eyes, but whether you have blue or brown eyes depends on which of the two genes happens to be present.

# Nature/Nurture

In the previous chapter it emerged that much of the controversy surrounding evolution centres on whether our behaviour is determined by the human genome, or whether it is a product of culture. To get a handle on human nature in our discussion of this nature/nurture problem, intelligence may be used as a proxy for human nature in the round.

The nature/nurture dichotomy may be caricatured thus: if our behaviour in life – our success or failure in solving life's problems and making a go of it – is determined by our inherited nature, of which intelligence is a salient component, then our fate is sealed at the time of our conception; there is little hope of improving our lot. If, on the other hand, our success in life is determined by our physical and cultural environment, in particular the socio-economic circumstances of our upbringing, our prospects may be improved by our having a better start in life.

Matt Ridley, in his book *Nature via Nurture*, summarises the evidence obtained from studies on twins for the heritability of several facets of human nature, including intelligence.[5] Identical twins have the same genes, the fertilised ovum dividing into two cells, each becoming an embryo. Differences between them as adults are therefore attributable to environmental differences during their upbringing. Non-identical, or fraternal, twins have different genes resulting from the fertilisation of two ova by different sperm. If they are born and brought up sharing the same environment, differences between them are attributable to their different genes. By studying populations of identical and fraternal twins brought up separately or together, the total variation in personality measurements can be partitioned between hereditary and environmental factors. Twin studies thus provide us with the best means of resolving the nature/nurture question, short of performing controlled experiments on babies from birth, to which there might be ethical objections.

Heritability is the percentage of the variation of a feature that can be attributed to genetic inheritance, and it can only be calculated for a group of subjects rather than an individual, and for a feature that varies. Thus, paradoxically, the heritability of having four limbs, or walking upright with a big brain, is said to be zero because these features are invariably present being almost certainly prescribed in the human genome. Heritability, because of the way it is calculated, is greatest when environmental variation is least. Thus the hereditary influence on adult height is only fully seen when adequate nourishment is available during growth, enabling everybody to achieve their full potential height. Similarly for measures of personality (openness, conscientiousness, extroversion, agreeableness and neuroticism): if the quality and quantity of family and social support and education is sufficient, the heritability of these factors is high, which is the case in Western society. Ridley concludes that more than 40% of the variation in personality is due to genetic factors, and the difference between one individual and another owes more to differences in their genes than in their family background.[6]

Intelligence, another personality feature likely to have a genetic basis, is measured as IQ. Particularly in children, however, it is influenced by socio-economic status. In poor families, variation in IQ scores relates to shared environment but not to heredity, while the opposite is true for children of richer families. Another finding is that the influence of environment on intelligence diminishes with age, and the importance of heredity increases.

The contribution of 'shared environment' to variation in IQ in Western society is roughly 40% in people younger than 20. It then falls rapidly to zero in older age groups. Conversely, the contribution of genes to explaining IQ variation rises from 20% in infancy to 40% in childhood to 60% in adults and maybe even 80% in people past middle age.[7]

From these empirical studies, two conclusions are warranted. First, some aspects of human nature, namely, personality, and intelligence (IQ) are hereditary, as the term is commonly used: other things being equal, identical twins with identical genomes are more alike than fraternal twins possessing different genomes. Second, the hereditary influence in identical twins, being far short of 100%, and in the case of intelligence, changing during a lifetime and affected by socio-economic status, cannot be described legitimately as genetic determinism.

It might be thought that the interactionist account proposed by Ridley – nature via nurture – with the genetic and environmental contributions being roughly 50:50, would satisfy both parties to the nature/nurture dispute. But no, this is seen by Lewontin, Rose and Kamin as an incorrect and ideologically led interpretation (pot calling the kettle black?).

> Interactionism takes the autonomous genotype and an autonomous physical world as its starting point... The hierarchical nature of human social organisation makes the subject-object dichotomy seem only natural when we contemplate the physical world. But that alienation is also of direct political relevance. The alienated organism must accommodate itself to the facts of life... Accommodation [is] a political goal...[8]

It is our class-ridden capitalist society which uproots us from our origins in the natural world, and which makes a nature/nurture distinction possible. Organisms, human or otherwise, are not naturally alienated from their environment but seek

172

out and create their own surroundings, the bond between them and their environment being dialectical, organisms creating environment, environment moulding organisms. Furthermore, the social milieu is just as important as the physical, so an organism is at the same time shaped by the environment as well as being part of it. This applies not only to organisms but to genes, which are not autonomous but have to be compatible with all the other genes comprising the gene pool: they are agents of heredity constrained by environment, while at the same time being part of that environment. Heredity and environment are inseparable.

While these criticisms have some validity, it has to be said that research in the social sciences can only be carried out in the society we have rather than the society we would like, and that it is often motivated by a desire to ameliorate the lives of the worst off, in recognition that many people get a raw deal with the present societal arrangements. A point particular to twin studies is that identical twins brought up separately have more in common than their genes: in the first formative months they also share the same ovarian factors and the same maternal intra-uterine environment. These elements may modify gene expression, so here too, nature and nurture are inseparable. However, these epigenetic factors are unlikely to be any more manipulable than the effects of genes themselves.

\*

In 1994 the results were published of a project to ascertain the relative importance of nature and nurture for the life prospects of 12,000 young Americans who were aged 14 to 22 when the study commenced, in 1979.[9] Cognitive ability was measured as IQ, and an assessment made of parental education, income and occupational prestige, all combined into a single numerical index known as socio-economic status (SES). The participants were followed up for ten years when a comprehensive assessment was again carried out, the participants then having a mean age of 30.

The data were analysed by the standard statistical technique known as multiple logistic regression analysis. The results show a powerful relationship between IQ at the start of the study and subsequent poverty, school dropout, unemployment, divorce, illegitimacy, welfare, parenting, crime and citizenship. Low IQ was a much stronger precursor than low parental SES for poverty at follow up. Similarly, the primary risk factor for being unemployed was neither socio-economic background nor education but low cognitive ability. The same was true of criminal behaviour except that most crime was committed by males and school drop-outs. There was a positive correlation between IQ and being married by the age of 30, and a negative correlation between IQ and the probability of divorce in the first five years of marriage. Low cognitive ability was a much stronger predisposing factor for having an illegitimate child than low SES, and the probability of a mother having a baby of low birth-weight was predominantly related to low IQ, an important contributory element being smoking; none of the smartest women smoked during pregnancy. A mother's IQ was more important than parental SES in predicting the worst home environments, and, in line with the evidence from twin studies, which supports inheritance of IQ, the mothers' IQ correlated closely with that of their children.

These empirical results demonstrate the much greater influence of IQ relative to SES on a wide range of behaviours. To a considerable extent, the dominant influence of intelligence pre-empts the possibility of amelioration of life prospects by modification of the socio-economic system. Furthermore, although an association between child deprivation and intel-

174

ligence has been shown, and environmental factors may contribute as much as 50% to the variance of IQ in children, it is another matter to break the link. Projects aimed at improving cognitive ability by early intervention have shown no long term improvement in IQ, so it is unlikely that in the foreseeable future the problems associated with low intelligence will be solved by outside interventions to make children smarter.[10] The authors write:

> Like many other disabilities, low intelligence is not the fault of the individual. Everything we know about the causes of cognitive ability, genetic and environmental, tells us that by the time people grow to an age at which they can be considered responsible moral agents, their IQ is fairly well set.[11]

This study, then, demonstrates that the nature/nurture dichotomy described above is, indeed, a caricature: there is no either/or dichotomy. Gould has written 'If we are programmed to be what we are, then these traits are ineluctable.'[12] The unspoken implication is that if our behaviour is not genetically programmed, but moulded by our upbringing, then it is readily modifiable. But the study just cited shows that the behaviour of young adults is influenced by both genes and environment in a sociobiological system where individuals interact with their physical and social environment in many complex ways. While genetic determinism is mollified by interaction with environment, behaviour is now seen to be much less malleable under the influence of environmental factors than was hoped.

This study was published as *The Bell Curve*, by Herrnstein and Murray, the title alluding to the normal distribution of IQ in a population. The book had vicious press reviews and rapidly achieved notoriety, a classic case of shooting the messenger bearing bad news. Also, like EO Wilson with *Sociobiology*,

Herrnstein and Murray broke a taboo concerning the study of human nature, in their case, its manifestation as intelligence, a topic badly tainted by association with eugenics. What attracted especially heavy fire was the authors' report that average IQ differed between racial groups, a finding that is now generally accepted, and which has important consequences.[14] There is not only an association between intelligence and life success at an individual level, but there is also a correlation between average IQ and wealth (GNP) at a national level.[15]

In fact, to forestall criticisms of racism, the authors of *The Bell Curve* excluded blacks and Latinos from the analyses summarised above, which were for whites alone. Nevertheless, criticisms there were, particularly from Gouldians, led by Gould himself. He had previously published *The Mismeasure of Man* in which he criticised the whole enterprise of measuring cognitive ability, claiming that general intelligence, g, is a reification of an idea that reflects scientists' racial, class and sexual prejudices, and which is used to justify and maintain the class system; he also had technical, statistical objections.[16] As to *The Bell Curve*, critics claimed that Herrnstein and Murray had made the mistake of confusing correlation with causation, inverting causation's direction: adverse social circumstances were the cause of low intelligence, not the other way round.

In an *Afterward* to a paperback edition published in 1996, the surviving author of *The Bell Curve*, Charles Murray, rebutted these and other criticisms. Intelligence as measured as IQ is not the reification of a means of social control, but represents a 'real property in the head' which has a major impact on an individual's ability to lead a successful and fulfilled life. Concerning intelligence:

> Genetically caused differences are not as fearful, or environmentally caused differences as benign, as

many people think. What matters is not the source but the existence of group differences and their intractability (for whatever reasons).[17]

## Consequences

David Hume in *An Enquiry Concerning Human Understanding* wrote:

> There is no method of reasoning more common, and yet none more blameable, than, in philosophical disputes, to endeavour the refutation of any hypothesis, by a pretence of its dangerous consequences to religion and morality…it is not certain that an opinion is false because it is of dangerous consequence.[18]

Gouldians, then, in the face of much evidence to the contrary, reject the idea of a genetic contribution to human nature because its acceptance would imply a fixity of human nature with all its shortcomings, with little hope of improvement. But experience shows that if human behaviour is determined instead by the environment, it is no less difficult to modify. The perfectibility of human nature is not therefore contingent on which view of human nature is correct.

Another reason for rejection of a determinist theory of human nature is that it appears to offer an escape from personal responsibility. If males have a gene for philandering, then they cannot be blamed for sleeping around; if women have genes for homemaking and motherhood, they have no hope of emancipation; and if a child's low intelligence is genetically determined, he cannot be blamed for doing badly at school. Men, women and children are all blameless puppets, and it is the genes that work the strings. To blame people for being what they are is to blame the victims for circumstances over which they have no control.

Box 12

The New Class System

Society used to be divided by social class, but it is now increasingly stratified by intelligence. In a country in which opportunity is open to talent there is social mobility for those with high IQs as never before. Moreover, in a post-industrial society, an increasing proportion of occupations require intellectual rather than manual skills, so that intelligence has growing value in the marketplace, resulting in a merger of the cognitive elite with the affluent. The old socio-economic upper class is being replaced by a new affluent cognitive elite which is becoming more and more segregated from the rest of the population, with whom its members have little in common and few contacts. Members of the new upper class live in secure, gated mansions and possess their own means of transport. They know how to work the system to best advantage, so have been well educated in school and university, and have access to the best health care. Their work is intellectual – eg in the financial sector or in information technology – and they pass much of their days at a computer. Leisure time may be spent at a subscription gym or golf club where they meet and marry their own kind. Their children, too, are bright and have every advantage at the start of their lives, in which most of them will emulate the success of their parents.

At the other extreme of the bell curve of intelligence is a new underclass of people with poor cognitive ability, trapped in poverty by their lack of intellectual and social skills and by the collapse of the market for manual labour. They are poorly educated with a reduced life expectancy, being ill-equipped to get the best from whatever education, health and welfare services may be available. They meet and mate with their own kind, and their children, although they may be brighter than their parents and closer in intelligence to the population mean, are severely disadvantaged at the start of their lives. Very few of them will make it to the upper echelons:

There is also an association between low IQ and teenage pregnancy which has important social consequences. Children of such single mother families are seriously disadvantaged by often having a less than competent mother and by not having a man who is able to sustain a long-term relationship as a resident role model. Boys may therefore model their behaviour on that of an older peer, who may well be unemployed and leader of a gang, having only casual encounters with the opposite sex. The effect of the absence of a father on girls is to make a repetition of the cycle of teenage pregnancy more likely. Single parent families, having only one potential wage-earner, are financially as well as socially impoverished.

This new class structure, with a widening gulf between haves and have-nots has a tendency to be self-perpetuating. It may be seen as an unintended consequence of an opportunity culture, an emergent property of a society stratified by intelligence.[13]

The philosopher Janet Radcliffe Richards deconstructs such arguments in her book *Human Nature After Darwin*.[19] She argues that it is important to distinguish the claims of evolutionary psychology, like there being a gene for philandering, from their implications should they prove to be true. Let us accept for a moment that there is such a gene. Does it follow that no blame can be imputed to a philanderer? One can say that if it were not for the genetic influence men would not be philanderers, and men cannot be blamed for the genes they have. The Gouldian alternative is that sex roles, including philandering in men, are culturally conditioned. But we cannot help our cultural conditioning any more than we can help which genes we inherit, and we cannot be blamed for what we cannot help. So whether or not we are blameworthy does not depend on the truth or falsehood of the evolutionary psychology account of human nature.

We have seen previously that genetic determinism is often wrongly taken to mean a rigid, electromagnetic type of causality, such as that implied by Gould's use of the word 'ineluctable'. But the causal chain between a supposed gene for philandering and the behaviour that it causes would have a great many links stretching for decades from conception, when the sex of the baby is determined, to adulthood, when the behaviour may be manifest. The causal chain – network might be a better metaphor – involves genes, sex hormones, brain structures and emotions, and is such that there would be many points where the sexual attraction felt by a would-be philanderer for his next conquest might be moderated. Variable attenuation of the effect of the gene for philandering means that the intensity of sexual passion will vary from person to person, and from time to time, and will rarely be overwhelming. Everyday criteria for responsibility can be applied quite properly to the sexual behaviour arising from possession of such a gene: being of sound mind, having reached the age of maturity, and not being physically or otherwise coerced so that no alternative course of action is possible. A person meeting these criteria, legally, and by common consent, would be held responsible for his actions, whatever an evolutionary psychologist might say in his defence.

But in a similar way, the causal chain between cultural conditioning and philandering behaviour would also be long and tenuous, and seldom so strong as to be unbreakable. Thus, whether our behaviour has genetic or environmental origins, we are responsible for it in the ordinary sense of the word 'responsible'.

But let us follow up this line of thought a little further. Suppose that our would-be philanderer, after considering his chances, passes up an opportunity for a fling. His decision to be faithful to his wife on this occasion is both a neural as well as a mental event.[20] And like all events at supra-atomic levels, this event is caused, in his case, by a multitude of factors that pull in different directions. Among those of which he is conscious is his frustrated lust, the thought that this affair might be difficult to keep secret, and his fear of the shame he would feel if he was found out. Then there is his genuine affection for his wife, and his appreciation of how upset she would be if she learned of his cheating on her. Among those factors of which he is unaware are his level of testosterone, the influence of his intended's pheromones, the long forgotten example set by his father and, of course, the actions of the gene for philandering that he inherited from him. His 'decision' is the outcome of a causal web where every event is caused, and every event becomes a cause; nothing happens in a causal vacuum. Given his entire life history up to now, his decision could not have been otherwise, though being finely poised, it might have been swayed by an external event – a stranger seen across a crowded room – at any time up to the very last moment before his mind was made up.

On this account our philanderer is responsible for his actions as ordinarily understood, but he cannot be held ultimately responsible, for two reasons. Although he is not coerced in any way, and has a choice between alternative courses of action, he cannot choose the state of mind in which he is able to exercise that choice. As the philosopher Quine puts it, 'You can will what you do, but you can't will what you will.'[21] The second reason is that even if he could determine the state of mind in which to make a choice, in the end he acts the way he does because of the way he is, and the way he is depends ultimately on events that occurred before he existed, for which he most certainly has no responsibility. Our philanderer has served to illustrate for us that materialism entails a form of determinism, and determinism renders the idea of ultimate responsibility incoherent.[22] Thus, Darwinism is sometimes rejected because it is a materialist doctrine entailing determinism, which precludes free will and ultimate responsibility for our actions.

Can free will be rescued if we allow indeterminism, the idea that not all events are caused? If anything, this makes us even less free and less responsible than if all events are caused.[23] If an action results from an uncaused event, an event unrelated to anything we are or do, then we are in no way accountable for the consequences. Being ultimately responsible for our actions is not therefore dependent on whether or not determinism is true. This conclusion may be extended to the materialist, and determinist, theory of evolution. Neither the hope of perfectibility of human nature, nor the assumption of ultimate responsibility for our behaviour, depends on whether or not Darwin's theory is true.

It is not just the idea of ultimate responsibility for our actions that is incoherent, but also that of free will itself. The notion of free will, *libre arbitre* in French, supposes a sequestered locus in the brain where decisions are made independently of any causal influence. It would be like having a trial jury not only isolated from the media and prevented from hearing prejudiced accounts of the alleged crime, but also denied access to the trial evidence: the jury's decision would be truly arbitrary.

## Consciousness

As evidenced in the epigraph to this chapter, consciousness was a particular problem for Wallace, who was quite unable to imagine that it had a bodily origin and so could have evolved by natural selection like any other faculty. He placed consciousness in the same category as life: a mystery which would never yield to scientific study but required a spiritual explanation. But with respect to life, molecular biology has proved Wallace wrong, just as scientific advances have confounded previous pronouncements concerning problems thought to be insoluble: it was once said that because of the remoteness of the stars and planets their composition would never be known, nor the nature of the force that moved them. At a time now when powerful new research techniques are being developed and results are flooding in, it is perhaps premature to designate consciousness as an insoluble, or even as a hard, problem.[24]

Setting aside the special nature of consciousness for the moment, we can readily think of just-so stories and adaptionist explanations for its evolution. Amongst the most plausible is the theory that consciousness allows us to negotiate better the complexities of community living by being able to imagine how other people are likely to feel and react.[25,26] Possession of such a 'theory of mind' would confer a survival or reproductive advantage in a fiercely competitive social environment. It is in consciousness, too, that we can anticipate fu-

183

ture events and carry out 'thought experiments' as a low risk means of solving problems; and we hold in consciousness long term aims and values with which to align moment-to-moment activity.

The special nature of consciousness consists of it being private and inexpressible. The philosopher Nagel encapsulated its unknowable quality in his provocative question 'What is it like to be a bat?' Being conscious is so unlike any other state of existence that we have no metaphors for it except those that contain a conscious being! The pervasive representation of 'what is it like to be me' is the Cartesian theatre deep inside my head where 'I' watch my life unfolding before me on a stage or screen. A third person description of my state of consciousness expressed in terms of neural correlates can never capture the marvellous intensity of my experience. But that is not to say that I experience something different in kind from that registered by a neuroscientist. It is just that I am connected differently to the inputs that give rise to my mental state. There are no grounds for thinking that my experience is a different phenomenon from that studied by a third person, or that it has a non-material basis or would continue if I were dead, or even just brain dead. Two very different descriptions may be made of the same event: consider accounts of a thunderstorm given by a landscape painter and a meteorologist; one account is experiential, the other causal and explanatory. But that parallel is not close enough, for the neuroscientist, though describing my experience in different terms from my own, would be able to gauge the strength of my emotional response to it. So although we do not know if one person's red is the same as another's, we do know that most people, and most monkeys, are aroused by the colour red, and calmed by blues and greens.[27] But personal experience need not be so very private because we do, after all, have language to describe how it feels. There may also be a more direct link

184

between your private experience and mine. If I see you being given a painful injection, so-called mirror neurones in my cerebral cortex, which normally fire when I am pricked with a needle, fire in sympathy with yours. In monkeys, the firing of different groups of mirror neurones accompanies the observation by a monkey of various very specific motor actions in another monkey. There is a preliminary report that mirror neurones were not found in a child with autism, a condition in which empathy is notoriously deficient.[28] The empathetic firing of mirror neurones may therefore be a means of knowing what it is like to be somebody else, if not a bat.

No locus of consciousness has been found in the brain; there is no part of the brain where consciousness is abolished by a single localised lesion. Consciousness is associated with a rhythmic synchronous firing of many neurones in large areas of the cerebral cortex linked to the intralaminar nucleus in the thalamus, deep in the middle of the brain.[29] Consciousness is therefore diffused in space within the brain, just as memories appear to be. The experience of time in consciousness is also smeared, and events may be represented in a different sequence from that in which they occur. Time is parsed in the brain, and two events are considered to be simultaneous if there is less than 100 milliseconds between them.[30] These distortions in the representation of time are understood to result from the circulation of coded sensory data round a network of parallel pathways and feedback loops. This has the effect of 'thickening the instant', prolonging the moment where the past meets the future. Under extreme stress time seems to slow down so that we visualise in slow motion the evolution of an accident in which we are involved. The recurrent processing of sensory data, what Dennett calls 'multiple drafts', results in the maximal extraction of meaning and generates working memory. Consciousness is thus diffusely localised in both space and time.                                                    .

Box 13

The Central Nervous System

The human brain consists of 100 billion neurones, each of which is connected to many others. The number of ways in which they could be connected up is said to be greater than the number of particles in the universe, which is another way of saying that the brain is very complicated indeed. This immediately raises a problem: the only instrument we have for understanding the brain is the brain itself. Although many aspects of its functioning are understood, there remains the possibility that there will be a persistent explanatory gap which will require an intelligence, an order of magnitude greater than our own to bridge. This applies particularly to what has been called 'the hard problem': how to explain the subjective, private and wonderful experience of being alive and conscious in terms of the neural activity of a kilogram and a bit of porridgy grey and white matter. The difficulty is in part a failure of the imagination when it comes to making conjectures about emergent properties of matter. Informed opinion is presently divided as to whether consciousness can be reduced to a physical explanation, or whether there will be an inexplicable residuum when the neuroscientists have done their work. Very broadly speaking, it is philosophers (and mathematicians) who come down on the side of the mystery of consciousness, some considering that consciousness somehow exists independently of brains, being part of the stuff of the universe. On the other hand, neuroscientists and psychologists are seeking what they call the neural correlates of consciousness, which they expect will provide at least a partial explanation for the phenomenon.

What is clear is that intuition is an unreliable guide to understanding brain function because so much neurological processing is inaccessible to us. Vision, for example, seems to be a simple matter, well, of just looking and seeing. The intuitive model is of a representation of the scene somewhere in the brain where 'I' view it. Neuroscientists say that this is wrong on many counts. The visual information captured in two dimensions by the retina is subject to an enormous amount of processing for the detection and recognition in three dimensions of edges, shapes, movement and colour. All this before we become conscious of what is happening. So a tennis player at Wimbledon returns a 125 mph serve before he or she has 'seen' the ball. And there does not seem to be any localised seat of consciousness, any theatre in which 'I' view my experience. Rather, there is a network of parallel pathways and feedback loops where sensory data or memories are processed again and again to extract maximal meaning. This iterative activity serves to prolong the present instant, and gives time for an appropriate response to be formulated. Consciousness is thought to arise from this circular activity within the brain's many layered systems. In this account, consciousness is an emergent property arising from a myriad neuronal interactions. As such, consciousness is not just an epiphenomenon, an ineffective byproduct of the brain's working, like the whistle of a locomotive, without effect on the engine. Rather, what happens in consciousness does have a causal effect on events at a lower level. Conscious thought is one of many factors influencing behaviour.

# Self and Free Will

Few dog owners doubt that their best friend is conscious, but it is questionable whether a dog is self-conscious. The recursive nature of human consciousness means that we go at least one better. As I write this I am conscious of the fact that I am conscious that I am conscious. But what is the nature of the 'self' of whom 'I' am conscious?

Descartes famously concluded that the only thing of which he could be certain was that he was thinking, and because he knew beyond doubt that he was thinking he knew he existed. He could imagine existence without a body, but not without thought. He concluded that he was therefore essentially a thinking thing, *res cogitans*, quite different from matter, *res extensa*, which, unlike thought, exists in and occupies space. Descartes' essence was the thinking, reasoning soul, which he located in the pineal gland in the centre of the brain behind the eyes, and likened to the pilot on the bridge of a ship. For Descartes his soul was his true 'self' and it was capable of existing independently of his body, and after his demise.

We may or not believe in life after death, but unless we have thought deeply about the matter, we too are likely to believe in self as somehow having an identity apart from the body, and comprising our personality, memories, feelings, hopes and aspirations. Self has coherence and continuity; after a night's oblivious sleep it is there when we wake up in the morning. And we locate self in the front row of the Cartesian theatre watching over our life as it unfolds. What's more, in this privileged position, self has agency, the capacity to choose between options, and to do what it chooses; we, our selves, have free will.

Here, as with consciousness, there is a marked disparity between first and third person points of view. Our personal experience, of which we, like Descartes, are absolutely certain, conflicts with scientific evidence and reasoned argument. The philosopher Bryan Magee writes:

> The fact of my own agency is something of which I have a knowledge so direct that it survives the most careful consideration of all the arguments to the effect that I do not have it.[31]

There are now two irreconcilable hypotheses: that all human behaviour has a cause or causes; or, that some human behaviour results from the exercise of free will. Can either proposition be confirmed or refuted?

The studies cited at the beginning of this chapter provide strong support for the notion that a high proportion of people's behaviour is *caused* rather than being arbitrary, being significantly correlated with environmental and genetic factors. Much individual behaviour can be accurately predicted: a healthy new-born baby can be expected to walk at age one, speak at two, read, write and do arithmetic by 11, and attain sexual maturity by 15 years. Failure to achieve these milestones is invariably caused by some disorder of development, not by exercise of free will. Grown-ups predictably get up in the morning, travel to work, take lunch, go home, watch television, and go to bed. The accuracy of these predictions is daily put to the test by the providers of services enabling people to do these things. At an individual level, knowledge of a person's habits and past behaviour enables accurate prediction of future conduct.

It will be objected, however, that a habit may be readily overridden by exercise of free will, and an individual may choose to behave differently from his personal or social group norm, thus falsifying any prediction. But this is to misunderstand the statistical nature of causality in a complex system, where every prediction comes with an estimate of its probability. Failure of a prediction of human behaviour is not proof of free will any more than the failure of a weather forecast is evidence of meteorological volition. It may rather indicate incomplete knowledge of the initial conditions, or else the apparently spontaneous, aberrant behaviour sometimes seen in a chaotic but deterministic system.

The scope for prediction of behaviour that results from exercise of free will is severely limited to that which is consciously and explicitly predicted by the individual himself. Self-willed behaviour is a small fraction of the total; nobody claims to exercise free will over digestion, or over respiration during sleep, or even falling in love. In spite of its very limited ambitions, the hypothesis that an individual can select for himself and determine even a small part of his own future behaviour is frequently falsified. The prediction that 'I will get up early tomorrow', 'I will lose weight', or, 'I will give up smoking' is unfulfilled, with the explanation that 'I didn't have the will-power'.

From a third person perspective, the idea that all human behaviour is caused and may be explained is quite consistent with our everyday thinking. Of behaviour which is considered to result from the exercise of free will we will ask, 'Why did you do that?' If the explanation we receive does not satisfy us, we may try to interpret the behaviour in terms of motives or influences of which the perpetrator may be unaware. Failure to find an explanation does not falsify the hypothesis of biological causation because we always have recourse to the argument that we have insufficient knowledge of the circumstances. Although determinism cannot be proved, the hypothesis that we have free will is falsifiable, and is falsified daily. We all experience the failure to do something which we are quite capable of doing, which we choose to do, want to do, predict we will do, and are not prevented from doing by any external constraint.

It is paradoxical, then, that there should be a widespread belief in the doctrine of free will, which is demonstrably false, but a widespread disbelief in determinism, for which there is abundant empirical and theoretical support. But this rehearsal of the arguments for determinism serves to underline the point made by Magee. When it comes to choosing between options – tea or coffee, one lump or two – we are perfectly free to do so, and this sense of our autonomous will prevails over any argument to the contrary. Is there any possible resolution of these two positions, of determinism and free will?

There is a famous experiment performed by a neurophysiologist named Libet that casts a bright light on the matter.[32] The electroencephalogram (EEG, brainwaves) was recorded by means of electrodes attached to the scalp in student volunteers who were asked to make a simple hand movement at a moment of their choosing, whenever they felt like it. The movement interrupted a beam of light falling on a photoelectric cell, enabling it to be timed. They also had to note the position of a dot rotating rapidly round a large clock face at the moment when they were aware of the decision to act. The results were surprising. The first indication of a voluntary action was the appearance on the EEG of an electrical spike known as the readiness potential, more than half a second before the movement started. But the reported time of decision was more than one third of a second *after* the readiness potential. The 'voluntary' movement was initiated subconsciously, and the 'decision', reported some time later, was therefore not the cause of the movement. The interpretation of this result favoured by Libet and many others is that free will is illusory.

A criticism of Libet's study is of timing inaccuracies in reporting awareness, and it has been argued that his observations are compatible with conscious deliberation having a contributory causal role in decision making.[33] However, a recent study using functional magnetic resonance imaging (fMRI) of the brain has shown that evidence of an upcoming decision can be detected as long as 10 seconds before it comes into awareness.[34] In relation to this long time interval, inaccuracies of timing are trivial. The volunteer subjects were asked to press one of two buttons whenever they had the urge to so, using either the right or left index finger. At the same time, a stream of letters was flashed on a screen every half-second. The subjects had to remember which letter had been on the screen when they first became conscious of their motor decision. Immediately after the movement they had to indicate the remembered letter, which enabled the interval between awareness and movement to be estimated. In a majority of cases it was within a second. Brain activity predictive of the movement was detectable up to 10 seconds beforehand, and its localisation in one or other brain region predicted whether the right or left finger would be used. Such a long subconscious preparatory period is compelling evidence that the left/right decisions had not originated in consciousness. The authors conclude that a network of high level control areas in the frontal cortex begin to shape an upcoming decision long before it enters awareness.

Experiments of this sort show that we have very much less conscious control over our decisions than we think. But conscious thought is not entirely an epiphenomenon, with no influence on decision making. When we ring a help line and a recorded voice tells us to press 1 to enquire about our account, or 2 for technical help, the content of consciousness held in short-term memory clearly has a major influence on our next action. In this example, our action in pressing one button rather than another is not a free choice – an exercise of free will – but a reaction dictated by our particular need for help. In the case of an experiment in which we are invited to press 1 or 2 as and when we wish, the only evidence that we are any freer in our choice is the *feeling* that another choice could have been made. The subconscious influences that caused us to press one button rather than another are hidden, and whatever reasons we adduce for our 'choice' are probably irrelevant. The experience of consciously willing an action is not evidence that the conscious thought has caused the action.[35]

Scientific evidence that free will is an illusion is accumulating, supporting the conclusion reached more than two centuries ago by Hume in his *Enquiry Concerning Human Understanding*.[36] Liberty, or free will, means no more than not being a prisoner or in chains – being free from external constraints or coercion.

*

We return to the question of whether any accommodation is possible between the rival notions of freewill and determinism. Perhaps the two positions are not totally irreconcilable. After all, the subjects of Libet's experiments were not puppets whose strings were operated by some external agency: the subjects moved their fingers of their own accord. The movements originated within their persons with neural activity manifesting as readiness potentials, and this scientific evidence is not in conflict with their *feeling* that they initiated the movements themselves. The difficulty arises from the concept of self.

The problem may be put like this. After a meal at a friend's house, the hostess, who is completely indifferent as to how I respond, kindly asks me which would I prefer, tea or coffee, both being immediately available. 'I' have an equal liking for both: do 'I' have a genuine choice? It certainly feels as if 'I' do. For a moment 'I' cannot decide – 'I' cannot predict what my brain is going to opt for – but then I say "coffee, please". Given the history of all previous similar decisions, each one of which alters the probable outcome of the next, and given all the influences operating subconsciously, including the latest TV advert working away subliminally, the outcome could not have been otherwise; it was not a genuinely free choice. But by expanding the definition of myself from my conscious self to my brain I regain, partially at least, my self determination. It was my decision, having been made by me, my brain. I have ownership of my decisions and am responsible for them as the word is ordinarily understood, even though they may be made unconsciously in part and their ultimate causes may be beyond my control. Moreover, I may be satisfied that my actions are in keeping with my values, or feel shame that they are not.

In the above account, a distinction has been drawn between the self-conscious, supposedly autonomous 'I' between apostrophes, and the I who is the object of the attention of others, the third person I. As with both consciousness and free will, where there are discrepancies between first and third person accounts, there are also different descriptions of self. Now while there is no place from which an entirely neutral point of view is possible, an a priori presumption must be that the first person account of oneself will be more biased, and in a direction favourable to oneself, than a third person account. That this is so is supported by a large body of psychological research reviewed in Cordelia Fine's amusing book *A Mind of its Own: How your Brain Distorts and Deceives.*

> Your unscrupulous brain is entirely undeserving of
> your confidence. It has some shifty habits that leave

the truth distorted and disguised. Your brain is vain-glorious. It deludes you. It is emotional, pigheaded and secretive. Oh, and it's also a bigot. This is more than a minor inconvenience. That fleshy walnut inside your skull is all you have in order to know yourself and to know the world. Yet, thanks to the masquerading of an untrustworthy brain with a mind of its own, much of what you think you know is not quite what it seems.[37]

To give just one trivial example, most of us consider, contrary to logic, that we are better than average drivers,[38] and many of us believe, against the evidence, that speed cameras are installed to raise revenue and do not reduce road traffic accidents.[39] More fundamentally, the first impression of someone we meet is influenced by factors of which we are quite unaware. This was strikingly shown in a psychology experiment in which someone's personality was rated using a standard inventory. The participants who were to do the rating were met individually by the experimenter's accomplice who, while going up in the lift to the research room, asked them to hold her drink while she noted their name and time of arrival on a clipboard; the drinks were either hot or iced-cold coffee. People who had briefly held the hot coffee cup rated the target person as being significantly warmer than did those who had briefly held the cup of iced coffee. The coffee manipulation did not affect ratings on traits unrelated to the warm-cold dimension.[40] The authors of this study surmise that the association between physical and emotional warmth is formed in infancy, and describe how both types of warmth are processed in the same area of the cerebral cortex, resulting in a type of synaesthesia.

So if the conscious self is so untrustworthy as a source of information and opinion about ourselves and other people, perhaps we should ignore it as far as possible. There are psychologists and philosophers, then, who consider that the conscious autonomous self, and free will, are both of them illusions that it is possible to live without.[41,42] But is it correct to identify the self with the brain?

There is a thought experiment in which a brain, complete with the memories of all of its owner's experiences, is removed from an old body, riddled with cancer, let us say, and transplanted into a younger, healthy one. Would that be the same person? People who pay for their heads to be deep frozen when they die believe the answer to be yes, hoping to resume their lives when brain transplantation becomes available in the future. But would the transplanted brain give rise to the same behaviour in the new body as in the old? Besides memories of experiences and of language, we have memories of skills: walking, talking, how to thread a needle or play the piano. While these latter skills are transferable between different sized needles or between a range of keyboard instruments, it is far from obvious that learned physical skills would be transferable between bodies with different developmental histories of the peripheral nervous system. The endocrine system, too, would have different settings of its many hormones, and there would be many other differences in the transplanted brain's biochemical environment, all of which would profoundly influence temperament, mood and libido of the new chimera. Moreover, a person's personality is mostly not manifested in isolation, but in the company of others, in interactions in which physical appearance plays a large part. Even if in all respects except height the new body was the same in appearance, structure and biochemical and hormonal composition as the old, the personality and behaviour of the transplanted brain would be different; looking down on somebody is more than a metaphorical expression. A person's height is the datum level for interpersonal relationships; how much more important are looks. So the brain

196

cannot be considered apart from the body, and a brain in a vat would literally die of boredom, or at least, go mad from sensory deprivation. But it is wrong to think of sensation as being purely passive; it is vigorously interactive. When we view a scene, our eyes dart between points of interest, and we may tilt our head to get a better view. What we see is not what we might record with a video camera balanced on our shoulders, but the image is edited to appear stationary while our eyes move, and rotated to compensate for the tilt of our head. When we make a gesture with a hand, the movement is monitored and we compare what we expect to feel with what we do feel, which is why we are unable to tickle ourselves and make ourselves laugh, the essence of a tickle being its unpredictability. The sensory and motor functions of the nervous system are inseparable, and the brain's role has been described as 'minding the body'.[43]

Our brains are embodied, and we saw earlier how our categories and concepts develop in infancy out of the tentative exploration of the world with our bodies. It was then that we felt that warmth is trust and comfort, saw that big is important, and grasped the basic properties of number. Throughout our lives we need to keep literally in touch with reality to preserve our sanity. Selfhood is not to be located in the brain, even less in that fragment of the brain that is conscious, the conscious self or soul. The truest account of my self is the third person one. My self is my body, one and the same.

*

Our invincible sense of free will, then, arises from our tendency to infer causation whenever two events are associated with each other: the experience of conscious will is associated with the occurrence of actions performed by our bodies; we take these to be cause and effect. But although free will is illusory, and the very idea is incoherent, the notion of conscious will has many positive aspects, and has been likened to the mind's compass.[44] Belief in free will enhances our self-esteem and gives us confidence in our abilities. By believing that we cause them, we take ownership of our actions, investing them with emotions of pride and joy, or regret and shame. Being morally responsible for our actions and their consequences enables us to learn from our mistakes so that our behaviour is modified accordingly. While bad behaviour makes us feel bad, good behaviour is reinforced by being emotionally rewarding.

## Agency is Other People

Our sense of free will, besides giving us ownership of our actions, also gives rise to the belief that we can change our behaviour if we so wish: become a better person, more loving, kind and considerate, or harder working perhaps. This year, we will keep our New Year's resolutions. But here again, we are under an illusion. For how can a deterministic system change itself? Certainly, it can evolve, changing in the course of time, but only in a direction determined by the clay of our inherited nature being moulded by nurture. It is not possible for a system to change the direction of causality from within, to choose for itself its destiny. A change of direction requires an outside agency.

It is in our relations with other people that change comes about. By means of language, as well as by non-verbal communication, we attempt to manipulate other people to do our will, and they do likewise to us. Verbal communication relies heavily on the concepts of self – myself and yourself – and our intentions for ourselves in relation to other people may be made explicit and supported by reasons. Our non-verbal communication projects our attitudes, expectations and feelings, which tend to evoke corresponding behaviour that fulfils our expectation, justifies our attitude and intensifies our feeling, whether of hostility or affection.[45] Both parties are changed in the encounter but not always in the anticipated direction; in a marriage of true minds, though, the changes in both may be profound indeed. When a couple becomes an item, their behaviour is not attributable to their separate agencies, but emerges from the dynamic of their relationship, and may not correspond to the intentions of either.

Babies are amongst the most potent change-agents on the planet, turning carefree fun-loving girls into loving mums, and boys behaving badly into lovely dads. But it is a two-way process, and while an inchoate baby is transforming its parents, it is itself being miraculously transfigured into a person.

It is in infancy that the first steps are taken, not only of walking, but of negotiating other minds. For the first couple of years, other minds can be manipulated to do baby's bidding without demur. But in the terrible twos comes the distressing realisation that the intentions of other minds may sometimes conflict with those of junior.[46] But little by little, the skill of mostly getting what one wants without causing hurt to oneself or rancour in others is acquired and employed in a widening circle of encounters with siblings, playmates and grownups outside the immediate family. These social skills are of immense lifelong importance, and are the basis of moral behaviour. Being good is a practical skill that is first learned in infancy.[47]

Someone acting under orders from a superior largely surrenders ownership of his actions, and has a diminished feeling of responsibility for their consequences. This was vividly illustrated by Milgram's notorious experiments in which volunteers obeyed instructions to give electric shocks of increasing severity to subjects in a study ostensibly about conditioned learning.[48] In fact, no shocks were given, and the subjects were stooges who faked electrocution. Some volunteers continued to obey the supervisor's instructions in spite of the howls of pain and pleas for mercy of their victims. Milgram wanted to know how it was that so many ordinary people had collaborated in the Holocaust, apparently without misgivings. The answer is all too simple: moral responsibility follows agency, and both are readily surrendered to a figure of authority.

A more subtle influence on our conduct results from our desire to conform with the behaviour of those around us, even if it means denying our own judgement. Other factors that may operate in group decision making are a desire to please the leader of the group, and a willingness to accept a greater risk than would be the case if the burden of responsibility was not shared. Decisions of a committee are therefore liable to be more polarised than the views of its members. If a group has a powerful leader, a prime minister of a war cabinet for example, there is a risk that any member who has the courage to express a dissenting opinion to that of the leader will be replaced, and legitimate counter-arguments to a proposal will not be heard.[49]

In *The Tipping Point*, Malcolm Gladwell describes how ideas, products, messages and behaviours spread through society in the manner of epidemics of infectious diseases, like measles or syphilis.[50] The spread of the latter is particularly dependent on a few sexually promiscuous individuals; similarly, trendy ideas or fashions are dependent on a few well-connected people who are considered 'cool' and worth emulating. The spread of the germ of an idea in this way is exponential, the number of 'cases' increasing rapidly once a threshold is reached, which Gladwell calls the 'tipping point'. Besides transmission by 'connectors', another factor influencing the spread of an idea is its infectivity or 'stickiness', its attractiveness to the people infected by it, which may be skilfully manipulated by a public relations department or an advertising agency. Amongst the many epidemics he describes are the harmless fashion of sporting Hush Puppies, and the lethal emulation of teenage suicide in Micronesia. In the latter case, the metaphor of *Ideas as Infectious Agents* is particularly apt. A closely related notion is contained in the nested metaphor *Ideas as Selfish Genes,* known also as memes.

Gladwell stresses the importance of context in influencing conduct: criminal behaviour in the New York metro is much more likely in graffiti covered trains than in freshly painted ones; children may cheat in an arithmetic test but not in a spelling test; and the likelihood of someone going to another's aid is strongly influenced by the number of people present: the more witnesses there are to an accident, the less likely it is that help will be given to someone needing it. This means that it is an error to attribute an essential nature to someone – law-abiding, honest or helpful – because how they behave will depend importantly on circumstances.

Alluding to non-linear system properties, the subtitle of *The Tipping Point* is *How Little Things Can Make a Big Difference,* and Gladwell concludes on an optimistic note:

> If there is difficulty and volatility in the world of the Tipping Point, there is a large measure of hopefulness. Merely by manipulating the size of a group, we can dramatically improve its receptivity to new ideas. By tinkering with the presentation of information, we can significantly improve its stickiness. Simply by finding and reaching those few special people who hold so much social power, we can shape the course of social epidemics. In the end, Tipping Points are a reaffirma-

tion of the potential for change and the power of intelligent action.[51]

On the other hand, knowledge of the mechanics of social epidemics may enable them to be engineered – our behaviour
may be manipulated, our voting intentions changed, or our
consumer wants stimulated, entirely to serve the purposes of
others. Or, a social epidemic may emerge in a society and
be no more intelligently engineered, nor any more welcome,
than is an epidemic of measles.

# Summing Up

In the previous chapter it was concluded that opposition to
Darwin's theory of evolution by means of natural selection
resulted in part from a fear that human nature would be found
to be fixed and unimprovable because of genetic determinism. But whether human nature is determined by nature or by
nurture is an empirical matter, and the available evidence is
well summarised by Ridley as 'nature via nurture'. Genes and
environment both play major roles in human development,
but the influence of genes is not so rigid as had been feared,
while the effect of environment is not so strong as had been
hoped. Whether determined by nature or nurture, human behaviour is no easier to modify. Rejection of Darwinism and
its implied genetic determinism in order to preserve the hope
of improving human nature is therefore not warranted.

Another fear was that genetic determinism would be used as
a way of denying free will and escaping from individual responsibility. But the concept of free will is incoherent and the
term 'free will' an oxymoron: if an action is willed it is not
free but caused; if it is free and not caused it is not willed.

While individuals may be held responsible for their actions in the ordinary, and legal, sense of the word, they cannot be held ultimately responsible because their very being results from events occurring before they existed and during their upbringing, over which they have no control whatsoever. This conclusion stands whether or not the theory of evolution is true, so escape from individual responsibility should not be used as an argument for Darwinism's rejection.

Repudiation of free will is not to deny human creativity and spontaneity, particularly when people come together in couples, groups or crowds. Our behaviour then is better understood as an emergent property arising from our interactions with each other, rather than as a manifestation of an essential nature possessed by each.

It is now generally accepted that consciousness is not a uniquely human characteristic but is widespread in 'higher' animals; indeed, apes, dolphins and elephants show evidence of self-consciousness.[52] The search is now on for the material basis – 'neural correlates' – of consciousness, whose evolution made possible the exploration of other minds and laid the foundations for the evolution of morality.

# Notes

## Chapter 5: The Evolution of Matter into Mind

1. Alfred Russel Wallace *cited in* Helena Cronin. *The Ant and the Peacock: Altruism and Sexual Selection from Darwin to Today*. Cambridge University Press, 1991: p354.
2. Robin Headlam Wells, Johnjoe McFadden. *Human Nature: Fact and Fiction*. London: Continuum, 2006.
3. Toga AW, Thomson PM. Genetics of brain structure and intelligence. *Annual Reviews of Neuroscience* 2005;28:1-23.
4. George Lakoff, Mark Johnson. *Philosophy in the Flesh: The Embodied Mind and its Challenge to Western Thought*. New York: Basic Books, 1999: p177.
5. Matt Ridley. *Nature via Nurture: Genes, Experience, and What Makes us Human*. London: Fourth Estate, 2003: p69-96.
6. Ibid, p82-3.
7. Ibid, p92.
8. RC Lewontin, Steven Rose, Leon J Kamin. *Not in Our Genes: Biology, Ideology, and Human Nature*. New York: Pantheon Books, 1984: p277.
9. Richard J Herrnstein, Charles Murray. *The Bell Curve: Intelligence and Class Structure in American Life*. New York: Simon & Schuster/Free Press Paperbacks, 1996.
10. Ibid, p389.
11. Ibid, p142.
12. Stephen Jay Gould. *Ever Since Darwin: Reflections in Natural History*. Harmondsworth: Penguin Books, 1980: p238.
13. Charles Murray. *Underclass +10: Charles Murray and the British Underclass 1990-2000*. Civitas, 2001.
14. Racial differences in intelligence: What Mainstream Science says. First published in *The Wall Street Journal,* 1994 and signed by 52 internationally known scholars. www.cpsimoes.net/artigos/bell_mainstr.html
15. The wealth of nations is mapped by their IQ. *The Times* 10 November 2003.
16. Stephen Jay Gould. *The Mismeasure of Man*. Harmondsworth: Penguin Books, 1984: p234-320.

17. Richard J Herrnstein, Charles Murray. *The bell Curve: Intelligence and Class Structure in American Life.* New York: Simon & Schuster/Free Press Paperbacks, 1996: p563.
18. David Hume. *Enquiries Concerning Human Understanding and Concerning the Principles of Morals* (1777). Oxford: Clarendon Press,1975: p96.
19. Janet Radcliffe Richards. *Human Nature After Darwin: A Philosophical Introduction.* London: Routledge, 2000: p131-4.
20. Ted Honderich. *Mind and Brain: A Theory of Determinism. Volume 1.* Oxford: Clarendon Press, 1990, p248.
21. WV Quine *in* Bryan Magee. *Talking Philosophy.* Oxford University Press, 2001: p146.
22. Janet Radcliffe Richards. *Human Nature After Darwin: A Philosophical Introduction.* London: Routledge, 2000: p145.
23. Ibid, p139.
24. Patricia Churchland: 'Many people suppose that by sheer contemplation of a problem, they can tell whether it is hard or easy. This is self-deception.' *Cited in* Susan Blackmore. *Conversations on Consciousness: What the Best Minds Think About the Brain, Free Will, and What it Means to be Human.* Oxford University Press, 2006: p51.
25. Nicholas Humphrey. *The Inner Eye of Consciousness. In* Colin Blakemore, Susan Greenfield (eds). *Mindwaves.* Oxford: Basil Blackwell Ltd, 1989: p377-81.
26. Paul M Churchland. *The Engine of Reason, the Seat of the Soul: A Philosophical Journey into the Brain.* Cambridge, Mass.: The MIT Press, 1995, p123-50.
27. Nicholas Humphrey. *Seeing Red: A Study in Consciousness.* Cambridge Mass.: The Belknap Press of Harvard University Press, 2006: p19-20.
28. Ramachandran, VS. *Mirror Neurons and Imitation Learning as the Driving Force Behind "The Great Leap Forward" In Human Evolution.* www.edge.org/3rd_culture/ramachandran/ramachandran_p1.html
29. Paul M Churchland. *The Engine of Reason, the Seat of the Soul: A Philosophical Journey into the Brain.* Cambridge, Mass.: The MIT Press, 1995: p215.
30. Rita Carter. *Consciousness.* London: Weidenfeld & Nicolson, 2002: p160.

31. Bryan Magee. *Confessions of a Philosopher*. London: Weidenfeld & Nicolson, 1997: p476.

32. Benjamin Libet. *Do We Have free Will?* In Benjamin Libet, Anthony Freeman, Keith Sutherland (eds). *The Volitional Brain: Towards a Neuroscience of Free Will*. Exeter: Imprint Academic, 1999: p47-57.

33. Daniel C Dennett. *Freedom Evolves*. London: Allen Lane, 2003: p232-42.

34. Soon CS, Brass M, Heinze HJ, Haynes JD. Unconscious determinants of free decisions in the human brain. *Nature Neuroscience* 2008; 11:543-5.

35. Daniel M Wegner. *The Illusion of Conscious Will*. Cambridge Mass.: MIT Press, 2002: p2.

36. David Hume. *Enquiries Concerning Human Understanding and Concerning the Principles of Morals* (1777). Oxford: Clarendon Press,1975: p95.

37. Cordelia Fine. *A Mind of its Own: How Your Brain Distorts and Deceives*. Cambridge: Icon Books, 2006: p2.

38. Ibid, p6.

39. www.speedcam.co.uk/index2.htm

40. Williams LE, Bargh JA. Experiencing physical warmth promotes interpersonal warmth. *Science* 2008;322:606.

41. Susan Blackmore. *The Meme Machine*. Oxford University Press, 1999, p235-246.

42. Ted Honderich. *The Consequences of Determinism: A Theory of Determinism. Volume 2.* Oxford: Clarendon Paperbacks, 1988.

43. Antonio R Damasio. *Descartes' Error: Emotion, Reason and the Human Brain*. London: Picador, 1995: p230.

44. Daniel M Wegner. *The Illusion of Conscious Will*. Cambridge Mass.: MIT Press, 2002: p317-42.

45. Ibid, p194.

46. Alison Gopnik, Andrew Meltzoff, Patricia Kuhl. *How Babies Think*. London: Weidenfeld & Nicolson, 1999: p38.

47. Paul M Churchland. *The Engine of Reason, the Seat of the Soul: A Philosophical Journey into the Brain*. Cambridge, Mass.: The MIT Press, 1995: p143-50.

48. Stuart Sutherland. *Irrationality: The Enemy Within*. London: Penguin Books, 1994, p35-39.

49. Ibid, p45-68.
50. Malcolm Gladwell. *The Tipping Point: How Little Things Can Make a Big Difference*. London: Little, Brown and Company, 2000.
51. Ibid, p259.
52. Elephants recognize mirror image; elephant ancestor found. http://www.world-science.net/othernews/061030_elephant.htm

# Chapter 6

# The Evolution of Morality

'The following proposition seems to me in a high
degree probable – namely, that any animal whatever,
endowed with well-marked social instincts, the parental and filial affections being here included, would
inevitably acquire a moral sense or conscience, as
soon as its intellectual powers had become as well,
or nearly as well developed, as in man... I do not wish
to maintain that any strictly social animal... would
acquire exactly the same moral sense as ours. In the
same manner as various animals have some sense of
beauty, though they admire widely different objects,
so they might have a sense of right and wrong, though
led by it to follow widely different lines of conduct.'
*Charles Darwin*[1]

As we saw in the last chapter, Alfred Russell Wallace, co-
founder with Darwin of the theory of evolution, was quite
unable to imagine that consciousness had a bodily origin,
believing that it had a spiritual explanation. 'The origin of
man as an intellectual and moral being' was another great
problem for Wallace, for whom the source of morality was
not evolution, as Darwin thought, but 'some different agency,
analogous to that which first produced organic life, and then
originated consciousness...in order to develop the higher intellectual and spiritual nature of man.' The agency alluded to
was presumably divine, even though Socrates had long ago
neatly demolished the argument that the gods were the arbi-
ters of what was good. Socrates questioned 'whether the pi-
ous or holy is beloved by the gods because it is holy, or holy

because it is beloved of the gods.' If behaviour is approved by the gods because it is holy, then there is a standard of holiness independent of and recognised by the gods; if an act is holy because it is arbitrarily beloved by the gods, then we can imagine ourselves sometimes disagreeing with what they approve. It is doubtful whether many fundamentalists are sympathetic to God's liking for animal sacrifice, nor do they endorse the biblical injunction to put to death someone who works on the Sabbath.[2] This shows that moral standards do not depend on God or gods for their existence, and the death of God does not entail the end of morality. Atheism used to be feared because it was thought that people would run amok and commit all manner of immoral acts if God was not in his heaven keeping a magisterial eye on us. These fears were unfounded: God is dead but morality lives on. But where does morality come from? What is the source of its authority, or as Darwin expressed it, the imperiousness of the little word 'ought'? Are our moral standards the result of our species' evolutionary history, or is there some absolute standard of right and wrong that exists independently of us? To update Socrates' probing question: is morality good because it was sanctioned by evolution, or sanctioned by evolution because it was good? Darwin was in little doubt about the answer:

> If, for instance, to take an extreme case, men were reared under precisely the same conditions as hive-bees, there can hardly be a doubt that our unmarried females would, like the worker-bees, think it a sacred duty to kill their brothers, and mothers would strive to kill their fertile daughters; and no one would think of interfering.[3]

The idea that morality – the best and most distinctive element of our human nature – had its origins in animals was abhorrent to Wallace, and remains unthinkable for many to this day. Are not 'animal' and 'bestial' derogatory terms for the very worst human behaviour? But before deliberating on whether morality has evolved, we must first consider some other possibilities: that morality derives from universal natural law; or, that morality derives from a happiness principle.

## Morality as Natural Law

The Prussian philosopher, Kant, though brought up as a Christian, endeavoured to construct a system of morality intended to guide us as to how we should behave. His system is therefore prescriptive rather than descriptive, and its foundations are neither divine nor human but part of natural law. Kant's is the most important attempt to develop a coherent non-religious ethical system, and he was driven to do this by Hume's claim that:

> Reason is and ought only to be the slave of the passions, and can never pretend to any other office than to serve and obey them.[4]

Kant rejected a morality based on passion, or, as we would say, feelings or emotion; and maximising happiness was certainly not his line. Happiness and morality have nothing to do with one another, and Kant, with a dig at JS Mill, found it 'astonishing how intelligent men have thought of proclaiming as a universal practical law the desire for happiness.'[5]

Kant rather based his morality on reason and duty. He argued that an act is good, not because of its good consequences nor because it is performed lovingly, with good intentions, but only if it is done with good will from a sense of duty. And what is our duty? Kant declares in his famous categorical imperative that:

> I ought never to act except in such a way that I could
> also will that my maxim should become a universal
> law.[6]

As well as arising from good will, our behaviour should be universalisable so that it would not be logically inconsistent if everyone were to behave similarly. Kant cites as irrational the making of a promise with the intention of not keeping it: if everybody did that it would undermine the institution of making promises; to always tell the truth entails no contradiction. Kant elevates this reason-based principle to that of a law of nature. Apart from its arid righteousness – the execution of a murderer is imperative even should he be the last person on a desert island – there are problems with absolute moral rules to which there can be no exceptions. It is difficult for most of us to think of any injunction that we would wish to be applied under all circumstances; we would not consider it wrong to lie to a mad axeman enquiring as to the whereabouts of our children, nor even to kill him if that were the only way to save the family. If there is more than one imperative, there is the possibility of an irresoluble conflict between them; there can be no hierarchy of absolute principles. The Old Testament edict to put to death those who work on the Sabbath clashes with the commandment 'thou shalt not kill'; presumably these are not thought to be absolute precepts even by fundamentalists. Kant's categorical imperative rules out maxims that cannot be universally applied, but does not say which maxims we should adopt. He instructs us that we ought to do our duty, but he does not say what that duty is. His categorical imperative is of little help in the conduct of an ethical life since many dilemmas arise where there is conflict between different claims. How do the rights of a foetus stack up against those of its mother? Should a politician work all day every day for the public good, or should he spend more time with his family? Kant is no help to us here.

Box 14

The Autonomous Self and the Autonomic Nervous System

Kant had the intuition that as well as the 'empirical self', subject to the laws of nature, we also possess an 'autonomous self'. The autonomous, or transcendental, self is independent of nature's laws but is subject to the laws of reason. It is the autonomous self which gives origin to free will, and it is free will which makes us morally responsible for our actions. This pre-scientific notion ignores the complete dependency of the brain, where the so-called autonomous self presumably resides, on an uninterrupted supply of glucose and oxygen for its metabolism. The autonomous self is no more autonomous than a person on a life support machine: it is utterly dependent on the silent operation in the background of what is known as the autonomic nervous system, autonomic here meaning self-regulating.

Walking upright with a big brain brings a number of physiological problems in its wake. The brain is responsible for 25% of the resting body's consumption of energy. The only fuel the brain can use is glucose, and as none is stored within the brain, a continuous supply is brought to the brain in the blood stream. A self-regulating mechanism ensures an adequate glucose concentration in the blood, but should it fall too low, as in diabetics who get too much insulin, rapid loss of consciousness – hypoglycaemic coma – is the result.

Standing upright poses another difficulty, manifested sometimes by guardsmen on parade: there is a tendency for blood to pool in the legs so that the pressure in the carotid arteries supplying the brain is inadequate to perfuse the brain with blood bearing glucose and oxygen. Again, loss of consciousness is the result. Mostly, though, this does not happen, because there are receptors in the carotid arteries which register when the pressure falls too low. A reflex action results in an acceleration of the heart rate and a contraction of the blood vessels supplying the gut so that blood is diverted from the digestive system to the more urgent task of keeping the brain alive.

Another function of the autonomic nervous system is to ensure that blood is fully oxygenated by the lungs: death of the brain starts within four minutes if its supply of oxygen is interrupted. The depth and rate of respiration is regulated by reflexes originating in carotid receptors which detect, not oxygen, but carbon dioxide, the product of the metabolic combustion of glucose, in which for every molecule of oxygen used up, one of carbon dioxide is produced. The accumulation of carbon dioxide, representing also a mounting debt of oxygen, reflexly stimulates more vigorous breathing and the intake of more oxygen, as well as the discharge of carbon dioxide.

In these and many other ways, self-regulating processes of which we are very largely unaware maintain a state of physiological equilibrium conducive to our getting on with whatever is our preferred activity, whether making moral judgements or working as a lumber jack. What we learn from biology is the extent to which different systems in a living organism, far from being in conflict, work together to form an integrated whole. To speak of an autonomous self somehow separate from the empirical self and not subject to its laws, but at the same time dependent on it, is incoherent nonsense.

My self is my body, one and the same.

In *Philosophy in the Flesh*, Lakoff and Johnson dissect the use of metaphor in moral reasoning, and lay out the very human origins of Kant's ethical system.[7] Prominent among the many metaphors for morality are wealth and health. The former is associated with a whole system of moral accounting in which moral credit is earned by generous acts, for which we give the benefactor his due, and to whom we are indebted; a wrong deed is worthy of punishment. Or, the behaviour of a malefactor may be said to be sick and to fill us with disgust; our children should be kept away from him for fear of moral contagion from his dirty talk. A good man is clean-living, well balanced and upright, but he may trip up and fall from grace. There are thus many metaphorical strands to morality, which is far from having a monolithic structure.

Lakoff and Johnson argue that individual morality is modelled on that of the family, whose ethos may range from harshly disciplinarian to empathetic, loving and nurturing. A child's concept of morality, and the metaphors by which it is interpreted and expressed, will depend on whether he is brought up in a 'strict father' or a 'nurturant parent' family. Kant's morality derives from his harsh, Prussian, protestant upbringing in a 'strict father' family where it was considered imperative to balance the moral books. He approved of strict discipline but had an abhorrence of sensuality, and considered that caressing, kissing and playing with a child harmed the child and shamed the parents; he never married.[8]

An element of Kant's philosophy which commands wide respect is the maxim that we should always treat other people as 'ends-in-themselves' and not as means to an end. While the sentiment of respecting each other's autonomy is of great importance, it is not immediately clear what is meant by an end-in-itself, nor how it relates to other elements of Kant's philosophy. To get at the underlying ideas we have to go

214

back to Aristotle and his four types of causation: material, efficient, formal and final. We recall the knife made of metal by a craftsman, its essence, the form and purpose of a knife, preceding its existence. And we remember that for an acorn, its final cause – its purpose or end – is to become an oak. The reason that the acorn becomes an oak is because that is its essential nature. Now the category of things called essences have this in common: existence. Moreover, essences have an existence that is transcendental, outside time and space (noumenal in Kant's terminology). So the essence of an oak simply exists; essence is not caused by anything other than itself, it is self-caused.

The essence of a human being, then, like that of the oak, is self-caused, a thing-in-itself. And as in the oak, our essence is also our end, an end-in-itself, self-caused and autonomous. But what is the essence of being human? For Kant, it is the possession of universal reason. So our end-in-itself is to live a life of reason according to 'the moral law... independent of all animality and even the whole world of sense.'[9] In our relationships with other people we must treat them as ends-in-themselves, respecting their reason above all else. But Kant goes further, eschewing friendship because it is 'a restriction of favourable sentiments to a single subject... proof that generality and good will are lacking... better to have no friends but to be equally well disposed towards everyone...'[10] He describes the love that inspires an act of kindness as 'pathological', as opposed to the 'practical' love that motivates a kind act done from a sense of duty.[11] Kant writes that 'it is laughable that a man wants to make himself loved by a young woman by means of understanding and great merits... the love of women is the last weakness.'[12]

We may therefore suppose from his writings and from the example of his own life that Kant believed that human relationships ought be based on reason alone, excluding as far as possible any passion, hot or cold. For it is only reason that is uniformly self-consistent and admits of no contradiction. By contrast, to show love is to be motivated by passion rather than reason, impinging on the autonomy of the loved one; to tell a white lie to avoid hurting someone's feelings is to destroy truth and undermine reason; and to be merciful and let a crime go unpunished is to impugn the categorical imperative. Morality, as part of natural law, is nothing if not consistent.

The Kantian ethical system, besides being difficult to apply, reveals a remarkable lack of psychological insight. Like Descartes, Kant considered that reason is universal, abstract, and passionless; but as argued previously, reason is embodied, metaphorical and involves the emotions. Of all topics, it is our relationships with other people which excite most passion, and these are the predominant concern of ethics. Thus, in requiring us to relate to one another without emotion, Kant is asking too much. Since 'ought' implies 'can', we are under no moral obligation to attempt the impossible.

Kant's notion of people as 'ends-in-themselves' derives from a discredited essentialism. It is an empirical finding, however, that our behaviour is determined to a large extent by the context and the company in which we find ourselves, belying our possession of an essential nature. As for an act of good will, cognitive psychology has shown us that we can never fully know our own motives, and that the autonomous self which has free will is a double illusion.

*

Kant had the worthy ambition of constructing a prescriptive ethical system based on reason, which he considered to be transcendental and objective. Such a system, based on self-evident propositions as incontestable as those of mathematics, would constitute a prescription for acting well, for being good. Once the system was set out, any rational person would want to abide by it. However, Kant had not reckoned on reason's lack of motivating power. As philosopher Simon Blackburn points out in *Being Good*, human reason has a limited domain.[13] While reason is a sine qua non in mathematics and logic, ethics is to do with preference, choice and values. He illustrates this point by getting us to imagine that a piano is on someone's foot. What is the rational response to be? It does not follow by inexorable logic that I should remove the piano, not even if there is a law to the effect that pianos should be removed from feet, nor even if this is God's law. I might be unconcerned about the person's suffering, indifferent as to the law, and defiant of God's wrath at my disobedience to it. No particular response follows necessarily from correctly reasoning that the poor man is in considerable pain; my response would be contingent, not logically necessary. To ignore someone's suffering is not irrational, but simply unfeeling. Rather than reason, what will motivate me to do something about the piano is fellow feeling, and sympathy for him in his unfortunate plight.

David Hume, in his great *Treatise of Human Nature*, recognised that the transition from description to prescription, from 'is' to 'ought', is not brought about by reason. This is what he meant by saying that reason is the slave of the passions. It is not reason but passion – sympathy – which is the engine of action, and it is the role of reason to analyse the nature of the problem and how best to solve it. Thus, moved by someone's howls of pain, I reason that it must be because there is a piano on his foot, and I work out the best way of lifting it off.

Kant's system of morality, founded on duty and reason, is thus an inadequate response to Hume's claim that reason is the slave of passion. Hume's position is further strengthened by recent neuroscientific studies which have shown that in the absence of emotion, moral reasoning is seriously impaired.

*

In *Descartes' Error*, Antonio Damasio describes clinical studies of patients with a disordered ability to feel emotion.[14] The patient who sparked his interest was a successful company lawyer known as Elliot, who developed a tumour that pressed on the frontal lobes of his brain. The tumour was removed but the affected part of the brain was permanently damaged. He appeared to make a complete physical recovery, and a battery of neuropsychological tests revealed no abnormality of intelligence, memory, reasoning skills or knowledge. His personality, however, had changed, and his life went to pieces. He lost his job and became bankrupt after several ill-advised business ventures. He divorced, remarried and divorced again. He was able to recount accurately his tragic life story, but in doing so he never showed any trace of emotion.

Another patient with similar damage to his frontal lobes, when asked to suggest a date for a clinic appointment, took half an hour detailing the pros and cons of alternative dates without choosing any one of them. The problem for these patients, then, concerns decision making, and the inability to place a value on any of the options which are quite correctly reasoned to be available. Elliot had no 'gut feelings' about possible business or life partners, no feeling that some choices were right and others wrong. He lacked what has been called 'emotional intelligence'.[15]

Research psychologists are able to demonstrate emotional responses using a slide show in which bland landscapes and abstract designs are interspersed with gory horror shots of people in accidents or other distressing situations. In a normal

218

subject, the horror slides provoke an increased heart rate and blood pressure, and the subject starts to sweat. This increases the conductance of the skin to electricity, which may be continuously monitored through a pair of electrodes. In the horror show Elliot and other patients with similar frontal lobe damage, while acknowledging the frightfulness of the scenes portrayed, felt no emotion and had no change in skin conductance. Further experiments by Damasio and his colleagues showed that in such patients choices were influenced by the anticipation of immediate high gain even when it was obvious that this strategy was not working and one of lower risk and lesser but more certain reward would have been better.[16]

The prefrontal cortical area damaged in these patients is where personal and social knowledge is organised and plans for the future generated; it is normally connected to the limbic system in the base of the brain where emotional responses originate. People who do not respond emotionally to social encounters are unable to adjudicate between the available options in accordance with their values and long-term aims; bad decisions based on short term advantage are the result.

The devastating effect on moral reasoning of a lack of emotion is also illustrated in Capras' delusion in which the recognition of family or friends excites no emotional response. A patient with this disorder may reason that, 'This woman looks like my mother, she tells me that she is my mother but I don't feel about her as I would feel if she really was my mother; therefore, she must be an imposter'.[17]

In *Descartes' Error* Damasio concludes that the error was:

> 'the abyssal separation between body and mind... Specifically: the separation of the most refined operations of mind from the structure and operation of a biological organism.'[18]

And it was Kant's error too: reason is not transcendent, abstract and objective, but embodied, metaphorical and passionate. Hume was right after all, reason *is* the slave of passion.

## Utilitarianism – the Happiness Principle

Utilitarianism is a moral system which is concerned, not with the motivation of acts, but their consequences. Its premises are that happiness is good, and pain and suffering are bad. It follows that an action is right insofar as it promotes happiness; the guiding principle of conduct should be to promote the greatest happiness of the greatest number – a not unworthy ambition. Utilitarianism has no pretensions to be a law of nature, but was devised by Jeremy Bentham (1748-1832) in an attempt to bring reason and fairness to the English penal system in the 18th century. At that time many legal decisions were made on the hoof by judges appealing to such 'principles' as Fitness of Things, Right Reason and Natural Justice, while the laws of England were said to have derived their validity from the Law of Nature, which ordained that pickpocketing goods to the value of one shilling, and being out at night with one's face blackened should be included in the list of 200 capital offences.[19] The arbitrariness of legal judgements as to which offences were punished, and the severity of the punishments, were condemned by Bentham as being adverse to the principle that happiness should be maximised. It hardly needed his 'felicific calculus' to show that the unhappiness of a poacher sentenced to deportation exceeded by far that of the landowner whose pheasant had been poached, and that justice, and the happiness principle, would be better served with a sentence which was proportionate to the offence. Bentham was against capital punishment partly on the pragmatic grounds that it would not be possible to compensate an innocent man if his punishment of execution was found later to have resulted from a miscarriage of justice.

It was John Stuart Mill (1806-73) who took Bentham's utilitarianism and changed it from a programme for penal reform into an ethical system. But happiness is a poor foundation for a universal system, meaning many different things to different people. As Bentham remarked, the 'quantity of pleasure being equal, push pin is as good as poetry'. Moreover, Mill had to hedge around the principle of maximising happiness with provisos and exceptions, particularly to safeguard the liberties of minority groups: Christians were not to be thrown to the lions even though that might result in the greatest happiness for the greatest number. And, *pace* Kant, it was sometimes admissible to tell a white lie, but on the other hand it was expedient for the sake of society at large to mostly abide by rules of conduct even if that meant foregoing happiness resulting from instant gratification of a desire. Mill's 'rule-based' or 'indirect' utilitarianism lacks the logical consistency of Kant's ethical system, but it addresses better the multifaceted nature of morality, which is reflected in the rich metaphorical language used to describe it.[20] But as with Kantian ethics, utilitarianism's generality is of little help in the day-to-day conduct of an ethical life. Certainly, being founded on the happiness principle, utilitarianism makes no claim to be transcendental or a law of nature.

There are several scenarios known as 'trolley problems' which have been used to examine how people react to moral dilemmas which have a utilitarian solution.[21] An empty runaway trolley (rail truck) is rushing towards a group of five children playing on the lines. Between the trolley and the children is a set of points which could be changed to divert the trolley to another line where a single workman is doing maintenance on the track. A bystander near the lever that operates the points correctly assesses that by pulling the lever he would avert the deaths of five children, but would be responsible for the death of a man. Most people judge that he should pull the lever and divert the trolley. A variation of this scenario is to imagine that instead of the trolley being diverted, it could be brought to a halt if an immensely fat man were to be pushed in front of it by the little man standing on the platform beside him. Most people now say that this action should not be taken. Killing a man with one's own hands is felt to be wrong, while killing a man remotely by pulling a lever is not, even though the consequential net saving of four lives is the same in each case. Interestingly, Damasio's patients with prefrontal lobe damage and a deficient emotional response have no difficulty in opting for whatever action causes least loss of life, and results in most happiness.[22] Thus, reason and emotion both play a part in making moral decisions, and they may be in conflict one with the other.

There are difficulties constructing a coherent ethical system, whether it is theistic, deontological (duty-based) or consequentialist (eg utilitarianism). If we believe that moral behaviour is ordained by God, as laid down in a holy book, we might balk at some ordinances, such as the requirement for animal sacrifice, or circumcision. In Kant's deontological scheme the categorical imperative 'never tell a lie' has to be qualified to deal with the case of the mad axeman, and the utilitarian principle of 'the greatest happiness for the greatest number' has to be qualified so that Christians are not thrown to the lions for our entertainment. All this should give us pause to consider whether the enterprise is not altogether misguided. Why should moral behaviour conform to a set of self-consistent rules when so many varied activities – from sex to dealing on the stock exchange – come under its umbrella, and the language used to describe it is itself incoherent?

To illustrate this latter point, recall that dominant metaphors for morality are wealth and moral accounting.[23] Thus, if I do you a good turn, I gain moral credit and you are indebted to me. But if I do you a bad turn, you are put in a dilemma. If you repay me in kind, an eye for an eye or a tooth for a tooth, by doing something harmful to me, you act immorally. On the other hand, if you let me get away with it, you are also acting immorally by failing in your duty to balance the moral books. If I do something terrible to you, something unpardonable, you may declare me morally bankrupt, or using a different metaphor, declare me sick. Either way, that puts you in a different position, for if I am bankrupt beyond redemption there is no point in your adding to my indebtedness, and if I am incurably sick you will wash your hands of me and leave me alone. What is judged to be the right thing to do will depend on the context and a host of other considerations, including the language used to depict the particular moral situation. Thus, the principle that requires that you do me no harm will apply under some circumstances, but not under others. What manner of principle is that?

Considerations of this sort have led some philosophers to question whether we need moral rules at all. In *Ethics Without Principles*, Jonathan Dancy expounds a particularist conception of morality, in which moral judgements are made on a case to case basis, without recourse to general principles.[24] Although certain moral statements are seen to be true, these statements are not considered to be instances of general moral principles, but are stand-alone moral facts. Thus, slavery, gratuitous violence against a person or animal, acceptance of bribes by judges, and insider dealing are all wrong, but for different reasons. Moral life is messy, and situations differ in a myriad subtle ways which general principles are unable to capture. Dancy argues that we can behave morally without moral principles, and that the application of principles may sometimes result in mistaken actions, or doing the right thing for the wrong reason.

Living the good life, then, requires many subtle judgements as we thread our way through a tangled web of social relationships of different shades. It is a practical skill which, like playing a musical instrument or making fine furniture, cannot be acquired from a set of principles or a book of instructions, but can only be learned by apprenticeship and lifelong practice. This was the view promulgated by Aristotle, who argued that:

> Ethical virtues do not come about by nature – but neither do they come about contrary to nature: we are naturally constituted so as to acquire them, but it is by habit that they are fully developed... Whatever we have to learn to do, we have to learn by doing it: people become builders by building, and lutanists by playing the lute... Thus the habits we form from early childhood are of no small importance; they matter a great deal – indeed, they make all the difference.[25]

We learn to be virtuous by living virtuously, and we start in childhood.

> Consider the child who, for whatever reasons, learns only very slowly to distinguish the minute-by-minute flux of rights, expectations, entitlements, and duties as they are created and cancelled in the course of an afternoon at the day-care centre, an outing with one's siblings, or a playground game of hide-and-seek. Such a child is doomed to chronic conflict with other children- doomed to cause them disappointment, frustration, and eventually anger, all of it directed at him... The boy…has not acquired the skills already flourishing in the others.[26]

Compare that latter account by the philosopher and neuro-computational scientist, Paul Churchland, with the following, in which David Hume speaks for the urbane, clubbable man who has served his apprenticeship and knows well how to behave in his society.

> It seems...superfluous to prove that the companionable virtues of good manners and wit, decency and genteelness, are more desirable than the contrary qualities... Would you have your company coveted, admired, followed, rather than hated, despised, avoided? Can any one seriously deliberate in the case? As no enjoyment is sincere without some reference to company and society, so no society can be agreeable, or even tolerable, where a man feels his presence unwelcome, and discovers around him symptoms of disgust and aversion.[27]

The society of others is the medium in which we live, and to ask what are society's rules and why should we obey them, is for a bird to ask 'How does one fly and why should one learn?'[28]

## The Evolution of Morality

Aristotle's dictum that 'Whatever you have to learn to do, you have to learn by doing it' is well illustrated by young chicks who have just flown the nest. Although a chick is constituted to fly, its first attempts are hazardous in the extreme – it may flutter onto foliage that does not bear its weight, fall to the ground, prey to prowling cats, or fly into a window, with possibly fatal consequences. Experience is a tough teacher, as Churchland's young lad also discovered in his early attempts at negotiating the hazards of pre-school life.

Being primates, we have been shaped by evolution to live together in social groups, so notwithstanding the discontinuity created by our unique possession of speech, we would expect our social behaviour to be on a continuum with that of our nearest primate relatives. They might differ from us in degree of sophistication, but their conduct would not be predicted to differ from ours in kind. Interpersonal relations being the principal subject matter of morality, it is possible to recognise in the comportment of chimpanzees the rudiments of our own moral behaviour. This is the thesis developed in *Primates and Philosophers* by Frans de Waal, a world authority on primates, who has been studying their social life for decades.[29]

Moral philosophers emphasise reason as the basis of moral behaviour, the latter being considered to be no more than a surface veneer restraining a fundamentally selfish nature, bad to the core: scratch an altruist and watch a hypocrite bleed.[30] De Waal takes a different view. While he fully accepts the 'selfish gene' account of evolution, he regrets Dawkins' use of the adjective 'selfish', with its connotation of conscious intention, and considers that 'self-serving' would better describe the evolutionary process. The irony of evolution is that a self-serving process has resulted in a human nature which is other-serving and good at its core. When we behave as moral beings we are not combating our animal instincts – we are behaving naturally.

The roots of moral behaviour are evolutionarily ancient. The common ancestors of chimpanzees and ourselves would have experienced a period of dependency after birth in order for their brains to grow to full size and maturity. And, of course, they were mammals, this fact also necessitating a period of reliance of the new-born on its mother. Darwin saw in the mutual bonding that arises from the 'parental and filial affections' the origin of moral behaviour, which was later extended to include the social group beyond the immediate family. The cries and smiles of an infant elicit the mother's sympathy; her caring behaviour has obvious survival value, greatly augmented by the commitment to the child's well-being that comes with the strong emotional bonding of mother and child, which has a well-established physiological basis. Stimulation of the nipple by the suckling infant causes release of the hormone oxytocin, which, as well as bringing about a flow of breast milk, also stimulates the limbic system, the structure at the base of the brain which is implicated in the generation of emotion. Oxytocin is also released in orgasm, contributing to the emotional bonding of a couple having intercourse.[32] Of such are the inherited physiological mechanisms which underlie the emotions, which in our evolutionary past have contributed to reproductive success and our evolution as moral animals. Emotions are physiological states, and empathy makes them contagious. Fear of a predator spreads rapidly through a group, uniting it in defence against a common enemy. Joy at the discovery of a generous source of food ripples through a foraging party, and all partake of the feast. The expressions of disgust at the smell of a rotting corpse are conveyed to others, who keep away, thereby avoiding contamination with disease.

Box 15

The Social System: Four Basic Forms of Human Relations

Moral behaviour may be seen as an emergent property arising from the interactions between people in a community. According to the sociologist Alan Fiske, there are four fundamental types of social relations each of which entails a different sort of moral behaviour.[31]

*Communal sharing.* Inter-individual differences are blurred and people identify with their community, which may be described as, or may actually be, a family. Kindness, kind and kin are words that apply to this type of caring relationship, in which goods are held in common and are used by each according to his need. This form corresponds to a 'nurturant parent' family.

*Authority ranking.* In this relationship of inequality there is a hierarchy of social status and authority which is accepted as legitimate, in which those at the top have an obligation to protect and look after their subordinates. Lower ranking subjects accept their position and look to their superiors for protection, aid and support, and are expected to be deferential, obedient and loyal. The number of people for whom responsibility is accepted, and the possession of goods and land, accords with rank. This form is the basis of a 'strict father' family.

*Equality matching.* This is an egalitarian relationship of individuals with equal status. Shares, contributions and influence are the same for everyone. Contributions are equalised, either by taking turns or by strict quid pro quo reciprocity, in which like is exchanged for like.

*Market pricing.* Different goods and services are priced and exchanged according to an agreed ratio against a common currency. Market pricing relationships are open to all competent and honest participants who have something to sell or money with which to buy. The market pricing relationship does not necessarily entail selfishness, competitiveness or materialism but does entail honesty and trust: that the goods are as described and are the vendor's to sell, and the purchaser has the money to buy, and will pay on time.

There are many variations on, and combinations of these basic relational forms, which are used to initiate social action, to understand what other people are doing, and to respond appropriately. For a relationship to be satisfying both parties should perceive it similarly. Misunderstanding of the type of relationship involved may lead to confusion or conflict.

Violation of the unspoken rules of any of these ways of relating has repercussions beyond the two parties primarily involved. A third party, observing such a violation, would be under an obligation to express disapproval of the offending party. If he fails to do so, he in turn would be liable to sanctions from a fourth party. In this way a rift in a primary relationship may cause widespread re-alignment of alliances in a community.

The four basic forms of human relations feature in a range of domains: the exchange and distribution of goods; contributions to community projects; the use of land; decision making; social identity and influence; moral judgements; moral interpretation of misfortune; conflict.

All four models may coexist within a community, and may be the source of inconsistent or incompatible rights, obligations and sentiments. This is most obvious in the distribution and use of land, where each model – communal sharing, authority ranking, equality matching and market pricing – is incompatible with all the others.

All the great apes closely related to us live in groups, and we can be sure that the first humans were social animals too; a zoologist would describe *Homo sapiens* as obligatorily gregarious. There never was a time when men were solitary noble savages, nor were the first humans members of a group where all fought against all. From the start we deployed cooperative behaviour supported by social instincts and emotional contagion. The basic mechanisms invoked to explain the evolution of social behaviour are kin selection and reciprocal altruism. The latter requires knowledge of group membership and its web of relationships and obligations, and memory, of slights received, favours granted and favours owed. All this necessitates a good deal of brain power, and it is noteworthy that, after adjusting for body size, there is a clear relationship in non-human primates between brain volume and size of social group. Accordingly, the size of the social group corresponding to the large human brain would be 150, which is approximately the number of family, friends and acquaintances that people do have on average.[33]

Chimpanzees live in groups of about 30-80 individuals that occupy a fairly well-defined home range over a period of years.[34] The entire group is seldom all together at one time, but parties form and reform in kaleidoscopic fashion, except for mothers and their offspring who remain together long after weaning. When parties of the same group meet, there are greeting ceremonies, especially between the adult males, who may embrace. When food is plentiful individuals eat separately, but when it is scarce food is shared. Adult males cooperate to hunt large prey, and the booty is usually shared with individuals of both sexes and all ages, following a complicated begging ritual. And reciprocal altruism has been confirmed: de Waal has documented that adults are more likely to share food with individuals who have groomed them earlier.[35]

230

While empathy is experiencing the same emotion as another, sympathy is the translation of that shared emotion into concern for another, by taking on their viewpoint. It is a cognitive leap from empathy to sympathy since it requires an individual to recognise that the source of the experienced emotion is not itself. Great apes have a concept of self, as demonstrated by self-recognition in a mirror, and this is associated with sympathetic, as opposed to empathetic, behaviour. Thus, consoling the loser of a fight by putting an arm around him is observed in chimpanzees but not in monkeys, who lack mirror self-recognition.[36] Empathy in monkeys has evolved into sympathy in chimpanzees, and sympathy has given rise to helping behaviour which is accurately targeted at other individuals' needs. De Waal stresses the strength of the ape's helping response. Chimpanzees cannot swim and will drown if they fall into deep water. Nevertheless, heroic attempts to save others from drowning are documented, including the case of an adult male chimpanzee who lost his life in an attempt to rescue an infant chimp who had fallen into the water.[37]

In chimpanzee communities, fights occur not infrequently, especially between young males. High-ranking males often police such brawls, physically separating the contestants in an even-handed manner and restoring the peace. High ranking females will later effect a reconciliation of the rivals.[38] De Waal interprets these efforts at mediation as concern for the community, each group member having a big stake in the community's harmony and integrity.

The most powerful force uniting chimpanzee community is enmity to outsiders. In the wild, intercommunity warfare is lethally violent, but out-group hostility cements in-group solidarity like nothing else. De Waal comments that 'the profound irony is that our noblest achievement – morality – has evolutionary ties to our basest behaviour – warfare. The sense of community required by the former was provided by the latter.'[39]

De Waal proposes that human morality has a three tiered structure, the lowest tier being much the same in humans as in chimpanzees, where social behaviour is largely at an automatic, affective level. The second tier is behaviour conforming to social pressure, complying with the rules and conventions of the community, and building a good reputation in so doing, so-called 'indirect altruism'. Compliance to social norms is bolstered by pride in a strong moral identity, while non-compliance is penalised by private guilt or public shame. The third tier is largely intellectual and verbal, self-consciously using abstract concepts of justice and fairness to extend the circle within which moral behaviour is considered to apply, going beyond one's own community, tribe or nation, or even beyond one's own species, by according rights to other animals.

*

Young infants are naturally disposed to acquire a moral sense in the same way as they are programmed to learn to speak, and a parallel has been drawn between the structure of morality and that of language.[40] Without being taught, three year olds acquire grammatical rules which they then apply, not always correctly: 'My teacher holded the baby rabbits and we patted them'.[41] Later, they learn that there are irregular verbs which make exceptions to the general rule for forming the past tense. In a similar way, children acquire and abide by rules of behaviour, and distinguish between moral rules that are always true, and rules of convention which might be different in other circumstances. Thus, children as young as three know that it is wrong to hit another child, but it would not be wrong to wear pyjamas to school if teacher said it was all right.[43] There are norms for a child's moral development which apply to all cultures, the four types of human relations described by Fiske (see box 15) emerging during development in an invariant sequence.[44,45] Even newborn babies show emotional contagion and a degree of empathy, crying in unison in the nursery. Later, empathy develops into sympathy, and a strong sense of fairness bursts forth at about age four.

Emotional responses of shame and guilt reinforce some actions and block others, building up an affective intuitional moral system, the particular system adopted being that of the family and culture in which the child grows up.

Anthropologists have identified three 'clusters' of ethical ideas in which moral goods consist of individual autonomy, being part of a community, or communication with the divine.[46] The relative importance of these conceptions of morality in different cultures gives rise to different intuitions of 'right' and 'wrong'. In 'autonomy ethics', predominant in the West, moral actions are those that maximise freedom and choice. In 'community ethics', prevalent in the East, the community has an identity and a hierarchical structure in which individuals know and accept their place. Leaders of the community are obligated to satisfy the needs of their subjects; in return they receive respect and loyalty, in bad times as well as good. Moral actions are those that foster good relations and interdependence, strengthening the community. In 'divinity ethics' the material world is considered to be imbued with the spiritual and there is a divine order in the universe. It is good to communicate with the spiritual, and act within the moral law, which is identified with natural law.

Box 16

Warfare

Human behaviour is on a continuum with that of chimpanzees, so warfare has gone on for millions of years, antedating the origin of our species. Warfare is conflict between independent political units leading to substantial deaths and loss of territory, or the expenditure of significant time and energy in defence; killing of the enemy is sanctioned by society. Warfare is an emergent property arising from people living in groups, and for most of prehistory it has been driven by population growth putting pressure on the availability of food.

There is abundant world-wide archaeological evidence of warfare in prehistoric times, of which the most obvious is the frequent settlement of hilltop sites defended by ditches and ramparts: these are inconvenient places to live in every respect except defence. Many such settlements show evidence of fire and of hurried evacuation consistent with having been attacked. Skeletons with embedded arrow or spear heads are a sure sign of warfare, as are fractures of the skull caused by a blunt instrument, or fractures of the forearm as a result of parrying a blow with a weapon. From such evidence it has been estimated that some 25% of adult males died from warfare. Depictions of battle scenes are found in prehistoric rock art, and warfare is prominent in accounts of the first encounters of explorers with indigenous tribes. Amongst tribes of foragers who have survived into the 20th century warfare has been largely suppressed, but conspicuous among their few possessions are offensive weapons and defensive protection such as the body armour made of bone worn by Eskimos.

Evidence of population pressure on the environment leading to shortage of food is less easily obtained, but it is known that when conditions are propitious, as on arrival in a virgin territory, numbers may double every 20 years, soon outstripping food supply. Thus the archaeological record of every continent shows the extinction of a great many large animal species within a short time of human occupation. Direct evidence of malnutrition is often found in skeletal remains, and in societies organised as chiefdoms or states, signs of malnutrition in the populace but not in their rulers suggests that there was not enough food for everybody. An even stronger indication of food shortage is cannibalism, evidenced by cuts on bones where they have been defleshed, and human bones cracked open to obtain the marrow.

Four types of prehistorical society are recognised: forager bands, tribal farmers, chiefdoms and states. For more than a million years our ancestors survived as nomad bands of hunter-gatherers with an equality matching organisation. This forager society was egalitarian though it is probable that men predominated in raiding parties, while women were more involved in defence. Similarly with tribal farmers, warfare served the interests of the whole community, and all participated on an equal footing as fighters and as victims of fighting. In a chiefdom, a warrior leader led the fighting, and the chief's position was hereditary and carried various privileges; chiefdoms have an authority ranking organisation. A state is a conglomeration of chiefdoms, with a hierarchical organisation of authority. With the development of these complex societies came a distinction between soldiers and civilians, and warfare began to serve, not the needs of the community as a whole, but the political and ideological ambitions of its rulers.

Reference: Stevan A LeBlanc. *Constant Battles: Why We Fight.*[42]

Examples of particular cultural differences in moral belief were obtained in a study comparing American and Brahmin children: American children thought it was wrong to eat with hands, while Brahmin children thought it right; American children thought addressing their father by his first name was right and Brahmin children thought it wrong; American and Brahmin children both thought that breaking a promise was wrong, while men holding hands was right.[47]

Many years later the same moral rules still have an unwonted hold over grown men and women. The question arises, why are they not as easily suspended as rules of grammar? Where does the authority of moral pronouncements come from? Whence comes the imperiousness of the little word 'ought'? According to philosopher Daniel Dennett, words like 'ought' and 'wrong' act as 'conversation stoppers'.[48] If somebody says 'I feel that I ought not to do it', then no further justification is required, the buck stops there If an act is deemed wrong, period.

In *The Evolution of Morality*, the philosopher Richard Joyce attributes the power of moral pronouncements to their arising from a moral sense, a sort of perception.[49] When we see the flames, feel the warmth and hear the crackle, these various sensations are collated in the cerebral cortex inside the skull, interpreted as a fire, and then projected out of the body back to their source in the grate. When we see a red ember, the colour red is to an extent a function of our visual apparatus, in particular, the number of different types of light-sensitive cells (cones) present in the retina; the colours in the fire are projected onto the scene. Nevertheless, seeing is believing, and our visual images owe their credibility to their truth, to their correspondence with reality, and the evolution of visual processing mechanisms is due to their truth function, their accuracy in obtaining a representation of reality. Our distant

ancestors owed their lives to the accurate recognition of predators lurking in the swamps of the Rift Valley, or prowling the
savannah.

When we have a moral perception, when we see that something is morally wrong, we project our feelings onto the object of our judgement. Something for which we feel disgust or
contempt becomes disgusting or contemptible; something we
commend or admire becomes commendable or admirable; a
possibility for action becomes an obligation; 'could' becomes
'ought'. Detached from us, these projected qualities seem to
have an objectivity and a greater authority than we possess
ourselves, and they compel other people towards our judgement and whatever action it entails. Joyce argues, however,
that moral projection is primarily a device for self-motivation.
Acting according to a moral intuition often means foregoing instant gratification. 'I would like another chocolate but I
ought not to because I'm trying to lose weight'. A cost-benefit
analysis of the decision whether or not to have a chocolate
would strongly support sticking to a diet and losing weight,
with all the health advantages which would follow later; compared with a few seconds of pleasure from sucking a truffle,
there is no contest. Nevertheless, instant gratification often
wins out. But by making the decision a moral-issue, the brain
short-circuits the reasoned analysis and pushes us towards the
decision which is better for us, not only as individuals, but
as obligate members of society. The brain's trick is to couch
those inclinations which are in our best long-term interest in
moral terms, as duty, obligation, fairness, loyalty, justice and
the like. We may feel like staying home and watching television, but we see it as our duty to attend a protest meeting at
the town hall. When someone offends us, instead of saying
'He made me angry, I would like to hit him' we say 'What
he did was wrong, he ought to be punished'. The feeling of
being angry is projected onto the cause of our anger and be-

comes a personal commitment to justice, and also an appeal to others to assist in seeing justice done.

Another of the brain's tricks is to clothe moral intuitions with a thick fabric of strong emotion. The anger at being wronged declares to the wrongdoer that he is dealing with a person of principle who will harm his own interests rather than see justice flouted. Thought of the shame of being caught with one's hand in the till protects us from the temptation to steal. We will be pierced with guilt if we do not stop to offer help at the scene of an accident. Emotions such as these are physiological states which in the distant past became linked with moral sentiments, thereby increasing their evolutionary utility.

Like the visual processing mechanisms, the brain's disposition to construe situations in moral terms has evolved, and is hard-wired: a moral sense is found in all cultures and develops by the same progressive stages in every normal child.[50] Like vision, the moral sense has evolved because of its utility, that is, its contribution to survival and reproductive success in an environment which importantly includes other people. The evolutionary usefulness of vision results from its truthfulness, its correspondence with reality. The evolutionary utility of morality, however, is not its truth, but its power to motivate individuals to participate fully in cooperative social behaviour. That motivating power is not owed to the accurate correspondence of moral perceptions with moral reality: we have no evidence for the independent existence of a moral reality, nor is it clear how moral facts would relate to naturalistic facts.[51] Morality's authority arises not from its correspondence with an absolute moral truth, but from the projection of our own sentiments outside ourselves, onto the surrounding gloom; it is a trick of light.

*

238

A uniquely human enterprise is an attempt to codify moral behaviour in terms of a set of self-consistent abstract principles.
This project is doomed to fail at all levels. The lowest tier of
human moral behaviour is an automated skill in balancing,
in Churchland's words, the 'minute-by-minute flux of rights,
expectations, entitlements, and duties as they are created and
cancelled in the course of an afternoon'. No general principles can be deduced from or applied to this set of learned reflexes, which are as varied as are the styles of playing a lute.
In the second tier of behaviour there is a continually changing
order of social obligations, from self-preservation and care
for one's kin, to tribal loyalty and patriotism for one's country; for most people citizenship of the world and saving the
planet are towards the bottom of the list; there are many ir-
resolvable conflicts of interest here. In morality's highest tier,
reason divorced from passion may proclaim equal rights for
all, for the out-group as for the in-group, but passion divorced
from reason does not agree, and who is to arbitrate between
the quarrelsome divorcees?

Thus, at every level of our behaviour as obligatory social animals there are conflicts: of kin and community, of instincts
and interests, and of reason and passion, priorities between
them changing from moment to moment. The sure negotia-
tion of this moral maze is an accomplishment for which no
rulebook can be written, and for whose mastery a lifetime is
too short.

*

Wallace's objections to Darwin's theory of evolution as applied to man – that the evolution of man is different in kind
from that of animals – cannot be sustained. Following Descartes, Wallace believed that consciousness was uniquely a
human attribute, divinely given in order that man should de-

velop his intellectual and moral nature. But familiarity with 'higher' animals leaves ethologists in no doubt about their being conscious, and if mirror self-awareness is a criterion, self-conscious to boot. As for intelligence, our close relatives make and use tools, and solve problems. They also have a 'theory of mind' as evidenced by deceitful and Machiavellian behaviour. In addition, primatologists such as Frans de Waal and Jane Goodall have also reported primate behaviour that in humans would be described as commendably moral: the devotion of parents to their offspring, the sharing of resources, working cooperatively to a common purpose, compliance with group behavioural norms, and above all, coming to another's aid, spontaneously and unstintingly to the point of self-sacrifice. The continuity in intellectual and moral behaviour between ourselves and our first cousins should not shock or surprise us in view of the close similarity of our anatomy, physiology and genetic endowment. But it does call for a recognition of the animal origins of our humanity, and a re-examination of what is meant by morality. There is an emerging scientific consensus that we share with primates a disposition to behave altruistically. But if such reflex behaviour based on affective subconscious judgements is deemed moral, then morality is dethroned as the supreme human accomplishment, and becomes a quality we share with beasts. The reaction of many philosophers is to redefine moral behaviour as that which is enacted by an autonomous self-conscious rational agent in conformity with universal moral principles.[52] Such a definition reasserts the difference in kind between ourselves and our nearest relatives, but it runs counter to the scientific evidence.

## Intuitive Morality

Reason is the stock-in-trade of philosophers, and most philosophical accounts of moral judgement, while allowing that moral sentiments such as sympathy may have some input into the process, give reason a privileged position. Moral reasoning is supposed to be a weighty matter of balancing considerations of fairness and freedom, harm and happiness, justice and generosity; after careful deliberation the judgement is delivered. However, the psychologist Jonathan Haidt reviews a considerable body of evidence which points to the conclusion that most moral judgements are made swiftly and effortlessly, and engage affective mechanisms; where reason is involved, it provides post hoc justification of an intuitive moral judgement, in particular, to give a convincing explanation of moral choices to other people.[53]

Moral behaviour, and the ability to make moral judgements, has evolved side by side with living in groups of increasing size. Other people are a supremely important part of the human environment, and the personalities they express through their body language and their words and deeds are continually and automatically evaluated by a 'sixth sense', a variety of perception which we describe in terms of the five special senses we recognise. Thus, we see what people are thinking, and we are touched by their concern, but we smell a rat, and an encounter leaves a nasty taste in the mouth; when we hear what they say, we hear more than the words with which they say it. In a similar way, truths are seen to be self-evident and actions perceived to be wicked. Just as the processes involved in visual perception are inaccessible to us, so are those for moral perception. This results in the illusion that reasons for a moral judgement thought up afterwards are those which led to it.

There are many factors operating unconsciously which may influence moral judgements. This has been shown in experiments in which subjects without their knowing are primed subliminally with emotionally charged words or images, or by suggestions made under hypnosis. When they are then asked to describe a scene or comment on a piece of writing, their responses are clearly biased by the emotions with which they have been primed. The reasons proffered for their responses are plausible but fabricated, and show no awareness of the manipulation of their thinking by the experimenters.[54]

Another indication that reason is not the primary means of reaching moral decisions is that it is a weak motivating force compared with emotion, as Damasio's patients showed. Moral judgements are strongly motivating, suggesting that it is emotionally based intuitions that give rise to them. Confirmation of the importance of emotion in moral behaviour comes from the study of sociopaths, in whom reasoning is dissociated from moral emotions. Characteristically, they have good intelligence and no delusional or irrational thinking, but they show a marked poverty of emotional reactions to other people's suffering, or to the condemnation of their sociopathic behaviour.[55] Sociopaths are able to anticipate the consequences for their victims of their criminal actions, and they know that their behaviour is wrong, but lacking empathy, they simply do not care, proceeding without guilt or remorse to lie and cheat, steal from friends, or even murder their parents for the insurance money. Some sociopaths have been shown to have underactivity of emotional processing areas in the prefrontal cortex, as did Damasio's patients. Damasio surmises that his patients would have been sociopaths if the impairment of their emotional responses had been present from birth rather than having been acquired in adult life.[56]

Haidt makes the observation that the style of post hoc moral reasoning is that of a lawyer defending a client rather than that of a scientist seeking the truth. A lawyer selectively uses whatever evidence supports his case; sometimes the arguments are pretty flimsy, as may be the reasons adduced for

242

acting in a certain way. A scientist, however, will give a more balanced appraisal, considering evidence which does not fit the hypothesis, as well as that which does. For moral judgements to result logically from reasoning, rather than from intuition, they would have to be more cogent than they often are, all the available evidence being taken into account, the balance being in favour of the judgement.

An important element of Haidt's 'social intuitionist' model of moral judgement is the description of the way in which people relate to one another in a dispute on a moral issue. The main function of the post hoc reasons adduced to support a moral judgement is to justify the judgement to somebody else. Reasoned persuasion does not engage directly with another person's dispassionate reasoning faculty but is evaluated intuitively, the intuition depending as much on the relationship of the disputants as on their reasoned arguments.

Sometimes a person's reasoning leads him to revise his judgement so that it does not accord with his intuition. This is the uncomfortable state of cognitive dissonance, reason warring with passion. Rarely, after much reflection and rigorous reasoning, the intuition may be changed so that it now agrees with the revised judgement and 'feels right'; more commonly, facts that are discordant with judgement are simply ignored.

\*

In *Judgement Misguided: Intuition and Error in Public Decision Making*, psychologist Jonathan Baron describes how a number of commonly held intuitions are brought to bear on moral issues.[57] Baron uses the term intuition to mean blind feelings, but also more reflective beliefs which appeal to some judgement or principle other than consequences. One such is respect for personal autonomy, a version of Kant's categorical imperative called the Formula of Humanity: 'So act that you use humanity, whether in your own person or in the person of any other, always at the same time as an end, never merely as a means'.[58] We may surmise that Kant had the intuition that every individual's autonomy is sacrosanct, and then, drawing on Aristotle, he adduced the essentialist justification for respecting people as ends-in-themselves. But this intuition also has a more straightforward utilitarian justification: that people themselves know best what they want and what is good for them. JS Mill also recognised the importance of respect for autonomy, but argued that it should not be an absolute principle, a categorical imperative. People should be free to do what they want, but only up to the point where their behaviour impinges on other peoples' freedom.

Whenever some limit on personal freedom is necessary for the greater good of society – from restricting free access to fishing grounds to population control – those whose freedom is threatened not infrequently appeal to the principle of autonomy for protection against encroachment on their rights. This appeal is often successful because intuitively, as Kant appreciated, individual autonomy is a moral absolute, in Dennett's terminology, a 'conversation stopper', for which there is no answer. The invocation of this intuited principle often results in worse consequences than if achieving the best outcome for everyone had been the sole basis for deciding on a policy. In the case of access to fishing, the appeal for protection of their autonomy by New England fishermen was important in preventing any agreement being reached on restricting access, with the result that fish stocks were depleted and everybody was worse off.[59]

Another commonly held intuition is epitomised by the Latin tag learnt by generations of medical students, *Primum non nocere*: firstly, do no harm.[60] As an example of the application of this maxim, many parents, and also some doctors, consider that vaccination of infants (against diphtheria, whooping cough and tetanus, and also mumps, measles and rubella) should not be undertaken because of the small risk of side effects, notwithstanding that the unvaccinated child faces a much greater risk of harm from these preventable diseases than from the vaccine itself.[61] The precept upheld by such well-meaning parents is not directed at vaccination per se, but against its occasionally harmful consequences. Thus the proposition 'Do no harm' has a consequentialist justification but is here elevated to become, if not a categorical imperative, a paramount parental duty, which is at odds with the overall aim of reducing the harm done to children by these infections. In many cases the parent's attitude results from misinformation or a misunderstanding of the relative risks associated with the vaccination or its being withheld. But in other cases the parental attitude is unreasoned and unreasonable, and results from an intuited apprehension that their child would be harmed by the procedure.

In fact, the practice of medicine is mostly consequentialist in its approach, there being scarcely any treatment, medical or surgical, without some risk or disadvantage; the risks are weighed against the benefits, and only if the balance is likely to be in favour of the latter is the treatment given. Part of the training of medical students is to overcome the intuition of *Primum non nocere*, and enable them to wield a scalpel or inject an infant with vaccine in the expectation that the eventual benefits will outweigh the initial harm.

Another widespread intuition consists of a feeling of responsibility for acts of commission but not for acts of omission. This may be traced back to the time in infancy when an association is made between consciously willing an action, and the occurrence of movement of a limb or a finger. Ownership

245

is assumed for movements of the body and the consequential events – the toppling of a tower of bricks, or the baby's mother picking up the spoon dropped from the high chair. Quite rightly, no responsibility is assumed for events which occur independently of any action of the child. However, in the adult world of morality, inaction may have consequences as grave as those of an action which is willed, but responsibility is only intuitively felt for the latter. Responsibility for the consequences of acts of omission may be accepted intellectually, but the onus is not *felt* as strongly as that for acts of commission.

As an example, doctors may feel responsible for the adverse side effects from giving a life-saving drug, but not for the loss of life from withholding it. Thus, general practitioners are reluctant to give 'clot-busting' thrombolytic therapy to patients having a heart attack, even though their giving this treatment has been shown to halve the mortality rate of what is the commonest single cause of death.[62] The doctors do not want to be responsible for the rare but unavoidable adverse effects of this treatment, which admittedly are serious, including, occasionally, stroke from cerebral haemorrhage. They feel little responsibility for the more numerous heart attack deaths occurring after admission to hospital which could have been prevented by their giving thrombolytic treatment at the first opportunity in the community. Here, a strong attachment to an intuition about which consequences one is responsible for cuts across the overall intention of saving life and minimising suffering. Unless we are afflicted like Damasio's patient Elliot, we can sympathise with the feeling of responsibility for the bad consequences of a well-intentioned action. Nevertheless, it is difficult to justify withholding life-saving treatment on the basis of an intuition when the treatment has been shown conclusively to be beneficial overall.

The standard method of evaluating a new medical treatment is with a 'randomised double-blind clinical trial'. In this experiment, patients are randomly allotted the new treatment or a placebo, and the outcome for the two groups of patients is compared. In order to minimise bias, neither the patients nor the evaluating doctors know until the trial has been completed which patients have received the active treatment; patients and doctors are both 'blinded'. Baron reports how intuitions about fairness prevented a planned trial of a treatment for AIDS from reaching a conclusion.[63] A consumer-advocacy organisation considered it 'unethical' that only half of those included in the study should receive active treatment, even though this was the only way to be sure that the new treatment was effective. If the drug continues to be used in ignorance of its efficacy, there is the possibility that patients will be subjected to risk and expense with no compensatory benefit. If the drug is withdrawn, because of lack of evidence of efficacy (not the same thing as evidence of lack of efficacy), there is the possibility that future patients will be deprived of an effective treatment. Either way, the outcome is worse than if the intuition of 'unfairness' had been ignored, and the trial completed as planned.

Fairness is a slippery concept, and the Kantian justification for treating everybody the same is that all have identical status and rights as ends-in-themselves. But there is also a utilitarian justification for treating people fairly: that to do otherwise would, at the least, result in resentment or jealousy in those less well treated, reducing overall happiness. There is also another argument from economic theory. Given the opportunity, people satisfy their most pressing needs first, so that as the amount of money at someone's disposal increases, the satisfaction obtained from spending it diminishes progressively.[64] Thus, if twin girls were each given £10 on their birthday, other things being equal, their satisfaction from spending it would be the same. But if one twin was given £12 and the

247

other £8, the total satisfaction would be less than if both had received £10. The lucky twin would gain less happiness from her extra £2 than was deprived from the unlucky twin by her loss of £2. The greatest happiness, or the least unhappiness, of the greatest number usually results from distributing goods, or burdens, equally.

There are many other commonly held intuitions cited by Baron: nature knows best; no arguments are needed for maintaining the status quo, only for changing it; loyalty is owed to the group one happens to belong to, whether or not it was freely chosen; retaliation should be in kind, an eye for an eye. Baron comments that:

> If we want a better world, one relatively inexpensive way to get it is to improve the way we make decisions. We need to think more about their effects, and less about the rules that might guide them.[65]

## Extending the Moral Family

Let us recapitulate the evolution of morality. Over many generations, by means of kin selection and reciprocal altruism, and perhaps also by sexual selection for 'niceness', selfish genes for unselfish behaviour increased in frequency in the hominid gene pool. To begin with, the moral behaviour engendered by these genes involved only the immediate family. Then, as our distant ancestors' brains enlarged, in step with their capacity to cope with more complex social structures, the circle within which morality operated extended to more distant members of the family. Within the confines of the extended family or tribe, moral sentiments and behaviour strengthened group cohesion and motivated cooperation. A basic requirement for group harmony is that group members should not kill one another. Mating with another's sexual partner is another potent cause of group disruption, so murder, sexual infidelity and other behaviours that threatened group solidarity were discouraged by the pressure of social disapproval, and, if found out, severely punished, often by death. Capital punishment for such behaviours would, incidentally, have exerted a selection pressure for socially acceptable conduct.

Our ancestors' living in groups resulted in a tendency for them to categorise other people as belonging to their own moral family and in-group, or as belonging to an out-group, a tendency which persists to this day. Identification of strangers as out-group is assisted by their possession of a different skin colour, language, or religion. While members of the in-group are trusted, the reaction to out-group members is one of distrust and hostility. Threats from them are met with unreasoning hatred, and conflicts settled by aggression.[66]

The behaviours described above evolved over hundreds of thousands of years, an immensely long period in comparison with the blink of an eye since the beginning of civilisation. Then, with the appearance of religion, basic moral rules for group living would often be attributed to a deity, and gained added authority by being written down in a holy book. Adherence to a particular religion provided a marker indicating the ambit of the enlarged moral family. Many religions developed a version of the golden rule 'do as you would be done by', which is a reformulation of reciprocal altruism, one of the mechanisms by which morality is thought to have evolved in the first place.[67] The golden rule, by encouraging a generous first move in an encounter, is an advance on the tit-for-tat, eye-for-an-eye, morality of much of the Old Testament, but like reciprocal altruism itself, the golden rule, at least in its biblical version, only applies to the in-group.[68]

Because general moral maxims such as the golden rule are of little help in living the good life, they were supplemented with numerous requirements concerning aspects of daily life: the Jewish mitzvoth with 613 commandments, or the sharia, the detailed sacred law of Islam. In some sects morality then came to be seen as compliance with the rules concerning, for example, what to eat or what to wear. In the parable of the good Samaritan and other teachings, Jesus advocated extending the moral family to other sects than one's own, and acting in the spirit of the golden rule rather than in compliance with the letter of sectarian law.

While the early Christians may have followed the exhortation 'do unto others as you would be done by', Christianity changed radically with its adoption by Constantine as the official religion of the Roman empire; Gibbon documents the murderous internecine strife over minutiae of doctrine as the Church became established as a powerful political institution.[69] In the dark ages following the collapse of the Roman empire, the Church became the sole repository of learning in the West, and the ultimate authority on morality. Amongst the medieval scholars, Thomas Aquinas stands out for integrating Aristotle's thought into Christian theology, and consolidating Church doctrine. As far as the Church was concerned, the moral family embraced only Christians who followed the approved doctrine. This is evident from its cruel treatment of heretics,[70] its abominable behaviour towards Moslems and Jews during the crusades,[71] its support for the conquest of Amerindians in the newly discovered Americas,[72] and many other examples of unspeakable behaviour towards an outgroup, including its complicity with the deportation of Jews to Nazi Germany.[73]

## Moral Progress

As we have seen, attempts to systematise morality have not met with much success, and after centuries of wrangling, phi-

250

losophers are still, metaphorically speaking, at each other's throats arguing whether deontology or consequentialism provides the better approach to moral philosophy; meanwhile, theologians maintain that they hold the keys to morality as well as to heaven and hell. Nonetheless, there has been some moral progress, by which is meant that some moral statements have come to be widely accepted as fact, regardless of philosophical or religious opinions held. Some acts are simply wrong, and, most importantly, they are wrong whoever is on the receiving end: with regard to certain actions, everybody, regardless of race, nationality, sex, age or religion is included in the moral family. Two examples will be given where significant moral progress has been made in recent centuries: the abolition of slavery, and the assertion of universal human rights.

While enlightenment philosophers were challenging the authority of the Church in matters of justice and morality, others were questioning the authority of their rulers to govern them. Hitherto, the prevailing view of society, and the one fully endorsed by the Church, had been taken from Aristotle. Society had a hierarchical structure in which everybody had their natural place in accordance with their inherited aptitudes and abilities, ranging from the king, ruling by Divine Right at the top of the pyramid, to the slaves – who were not capable even of ruling themselves —taking their place at the bottom of the heap. But revolutionary new ideas were now emerging – of a two-way social contract between the ruler and the ruled, and of the Rights of Man. The latter notion, of human rights, found its trenchant expression in the American Declaration of Independence: 'We hold these truths to be self-evident, that all men are created equal, that they are endowed by their Creator with certain unalienable rights, that among these are life, liberty and the pursuit of happiness.'

It soon became apparent in the newly formed United States of America that the coolly rational moral principles set out by the Founding Fathers were in conflict with the practice of slavery, widespread in the plantations in the Southern states. This was cognitive dissonance, the conflict of reason and passion, the state of mind where a reasoned position is at odds with the felt position. It has to be said that as well as slavery not *feeling* wrong to many people, there were also many economic interests vested in it. Although the issue of slavery came to a head in the bitter Civil War, the war was fought, not in defence or defiance of slavery, but in defence of the Union on the one hand, and the slave states' right to secede from the Union on the other. President Lincoln considered that the Union was much more important than slavery, on which point he was prepared to be pragmatic and do whatever was necessary for the Union's preservation.[74]

After the civil war, which ended in 1865, slaves were emancipated and granted citizenship by amendments of the constitution. But the prejudiced view of Negroes which had made possible the acceptance of their enslavement persisted. Slavery may have been outlawed, but racial segregation took its place; that too was later outlawed, but racism is ever present in America and elsewhere.[75] Nonetheless, the abolition of slavery represented moral progress whatever the motives that were responsible for bringing it about. The moral family, within which slavery is unconscionable, had been enlarged, by decree, if not by sentiment.

The abolition of slavery took a different course in France, where Jean-Jaques Rousseau was appalled at the excesses and abuse of power of the ancien régime while at the same time the peasants were starving. He declared that 'Man is born free, and everywhere he is in chains', and in so saying inspired revolution, though he did not incite it: his writings containing no revolutionary programme, nor any revolutionary tactics. In 1789 when the French revolution started with the storming of the Bastille, it caught almost everyone unawares, and all were surprised by the violent direction it took.[76] The newly formed Constituent Assembly incorporated the views of Rousseau and other enlightenment thinkers in the Declaration of the Rights of Man and of the Citizen, which laid down the principles of the new regime. The first article says 'men are born and remain free and with equal rights'. This declaration, and the rallying cry of the revolution – 'Liberté, égalité, fraternité!' – were taken literally by black slaves in the French colony of Saint-Domingue (now Haiti), who staged a successful rebellion, which perhaps was not too difficult since they comprised 90% of the population. In response, the Constituent Assembly at first declined to change the status of coloured people until the white settlers had been asked for their opinion. But five years after the revolution, freedom and French citizenship were granted to all slaves in the colonies. In reaching this decision, the ruling body was influenced by the thought that slaves in English colonies might be encouraged to rise up and damage English interests. However, the emancipation decree was revoked by Napoleon in 1802, and slavery was not finally abolished in French colonies until 1848.

In Great Britain the course of the abolition movement was different again. In the 1780s, about half of the 70,000 African slaves a year that crossed the Atlantic were carried in British ships.[77] Huge profits enriched the great cities of London, Liverpool and Bristol, as well as many smaller ports. Manufactured goods were shipped from Britain to West Africa, where they were traded for slaves captured by African intermediaries. In the notorious 'middle passage' the slaves, chained, shackled, overcrowded, thirsty and underfed, crossed the Atlantic to be sold to work in sugar or cotton plantations in the Caribbean or the Americas. From there, the products of their labour were shipped back to Britain, completing a triangular circuit. In the middle passage, which lasted several weeks, between 15-30% of the human cargo was expected to die, and it was the suffering entailed in this crossing which aroused the sympathy of the Quaker pioneers of the abolitionist movement.[78]

The campaign led by the Anti-Slavery Society was directed not at slavery itself, but at the slave trade, and it had widespread public support. The founders of the society were Thomas Clarkson, an evangelical Anglican, and some Quaker friends, soon to be joined by William Wilberforce the member of parliament for Hull. He was an eloquent and indefatigable sponsor of antislavery legislation, and before the Anti-Slavery Act was finally enacted he presented numerous bills to parliament which were either not passed by the Commons, or else were rejected by the Lords, where the opposition to abolition was led by the Duke of Clarence, the future King William IV. In the Commons, Wilberforce had the backing of the Prime Minister, William Pitt the younger, but that was not enough because there were many in both Houses with vested interests in the lucrative trade. With the start of the revolution in France, support for abolition dwindled because of the fear of an uprising of slaves in British colonies, such as had taken place in the French colony of Saint-Domingue. But the restoration of slavery in French possessions by Napoleon, and the outbreak of war between England and France, aroused anti-French sentiment and revived the opposition to the slave trade, which was eventually outlawed in 1807. By a happy coincidence the slave trade in America was prohibited by Congress in the same year. Slavery itself was abolished in British possessions three decades later by an 1833 Act which came into force five years later. The compensation to slaveholders, amongst whom was the Church of England, was £20 million, while the liberated slaves received nothing.

Between 1807 and 1870, Britain, poacher turned gamekeeper, had naval squadrons off the coast of West Africa to search, detain and capture traders who continued to supply slaves, especially to Brazil and Cuba. In that period some 200,000 were freed from slave ships, out of some 2 million who were transported out of Africa.[79] It is estimated that from the 16th to the 19th century between 10 and 20 million Africans were sold into slavery and transported across the Atlantic.

The passing of the Anti-Slavery Act has been celebrated as a victory of the philanthropists led by William Wilberforce, but there is another side to the picture. Adam Smith had claimed that because a slave has no hope of owning property he works less hard than a freeman, whose work is cheaper in the end than that of a slave. Slavery also contravened the principle of free movement of labour, and thus reduced the efficiency of the market. Others have argued that the availability of slave labour curbs inventiveness and dampens the initiative for economic improvement. There were thus direct economic arguments for abolishing slave labour. But there was another motive for the belated interest in African emancipation by Britain and other European countries: the scramble for colonial conquest of Africa in order to gain access to its raw materials. Britain's prize was Nigeria.

Nonetheless, the abolition of slavery represented a huge moral advance. Slavery had been practised since antiquity, and when the abolition movement started, slavery had almost universal acceptance. But from a nexus of people and movements with varied motives, beliefs and interests there emerged a conviction that slavery was morally wrong, and that it should be abolished by law. This change in attitude took place over centuries, and cannot be attributed to any individual, or government, or non-governmental organisation, but rather, to the power of ideas. The abolition of slavery was a triumphal marriage of reason and passion.

The conclusion of the long campaign for the abolition of slavery came in 1948 with the adoption by the General Assembly of the United Nations of the Universal Declaration of Human Rights, in which Article 4 prohibits slavery and the slave trade. Slavery persisted in Saudi Arabia into the 1960s but was finally made illegal in the Arabian Peninsula in 1962.

*

The United Nations Organisation was set up in 1945 in the aftermath of World War II, when the Holocaust was fresh in everybody's memory, and genocide and racial discrimination were sensitive issues. The Declaration of Human Rights asserts that all are equal before the law, and entitled to all the rights and freedoms set forth in the Declaration, without distinction of any kind, such as race, colour, sex, language, or religion.

Article 1 declares that 'All human beings are born free and equal in dignity and rights', reiterating the claims made in the American Declaration of Independence nearly two centuries previously. In that Declaration, 'certain unalienable rights' were considered to be endowed by the Creator to all humankind. The 1948 Declaration does not go into the question of the origin of human rights, but the answer is not far to find. The rights accorded to every one of us born into any of the 192 member states of the UN consist, in effect, of a promissory note underwritten by the government vouchsafing the delivery during our lifetime of the moral goods described in the 30 articles of the Declaration. If we think we have had a raw deal and the goods are not as promised or not delivered on time (they include free primary education), then we have recourse to national and international human rights law, of which the Declaration forms the basis.

For our part, during our lifetime we are expected to reciprocate by giving back to society at least as much as we receive. This means behaving towards other people in a way which is respectful of their rights. Thus, human rights constitute one side of a social contract between the government and the governed. But the government is representative of the people, so human rights are part of an intra- and inter-generational social contract. In effect, then, we accord human rights to each other. Human rights constitute a reformulation and codification of reciprocal altruism, applied, not just to immediate kith and kin, but to the global human family, and underwritten by law. The Universal Declaration of Human Rights is reciprocal altruism writ large.

Not all people have equal enjoyment of their human rights, and the Declaration is not an enforceable treaty; nor does the UN have international legal powers of enforcement. Nevertheless, the Declaration provides a moral benchmark for political systems, and asserts a minimal standard of social behaviour which people world-wide have a right to expect.

*

Our moral concepts and categories are acquired in the setting of the family during infancy and childhood, a time of life when passions run high, and the emotional feel of good and bad behaviour is quickly learnt. The intense emotional associations forged in the family in childhood persist into adulthood where in a metaphor of the family, government takes the role of parent, and citizens become children.

This metaphor of *Society as Family* explains the paradox that a nation launched with the mission statement of 'Life,

257

liberty and the pursuit of happiness' should ever deny these very rights to certain groups of people living within its shores, on account of their colour, for example. The solution to this puzzle is to understand that moral behaviour is only required between family members; the zone of morality is the family circle. Outside every tribal, racial or national family circle is an amoral zone where there are few restraints on the treatment meted out to non-family members. Moral progress in society consists of extending the boundaries of the moral family to include more of the people – and animals – who were previously relegated to the amoral zone. There are two moral forces that may be brought to bear on shifting the boundary between Them and Us and extending the circle of the human family: reason based on scientific knowledge, and human sympathy.

Although it cuts little ice against deep-seated racial prejudice, an argument that may be used against racism is that there is no scientific basis, in anatomy, physiology or genetics, for the concept of race.[80] Average differences in genetically determined characteristics between races are much less than the range of variation within a racial group. Taking intelligence as an example, the differences in average IQs between various racial groups are at the most 10-15 points, but these differences are swamped by the span of IQs found in the population at large, which ranges roughly from 50 to 150, with a mean of 100. There is no legitimate argument why any encounter between individuals of different racial groups need be affected by the knowledge that an aggregate ethnic difference in IQ exists.[81] But that statement, however true it may be, misses the point that when we encounter other people, a scientific, quantitative mode of thought is seldom used; instead, we use stereotypes.

A stereotype is a generalised description of a group of people all of whom are assumed to possess one or more characteristic traits; they are all tarred with the same brush. This intuitive, essentialist, qualitative thinking is a rough and ready method of classifying people on a first encounter. There is a large body of research showing that racial stereotypes are very prevalent, and have a powerful and unconscious effect on our behaviour towards one another.[82] Moreover, our expectations of people acting according to type tend to be self-fulfilling. If there is any truth in the stereotype it is that the trait in question has a roughly bell-shaped distribution within the target population, of whom about 50% will manifest an above average score, while 50% will be below average. Perhaps, too, the average value will differ slightly from that of the group to which the user of the stereotype belongs. But stereotypes are very resistant to reasoned attack because they are constructed unconsciously and reflect the need of the user to maintain a relationship of superiority to the stereotyped group.[83]

Much more powerful than reason at crossing the frontier of the moral family is sympathy. At times of natural disasters, such as the Asian tsunami or the Pakistani earthquake, human sympathy breaks through boundaries of class, creed, race or ideology with generous offers of help for the unfortunate victims. What moves us most are video images of people stricken with grief at the loss of loved ones. We have empathy – we experience their emotion – and we are moved to help them; our empathy translates into sympathy. However, where the disaster is one of human warfare and the victims are civilians or combatants, particularly of hand-to-hand fighting, any sympathy with the enemy on the part of the soldiers would undermine military discipline and perhaps the mission itself. This possibility is largely pre-empted by military training in strict obedience to orders, together with indoctrination in which the enemy is totally dehumanised and placed outside the circle of the human family: Vietcong are gooks, Iraqi soldiers are cockroaches,[84] and people held as suspects in the

259

detention centre at Guantanamo Bay are simply dogs, or at best, detainees; never men or even prisoners.[85]

## Summing Up

Attempts to construct a coherent theoretical account of morality have been unsuccessful, though there are some moral statements which are almost universally agreed: that killing people is wrong is one of these. Other particular statements, such as that slavery is wrong, have come to be widely accepted as true over a period of time.

Morality is best viewed as a learned skill in social interaction, and as such it is incapable of being codified except in very general terms which are of little help in daily life. Moral behaviour is an evolved adaptation to living in groups, and may be seen as an emergent property arising from the interactions of people living cooperatively, its function being to motivate cooperative activity and strengthen group cohesion. Four main modes of interaction have been described, each of which results in a different pattern of normative behaviour inconsistent with the others.

Children have an innate disposition to acquire moral intuitions, but particular intuitions of 'right' and 'wrong' derive from the culture in which they are brought up, may be different in different cultures, and may change with time. Moral intuitions are highly charged with emotion, resistant to reason, and strongly motivating; their authority may be further enhanced by projection outside one's self where they may be construed as absolute standards, or as originating from a deity. The realisation that moral standards are of our own making opens up the possibility of their being revised to take account of modern knowledge, and modified in such a way as to assist

260

rather than hinder us in solving the many problems facing us. At the same time, however, realisation of the human origin of moral standards reduces their authority and the likelihood of their revision and acceptance. Extending the boundaries of the human family to include zones where behaviour is at present amoral is a major challenge.

# Notes

## Chapter 6: The Evolution of Morality

1.  Charles Darwin. *The Descent of Man, and Selection in Relation to Sex.* London: Penguin Books, 2004: p120-3.
2.  'An altar of earth thou shalt make unto me, and shalt sacrifice thereon thy burnt offerings, and thy peace offerings, thy sheep, and thine oxen.' Exodus 20:24. 'Six days shall work be done, but on the seventh day there shall be to you an holy day, a sabbath of rest to the LORD: whosoever doeth work therein shall be put to death.' Exodus 35:2.
3.  Charles Darwin. *The Descent of Man, and Selection in Relation to Sex.* London: Penguin Books, 2004: p123.
4.  David Hume. *A Treatise Upon Human Nature* bk2, pt 3 (1739), *cited in* John Cottingham. *Western Philosophy: An Anthology.* Oxford: Blackwell Publishers Ltd, 1996: p375.
5.  Immanuel Kant. *Critique of Practical Reason, cited in* Ben-Ami Scharfstein. *The Philosophers: Their Lives and the Nature of their Thought.* New York: Oxford University Press, 1989: p227.
6.  Immanuel Kant. *Groundwork of the Metaphysic of Morals* (1785), *cited in* John Cottingham. *Western Philosophy: An Anthology.* Oxford: Blackwell Publishers Ltd, 1996: p385.
7.  George Lakoff, Mark Johnson. *Philosophy in the Flesh: The Embodied Mind and its Challenge to Western Thought.* New York: Basic Books, 1999: pp415-39.
8.  Ben-Ami Scharfstein. *The Philosophers: Their Lives and the Nature of their Thought.* New York: Oxford University Press, 1989: p210-30.
9.  Ibid, p211.
10. Ibid, p216.
11. Immanuel Kant. *Groundwork of the Metaphysic of Morals* (1785), *cited in* John Cottingham. *Western Philosophy: An Anthology.* Oxford: Blackwell Publishers Ltd, 1996: p384.
12. Ben-Ami Scharfstein. *The Philosophers: Their Lives and the Nature of their Thought.* New York: Oxford University Press, 1989: p229.

13. Simon Blackburn. *Being Good: A Short Introduction to Ethics*. Oxford University Press, 2001: p111.
14. Antonio R Damasio. *Descartes' Error: Emotion, Reason and the Human Brain*. London: Picador, 1995: pp34-51.
15. Daniel Goleman. *Emotional Intelligence: Why it Can Matter more than IQ*. London: Bloomsbury, 1996.
16. Antonio R Damasio. *Descartes' Error: Emotion, Reason and the Human Brain*. London: Picador, 1995: pp212-22.
17. Cordelia Fine. *A Mind of its Own: How Your Brain Distorts and Deceives*. Cambridge: Icon Books, 2006: pp71-4.
18. Antonio R Damasio. *Descartes' Error: Emotion, Reason and the Human Brain*. London: Picador, 1995: p250.
19. Roy Porter. *England in the Eighteenth Century*. London: The Folio Society, 1996: p127.
20. Simon Blackburn. *Being Good: A Short Introduction to Ethics*. Oxford University Press, 2001: pp86-93.
21. Peter Singer. *Morality, Reason, and the Rights of Animals*. In Frans de Waal. *Primates and Philosophers: How Morality Evolved*. Princeton University Press, 2006: p147.
22. Brain mishaps produce "cold" morality. www.world-science.net/othernews/070320_morality.htm
23. George Lakoff, Mark Johnson. *Philosophy in the Flesh: The Embodied Mind and its Challenge to Western Thought*. New York: Basic Books, 1999: p294.
24. Jonathan Dancy. *Ethics without Principles*. Oxford: Clarendon Press, 2004.
25. Aristotle. *Nicomachean Ethics*. In John Cottingham. *Western Philosophy: An Anthology*. Oxford: Blackwell Publishers Ltd, 1996: p367-8.
26. Paul M Churchland. *The Engine of Reason, the Seat of the Soul: A Philosophical Journey into the Brain*. Cambridge, Mass.: The MIT Press, 1995: p148-9.
27. David Hume. *Enquiry Concerning the Principles of Morals* (1751). In John Cottingham. *Western Philosophy: An Anthology*. Oxford: Blackwell Publishers Ltd, 1996: p379-80.
28. Paul M Churchland. *The Engine of Reason, the Seat of the Soul: A Philosophical Journey into the Brain*. Cambridge, Mass.: The MIT Press, 1995: p150.
29. Frans de Waal. *Primates and Philosophers: How Morality*

*Evolved*. Edited and introduced by Stephen Macedo and Josiah Ober. Princeton University Press, 2006.

30. Ibid, p10.
31. Alan Page Fiske. *Structures of Social Life: The Four Elementary Forms of Human Relations*. New York: The Free Press, 1993.
32. Matt Ridley. *Nature via Nurture: Genes, Experience and What Makes us Human*. London: Fourth Estate, 2003: pp42-48.
33. Steven Mithen. *The Prehistory of the Mind: The Cognitive Origins of Art and Science*. London: Thames and Hudson, 1999: p133.
34. Edward O Wilson. *Sociobiology: The New Synthesis*. 25th anniversary edition. Cambridge Mass: The Belknap Press of Harvard University Press, 2000: p539.
35. Frans de Waal. *Primates and Philosophers: How Morality Evolved*. Edited and introduced by Stephen Macedo and Josiah Ober. Princeton University Press, 2006: p43.
36. Ibid, p36.
37. Ibid, p33.
38. Ibid, p170.
39. Ibid, p55.
40. Marc D Hauser. *Moral Minds: How Nature Designed our Universal Sense of Right and Wrong.* New York: HarperCollins Publishers, 2006.
41. Steven Pinker. *Words and Rules: The Ingredients of Language*. London: Weidenfeld & Nicolson, 1999: p196.
42. Steven A LeBlanc, with Katherine E Register. *Constant Battles: Why We Fight*. New York: St Martin's Griffin, 2003.
43. Richard Joyce. *The Evolution of Morality*. Cambridge, Mass: The MIT Press, 2006: p136.
44. Alan Page Fiske. *Structures of Social Life: The Four Elementary Forms of Human Relations*. New York: The Free Press, 1993.
45. Haidt J. The emotional dog and its rational tail: A social intuitionist approach to moral judgement. *Psychological Review* 2001; 108: 814-34.
46. Richard A Shweder, Nancy C Much, Manamohan Mahapatra, Lawrence Park. *The "Big Three" of Morality (Autonomy, Community, Divinity) and the "Big Three" Explanations of*

*Suffering. In* Allan M Brandt, Paul Rozin (eds). *Morality and Health.* New York: Routledge, 1997: pp130-150.

47. William Damon. *The Moral Child: Nurturing Children's Natural Moral Growth.* New York: The Free Press, 1990: p106.

48. The term 'conversation stopper' was coined by Dennett as a non-rational 'magic word' which closes a decision process that otherwise 'spirals fruitlessly to infinity.' Daniel C Dennett. *Darwin's Dangerous Idea: Evolution and the Meanings of Life.* London: Penguin Books, 1996, p506.

49. Richard Joyce. *The Evolution of Morality.* Cambridge, Mass: The MIT Press, 2006: p125-33.

50. Ibid, p135.

51. Ibid, pp184-5.

52. John Gray. Are we Born Moral? *The New York Review*, May 10, 2007.

53. Haidt J. The Emotional Dog and its Rational Tail: A Social Intuitionist Approach to Moral Judgement. *Psychological Review* 2001; 108: 814-34.

54. Richard Joyce. *The Evolution of Morality.* Cambridge, Mass: The MIT Press, 2006: p130.

55. Haidt J. The Emotional Dog and its Rational Tail: A Social Intuitionist Approach to Moral Judgement. *Psychological Review* 2001; **108**:814-34.

56. Antonio R Damasio. *Descartes' Error: Emotion, Reason and the Human Brain.* London: Picador, 1995: p178.

57. Jonathan Baron. *Judgment Misguided: Intuition and Error in Public Decision Making.* Oxford University Press, 1998: p5.

58. Simon Blackburn. *Being Good: A Short Introduction to Ethics.* Oxford University Press, 2001: p120.

59. Jonathan Baron. *Judgment Misguided: Intuition and Error in Public Decision Making.* Oxford University Press, 1998: p26.

60. Raanan Gillon. *Philosophical Medical Ethics.* Chichester: John Wiley & Sons, 1985: p80-85.

61. Jonathan Baron. *Judgment Misguided: Intuition and Error in Public Decision Making.* Oxford University Press, 1998: p111.

62. Rawles J. Halving of mortality at 1 year by domiciliary thrombolysis in the Grampian region early anistreplase trial (GREAT). *Journal of the American College of Cardiology*

1994; 23: 1-5.

63. Jonathan Baron. *Judgment Misguided: Intuition and Error in Public Decision Making*. Oxford University Press, 1998: p52.

64. Ibid, p48.

65. Ibid, p1.

66. Edward O Wilson. *On Human Nature*. Cambridge, Mass.: Harvard University Press, 1978: p119.

67. 'Whatsoever ye would that men should do to you, do ye even so to them'. Matt 7:12.

68. Richard Dawkins. *The God Delusion*. London: The Bantam Press, 2006: p254-62.

69. The relationship between Father and Son in the Godhead was the issue, 'almost invisible to the nicest theological eye', which divided the Athanians from the Arians. It hinged on the Greek words Homoousion (of one substance), and Homoiousion (of like substance). Gibbon writes 'The profane of every age have derided the furious contests which the difference of a single diphthong excited between the Homoousians and the Homoiousians'. Edward Gibbon. *The History of the Decline and Fall of the Roman Empire*. Volume III. *The Revival and Collapse of Paganism*. London: The Folio Society, 1985: p35.

70. Stephen O'Shea. *The Perfect Heresy: The Life and Death of the Cathars.* London: Profile books, 2000.

71. When the first crusade reached Jerusalem there was wholesale slaughter of Moslems and Jews, including those taking refuge in the Al-Aqsa Mosque and in the Synagogue. The victorious Christians then gave thanks to God in the Church of the Holy Sepulchre. Terry Jones, Alan Ereira. *Crusades*. London: BBC Books, 1994: p71-75.

72. A year after Columbus' discovery of the West Indies, the Pope generously gave the mainlands and islands together with the peoples of the New World yet to be discovered, to the east of longitude 50° W to Portugal, and to the west to Spain. Brian Moynahan. *The Faith: A History of Christianity*. London: Aurum Press, 2002: p504-24.

73. John Cornwell. *Hitler's Pope: The Secret History of Pius XII*. London: Viking, 1999: p298-318.

74. President Lincoln: 'If I could save the Union without freeing any slave, I would do it; and if I could save it by freeing all the

slaves, I would do it; and if I could save it by freeing some and leaving others alone, I would also do that.' *Alistair Cooke's America.* London: British Broadcasting Corporation, 1973: p218.

75. James A Morone. *Hellfire Nation: The Politics of Sin in American History.* New Haven & London: Yale University Press, 2003: p463.
76. J S McClelland. *A History of Western Political Thought.* London and New York: Routledge, 1996: p311.
77. Hugh Thomas. *The Slave Trade: The History of the Atlantic Slave Trade 1440-1870.* London: Picador, 1997: p447.
78. Kevin Shillington. British Made: Abolition and the Africa trade. *History Today* 2007; 57 (3): 20-27.
79. Hugh Thomas. *The Slave Trade: The History of the Atlantic Slave Trade 1440-1870.* London: Picador, 1997: p784.
80. Steve Jones. *In the Blood: God, Genes and Destiny.* London: Harper Collins Publishers, 1996.
81. Richard J Herrnstein, Charles Murray. *The Bell Curve: Intelligence and Class Structure in American Life.* New York: Simon & Schuster/Free Press Paperbacks, 1996: p313.
82. Cordelia Fine. *A Mind of its Own: How Your Brain Distorts and Deceives.* Cambridge: Icon Books, 2006: pp139-64.
83. David Berreby. *Us and Them: Understanding your Tribal Mind.* New York: Little, Brown and Company, 2005: pp157-81.
84. Jonathan Glover. *Humanity: A Moral History of the Twentieth Century.* London: Jonathan Cape, 1999: p50.
85. Clive Stafford Smith. *Bad Men: Guantanamo Bay and Secret Prisons.* London: Weidenfeld & Nicolson, 2007: p00.

# Chapter 7

# The Evolution of Capitalism

'You cannot buck the market.' *Margaret Thatcher*

In the previous chapter it was argued that morality is a learned skill in social living, reducing interpersonal conflict by motivating cooperative behaviour and strengthening group cohesion. Four basic types of interpersonal relations were described, each with its own behavioural conventions supported by moral intuitions. Moral behaviour is first learned in the bosom of the family in childhood, family relationships tending to conform to communal sharing or authority ranking models. Later, children develop a sense of fairness as they experience personal relations corresponding to equality matching mode. Last of all to be acquired, and the least emotionally reinforced, is market pricing behaviour where personal relationships are minimal, consisting merely of what is necessary for an economic transaction.

Economic activity is defined as the production, distribution and exchange of goods and services. At its most basic this could be the production of meals for the family. In communal sharing each family member is fed according to need with no consideration of equity or rank. In authority ranking, the head of the household has first claim, particularly on the most nutritious items of diet; the others accept their position in the pecking order. In equality matching, equal shares for all is the rule, any violation of which causes ructions. In market pricing mode meals are purchased, perhaps in a café or restaurant. Economic transactions of this sort are open to all, the only constraints being that the goods must be as described and be the vendor's to sell, and the purchaser must have the funds to buy at the agreed price, and will pay on time. These minimal conditions of honesty and trust are backed by contract law. Economic transactions are *felt* to be right or wrong to the extent that they involve personal relations. We may express the gratitude felt for receiving a good meal in a restaurant by giving a tip; the restaurant staff are temporarily included in our moral family. Much economic activity, however, entails little personal interaction, and with internet bidding and electronic transfer of funds, many deals are completely impersonal and dispassionate. Where the human consequences of such activities are invisible, dealing in shares or foreign currency for example, this behaviour seems neither right nor wrong, but is simply amoral.

This chapter deals with economics, particularly with the highest level of economic activity, namely, capitalism. Capitalism emerges as a major player in the final episode of the immensely long human saga recounted in the preceding chapters, and which had its origins in the Big Bang. An important characteristic of the story so far has been the pivotal role of chance in determining the course of our evolution, notably in the acquisition of our distinctive feature of walking upright with a big brain. Chance has played a large part too in the development of capitalism, as will be described in this last instalment of our history. Capitalism is a driving force behind unsustainable economic growth, central in the group of nine problems featured in the schema shown in the frontispiece. It is necessary to review its history if we wish to reach an understanding of our human predicament.

# Growth of the Market Economy

Division of labour has long been a feature of human society, dating at least from the time of the hunter-gatherer communities. While the men were away hunting, so the story goes, the womenfolk remained close to the homestead gathering nuts and berries and minding the children. No doubt further specialisation developed within and between the sexes according to aptitude, custom and status within the tribe. Wealth of a sort was created by the women gathering, preparing and preserving foodstuffs, and craftsmen adding value to raw materials of clay, flint, wood and bone. Within and between tribes, goods and services would be exchanged, and bartering would become the framework for a body of social relationships in which money played no part. *as money did not then exist*

In developed societies today it is estimated that 30-40% of all economic activity is still accounted for by what the French economic and social historian Fernand Braudel calls *la vie matérielle*, which may be translated as 'material life', or the structures of everyday life.[1] This informal, autonomous, and largely cashless economy takes place within and between households and neighbourhoods. It is not susceptible to boom or bust, is beyond the reach of government but is regulated by mutual bonds of affection, obligation and trust. It is what provides people with basic necessities even when the money economy has completely collapsed.

With the growth of towns, and the invention of money, the true market economy came into being.[2] Once or twice a week smallholders and farmers would bring their produce to the market place in the town centre, to set up their stalls alongside those of artisans selling goods for home or farm made in their urban workshops. According to Karl Polanyi, the author of *The Great Transformation,* the idea of any person or enterprise acting solely for financial gain was virtually unknown until the 18ᵗʰ century, economic activity being embedded in a society knitted together by a web of mutual dependencies in which finance played but a small part.[3] Moreover, communities, villages, towns, or at the most, regions, were largely autonomous in their staple needs. People primarily worked, not so much to gain a living, but to fulfil a role in their community; certainly not to make a fortune. In turn, the community had a responsibility towards its members, especially those who were poverty stricken through age, infirmity or unemployment. Social obligations were acknowledged as being reciprocal in the long term, so an individual who disregarded the accepted code of honour and generosity and accumulated a personal fortune would be seen as a miser and an outcast.

It was in this pre-industrial setting that Adam Smith (1723-90) recognised the importance of division of labour for increasing productivity. A task like making a pin is broken down into a number of stages, each worker carrying out one stage rather than doing the whole process himself. Smith also observed that in a market economy, although every individual acts in his own interest, by means of the invisible hand of the market this essentially selfish activity meets other people's needs and leads to the enrichment and well-being of society as a whole. For optimal efficiency, however, the market must be free, and its self-regulating mechanisms must not be obstructed by interference from government tariffs or business monopolies. Commodities such as grain or cotton attain their natural price by the law of supply and demand; it could be demonstrated mathematically that the economy achieves optimal efficiency through this pricing mechanism, but it requires that the market be fully informed and freely competitive.

Box 17

The Law of Supply and Demand (Say's Law)

Adam Smith (1723-90) was a moral philosopher who is better known for *An Inquiry into the Nature and Causes of the Wealth of Nations*, a foundational text in political economy. Wealth arises from the accumulation of capital, from technical progress, and from specialisation, which greatly increases the productivity of labour. According to Smith, 'Every individual necessarily labours to render the annual revenue of society as great as he can. He generally neither intends to promote the public interest nor knows how much he is promoting it. He intends only his own gain, and he is, in this, as in many other cases, led by an invisible hand to promote an end which was no part of his intention.'

Smith describes how in a self-regulating market free from outside interference, and in which the producers and consumers are fully informed, the price of goods is optimal for all parties, and comes to be such that the demand for goods is in equilibrium with their supply. Increased national wealth is an unintended consequence of this attempt by producers and consumers to maximise their gain in their dealings with each other.

It was the French economist Jean-Baptiste Say (1767-1832) who attempted a proof of this 'law' by arguing that supply and demand are not independent variables since producers are also consumers. Taking all goods and services together, the profit from their production constitutes the income of the producers, and is in turn spent on consumption. Supply and demand are therefore necessarily the same, the supply of goods influencing its own demand. A temporary surplus of goods is quickly rectified by a price reduction which increases sales; conversely, a shortage of goods leads to increased demand and a price rise, encouraging greater production.

The law of supply and demand may be seen as an emergent property of a society in which people relate to each other in Market Pricing mode, to use Fiske's terminology. But the model of society breaks down, and the 'law' of supply and demand no longer holds, if people relate to each other in another mode, for instance, in Communal Sharing – 'to each according to his needs', or in Equality Matching, where everybody has an equal share of goods. Another circumstance in which the law of supply and demand breaks down is when there is uncertainty and loss of confidence in future prosperity. Under these conditions people save their earnings as a security against hard times ahead, and there is a surplus of goods in spite of price reductions. If sustained, lack of confidence may result in mass unemployment and a collapse of the economic system, as in the Great Depression in 1929.

Another important principle is that of comparative advantage, enunciated by David Ricardo (1772-1823). This states that to maximise economic benefit, trading partners should each produce and trade the commodity which they manufacture or grow most efficiently. It is easily shown that this would be economically advantageous to both countries, even if the product that the poorer country is best at producing is made less efficiently than the same product in the richer country. Malthus' (1766-1834) prediction of exponential population growth led Ricardo to envisage the cultivation of increasingly infertile land, from which followed the law of diminishing returns. As land then becomes scarce, landowners' rental income inevitably rises. These theoretical notions of society's economic mechanisms were taken to be laws of Nature, and as such, they were as ineluctable as the law of gravity, which had been recently enunciated by Newton (1642-1727).

Ever since their formulation, these so-called laws of economics have been used to justify all manner of exploitative behaviour, from subsistence wages for industrial workers to free trade with developing countries. But the decision of a developing country to comply with Ricardo's law and to turn from mixed farming to a cash crop is not simply one of economics. It concerns also the social upheaval that goes with overturning traditional agricultural practices, and the political consequences of exchanging nutritional self-sufficiency for dependency on world markets and international transport.

On the World Trade Organisation (WTO) website there is a quotation by Nobel laureate economist Paul Samuelson concerning Ricardo's law of comparative advantage:

> ...arguably the single most powerful insight into economics... That it is logically true need not be argued before a mathematician; that it is not trivial is attested by the thousands of important and intelligent men who have never been able to grasp the doctrine for themselves or to believe it after it was explained to them.[4]

274

Perhaps the difficulty which important and intelligent men have with this insight is its fallaciousness. Academic economists are so beguiled by the logical argument for comparative advantage, which is completely in tune with their free market ideology, that they are loath to re-examine it. For when Ricardo formulated his principle, neither capital nor labour was able to move easily from one country to another. Once free movement of capital is allowed, absolute rather than comparative advantage becomes the basis of trade, which is no longer necessarily advantageous to both trading partners. Ricardo's principle cannot therefore be used to argue for free movement of goods, capital and labour when the principle itself depends on immobility of capital and labour. The cornerstone of the WTO's case for free trade has crumbled.[5]

Another example of undue respect being given to an economic principle was Mrs Thatcher's dictum, 'You cannot buck the market'. She was referring to the 'law' of supply and demand where a multitude of traders supply the needs of a multitude of fully informed consumers, and where commodity prices achieve so-called 'Pareto-efficiency', that is, no one would be able to make a better bargain without somebody else being worse off. But these idealised market conditions scarcely exist anywhere nowadays, certainly not in the high street where one or two supermarket chains compete for our custom. Perhaps the stock market is closer to Adam Smith's market than the high street, but even there, behaviour is not as theory predicts. When share prices fall buyers offload their goods rather than buy, and when they rise buyers are plentiful. From time to time economically irrational exuberance leads to gross inflation of the prices of commodities, from dotcom shares to houses; when these 'bubbles' burst there is economic havoc. The hand that guides the market is invisible because it does not exist. Economic theory has succumbed to the fallacy of misplaced concreteness: conjecture has been reified into ideology.[6] What's more, like religious and political ideologies, economic ideology is used by the strong to justify exploitation of the weak – human needs are made subservient to human notions.

Box 18

Ricardo's Law of Comparative Advantage

While Adam Smith demonstrated that division of labour improved economic efficiency, David Ricardo (1772-1823) extended the principle internationally. He showed that if countries specialise in producing and trading the goods they are best at making, this is preferable to each country being self-sufficient and meeting all its own needs. Consider two countries, England and Portugal, and two goods, wine and cloth. Suppose that to produce one barrel of wine or one length of cloth each take five hours of labour in England, and two and eight hours respectively in Portugal. Two being less than eight, Portugal is said to have a comparative advantage in the production of wine. The production in each country of a barrel of wine and a length of cloth requires 10 hours in England and 10 hours in Portugal, a total of 20 hours' labour altogether. If Portugal specialises in the sector corresponding to its comparative advantage, namely wine, and if England produces all the cloth, production of the same quantities of these goods as before now requires 10 hours in England for two lengths of cloth, and four hours in Portugal for two barrels of wine, a total of 14 hours. Both countries stand to gain from trading the goods produced more cheaply following this specialisation.

The above argument for Portugal specialising in wine production holds even if Portugal has an absolute disadvantage, and production of both wine and cloth takes more labour there than in England, perhaps because the labour force is less skilled or less well provided with labour-saving equipment. If we suppose that six hours' labour is needed to produce a barrel of wine in Portugal, other labour costs being the same as in the previous illustration, the totals for England and Portugal are 10 and 14 hours before specialisation and 10 and 12 hours after. As long as there is a comparative advantage in one commodity, goods which may be traded are produced more cheaply with specialisation than without. Ricardo's law of comparative advantage thus provided strong support for international free trade.

But there is an assumption underlying the above argument: that neither capital nor labour can be moved from one country to another. That assumption was largely true in Ricardo's day, but is true no longer. Nowadays it would be possible for an English company to set up as a wine grower in Portugal and even to employ English labour, ensuring that the profits of its capital investment would return to England, while taking advantage of Portugal's favourable climate for growing vines. Thus the free movement of capital and labour undermines the case for free trade.

# The Industrial Revolution

The industrial revolution created a need for up-front capital for machinery and factories, which to be most efficient economically needed to be worked night and day. Hitherto, labour had been closely linked to the land in a predominantly agricultural society, but the industrial revolution created a demand for labour as a commodity, uprooted from the soil, severed from pastoral links, and available to be hired or fired according to the ups and downs of the order book. But what was the natural price of labour? According to the law of supply and demand, if labour was plentiful, as it was at the turn of the 18th century, its price in wages was no more than subsistence, the 'threshold of wretchedness'. Advocating the reform of the Poor Law, which distorted the labour market by paying people who were not working, one Joseph Townsend wrote that 'In general it is only hunger which can spur and goad them [the poor] on to labour.'[7] Poverty in a substantial section of society was therefore part of the natural scheme of things, the necessary motivating factor for the labourer, and the price to be paid for the overall prosperity wrought by the industrial revolution. It was a price paid in full by several generations of British working people.[8]

The industrial revolution also created a demand for land for building factories and new industrial towns. In the 19th century, a relatively small number of landowners still owned two thirds of the land of the British Isles.[9] Because of the right of primogeniture, large estates were passed intact from generation to generation, entailing stewardship rather than ownership, sustainable development rather than exploitation. Land for new development, therefore, was, and remains, scarce and expensive.

Another important sequel to the industrial revolution was the growth in the money market. In the 18<sup>th</sup> century, the flow of money closely matched the flow of traded goods, which was very largely in the domestic market. Now, there is a gross disparity between the movement of money and that of goods. World financial flows have increased exponentially, and the annual turnover of foreign exchange is now more than 60 times the value of world trade.[10]

## The Transformation of Society

The great transformation of which Polanyi wrote, was not therefore the industrial revolution itself, but the upheaval in society caused by industrialisation's demand for, and creation of, new markets for labour, land, and capital.[11] The natural prices reached for these pseudo-commodities were respectively the wages of the labourer, the rent of the landowner and the interest of the banker. From now on society was to be radically different: for many people, work was wrenched from its social context and became the means of making a meagre living. For others who were more fortunate, great wealth was to be had by dealing in these new pseudo-commodities of land and money. Making money was now deemed to be an acceptable activity in its own right, and no longer carried any constraining social obligations – *richesse n'oblige pas*. Although faith was the route to heaven, for the hard working protestant, business success was the sign of heavenly approval; the obverse of this coin revealed poverty as a moral failing.[12] Charity directed at the indigent removed the motive for self-improvement, and if the treatment of the labouring class appeared inhumane, that was because natural law is merciless. That morality and natural law both suited the nouveau riche industrialists was a happy coincidence.

The industrial revolution and the great transformation of human society that accompanied it was brought about, not by any external non-human agency, but by humans themselves. Nevertheless, restructuring of society soon became irreversible and beyond human control. It was directed neither by destiny, nor by human aspiration. Indeed, the significance of the tentative origins of the industrial revolution was not recognised even by Adam Smith,[13] and no one foresaw where it would lead, or anticipated its ultimately injurious consequences. That it took off in Britain and not elsewhere was contingent on a host of factors, including a population spurt, increased agricultural productivity, the existence of wealthy landowners with surplus capital, the exhaustion of wood supplies and the increased use of coal as a fuel for the new steam engines, an effective transport system, the availability of raw cotton from our American colonies, and a well-fed and available workforce.[14] Other factors, considered secondary (necessity being the mother of invention), were the flying shuttle and the spinning jenny. But what appears to have lit the fuse was the threat to our primitive fustian industry posed by the import of fine cheap printed cotton material from India. Had any one of these factors been missing or lacking in capacity, the industrial revolution might never have happened. Anywhere; ever.

Rather than being something that was willed by the people of Britain, the industrial revolution, with its accompanying social upheaval, was something which happened to them. Had a visionary government wanted to bring about such a rapid change, anticipating just some of the power and prestige which would ensue, it would not have got the ship of state off the chocks. Not until two centuries later would the government have had either an adequate command of the economy or the administrative capability for such an enterprise, even supposing there had been sufficient popular support. But even if these conditions were met, such a concurrence of circumstances, each of which was essential for the launch of the revolution, could not possibly have been engineered, because much of the science and technology on which the industrial revolution was based had yet to be discovered and invented. It is the nature of future discoveries and inventions that they are unpredictable and mostly unimaginable before their appearance.

In fact, increasingly during the 19th century, the role of the state was to act as a buffer between capitalism and the proletariat, and to oppose the exploitation of working people. Legislation was enacted to limit the employment of children and women, and to mitigate the worst effects of industrialisation on working conditions. Working people themselves formed trade unions, initially for mutual insurance to cover sickness and burial, later to improve rates of pay and conditions of work, to become later still an arm of the Labour party. By the beginning of the 20th century, society had adapted to the industrial revolution, and the outlook was optimistic. A century later, however, we view the long-term consequences of industrialisation with growing alarm.

## Capitalism: High Finance

The terms 'market economy' and 'capitalism' are often used interchangeably, but Braudel makes a clear distinction between them.[15] In the market economy, there is a direct link between traders and consumers, and the terms of trade are public; it is a public market. Capitalism, by contrast, operates in a private market, where the capitalist is an intermediary between producer and consumer; he alone knows how much is the producer's reward and how much the consumer pays, and hence the profitability of the deal. His is a private or anti-market (*le contre-marché*), where the intention is to circumvent the law of supply and demand which restrains profit in a public market. The public market is competitive, but the private market is monopolistic. While the anti-market is not without risk, the profits may be huge, and unlike the trader, who tends to specialise in the goods he sells, the capitalist is adaptable and will use his money on any profitable venture. Reminiscent of a selfish gene, the capitalist's money breeds money.

Thus for Braudel the economic system has three tiers, the uppermost being the high finance of capitalism, which merges with and is supported by the market economy, the whole edifice being grounded on the structures of everyday life, *la vie matérielle*. What counts as capital is not just the money available to the capitalist, but also those of his goods that are instrumental in making more money – his factory, newspaper or shipload of spices, in fact, anything that is giving a good return on investment. To pursue the selfish gene metaphor a little further, while money represents genotype, goods are phenotype, the embodiment of money, fittingly adapted to the current financial environment so as to beget the most progeny. The life cycle of capitalism starts with surplus money capital, which is then invested in commodities; in its maturity, capitalism spawns redoubled money capital which seeds the next capitalist cycle.

Although the accumulation of capital accelerated with the industrial revolution, capitalism as described by Braudel is ancient. Starting in the 15<sup>th</sup> century four long cycles of capital accumulation have been described, centred successively on Genoa, Amsterdam, London and New York, increasing in size and world power at each stage.[16] The latter two phases in particular demonstrate the interdependence of capitalism and the state, represented by Great Britain and the United States respectively. It is this emerging symbiotic relationship between capitalism and state government which will now be explored.

## Capitalism's Epicentre Comes to London

A key factor in Britain's capital growth in the 19th century was her access to raw materials and the immense markets afforded by her colonies, India in particular. In 1600, Queen Elizabeth granted a royal charter to the English East India Company which gave it a monopoly of trading rights in the east, where it acted as an agency for the British government until after the Indian mutiny in 1857. The company's private army successfully waged war against Dutch and French competition in India, and during the 19th century the company methodically conquered and annexed Indian territory until the English were in control of almost all of the sub-continent. The domiciliary textile industry there was destroyed by England's aggressive trade in machine made cotton goods, causing widespread unemployment and poverty, as did the reorganisation of agriculture to provide export crops. All military spending was covered by the Indian treasury, 70% of whose budget was earmarked for 'defence expenses'.[19] The upshot of the 'White man's burden' in India during just the 50 years from 1750-1800 was a return on investments of about £100 billion.[20]

Box 19

Capitalism

Economic historians have postulated a causal association between Christian ideology and the rapid expansion of capitalism in Western Europe, in particular, during the industrial revolution in Britain in the 18th century.[17,18] Root influences may be traced back at least to the sixth century and a ruling of Pope Gregory I to Augustine of Canterbury that marriage was to be based on mutual affection and consent rather than be, as hitherto, a means of forging political alliances and maintaining or increasing ownership of land. Close marriages and concubinage were forbidden, and adoption of orphaned children and remarriage of widows was discouraged. As a result, the number of families without male heirs increased and, as intended, the Church was the beneficiary, becoming a major land owner from bequests of land and property. An unintended result was the promotion of personal independence and individualism as families came to have a nuclear structure, with couples setting up on their own when they could afford to get married, often having already left the parental home to find work.

The political power of the Church was consolidated by Pope Gregory VII, who in 1075 asserted the ultimate supremacy of the papacy in secular as well as in church affairs, including the right to make or depose heads of state, his authority being backed by the threat of excommunication and eternal damnation. The increasing worldliness of the Church culminated in the gross excesses of the renaissance popes financed by taxes, tithes and the sale of remission for sins past and future in the shape of masses for the dead and indulgences for the living.

The papacy was the avaricious centre of the most highly organised financial, legal and administrative system of the age. Usury – charging high rates of interest on loans – was denounced from the pulpit but widely practised, and had papal protection. This was prototypical capitalism, in which a monopoly supplier was able to create the demand for spiritual goods for which it set the price.

The sale of indulgences – passports to paradise – was the main target for Luther's 95 theses nailed to the church door at Wittenberg in 1517, triggering the protestant revolution as well as his excommunication. His German translation of the New Testament was a breach in the Church's monopoly, making the scriptures available to the masses and showing that there was no biblical basis for the intermediacy of the priesthood between believers and their God. Luther's stand led to the establishment of protestant churches whose beliefs may be summarised as salvation by faith, as opposed to salvation by good works or cash in the unreformed Catholic Church. For protestants, individual freedom of conscience is paramount, and there is no central doctrinal authority other than the Bible, whose interpretation allows a wide range of beliefs. Thus, from the start, protestantism was characterised by its schisms: Luther believed in transubstantiation but condemned usury, while the Swiss reformer, Calvin, denied the former and accepted the latter; there are now hundreds of protestant sects differing in the minutiae of their beliefs and practices.

King Henry VIII's desire for a male heir, and his wife's failure to give him one, led to his requesting a divorce, a request which was difficult for the pontiff to grant since he had made a special dispensation for the marriage in the first place, Catherine of Aragon being the widow of Henry's elder brother. Henry's defiance in divorcing Catherine and marrying Anne Boleyn led to his excommunication and the establishment of the Anglican Church with the sovereign of England at its head. Dissolution of the monasteries followed, with seizure of church revenues and treasure, and sale of church lands. In respect of his beliefs, Henry remained a Catholic and, papal supremacy apart, he enforced Catholic dogma, though he did order a Bible in English to be placed in every parish church.

Protestantism was fully established in England when the Church, headed by Elizabeth I, adopted the Book of Common Prayer and 39 articles of faith which were sufficiently ambiguous for most of her subjects to accept, though there were some dissenters. An Act prohibiting all interest on loans – 'a vyce moste odyous' – was repealed by Elizabeth's government, and the Church of England could but acquiesce since Elizabeth was its head. During the next century ecclesiastical courts were swept away and the Church ceased to have any jurisdiction over social or economic matters. Notwithstanding the diminished sphere of influence of the Anglican Church, there were many Calvinists, known as Puritans, who were unwilling to conform to its liturgical practices or submit to the authority of its bishops and its sovereign head. Puritans tended to be members of the growing bourgeoisie of small traders and independent artisans who brought a new sense of vocation to their work. Rather than being a punishment for the sin of Adam – 'in the sweat of thy face shalt thou eat bread' – to toil was a calling in which Puritans engaged wholeheartedly for the greater glory of God. Salvation was a gift from God, and could not be attained by good works. Nevertheless, success in one's business was evidence of God's grace, a sign of being one of the Elect who had been saved. Conversely, being unsuccessful and poor was construed as a lack of God's grace and a moral failing. Whereas society was strengthened by charitable deeds inspired by the Catholic belief in salvation by good works, society was weakened by the solipsist protestant belief in salvation by faith, though the protestant contribution to philanthropic projects is undeniable. The successful Puritan merchant was required by his religion to be sober, modest, industrious and thrifty, but to be no more than honest and fair in his business affairs and in his dealings with people less fortunate than himself, from whom he generally kept himself and his family apart.

With the growth of world trade financed on an enlarging and impersonal scale, and a capitalist organisation of industry, the opinion grew that economic life was an area best left to businessmen, where moral principles had little place. The reversal of attitudes was complete in the 18th century with the development of economic theory which claimed that unfettered operation of the free market worked providentially for the benefit of society; to interfere with its operation would be wrong, going against natural law.

Thus, capitalism has its origins in the legal and financial infrastructure of the Catholic Church, whose cupidity had the unintended consequence of promoting individualism and defiance of authority, leading to the protestant revolution. Protestant values contributed to the blossoming of science in the Enlightenment, fuelling capitalism's rapid expansion in the industrial revolution. Capitalism is an unintended outcome of Christianity which could never have been predicted; it is now self-sustaining and operates in an amoral zone completely cut off from its origins.

The most notorious of the 'nabobs' returning from India to England having made a fortune, was Robert Clive. He started out as a clerk with the English East India Company, but came to lead his company's forces successfully against those of the French company. He spent three periods in India where he ended up as governor and commander-in-chief after a string of military victories which included Plassey, where he secured control of Bengal. When he finally returned to England, Clive had amassed a fabulous fortune with which he bought his way into parliament and acquired the title of First Baron Clive of Plassey. Assailed in the House of Commons, he defended himself eloquently pointing out that the directors of the East India Company had acquired an Empire more extensive than any kingdom in Europe. They had also acquired a revenue of £4 million and trade in proportion. Concerning his own fortune he said, 'I stand astonished at my own moderation.'[21]

As an aside we should note that it was the British government's desire that the East India Company should enjoy a monopoly position that precipitated the American war of independence and the loss of the American colonies.[22] The king himself and many members of the government were stockholders in the company, which had a large store of tea to dispose of. The company successfully sought to have its tea selectively exempted from tax, to enable it to undercut and put out of business the smugglers and independent tea merchants who were supplying the lucrative market of the American colonies. Thus, the Boston tea party was the first popular demonstration against the power of a multinational corporation to dump its subsidised produce on an unwilling market.

These British exploits in India and America illustrate some of the ways in which there developed a symbiotic relationship between the State and capitalism. With the formation of the United Kingdom with its excellent transport system and no internal trade barriers, the domestic market was greatly expanded to the benefit of those capitalists willing to exploit it. But while in the 18th century production for the domestic market increased by 52%, that for export rocketed by 450% as new markets were forcibly opened up by companies established and initially supported at arm's length by the mother country, and in the case of India, to be later placed directly under the protection of the government of Great Britain and her Royal Navy.[23] Her unilateral free trade policy meant that Britain was also a natural market for raw materials from the colonies, which needed sterling to pay for their imports of Britain's manufactured goods.

The Napoleonic wars served to weaken Britain's competitors in Europe, while at home the iron industry expanded rapidly in response to wartime needs, attracting capital from the cotton industry where the returns, initially 'fantastic', were now more modest. The battle of Waterloo (1815) marked the beginning of a hundred years of relative peace for Britain, though not for her European competitors, and the now surplus capacity of the iron industry came to provide railways and ships for Britain and the world.

As in Clive's case, the influence of the State and capitalism was mutual. Resourceful capitalists, beneficiaries of direct or indirect state support, promoted themselves into the realms of the good and the great whence they could influence government policy in their own favour. At the turn of the 19th century, the benches of the House of Lords were no longer the reserve of the landed aristocracy but were occupied by bankers, brewers, newspaper proprietors, and magnates from shipping, iron and engineering industries.[24] Many of these new plutocratic peers bought land with their plentiful millions on a massive scale, attempting to emulate the old territorial nobility. This abundance of money capital marked the maturity of this phase of capital accumulation centred on London.

## Capitalism's Epicentre Moves from London to New York

In America after the civil war there was a period of unprecedented expansion. Settlement spread through to the Pacific coast, closing the western frontier; east met west in 1869 as Union Pacific and Central Pacific railway tracks were joined in Utah. As the central plains were opened up, population increased from 50 to 75 million in just 20 years, 1880-1900.[25] A driving force behind American capitalism at this time was the development of the railways, and it was the railroad companies that instituted a new type of business management with so-called 'vertical' integration, combining within one corporation all the processes and transactions necessary for setting up and running the enterprise.[26] In the case of a railroad company, this would range from acquisition of land across a continent, laying track, building bridges, tunnels and stations, to printing tickets and training the ticket collectors. In the ten years after the civil war, 40,000 miles of track were constructed,[27] much of it with the aid of massive government subsidies and gifts of land.[28] Thus was opened up a huge market for the mass distribution of mass-produced goods from vertically integrated companies whose management structure set the pattern for today's corporations.[29] A number of these pioneering companies are still trading and are on the Fortune 500 list of wealthiest corporations (Union Pacific, Wells Fargo, and Sears Roebuck for example). American capitalism had from the start a symbiotic relationship with government, which was described as a paid agent, its scandals and deals becoming blatant.[30] The prospect of rich pickings attracted huge capital investment from London and elsewhere, well illustrated by Mr Melmotte's fraudulent promotion of the South Central Pacific and Mexican Railway in Trollope's *The Way We Live Now*.[31]

The 35 years between the end of the civil war and the end of the century was the golden time of American inventiveness, with McCormick's mechanical reaper, Edison's electric light bulb and phonograph, Bell's telephone, Eastman's Kodak camera and many more household and farm appliances now taken for granted.[32] It was an age of millionaires, of Rockefeller, Carnegie, Vanderbilt, Frick and Harriman, whose monopolistic empires were based respectively on oil, steel, steamers, coal and railroads, and of course, there was a banker, JP Morgan.

The 90s saw a reaction against capitalist excesses with the passage through Congress of the Sherman Antitrust Act against 'contracts and combinations in restraint of commerce...'.[33] Although this Act was aimed at the 'evils of massed capital', one of its first applications was against union leaders who had organised a strike, finding them guilty of conspiracy in restraint of commerce.

An economic downswing revealed the extent of discontent amongst industrial and farm workers, all hit by falling wages. Their cause was taken up by Bryan, the Democratic presidential candidate in the 1896 election. He was defeated, however, by the Republican McKinley with the aid of a large war chest raised from his industrialist supporters. This set the pattern for future presidential elections, in which the laurels were to be awarded usually to the candidate who raised most money, big business sponsoring the runner who would most likely further its aims.

Meanwhile, in the half-century preceding the Great War, Britain was earning substantial foreign exchange from the export of raw materials from her empire, much of which was invested abroad rather than being used to modernise industries at home. The greater part of Britain's foreign investments were made in the United States where the best returns were to be found, and the United States was accumulating a large foreign debt in loans and interest, amounting to $3,700 million (equivalent to about £760 million) in 1914.[34]

Historians still debate the causes of the First World War, but economic competition between Britain and Germany undoubtedly played a part. This was reflected in the race to assemble the largest navy, directed in England by Winston Churchill and on the German side by Kaiser Wilhelm II himself. The latter had been persuaded of the importance of mastery of the seas by *The Influence of Sea Power on History*, written by Captain Mahan, president of the American Naval War College, a copy of whose book was to be found, by order of the Kaiser, in every ship in the German navy.[35] That the Kaiser had learned his lesson well is borne out by the fact that while the combatant armies were bogged down on land, the most effective German weapon was the U-boat directed at Britain's supply lines at sea. Indeed, it was Germany's U-boat onslaught against American merchant shipping that brought the United States out of its state of neutrality in 1917.

Britain's wartime need for armaments, machinery and raw materials was largely supplied by the United States, and paid for by British stock liquidated at discount prices on the New York stock exchange. By the time the United States entered the war, Britain had run up huge American debts, and from then until the armistice had to borrow nearly £1000 million from the United States' government for bare essentials.[36] Thus, by the end of the first world war, Germany was out of the economic race and the relative financial positions of Britain and the United States had been substantially reversed.

The economic consequences of the Second World War were similar to those of the Great War, but greater in extent. America was Britain's granary, and its main source of materiel. Negotiations over the extent of the lend-lease programme were at times acrimonious, as neither Congress nor the treasury department had any great desire to assist an imperial power and economic rival.[37] With the surrender of Japan in August 1945, America's lend-lease programme to Britain was abruptly terminated, with Britain having a huge balance of payments deficit. Keynes, the economist who led British treasury negotiations, felt that since Britain had made much greater sacrifices for the common cause than the United States, a partial write-off of British debt and an American loan at a token interest rate would have been a just settlement. The Americans, however, never accepted that they owed Britain a moral debt, so Britain had to settle for a loan at a commercial rate of interest which was linked in negotiations at Bretton Woods to free-trade conditions targeted particularly at Britain's preference for imports from her empire.[38] The last instalment of the debt was paid on New Year's Eve, 2006.[39] The Special Relationship.

World War II had laid waste every major industrial area of the globe except North America. The result was that in 1945-6 the United States accounted for almost half the gross world production of goods and services, and enjoyed a technological lead symbolised by its atomic monopoly.[40] The arrival of peace thus saw America as the world's leading military and economic power, to which Britain was deeply in debt. Britain's policy of sparing no expense had enabled her to win the war with the Axis, but had lost her the economic race with her ally.

The United States' strong creditor position meant that its economy faced post-war stagnation because of a dollar shortage in its former markets in Western Europe, still dislocated

293

by poverty and unemployment, conditions in which the communist party had enhanced attractiveness for voters. Where Keynes' appeal to justice had failed, fear of communism then succeeded in winning the approval of Congress for the Marshall plan in which some $13 billion was given to 17 European countries, of which Britain's share was $2.7 billion.[41] The plan successfully initiated economic recovery in the recipient countries but there was a continuing dollar shortage at its expiration in the late 1940s. This liquidity problem was solved by US and European rearmament, with massive military aid to foreign governments and direct US military expenditure abroad during and after the Korean war.[42]

## Bretton Woods and After

In 1944 plans were being made for reconstruction in Europe after the war, which the Allies were now confident of winning. Negotiations were held in the United States at Bretton Woods in New Hampshire, where the British team was lead by John Maynard Keynes, and the American team by Harry Dexter White. Lord Keynes, knighted in 1917, had an aristocratic bearing and was considered to be the greatest economist of the day; the position of Britain, however, was that of supplicant. White had the reputation of being one of the pushiest, least agreeable men in town, and Keynes would have reinforced his instinctive prejudices against the ruling class of a decaying colonial power.[43] Furthermore, White represented the United States – the world's biggest creditor, and determined to stay that way.

Keynes had foreseen the post-war problem of lack of liquidity resulting from America's strong creditor status, and also that creditor and debtor countries would become locked into their respective positions of economic dominance and poverty if payment of interest from debtor to creditor was required. It was soon apparent, however, that Keynes' scheme of capital controls and creditor as well as debtor adjustment was a non-starter, and it would be the American proposal of an International Stabilisation Fund and the International Bank for Reconstruction and Development that would prevail; the former became the International Monetary Fund (IMF), and the latter the World Bank. Participating countries would contribute to the fund, and the amount of their contribution would determine their borrowing limit and their voting rights. The United States contributed the most, which gave it enough votes to block any proposal of other countries should it so wish. All exchange rates were fixed against the dollar which was the only currency convertible to gold, thus ensuring the hegemony of the dollar as the world's reserve currency. Finally, White determined that both the fund and the bank would be sited in Washington with a staff of 300 and fulltime executive directors who would be lavishly reimbursed.[44] This proved to be a perfect formula for continued US economic dominance and the permanent indebtedness of the poor nations.[45]

The problem of Europe's post-war indebtedness was solved, not by IMF loans, but by the Marshall plan' and by United States' and European rearmament. Impoverished developing countries outside Europe, however, had to depend on loans from the IMF, the World Bank or the United States' Agency for International Development (USAID), but crippling terms and conditions often lead to entrapment in poverty. John Perkins in *Confessions of an Economic Hit Man* describes how an exaggerated forecast would be made of the benefits of investment in a developing country so as to encourage the acceptance of a large development loan that ensured perpetual indebtedness and political loyalty; contracts would be with United States' engineering and construction companies.[46] In this way, development funds pass directly from bank to corporation, and the 'beneficiary' is left to repay the loan from the economic growth that is never as great as predicted.

The "Core of Engineers"

Thus each person born in Latin America in 2003 already owed $1600 in foreign debt, or $336 if born in Sub-Saharan Africa. Between 1980 and 2000 the total debt of Southern countries increased from $567 billion to more than $2 trillion, in spite of their having paid off $3.45 trillion in interest and write-offs during that time.[47] In 2008, the world's 142 emerging and developing countries owed $2.7 trillion to rich country creditors and in that year paid them $514 billion in a combination of interest charges and repayment of capital. For every $1 the developing countries receive in aid, they pay $5 in debt service.[48] The extent of third world indebtedness is all the more shocking when it is recalled that the developed countries owe much of their wealth to the exploitation in the past of these former colonies.

Another institution that was conceived at Bretton Woods was The General Agreement on Tariffs and Trade (GATT). This was a forum for negotiating international trade agreements and treaties. Under the American constitution, a treaty ratified on behalf of the United States becomes the supreme law of the land, overriding any federal, state or local law to the contrary. Concerns about the loss of sovereignty entailed by GATT kept it from being ratified for half a century, but under the Reagan administration, which looked favourably on deregulating big business, multinational corporations lobbied for ratification of GATT, which would ease restrictions on their activities overseas. Eventually in 1995, Bill Clinton, in the final days of his first four year term, and just before the Christmas recess, brought the GATT agreement to pass.[49] With its ratification, GATT was superseded by the World Trade Organization (WTO) with its headquarters in Geneva.

By 2009 the WTO had 153 member nations accounting for more than 97% of world trade,[50] of which 70% is conducted by multinational corporations.[51] All member nations agree to surrender their own sovereignty in matters of trade to the supremacy of the WTO. Whereas GATT had mainly dealt with trade in goods, WTO agreements also cover trade in services, inventions and other intellectual property. The mission statement of the World Bank is 'Our dream is a world without poverty', but the narrow aim of the WTO is 'to help producers of goods and services, exporters, and importers conduct their business.' The first among its list of benefits is 'The system helps promote peace'. There is no doubt that peace and international trade do go hand in hand – this was also the rationale behind the establishment of the European Economic Community after the Second World War. But the functioning of the three institutions that arose from Bretton Woods – the IMF, the WTO and the World Bank – may be seen now as a neoliberal economic project that furthered the United States' hegemonic ambitions.

The narrow economic agenda of this 'Washington consensus' is free trade, free flow of capital, flexible exchange rates, market determined interest rates, the deregulation of all markets, and transfer of assets from the public to the private sector.[52] Joseph Stiglitz, former chief economist of the World Bank, has described how the rigid application of these principles to developing countries has often exacerbated poverty and corroded the very fabric of the societies they were meant to be helping.[53] Free trade for a developing country may mean opening up its domestic market to imports of subsidised agricultural produce from developed countries. Thus 80% of tomatoes in West Africa come from Europe, and the local industry has been nearly destroyed. In accordance with Ricardo's law of comparative advantage, free trade also means turning from traditional mixed agriculture to production of a cash crop for export. This may result in overproduction and falling prices as other developing countries do the same. Thus cotton prices fell 47% from 1998-2001 and coffee by 69%. Free

297

flow of capital often comes with conditions such as flexibility of labour regulations, meaning that working people have to work longer hours and take a reduction in wages. Thus salaries in Mexico fell so much after the country joined the North American Free Trade Agreement (NAFTA) that a worker in an American owned factory could no longer support a family. Privatisation may mean the acquisition of public utilities by multinational corporations at bargain prices, with subsequent price hikes for consumers. Thus the people of Cochabamba were unable to pay for their water after a take-over by multinational Bechtel.[54] *The same with Privatised Water in UK.*

Although we cannot draw general conclusions from these particular examples, and counter examples could surely be found, it does appear that developing countries within the WTO are at a disadvantage compared with the major industrialised nations. Although every country in WTO has one vote, this cannot be considered truly democratic as long as Iceland has the same voice as India, no account being taken of a country's population. Moreover, although developing countries outnumber industrialised ones, agreements are made by consensus, so that a majority wish may be thwarted by a single veto. In fact, negotiations between the most powerful members take place behind closed doors, and their decisions are then presented as a fait accompli to the whole membership, pressure being applied to developing countries to be compliant.[55] Disputes between member states, or between corporations and national governments, are adjudicated by a disputes resolution panel consisting of three to five unnamed experts who meet in secret and whose deliberations are never made public.[56] In these various ways the power structure of the WTO is unfavourable to developing countries compared with the United States, other major industrial nations and their multinational corporations.

The moral philosopher Peter Singer considers four charges made against the WTO: that it places economic considerations ahead of concerns for the environment, animal welfare, and even human rights; that it erodes national sovereignty; that it is undemocratic; and that it increases inequality.[57] He concludes that the WTO is guilty on the first three charges but the verdict is not proven on the last, that it makes the rich richer and the poor poorer. Nevertheless, the gap between the world's poorest and richest states is now greater than it has ever been, and is increasing.[58] The richest 20% of the world population have 82.7% of world income, while the poorest 20% have only 1.4%, a 'champagne glass' distribution of wealth, wide at the top and narrow at the bottom.

In Africa, for example, in spite of long IMF involvement, and many structural adjustment loans and stand-byes, the gross domestic product (GDP) per capita has not moved from its level of 20 years ago, and in 24 African countries it is less than in 1975; in 12 countries it is even below its 1960s level.[59]

## The Rise of the Corporation

We have already encountered the English East India Company that was established in the 17th century to promote trade to the Far East. This was a joint-stock company, in which a small number of shareholders pooled their resources to own and run the company, and for whose debts they were personally responsible. The expenses they would incur if one of their ships was lost with all hands, for example, could entail the shareholders in the loss of far more than their initial investment; shareholding therefore tended to be a rich man's pursuit.

Box 20

The Banking System

The banking system came into existence as a means of providing credit to enable people and companies to obtain goods and services before payment (Latin *credere* – to believe, to trust). The simplest system is represented by a non-profit mutual building society where depositors' funds are borrowed for house purchase, the administration costs being met from the difference in interest rates for deposits and loans; the society is in effect owned by the depositors. If loans are less than the value of the properties bought with them, and no more than 2-3 times the annual income of the borrower, the deposited money is 'as safe as houses'. If a borrower defaults on repayments, the property can be repossessed and the mortgage redeemed. Even with a conservative lending policy, about 90% of depositors' money is out on loan, so the money remaining in the society's vaults is the security for a loan nine times as great: the 'leverage' is 9:1.

A commercial or 'high street' bank is owned, not by the depositors, but by the shareholders, who receive a dividend and expect their shares to increase in value. The needs of the shareholders compete with those of the customers, and this may result in a bigger difference in interest rates for depositors and borrowers than in a mutual society. To increase its income further, the bank may make riskier loans justifying higher interest rates, at the same time as having higher leverage. To meet a sudden demand for cash in excess of reserves, banks may borrow from each other or from a central bank.

The 'shadow' banking system, which includes investment banks, hedge funds and markets for bonds, futures and other derivatives, provides a range of financial services and products to banks and business which are not directly available to the public. Regulation is much less strict than for high street banks, and transactions are on a larger scale, with high profits and bonuses allied to greater risk. Investment banks may have leverages as high as 40:1 as borrowed funds are used for investment, exposing them to huge losses.

A derivative is not a commodity itself – such as a wheat harvest – but might be its future price. A farmer's risk may be 'hedged' by a contract agreeing the price at which next year's harvest will be bought. While providing some security for the producer, derivatives also form a vehicle for risky speculative trading using hedge funds.

Traders also deal in shares, or in a national currency, and may make a profit whether prices are rising or falling. The financier George Soros famously made $1 billion on Black Wednesday by gambling on a fall in the value of the pound, forcing Britain out of the exchange rate mechanism (ERM). He sold $10 billions' worth of sterling (some of it borrowed), then bought it back at a reduced price after devaluation.[61] Deals like this are 'zero sum', not adding any value to the global economy. Soros' gain was the British people's loss since they then had to pay more for foreign imports.

Globally, the volume of money exchange is many times that of traded commodities, and an army of brokers, dealers, traders, fund managers, accountants and lawyers, all taking their cut, comes between investors and would-be borrowers needing credit. The banking system has become self-serving and parasitic on the real economy. Because of its size, complexity and hyperactivity it is a chaotic system liable to act in unprecedented and unforeseen ways, of which the collapse in 2008 provides a good example.

In the 19th century, the great expansion of industry created an unprecedented need for more capital, which could only be met through wider share ownership. This was encouraged by a change of the law to permit the establishment of limited liability companies in which shareholders' liability is limited to the amount of their investment; shareholders are liable neither for debts nor for any illegal actions of the company.[60] Limited liability companies are run on behalf of the shareholders by a board of directors. Although shareholders have the right to vote on a company's policies and appointments, it is a right more honoured in the breach than the observance, and the directors usually have a free hand in running the company, or the corporation as it is known in the United States.

In America, individual states authorised the setting up of corporations, and vied with each other to attract them. This led to the repeal of rules restricting corporations to a narrow range of activity, or for a limited tenure, or for operation in a defined location. Rules on mergers were also relaxed and as a consequence some 1800 corporations were consolidated into 157 between 1898 and 1904.[62] Millionaire Rockefeller's Standard Oil Company notoriously took over many small businesses by fair means and foul until it controlled 80% of oil output and was sanctioned by the Supreme Court under the Sherman Antitrust Act.[63]

Another of the large American corporations was the Ford Motor Car Company, where the hugely successful Model T was the first car in history to be built on an assembly line. The workers were paid substantially more than the going rate, but the thinking here was not entirely altruistic as Henry Ford saw the possibility of creating a large new market among the workers themselves. In 1916 he decided that he would cancel the dividend due to shareholders, and use the money to reduce further the car's price.[64] Some of the shareholders were not pleased at this unwonted generosity at their expense, and brought a successful action against him. The judge ruled that the overriding obligation of a corporation and its directors is to maximise profit for the shareholders – so Ford was compelled to restore the dividend. This ruling means that it is illegal for a public limited company or corporation to have any objective, however worthy it might be, other than to be maximally profitable. The welfare of its workers, or care for the environment, is not a legitimate company aim except insofar as it might increase profitability. Any activity under the banner of corporate social responsibility is not undertaken in good faith, but for ulterior motives. A corporation's obligation to maximise profit often conflicts with its obligation to comply with the law, concerning working conditions or the environment, for example. If the chances of getting away with a breach of regulations are good, and the fines are in any case less than the cost of compliance, then the less expensive path will be followed, the fine being considered an unavoidable cost of doing business.[65] Because corporate decisions are often taken jointly by a number of people, culpability is seldom attributed to an individual but to the corporation.

In 1886 there was another change in the corporation's legal standing which has had far-reaching consequences, such that today the corporation is the most dominant institution in the world.[66] It arose out of a case before the United States' Supreme Court, *Santa Clara County v Southern Pacific Railroad Company*, in which the railroad company disputed six years' property taxes owed to Santa Clara County in California.[67] Among the arguments used by the defence was that the county was attempting to impose a burden of taxation on the corporation which it would not have imposed on a natural person. In several previous cases, corporation lawyers had made the claim that the corporation is a person within the meaning of the 14th amendment, which forbids a state to deny to any person within its jurisdiction the equal protection of the laws. This amendment had been added to the constitution after the civil war with the intention that freed slaves should enjoy the same legal privileges as whites. Although the corporation was obviously not a natural person, as a defence ploy it was worth a try, since historically, corporations had been referred to as artificial persons. In the event, the railroad company won the case, but on the simpler grounds that the tax had been wrongly assessed. The Chief Justice did not formally rule on the more contentious issue of whether or not a corporation is a person, but the court reporter had added a note to the court record to that effect. Although this note had no legal standing whatsoever, this case has been cited ever since, and the principle, that corporations have the status of natural persons, is now deeply embedded in American law.

Although the 14th amendment was intended to protect Negroes, it has in fact been invoked much more often to provide protection for corporations, which, like natural persons, now have the right to freedom of expression, as contained in the first amendment. Hence, corporations have the right to spend whatever they want on lobbyists, of whom there are 20,000 in Washington, in order to get their point of view heard by members of congress. It is significant that while corporations have the right of freedom of expression, trade unions do not because they are considered to be artificial rather than natural persons. The fourth amendment gives corporations the right to privacy and freedom from unreasonable searches, including random inspections from the Environmental Protection Agency (EPA). The fifth amendment gives corporations the right to decline to testify against themselves, or to be tried twice for the same crime.[68]

A business enterprise, such as a quarry, factory or office block, will often have a substantial impact on the environment and infrastructure of the locality where it is sited. As far as possible the corporation that owns the enterprise will try and 'externalise' the costs of any third party consequences of its operations. The community rather than the corporation will thus find itself having to pay for environmental clean-up, transport links, provision of emergency services, and so on. But the implications of externalising costs go further. Just as a company may make a cost-benefit calculation and conclude that the most profitable course is to act illegally and pay the penalty if found out, it may also conclude that it would be cheaper to pay compensation claims rather than to install a safety feature that would prevent an accident from occurring. Thus, General Motors notoriously included in its cost-benefit calculations the cost of compensation for 500 fatalities caused by vehicle fires, and concluded that it would be cheaper to pay up than to relocate the fuel tank so that a fire was less likely to occur following a rear impact collision; $6 per vehicle was saved by this decision.[69]

A corporation's ultimate purpose, then, is to maximise profit, which, as Joel Bakan has described in *The Corporation*, it does with the ruthlessness of a psychopath. As such, the corporation is very much the creature of capitalism in the sense of the word as used by Braudel: the very antithesis of the free market in which a multitude of producers compete to sell their goods to a multitude of informed consumers. A corporation's preferred way of working is to engulf or form a cartel with a rival rather than compete with it, and to do its deals in secret. In the past, corporate capitalism has thrived from its symbiotic relationship with government, and true to form, it has today achieved its full flowering implanted in Washington. Located there is a huge public relations industry which, as well as lobbying Congress, runs publicity campaigns to influence public opinion according to the brief of the employing industry.[70] The tobacco industry notoriously ran a disinformation campaign concerning the health effects of smoking, and the fossil fuel industry continues to deny global warming.

Big business also contributes millions of dollars to support election campaigns, for which the expected payback may be repeal of regulating legislation, a government contract, or a tax break. It is, of course, difficult to establish a direct connection between a donation to a political party and ensuing beneficial legislation, but knowing the pivotal role of profit in big business, it would be surprising if politicians did not make it worthwhile for businessmen to support them. And then there is the 'revolving door' between big business and government, through which high ranking ministers or officials pass from government to industry taking commercially useful inside information with them. Or, corporation lawyers may pass in the reverse direction, having been seconded to government to assist in formulating legislation for monitoring the industry for which they work.[71] One of the results of this collusion is an increasing reliance on industry itself to monitor compliance with such regulations that still remain in force, which has been likened to asking the fox to guard the chicken coop.

It should not be thought that this symbiosis with government and subversion of democracy is confined to the United States. Multinational corporations operate with the same ruthlessness in dozens of countries, with loyalties to none. Wal-Mart, top of the Fortune 500 list, and with an appalling history of labour relations in the United States, is operating in Britain as Asda.[72] Multinational Tesco with 2282 stores in Britain, and 1640 stores in 14 other countries in Eastern Europe and the Far East, announced record £3 billion profits in April 2009.[73] George Monbiot in *Captive State* has exposed the extent of collusion between big business and local and national government in Britain, particularly concerning supermarket planning applications. He devotes a whole chapter to *The Fat Cats Directory* in which he details the movement of senior personnel between big business and government, starting with Lord Marshall of Knightsbridge, who, as chairman of British Airways, campaigned against an aviation fuel tax as a means of reducing greenhouse gas emissions; he was subsequently in charge of Gordon Brown's energy tax review that was set in the context of global warming.[74] In Brussels, 15,000 lobbyists, largely representing big business, attempt to sway decisions of the European Union; a group of NGOs is petitioning that their influence should be curtailed.[75]

Big business is now involved in domains that hitherto have been public: education, health, the care of prisoners, or the elderly. Naomi Klein, in *No Logo*, has drawn attention to the intrusion of big business into daily life, with loss of public space, loss of choice and loss of jobs arising from our increasingly branded world.[76] We no longer shop in the high street, but in a mall where no dissent or political demonstration is allowed, and from which undesirables will be ejected. Choice is restricted to the same handful of chain stores in every city, as small independent businesses are driven out. Jobs in manufacturing and assembly are lost as this work is outsourced to sweat shops in developing countries. Big business puts its logo on sport, music and art, and infiltrates schools and universities. The corporation has indeed become the dominant institution in the world.

## The World Economic Crisis

The economic crash of 2008 was considered by some to herald the end of capitalism.[77] Rather, it indicated the creative ingenuity of capitalism, and the extent to which capitalism and government are locked in an interdependent relationship, each reliant for its survival on the other. The crash had many causes, amongst which was the deregulation of financial markets for which the industry had lobbied during the Reagan/ Thatcher era. In the US the Glass-Steagall Act separating investment and commercial banks was repealed, and in the UK demutualisation of building societies was allowed; also, the rules concerning the amount of capital to be held by banks were relaxed. The ideology of free trade, free movement of capital, flexible exchange rates and deregulation of all markets having been widely implemented, any local economic difficulty was then liable to become global.

The immediate cause of the global crash was the bubble in the US housing market, in turn encouraged by low interest rates intended to boost the US economy after the 9/11 attack.[78] Mortgages were sold aggressively to sub-prime borrowers by dealers paid on commission. The loans were then packaged into securities and conveyed to specially created legally independent 'vehicles', from which they were then sold to investment banks as mortgage backed securities. The initial loans having been passed on, mortgage banks were then able to issue more housing loans to less and less credit-worthy borrowers, many of whom defaulted in their repayments. These sub-prime mortgages now became 'toxic' assets of investment banks around the world. Because of the way they had been packaged, mortgage backed securities were far from secure, though the degree of risk was unknown since the number of borrowers who would later default in their repayments could not be known. The result was a widespread loss of confidence so that inter-bank lending came to a halt, and credit for the conduct of business dried up.

Amongst those holding toxic assets was the British bank, the demutualised Northern Rock.[79] As mortgage backed securities became unsaleable its investment branch incurred heavy losses, resulting in a run on its savings bank which was subsequently nationalised. Other banks which were said to be 'too big to fail' were similarly bailed out by government, at the same time as the scale of bankers' and traders' salaries and bonuses became known. Even as the stock market was in free fall, traders were profiteering by 'short selling'. It was justly said that bankers took the profits while taxpayers, through their governments, paid for their losses.

When an economy is growing and there is low unemployment, the government takes the credit and reaps the electoral rewards. Conversely, when there is a recession, with financial and job insecurity, the government of the day takes the rap, and has to be seen to be acting decisively to deal with the crisis, while not accepting responsibility for it. In the US and the UK, as well as there being a meltdown of the economy, government and private debt were both at an all-time high. Action was needed, but in contrary directions: the government needed to invest heavily in infrastructure projects – including renewable energy and energy efficiency – to stimulate the economy, while reducing its public spending to bring down its debt. Similarly, domestic consumption needed to be increased or at least maintained, while personal debt had to be reduced. And the banks were required to make more credit available for business, at the same time as increasing their capital reserves. The former 'spend now, repay later' approach prevailed, with future repayments of national and private debt being predicated on economic growth.

Thus, government needs the capitalist enterprise to provide economic growth, essential for electoral support, while capitalist ventures, in order to thrive, need the backing of government for handouts in hard times, and a hands-off approach in good times. This mutually dependent relationship is self-serving and self-perpetuating, and begs the fundamental question as to what economic growth is for. ⁊?

## The Pursuit of Happiness

In developed countries economic growth has resulted in large improvements in living standards, and this is its strong justification. Increased prosperity, however, has not generally made people happier. In the United States, although real income per head has more than doubled in 50 years, the proportion of people describing themselves as 'very happy' has not increased, nor has the proportion 'not very happy' fallen.[80] Similarly, in a group of affluent western countries, additional income was not associated with greater happiness.[81]

Increased affluence during the last century has had a favourable impact on health, and this is reflected in increased life expectancy. Rising incomes and the decline of poverty have lifted populations out of absolute material need, but once the basic conditions for health have been established, the curve of rising life expectancy with increasing wealth levels off. Thus, life expectancy among the richest countries is no longer related to how rich they are, and although the United States, for example, is the richest country in the world, life expectancy there is shorter than it is in most other developed countries – including some that are only half as rich.[82]

In *The Impact of Inequality: How to Make Sick Societies Healthier,* sociologist Richard Wilkinson claims that what *does* influence expectation of life in developed countries is not absolute, but relative poverty, indicated by inequality of incomes between the richest and poorest classes in society. The negative correlation between income inequality and expectation of life is very robust and has been shown in many studies comparing different countries, or different regions within countries. The magnitude of the effect of inequality on health and longevity is substantial, and a study from the United States showed that the difference in life expectancy between 16-year old blacks in poor areas and 16-year old whites in rich areas was about 16 years. At birth, taking account of deaths in infancy and childhood, expectation of life was 20-25% less for blacks than for whites.[83] Differences in incomes almost wholly accounted for differences in black and white death rates.

The period of Mrs Thatcher's premiership saw a large rise in inequality also in Britain, which is one of the most unequal societies in Western Europe. Inequality has not fallen significantly under subsequent labour governments, and although there has been some reduction of child and pensioner poverty, income inequality is now at its highest level since comparable series began in 1961.[84]

Besides being related to life expectancy, the extent of income inequality correlates positively with homicide rates, and negatively with social capital, a measure of the strength of civic life. Wilkinson argues persuasively that besides loss of life expectancy for poor people, inequality leads to a decline in the quality of social relationships which become less caring and more conflictual. Less egalitarian societies have more violent crime, less trust, less involvement in community life, and more racism, so that the quality of life for all members of society is reduced. The psychosocial mechanisms activated by relative poverty involve a powerful sense of shame at loss of status.

Thus, in developed countries continued economic growth is no longer contributing to greater happiness or health. Indeed, insofar as increased affluence is associated with greater inequality, it is detrimental to the health of the less well off and inimical to social relations and quality of life throughout society. Moreover:

> [G]reater inequality is perhaps the most significant obstacle to the development of an environmentally sustainable level of economic activity. By increasing status competition, inequality adds to the pressure to consume as a way of expressing social status. It

condemns us to ever-spiralling economic growth, destruction of resources, and environmental pollution.[85]

## Whither Capitalism?

The English edition of the communist manifesto was published in 1882, and its opening words are 'The history of all hitherto existing society is the history of class struggles.'[86] Marx and Engels asserted that the many layers of society had become condensed and polarised into two irreconcilable classes, the proletariat and the bourgeoisie, implacably hostile to each other. In the 21st century this basic premise is clearly false, and even in Marx's time there was movement between the classes, of workers who made good and became capitalists, and of capitalists who failed and became workers. We have seen too how that arch-capitalist Henry Ford saw the value of mutual cooperation, if not of collusion, between the capitalist enterprise and the workers.

According to classical economic theory, privation, inequality of wealth, and a measure of insecurity are all necessary for the efficient functioning of our economic system, which, according to Karl Marx, will ultimately self-destruct. Capital, the means of production, will come to be concentrated into so few hands that it will then be easily overthrown by violent revolution of the proletariat who have been moulded into a unified and disciplined force by the capitalist system itself.

> The development of modern industry…cuts from under its feet the very foundations on which the bourgeoisie produces and appropriates products. What the bourgeoisie, therefore, produces, above all, is its own grave-diggers. Its fall and the victory of the proletariat are equally inevitable.[87]

312

That prediction, being based on the false premise of a polarisation of society into just two classes, seems unlikely to be fulfilled. If ever there was a time when the proletariat revolution might have taken place it was surely in 1914 when the Socialist International urged workers of different countries not to fight each other in the imminent war. Unfortunately, national loyalties prevailed over international and revolutionary aspirations.

In the past century working people in developed countries have benefited from economic growth at least as much as capitalists, and they now enjoy a standard of living which is far above the 'threshold of wretchedness' of classical economic theory. The proletariat has been transformed into a willing domestic market for the products of capitalism. But the collaboration between working people and capitalism goes beyond the acquisition of material goods as more and more people become reliant on personal pensions derived from investments in capitalist enterprises. And with the extension of investment accounts and share ownership, ordinary folk literally buy into the capitalist idea that one can make money simply by playing the stock market. Marx's interpretation of history as a class struggle was very much of its time, and if it had some validity then, it has lost it now.

The economist Joseph Schumpeter advanced the thesis that while there is no inherent flaw in capitalism itself which would bring about its destruction, its very success would undermine the social institutions that sustain it, leading inevitably to its demise; for Schumpeter, socialism would be the successor to capitalism.[88] Thus, arguing from different premises he reaches much the same conclusion as Marx, though differing from him on the way. For a start, the capitalist engine of mass production, far from exploiting them ruthlessly, benefits the masses more than those better off.

Queen Elizabeth [I] owned silk stockings. The capitalist achievement does not typically consist in providing more silk stockings for queens, but in bringing them within the reach of factory girls in return for steadily decreasing amounts of effort.[89]

Schumpeter considered that the threat to capitalism would arise not in the lower but in the higher strata of capitalist society. He speaks of 'the obsolescence of the entrepreneurial function' brought about by the replacement of proprietors having a personal interest in the company, with salaried executives who are, in effect, office workers, totally lacking in vision, social position and prestige.[90] It suffices to point out that his predictions concerning entrepreneurial obsolescence are not borne out by the likes of Richard Branson, Bill Gates or the creators of Google, and evidence of social position and prestige, not to mention political influence, is there for all to see in the pages of *The Fat Cats Directory*.[91]

A better case for the decline, if not the demise, of capitalism is presented by Immanuel Wallerstein.[92] There are three areas where capitalism is increasingly constrained, with consequent reduction of profits: wages, raw materials, and taxation. With unionisation of the workforce and legislation on wages and hours of work, the cost of labour as a proportion of the cost of the final product is going up. Prices of raw materials, too, are rising due to their growing scarcity and the increased costs of extraction. In addition, companies are having to internalise the costs of mitigating the environmental impact of their operations. Finally, business is an obvious source of tax to fund increasing welfare benefits which governments of countries in which capitalist enterprises operate are expected to provide.

Although these factors may restrain capitalism and limit its profitability, they do not constitute a fatal attack. Moreover, they apply across the board to all capitalist enterprises, which will continue to compete with each other, in particular, by trying to escape these constraints. Schumpeter considered the possibility, only to dismiss it, that capitalism would eventually come to an end because there would no longer be any investment opportunities, all our material needs and wants having been sated.[93] A more plausible scenario is that supplies of raw materials would become exhausted, but in this case, such is the versatility of capitalism, we would end up paying through the nose for fresh air and sunshine. Schumpeter argued rather that capitalism would perish because of its destruction of the social institutions that support it. That thesis may be reformulated: capitalism will survive, but the society which hosts it will be irreparably damaged.

Big business, in seeking to reduce labour costs may relocate to another country, leading to job losses in the host country, causing much social distress and tension. Or the host country may seek to prevent this outsourcing of jobs by deregulation of labour conditions, in effect maintaining the company's profits at the workers' expense. Non-compliance of industry with environmental regulations may be abetted implicitly by government when funding for environment agencies is reduced. Or environmental regulations may be repealed, so that the financial costs of 'externalities' are again borne by the community, or else pollution is unmitigated and the community's quality of life is degraded. In order to avoid tax, a corporation may relocate its headquarters offshore, or relocate its whole operation elsewhere. To obviate this, the government may give the industry a tax break and cut back on welfare spending to compensate for its loss of revenues. At the same time as companies are seeking to evade paying their way, chief executive officers are awarding themselves ever larger salaries, now averaging more than £3 million per annum for directors of FTSE 100 companies, greater than 100 times the pay of the average worker.[94]

In these various ways society is being harmed by its accommodation with capitalism, but the damage goes deeper still with spreading legitimation and acceptance of greed and selfishness. As Adam Smith said, it is not from the benevolence of the baker and the brewer that we expect to get our sustenance, but from their self-interest. *Homo economicus* strives to maximise his interests in market transactions; pursuit of private gain is rational, but by insinuation, other modes of behaviour are not. *Homo economicus* does not concern himself with other people except perhaps those of his immediate family. This is what Mrs Thatcher meant when she said 'There is no such thing as society. There are individual men and women, and there are families.'[95]

The Reagan/Thatcher era saw selfishness legitimised, and *Greed is good* become the watchword.[96] Extension of share ownership exemplifies the zeitgeist. Neither the nature of the business in which people are investing, nor its provenance is of interest, only its profitability. Share ownership does not imbue any loyalty to the company or to the country where it is registered. Any hint of a fall in share value and the investment is withdrawn and placed somewhere more profitable. In this way investors' behaviour has come to reflect and reinforce that of the psychopathic multinational corporations in which they are investing.

There is a more fundamental reason for being wary of our capitalist economic system: its growth. There is growth at corporate, national and global levels; growth in service and manufacturing industries; growth in money markets; growth in banking. Exponential growth of any human enterprise depends ultimately on the availability of energy and raw materials; an increasing quantity of waste is also generated. On a finite planet, an economy predicated on indefinite growth would appear to be foredoomed.

In the economics literature the words 'momentum', 'dynamic' and 'organic' keep cropping up, as well as the phrases 'taking on a life of its own' and 'out of control'. In *The Communist Manifesto* we read of:

> ...a society that has conjured up such gigantic means of production and of exchange, is like the sorcerer, who is no longer able to control the powers of the netherworld whom he has called up by his spells.[97]

The authors were well aware of the theory of evolution, and hoped that they would do for history what Darwin had done for biology.[98] Schumpeter is explicit in his use of an evolutionary metaphor, speaking of industrial mutation that incessantly revolutionises the economic structure from within, a process of Creative Destruction being the essential fact about capitalism.[99] Braudel, too, emphasises capitalism's flexibility and its capacity for change and adaptation, describing the anti-market as a zone in which great predators roam and the law of the jungle operates.[100]

## Summing Up

Economic growth, that is, growth in the production and exchange of goods and services, has raised the standard of living in developed countries to such an extent that our material needs for survival are amply met, and further increase in wealth will neither extend our longevity nor increase our happiness. Indeed, during the last quarter century, increased wealth has been associated with an increase in inequality and relative poverty, both nationally and globally. Because of our evolutionary history as an intensely social species, the low status associated with poverty has an adverse effect on happiness and health, leading to reduction of life expectancy and degeneration of civic society.

Capitalism, the upper layer of the economic system, exhibits an evolutionary history, which though instigated and perpetuated by human action is now out of control due in large part to its symbiotic relationship with government. Capitalism's Darwinian advance is causing environmental degradation, depletion of resources and societal collapse, and has given origin to great predatory institutions of which the dominant species is the multinational corporation. As with the evolution of life, an awareness and understanding of the evolution of capitalism does not enable us to direct it, and its course is blind with no purpose other than self promotion and self perpetuation. If we were to rewind the tape of history and play it again the result would be different because at many points in time the route taken has been a matter of pure contingency, as in the case of *Santa Clara County v Southern Pacific Railroad Company*. Or it has resulted from a unique concurrence of circumstances, like the industrial revolution starting in Britain, or a clash of personalities, as at Bretton Woods. While individual actions have altered the outcome of events, this is often apparent only in retrospect, and in ways different from planned: Kaiser Wilhelm's espousal of mastery of the seas had the unintended consequence of bringing America into the First World War, leading to Germany's defeat.

For most of the time, most of us are merely bystanders caught up and swept through history by an economic system, which, like ourselves, is the result of a haphazard evolutionary process with its own dynamic over which we have little or no control.

# Notes

## Chapter 7: Evolution of Capitalism

1   Fernand Braudel. *Civilisation Matérielle, Économie et Capitalisme XVᵉ-XVIIIᵉ siècle. 3. Le Temps du Monde.* Paris: Armand Colin, 1979, p798. *La Vie Matérielle* is translated rather unsatisfactorily into *material life*, which is why the original French is retained here.

2   Fernand Braudel. *La Dynamique de Capitalisme.* Paris: Flammarion, 1985: p21.

3   Karl Polanyi. *The Great Transformation: the Political and Economic Origins of our Time.* Boston: Beacon Press, 2nd ed, 2001: p48-49.

4   World Trade Organization website: www.wto.org/english/res_e/reser_e/cadv_e.htm

5   Herman E Daly, John B Cobb Jr. *For the Common Good: Redirecting the Economy Toward Community, the Environment, and a Sustainable Future.* Boston: Beacon Press, 2nd ed 1994: p216.

6   Ibid, p25.

7   Joseph Townsend, *Dissertation on the Poor Laws 1786 by a Well-Wisher of Mankind.* Quoted in Karl Polanyi. *The Great Transformation: the Political and Economic Origins of our Time.* Boston: Beacon Press, 2nd ed, 2001: p118.

8   Fernand Braudel. *Civilisation Matérielle, Économie et Capitalisme XVᵉ-XVIIIᵉ siècle. 3. Le Temps du Monde.* Paris: Armand Colin, 1979, p 774-6.

9   David Cannadine. *The Decline and Fall of the British Aristocracy.* London: Papermac, 1996: p9.

10  David Held. *Global Covenant: the Social Democratic Alternative to the Washington Consensus.* Cambridge: Polity Press Ltd, 2004: p26.

11  Karl Polanyi. *The Great Transformation: the Political and Economic Origins of our Time.* Boston: Beacon Press, 2nd ed, 2001: p71-80.

12  RH Tawney. *Religion and the Rise of Capitalism.* Lon-

don: Penguin books, 1977.

13  Fernand Braudel. *La Dynamique du Capitalisme*. Paris: Flammarion, 1985: p109 'Adam Smith lui-même a vécu au milieu des premiers signes de cette Revolution sans s'en rendre compte.'

14  Fernand Braudel. *Civilisation Matérielle, Économie et Capitalisme XVᵉ-XVIIIᵉ siècle. 3. Le Temps du Monde*. Paris: Armand Colin, 1979, p 697-721.

15  Fernand Braudel. *La Dynamique du Capitalisme*. Paris: Flammarion, 1985: p 52-67.

16  Giovanni Arrighi. *The Long Twentieth Century*. London: Verso, 1994.

17  Deepak Lal. *Unintended Consequences: The Impact of Factor Endowments, Culture, and Politics on Long-Run Economic Performance*. Cambridge, Mass.: The MIT Press, 1998.

18  RH Tawney. *Religion and the Rise of Capitalism*. London: Penguin books, 1977.

19  Instituto del Tercer Mundo. *The World Guide 2003/2004: An Alternative Reference to the Countries of our Planet*. Oxford: New Internationalist Publications Ltd, 2003: p294.

20  Fernand Braudel. *Civilisation Matérielle, Économie et Capitalisme XVᵉ-XVIIIᵉ siècle. 3. Le Temps du Monde*. Paris: Armand Colin, 1979, p729.

21  Winston S Churchill. *A History of the English-speaking Peoples. Volume III: The Age of Revolution*. London: Cassell and Company Ltd, 1957: p183.

22  Thom Hartmann. *Unequal Protection: The Rise of Corporate Dominance and the Theft of Human Rights*. Rodale Inc, 2004: p45-63.

23  Fernand Braudel. *Civilisation Matérielle, Économie et Capitalisme XVᵉ-XVIIIᵉ siècle. 3. Le Temps du Monde*. Paris: Armand Colin, 1979, p728.

24  David Cannadine. *The Decline and Fall of the British Aristocracy*. London: Papermac, 1996: p202.

25  Barbara W Tuchman. *The Proud Tower: a Portrait of the World Before the War 1890-1914*. London: The Folio Society, 1995: p109.

26  Giovanni Arrighi. *The Long Twentieth Century*. London: Verso, 2002: p240.

27  Clifton Daniel (Ed dir). *Chronicle of America*. Farnborough: Chronicle Communications, 1993: p431.

28  Alistair Cooke. *Alistair Cooke's America*. London: British Broadcasting Corporation, 1973: p228.

29  Giovanni Arrighi. *The Long Twentieth Century*. London: Verso, 2002: p242.

30  Barbara W Tuchman. *The Proud Tower: a Portrait of the World Before the War 1890-1914*. London: The Folio Society, 1995: p109.

31  Anthony Trollope. *The Way we Live Now*. London: The Folio Society, 1992.

32  *Alistair Cooke's America*. London: British Broadcasting Corporation, 1973: p247-71.

33  Clifton Daniel (Ed dir). *Chronicle of America*. Farnborough: Chronicle Communications, 1993: p485.

34  Giovanni Arrighi. *The Long Twentieth Century*. London: Verso, 2002: p270.

35  Barbara W Tuchman. *The Proud Tower: a Portrait of the World Before the War 1890-1914*. London: The Folio Society, 1995: p120-3.

36  Giovanni Arrighi. *The Long Twentieth Century*. London: Verso, 1994: p271.

37  Robert Skidelsky. *John Maynard Keynes. Fighting for Freedom. 1937-1946*. New York: Penguin Books, 2000: p99-107.

38  Ibid, p453-58.

39  According to figures released by the Treasury, Britain borrowed a total of $4.3 billion from the US and repaid a total of $7.1 billion at an interest rate of 2 per cent per year. *The Scotsman*, 30 December 2006.

40  *Wasteland: The World After 1945*. Britannica CD 99 Multimedia Edition   1994-1999 Encyclopdia Britannica, Inc.

41  Robert Skidelsky. *John Maynard Keynes. Fighting for Freedom. 1937-1946*. New York: Penguin Books, 2000: p492.

42  Giovanni Arrighi. *The Long Twentieth Century*. London:

Verso, 1994: p296-7.

43 Robert Skidelsky. *John Maynard Keynes. Fighting for Freedom. 1937-1946*. New York: Penguin Books, 2000: p241.

44 Ibid, p465.

45 George Monbiot. *Manifesto for a New World Order*. New York: The New Press, 2004: p168.

46 John Perkins. *Confessions of an Economic Hit Man*. San Francisco: Berrett-Koehler Publishers, Inc., 2004: p15-17.

47 Instituto del Tercer Mundo. *The World Guide 2003/2004: An Alternative Reference to the Countries of our Planet*. Oxford: New Internationalist Publications Ltd, 2003: p58.

48 Peter Stalker. *The No-nonsense Guide to Global Finance*. Oxford: New Internationalist Publications Ltd, 2009: p114.

49 Thom Hartmann. *Unequal Protection: The Rise of Corporate Dominance and the Theft of Human Rights*. Rodale Inc, 2004: p141.

50 World Trade Organization website: www.wto.org

51 David Held. *Global Covenant: The Social Democratic Alternative to the Washington Consensus*. Cambridge: Polity Press Ltd, 2004: p23.

52 Ibid, p55.

53 Joseph Stiglitz. *Globalization and its Discontents*. London: Penguin Books, 2002.

54 'Free trade – the facts'. *New Internationalist* Dec 2004;374:16-25.

55 Instituto del Tercer Mundo. *The World Guide 2003/2004: An Alternative Reference to the Countries of our Planet*. Oxford: New Internationalist Publications Ltd, 2003: p73.

56 Joseph Stiglitz. *Globalization and its Discontents*. London: Penguin Books, 2002. p227-8.

57 Peter Singer. *One World: the Ethics of Globalization*. Yale University Press, 2002: p55-91.

58 David Held. *Global Covenant: the Social Democratic Alternative to the Washington Consensus*. Cambridge:

322

Polity Press Ltd, 2004: p35.

59  Ibid, p54.

60  Thom Hartmann. *Unequal Protection: The Rise of Corporate Dominance and the Theft of Human Rights.* Rodale Inc, 2004: p167.

61  Peter Stalker. *The No-nonsense Guide to Global Finance.* Oxford: New Internationalist Publications Ltd, 2009: p99.

62  Joel Bakan. *The Corporation: The Pathological Pursuit of Profit and Power.* London: Constable, 2004: p14.

63  Clifton Daniel (Ed dir). *Chronicle of America.* Farnborough: Chronicle Communications, 1993: p571.

64  Joel Bakan. *The Corporation: The Pathological Pursuit of Profit and Power.* London: Constable, 2004: p36.

65  Ibid, p79-80.

66  Ibid, p5.

67  Thom Hartmann. *Unequal Protection: The Rise of Corporate Dominance and the Theft of Human Rights.* Rodale Inc, 2004: p95-109.

68  Ibid, p126-222.

69  Joel Bakan. *The Corporation: The Pathological Pursuit of Profit and Power.* London: Constable, 2004: p63.

70  Thom Hartmann. *Unequal Protection: The Rise of Corporate Dominance and the Theft of Human Rights.* Rodale Inc, 2004: p241.

71  Ibid, p161-164.

72  Simon Head. Inside the Leviathan. *New York Review of Books* Dec 16, 2004.

73  Tesco sales top £1bn a week – now retailer targets banks. *The Guardian* April 21, 2009.

74  George Monbiot. *Captive State: The Corporate Takeover of Britain.* London: Pan Books, 2000: p208-224.

75  Ending corporate privileges and secrecy around lobbying in the European Union www.corporateeurope.org/alter-eu.html

76  Naomi Klein. *No Logo.* London: Flamingo, 2001.

77  See the website: http://endofcapitalism.com

78  Peter Stalker. *The No-nonsense Guide to Global Finance.* Oxford: New Internationalist Publications Ltd,

323

2009: p128-142.

79 Vince Cable. *The Storm: The World Economic Crisis and What it Means*. London: Atlantic Books, 2009: p10-27.

80 Richard Layard. *Happiness: Lessons from a New Science*. London: Allen Lane, 2005: p29.

81 Ibid, p32-33.

82 Richard Wilkinson. *The Impact of Inequality: How to Make Sick Societies Healthier*. New York: The New Press, 2005: p10.

83 Ibid, p14-15.

84 Institute for fiscal studies. IFS Commentary C109. *Poverty and Inequality in Britain: 2009*: http://www.ifs.org.uk/comms/c109.pdf

85 Richard Wilkinson. *The Impact of Inequality: How to Make Sick Societies Healthier*. New York: The New Press, 2005: p30.

86 Karl Marx, Friedrich Engels. *The Communist Manifesto*. Oxford University Press, 1998: p8.

87 Ibid, p4.

88 Joseph A Schumpeter. *Capitalism, Socialism and Democracy*. New York: HarperPerennial, 1975: p83.

89 Ibid, p67.

90 Ibid, p131-4.

91 George Monbiot. *Captive State: The Corporate Takeover of Britain*. London: Pan Books, 2000: p208-224.

92 Immanuel Wallerstein. *The Decline of American Power*. New York: The New Press, 2003: p58-64.

93 Joseph A Schumpeter. *Capitalism, Socialism and Democracy*. New York: HarperPerennial, 1975: p111-120.

94 Income Date Services annual report on chief executives' salaries, 2007: http://www.incomesdata.co.uk/mpr/dirpay07.htm

95 *Women's Own* 31 October 1987.

96 Ivan Boesky gave an infamous speech on the positive aspects of greed at the University of California in 1986 where he said in part 'I think greed is healthy. You can be greedy and still feel good about yourself'. This inspired the key speech in the movie in which are the lines

'Greed – for lack of a better word – is good. Greed is right. Greed works.' Boesky later received a prison sentence of 3.5 years and was fined $100 million for his prominent role in a Wall Street insider trading scandal. http://en.wikipedia.org/wiki/Ivan_Boesky

97  Karl Marx, Friedrich Engels. *The Communist Manifesto.* Oxford University Press, 1998: p8.

98  Ibid, p48

99  Joseph A Schumpeter. *Capitalism, Socialism and Democracy.* New York: HarperPerennial, 1975: p83.

100 Fernand Braudel. *Civilisation Matérielle, Économie et Capitalisme XV<sup>e</sup>-XVIII<sup>e</sup> siècle. 2. Les Jeux de L'échange.* Paris: Armand Colin, 1979, p514. The apt metaphor of predators roaming in the jungle appears in the English translation quoted by Giovanni Arrighi in *The Long Twentieth Century.* London: Verso, 2002: p10. The original French is not so picturesque.

# Chapter 8

# The Matter With Us

'If...the ends of men are many, and not all of them are in principle compatible with each other, then the possibility of conflict – and of tragedy – can never wholly be eliminated from human life, either personal or social."*Isaiah Berlin*[1]

We come now to the nub of our enquiry. We are today facing several inter-related problems – all of our own making – which threaten to overwhelm us. How did we get ourselves into such a predicament? And why do we cause each other so much suffering? What is the matter with us?

On the face of it, being self-inflicted, our most pressing problems must result, at least in part, from the way in which we think, how we reason and understand ourselves and the world, and how, in accordance with our beliefs, we behave. In preceding chapters various flaws in our thought processes and the ways in which we acquire and use knowledge were identified; how these defects contribute to our predicament will now be considered. These faulty ways of thinking may be grouped under three overlapping headings: reification – the projection of human concepts and categories onto the external world; over-reliance on intuition; and holding beliefs for which there is no evidence or which are contradicted by the evidence.

## Faulty Ways of Thinking

***Reification, or misplaced concreteness.*** Many of our categories and concepts are acquired in infancy and are determined
by the way in which our minds are embodied. It is in infancy
that we develop the concept of causality as an association of
cause and effect, and the notion of causes as reasons, or as actions to achieve a purpose. It is thus in infancy that we learn
to interpret the world teleologically by projecting our own
experience of causality onto it. It is in infancy that we learn
to categorise things as non-living or living, as animal or human; to classify people as family or strangers, us or them. We
develop concepts of number and of mathematics; we learn to
name the colours of things; we learn the difference between
right and wrong, and their different emotional feel. And we
come to believe that all of these concepts and categories have
an objective existence independent of us – we reify them.

As adults we reify our moral beliefs and continue to be constrained by the notions of right or wrong that we acquired as
infants. Projecting our concepts onto the world, we are inclined to believe, as did Plato, in the existence of Good and
Evil, of Truth and Beauty, and of Mathematics as a Law of
Nature. These beliefs, though quite natural to us, are erroneous, and may be misleading, if not harmful.

Projection of our notions of causality onto the universe has
given rise to the belief that the world is there for a purpose,
and that purpose has to do with ourselves. But fine tuning
of a mathematical model of the universe is not evidence of
a fine tuner who designed a universe for us to live in, but
rather, it reflects the self-organising properties of matter, and
the nature of the human invention of mathematics which we
use to describe those properties. Similarly, the appearance
of design in nature is not evidence of a purposeful designer
and creator, but results from the evolution by a process of
natural selection of all living things from a common ances-

tor. The consequences of interpreting cosmology, evolution or history teleologically are that we develop ideas above our station: that the universe was created, and made habitable, for our sakes; that evolution was preordained to culminate in *Homo sapiens*; that Britannia was meant to rule the waves; that America has a manifest destiny.

The fallacy of reification, or 'misplaced concreteness', often arises from our ability to describe the workings of nature in terms of mathematics, and our taking the mathematical model to be the real thing. But it does not follow from the 'law' of supply and demand that you cannot buck the market, nor that attempts to relieve the poverty of working people are wrongheaded because economic theory says that they should be paid no more than 'the threshold of wretchedness'. Nor can it be inferred, from the fact that in a mathematical model a promiscuous mating strategy maximises the replication of a selfish gene, that licentious sexual behaviour is genetically determined and cannot be modified, or that we cannot be held responsible for it.

But the most egregious reification – nay, deification – error, is to believe that we are made in the image of an omnipotent and omniscient God. This belief, which has had appalling consequences, is held by many people born into the three monotheistic religions based on the Old Testament. But we are not made in the image of God, rather, the reverse: the jealous and vindictive deity of these monotheistic religions is no more than a projection of our own nature, reflecting also an exaggerated opinion of human power and knowledge. This mistaken belief results in an abominable aggravation of many of the problems which we face. Affiliation to any one of these religions provides a marker which distinguishes 'us' from 'them', defining the extent of the moral family. All three religions make claims to be the one true religion, and their holy books each contain passages which may be interpreted as supporting persecution of those who do not believe in that religion. In countless conflicts unspeakable treatment has been, and continues to be, inflicted onto fellow humans in the name of fictitious deities who are considered to set the standard for morality. These religions also promise an afterlife in which misery and sacrifice in this life will be compensated and rewarded in the next. This has the effect of devaluing life on earth and undermining the incentive to ameliorate conditions of life here and now in the only life any of us will ever experience.

At the beginning of the third millennium of the common or Christian era, it might be supposed that religious belief would now be somewhat outdated, and the objections above would be losing their force. Scholars of religion, in enumerating the many contradictions and inconsistencies of the foundational texts of these religions, have clearly shown their human, and specifically masculine, origin.[2,3] Science provides a comprehensive explanatory account of our origins which is infinitely more credible than the creation myths written thousands of years ago by ignorant scribes who had no knowledge of the world beyond the Middle East. So does belief in a god whose existence is a fanciful human invention really matter? What's the harm? Three examples, one from each of the monotheistic religions, are sufficient to show that religious belief of this sort can be lethally dangerous.

The wave of suicide bombings by Moslems in recent years has been inspired, at least in part, by the belief in the hereafter, where there are rich rewards. This is evidenced by martyrdom videos dedicated to Allah, and the frequent jubilation of the bombers' families that their relative has gone to paradise. While suicide is forbidden, martyrdom in the cause of jihad is praised and encouraged. It is unlikely, though, that quite so many young men would sacrifice their lives for political causes such as al-Qaeda or Hamas if they were not expecting to go to paradise, with its promise of sexual pleasure (and permission to drink alcohol).

> They shall recline on jewelled couches face to face, and there shall wait on them immortal youths with bowls and ewers and a cup of purest wine (that will neither pain their heads nor take away their reason); with fruits of their own choice and flesh of fowls that they relish. And theirs shall be the dark-eyed houris, chaste as hidden pearls: a guerdon for their deeds.[4]

The number of 'dark-eyed virgins sheltered in their tents, whom neither man nor jinnee will have touched before',[5] is not specified in the Koran, but elsewhere in Islamic literature it is said to be 72.[6]

In the Middle East, an intractable problem results from the Jewish belief that the Jews are God's chosen people to whom he has promised the land of Israel, in spite of its having been inhabited by Arabs for centuries. The promise is alleged to have been made about 1200 BCE and is recounted in Exodus, the second of the first five books of the Old Testament, which are traditionally attributed to Moses. But Moses cannot have been the author, for the simple reason that his death as well as his life is reported, all in the third person. There are now thought to have been at least four different sources of these five books known at the Pentateuch or Torah, some of which originated centuries later than the stories which they relate. Notwithstanding this scholarship, in 2008, in a radio interview with Joan Bakewell, chief rabbi Jonathan Sacks, who had studied philosophy at Cambridge University, said:

> The authorship of Genesis to Deuteronomy we ascribe to God himself directly without intermediaries…He

set his seal of authority on it and this five book text is the text of our covenant with God at Mount Sinai, what I would call our written constitution as a nation under the sovereignty of God.[7]

He added that:

> What in politics is a virtue, in religion is a vice, namely, compromise.

For the 60 years of Israeli occupation, Palestinians have been paying with their lives for this uncompromising religious belief, which is based on ancient texts of dubious provenance, and which carry a clear incitement to genocide:

> I am come down to deliver them out of the hand of the Egyptians, and to bring them up out of that land unto a good land and a large, unto a land flowing with milk and honey; unto the place of the Canaanites, and the Hittites, and the Amorites, and the Perizzites, and the Hivites, and the Jebusites...[8] But of the cities of these people, which the Lord thy God doth give thee for an inheritance, thou shalt save alive nothing that breatheth: But thou shalt utterly destroy them; namely, the Hittites, and the Amorites, the Canaanites, and the Perizzites, the Hivites, and the Jebusites; as the Lord thy God hath commanded thee.[9]

The third example of a religious belief with potentially lethal consequences is the peculiarly Christian notion of the apocalypse, or unveiling. The apocalypse is the day of judgement and final destruction of the world, which is to be followed by God's reign on earth, an eventuality which is regularly entreated in the Lord's Prayer – 'Thy kingdom come'. After the death of Jesus, the early Christians thought that he would return 'in clouds with great power and glory', to overthrow and avenge the Romans for the siege of Jerusalem and the destruction of its temple, and to redeem his followers. Sixty years after Jesus' death, St John of Patmos wrote the Book of Revelation to encourage the faithful in their long wait. In it he imaginatively depicts violent apocalyptic events, and tells how the 144,000 of the Elect will be taken up into heaven at the commencement of the millennium, a thousand year reign of peace and harmony. Four hundred years and many generations later, Jesus had still not returned. By this time, however, the Romans were no longer an enemy but the Church's powerful promoter, Christianity having been adopted by Constantine as the official religion of the empire. Doctrine was hence realigned with the changed circumstances and the kingdom of God, also known as Zion, was deemed to be spiritual rather than terrestrial, and millennialism was denounced. Nevertheless, throughout the centuries there have arisen many millennialist movements, when the imminent end of the world has been forecast, with adherents vainly preparing themselves to be taken up into heaven. Such movements tend to occur at times of pestilence, warfare, famine and death – the four horsemen of the Apocalypse –for which the prophetic books of the Bible provide a spurious explanation in terms of vague predictions of an approaching cataclysm.

In *An Angel Directs the Storm,* theologian Michael Northcott tells of a resurgence of millennialism in America in recent years, particularly in various protestant sects which were close to President Reagan, and had the ear of President George W Bush and his advisers.

> New World millennialism involves the claim that Americans are in some exceptional sense in charge of human history, that their story represents the fulfilment of Biblical passages about the end of history, the last judgement and the final revelation of the millennial rule of the saints in which human history is finally redeemed.[10]

Since 9/11 a predominant strain of millennialism holds that turbulent international affairs presage the apocalypse. At that day 'we which are alive and remain shall be caught up together with them in the clouds, to meet the Lord in the air.'[11] After this 'Rapture', sinners will be left behind to face the tribulation of the 'last times' in which, after a long struggle, evil will eventually be overcome. These far-fetched beliefs have significant consequences for US government policy in three important areas, the environment, social welfare, and Israel.

If the end of the world is nigh, there is no point in conserving the environment, and the Elect, who will be taken up to heaven in the Rapture, have nothing to fear from global warming, nor need they take any measures to prevent it. Thus, US anti-environmental policies appeal to the religious right, amongst whom the environment is not one of the celebrated 'moral values'.[12]

The names of the Elect are already known to God, so there is no point in attempting to deflect the predestined fate of non-believers by proselytising or attempting any programme of social betterment: that would be to thwart the divine purpose and even delay the advent of Christ.[13] Consistent with this belief, federal support for public services and welfare may be cut, encouraged by a constituency who believe that this policy has religious and moral backing.

For more than a century, a belief in a divine plan for resettling Israel has exerted much influence on British and American foreign policy. America is now committed financially and strategically to rebuilding Zion as the State of Israel, condoning Israel's draconian, if not genocidal, treatment of the Palestinians. The Israeli ambition for Jerusalem is to build the Third Temple on the site currently occupied by the Dome of the Rock and the Al-Aqsa Mosque.[14] Many millions of American evangelical Christian voters believe that pursuit of this policy will bring forward the time of the Rapture, when they will be taken up to heaven.[15] America's policy with respect to Israel naturally has the support also of the powerful Jewish lobby. It has been argued that support for Israel is against America's best interest because of its financial cost, but more importantly, because of the intense hostility it provokes in the Moslem world.[16] But to some on the Christian right, conflict in the Middle East is welcome evidence of a build-up to Armageddon, the terminal catastrophic battle prophesied in Revelation, in which evil is finally overcome. Although this is a minority view, it is a cause of concern that there exists an influential group of Americans who are opposed to any rapprochement between Israelis and Palestinians, and who express a yearning to see in their lifetime an event which is invariably conceived as a nuclear holocaust. Thus an apocalyptic preacher with a large following, author of a best-selling book on Armageddon, has appeared on Fox News as an expert on Middle East affairs advocating an attack on Iran.[17]

In these three examples of religious beliefs with potentially lethal consequences – Islamic martyrdom inspiring suicide bombing, Jewish Zionism inciting genocide, and Christian millennialism hoping for a Middle East showdown – the basic, and completely unfounded, premise is that there exists a God who is involved in human affairs. The written foundational legends of these religions, which down the ages have been adapted and selected for their 'stickiness' and their aptness at making sense of tribulation at the time when they were written, have been taken out of their historical context and applied to current events of which the authors of these myths could have had no inkling whatsoever.

The erroneous belief in a god, who in any conflict invariably sides with those who believe in him, has been the justification for countless atrocities, and continues to be a cause of much strife. These religions are divisive, repressive, particularly for women, and mutually incompatible. While it would be an exaggeration to declare that life would be unproblematic were monotheistic religion to be abolished, nevertheless, the world would surely be a better place without such a potent cause of conflict. But, although religious belief is a major contributor to our predicament, it is natural, universal and part of what it is to be human. Religious belief, largely inculcated in childhood, is ineradicable. It is a problem for which there is no solution.

***Over-reliance on intuition.*** Many of our beliefs, values and preferences are acquired in infancy and childhood, when we are strongly influenced by our families and the style of parenting we experience; and as the Jesuits boasted, religious beliefs indoctrinated in the first few years may last a lifetime. Emotions run high in childhood, ensuring that we have a strong emotional attachment to convictions acquired at that time, to which we revert intuitively in adult life. But when we feel that an act would be wrong, when we choose between the policies of political parties, or have insight into our own or somebody else's behaviour, we are unaware of all the influences brought to bear on these intuitions, and the predominant role in arriving at them of emotion rather than reason. Nevertheless, in spite of their dubious origins, intuitions carry a strong conviction of their own truth.

It was argued in Chapter 6 that resolving the swarm of conflicting moral claims encountered in daily life is a doomed enterprise. We also saw how, in discussion of contentious moral issues, other peoples' reasoned arguments mostly receive an intuitive response, reason seldom engaging directly with reason. Thus, the desire to achieve a particular beneficial outcome is often thwarted by running up against somebody's moral intuition that, even if the end is virtuous, the means of reaching it is not; moral intuitions are unyielding 'conversation stoppers'.

In *Moral Politics: How Liberals and Conservatives Think*, George Lakoff, on the basis of linguistic and cognitive analysis, reveals the moral systems underlying contemporary American party politics.[18] Many of the metaphors used in moral discourse are held in common, but their hierarchical ordering differs in such a way that liberal and conservative moral systems, and the policies to which they intuitively give rise, are often mutually incompatible and, indeed, incomprehensible. Moral values are acquired in childhood, and in a 'strict father' family, obedience to parental authority is paramount and is reinforced by rewards and punishments (often corporal) according to a system of moral book-keeping in which people receive their just deserts, and debts have to be paid. The aim is to promote self-discipline and strength of character, and ultimately, independence and self-reliance. Pursuing self-interest is a moral activity since it maximises everybody's wealth through the mechanism of the invisible hand of the free market. Life is a competitive struggle and people are therefore categorised as being for us or against us, good or evil; you do not empathise with an opponent. If strength is moral, weakness is immoral: a weak person lacks self-discipline and is likely to succumb to evil forces. In this model of the family, concepts to do with moral strength – authority, order, essence, health – have priority over those to do with nurturance.

In a 'nurturant parent' family there is no system of awards and punishments, but children learn by attachment to, and modelling themselves on, their parents; obedience comes less from fear of punishment than from love and respect. Empathy, a precondition for nurturance, is pre-eminent, and is expressed

336

as 'I know how you feel' or 'my heart goes out to you'. Feeling as someone else does means experiencing their needs and wanting to meet them, and sharing their suffering and wanting to relieve it. Strength serves nurturance rather than the reverse, and nurturance serves self-development, moral growth and happiness, without which empathy with other people is not possible. The aim is to produce happy, self-fulfilled, responsible and nurturant adults. In this model of the family, concepts to do with nurturance – empathy, self-development, happiness and fair distribution – have priority over those to do with strength.

The above sketches outline the complex metaphoric structure of these two idealised but recognisable family models. From the common experience of growing up within a family, very different hierarchies of values are established at an early age, and in many cases they pass over into incompatible political attitudes in adult life. The family in which moral behaviour is first learned becomes a metaphor for society, with government taking the role of parent, and citizens becoming children in this extended family. The intense emotional associations forged in the family in childhood persist into adulthood where they are transferred to society and government at large.

As an illustration, conservatives, typically brought up in a strict father family, see income and wealth as being just deserts. Thus, progressive, redistributive taxation, taking money from the rich to give to the poor, is perceived as being doubly immoral and contrary to reason. Rich people are denied their due rewards for being successful, and poor people, besides receiving benefits which they do not deserve, have their self-discipline undermined and are put into a state of dependence against their own and society's best interests. For liberals, on the other hand, it is morally right to empathise with people who, through no fault of their own, are poverty-stricken through unemployment, ill health or plain incompetence; feeling their wretchedness, it would be unreasonable as well as immoral for liberals not to want to help them with generous benefits. Thus, both for conservatives and liberals, reason follows the dictates of passion, but in diametrically opposite directions. The post hoc reasons adduced by conservatives for their intuition (*benefits create dependency, which is bad*) are rejected by liberals' intuition (*helping people is good*), and the post hoc reasons adduced by liberals (*it's unfair that some people should be so rich when others are so poor*) is rejected by conservatives' intuition (*it's right that people should get what they deserve*). Stalemate. Unquestioning trust in the correctness of their moral intuitions has brought the conversation between conservatives and liberals to a halt. The way to get it restarted is to open out a debate about core values, and base decisions on public issues more on a consideration of the desired and expected results of a policy, and less on a gut feeling for the ethical principles involved.[19]

*

In shaping policy and making decisions, the over-reliance of political leaders on intuition may have far reaching consequences, for themselves, as well as for those on whose behalf they are supposed to be working. Thus Margaret Thatcher's persistence with the unpopular poll-tax contributed significantly to her downfall as prime minister. Conviction politicians such as her come to believe in the infallibility of their intuitive political judgements, and they collect around themselves people who defer to their leader's beliefs and keep contrary opinions to themselves. Particularly where there are no great moral principles involved, for example, in evaluating schemes for teaching children to read, it would be better to proceed on the basis of a cost-benefit analysis, looking at

338

all the possible consequences and costs of a policy, rather than putting trust in a passionately held belief for which there is no empirical evidence. Even better would be to evaluate competing schemes in a formal trial, and then gain experience of working with the better scheme in a pilot study.

*Belief Without Evidence.* As infants we construct the concept of causality from an appreciation of the contiguity of events, sometimes confounding true cause-and-effect sequences with paired events which simply occur together. As adults we retain an acute sensitivity to cause and effect, and we are masters at drawing conclusions from incomplete information, though not infrequently we see connections where there are none. If we suspect causation, the natural way to confirm it is to seek additional instances of it, and we tend to ignore evidence which is contradictory. But no amount of coincidences can provide proof of causation, and the only certain knowledge we can have is that something is not so: a hypothesis can never be proved, it can only be disproved. But stable, reliable knowledge is possible if it constitutes part of an explanatory theory which enables verifiable predictions to be made, the theory having withstood attempts at its falsification.

The importance of distrusting beliefs which are not evidence-based is clearly seen in health care. Individual experience of illness is necessarily limited, so the onset of an ailment may be falsely attributed to an activity which preceded it, and spontaneous recovery wrongly credited to a nostrum taken in the belief that it would be curative. For an individual to be irrational in this way may be no more than a harmless indulgence, but a public health policy which is not based on scientific evidence may have tragic consequences. An extreme example is the recommendation of beetroot, garlic and African potatoes rather than antiretroviral drugs for treating HIV/Aids, a regime advocated in South Africa by the minister of health

339

and endorsed by the prime minister, Thabo Mbeki.[20] He challenged the scientific consensus that HIV is the cause of Aids, claiming that the disease is the outcome of colonialism and apartheid. About one in ten of the population of South Africa have HIV infection, of whom some 500,000 are in need of antiretroviral drugs which they are not receiving.

Other areas of public policy besides health would benefit from being based on results from scientific studies designed to discover, for example, the best method of teaching children to read, or stopping criminals from reoffending. All too often, however, public policy is based on ideology, or on intuitions which are unfounded. But even scientists are not immune from irrationality, being quite capable of believing in inviolable physical laws during the week, only to avow on Sunday that they have faith in miracles which contravene those laws. Or, in defiance of the scientific evidence in support of it, they may reject a theory because its implications are unwelcome or conflict with a political ideology. The latter seems to be the case with Gouldians when they reject the role of heredity in contributing to human nature.

These, then, are some of the problem areas of our individual thinking. We project our own concepts and categories onto the world and then give them undue deference, even to the extent of bowing down and worshipping them. The fallacy of misplaced concreteness results in our needs becoming subservient to our notions. The misconception that causality entails purpose leads to a teleological view of the universe and an inflated opinion of our place in the world. Beliefs and intuitions forged in the emotional heat of childhood resist critical appraisal and the passage of time, to be passed on to our children, who, naturally trusting, accept as truth whatever they are taught by their parents, however fanciful and incoherent it may be. For most people an attitude of scepticism concerning the source of their beliefs and values does not come naturally, and is seldom acquired; the scientific method goes against the human grain.

## Tony Blair's Faulty Ways of Thinking

These errors of thought – reification, over-reliance on intuition and belief without or contrary to evidence – were manifested during the premiership of Tony Blair, as laid bare in the monumental two volume biography written by Anthony Seldon.[21,22]

Blair was born into a family which fully fits the description of being 'nurturant'. Of his parents, his mother had the greater influence in his life, his father, a self-made man, having had a stroke when Tony was 11. Although full of admiration for his father, who against the odds made a good recovery, it was from his mother that Tony obtained his religious faith, social conscience and empathetic outlook. As a law student at Oxford Blair was easy-going, happy and self-confident, and he later developed liberal political views corresponding to his 'nurturant parent' upbringing. According to Seldon's sources, Blair's policies as Prime Minister were totally influenced by his religious beliefs, which permeated his whole life.[23] The sincerity of his faith is evident from his joining the Roman Catholic Church after his demission from office in 2007.[24] In the classification of errors of thought outlined above, religious belief falls into all three categories. Faith in God is at the same time a belief without evidence and a reification error, and it also gives rise to moral and religious intuitions which carry strong but false conviction of their own truth.

*Reification.* Soon after the terrible events of 9/11 in 2001, Blair committed, or colluded with, a reification error when he declared his support for President Bush in his 'war on terror'.

Here, terror is an umbrella term for a great many different terrorist acts, using a wide variety of techniques, aiming to achieve a multiplicity of objectives, mostly political. Terrorism is as old as history, and includes violent acts committed by nationalist, separatist, anti-colonial and revolutionary movements. For Blair to say that 'we will not rest until this evil is driven from the world' was to announce a utopian project which could never be accomplished.[25,26] Terrorism is defined as the calculated use of violence or the threat of violence to attain goals that are political, religious or ideological in nature.[27] The US has rescinded this catch-all definition because many of its own activities would be included in it. Rather, terrorism is what rogue states and terrorist organisations which are on their blacklist do. In standing 'shoulder to shoulder' with Bush in the 'war on terror', Blair camouflaged the fact that terrorist acts are usually motivated by a grievance, which in the case of Al-Qaeda was the presence of US forces in the Moslem holy land of Saudi Arabia; US support for Israel in the Israeli-Palestinian conflict was another motivating factor.[28,29] An understanding of the political objectives behind each terrorist act may lead to a dialogue between the disputants and the eventual resolution of the unequal conflict between a guerrilla terrorist group and regular forces, a battle which is never likely to be solved by military means alone. It suffices to mention Northern Ireland, South Africa and Algeria, where terrorism eventually ceded to diplomacy. But the US declaration of war on terror in the abstract exacerbated the conflict with Al-Qaeda, and was seen as an opportunity to embark on regime change in Iraq, for which planning started as early as November 2001.[30] In addition, the declaration of war gave the US government justification for assuming new powers to curtail the rights and liberties of their citizens, and to abrogate the Geneva Convention on the treatment of prisoners of war and enemy suspects. Further, the co-option of President Putin into the war on terror gained him the West's acquiescence in his own 'war on terror' against Chechnyan separatists.[31]

On 12 September 2001 Blair wrote a long memorandum to Bush advocating a measured, legalistic response to the 9/11 attack: first establish the complicity of Al-Qaeda, publish the evidence, demand that the Taliban hand over Bin Laden, and only if they do not, take tough action with international support. He also wrote that restarting the Middle East peace process would help build Arab support for military action.[32] This sound advice to Bush, rendered privately, was overridden by Blair's public affirmation of his support for Bush in his 'war on terror'. Subsequently, 'war on terror' became a stand-alone justification for a variety of aggressive and repressive measures. 'War on terror' had been reified, with detrimental results.

***Over-Reliance on Intuition:*** In Chapter 6 it was explained just how very easily our behaviour may be influenced without our realising it, and how biased we are – invariably in our own favour – in judging our own motives and actions. Also considered was Haidt's social intuitionist model, in which moral judgements are said to be made swiftly and subconsciously, the reasons given for reaching a decision being post hoc rationalisation with the function of justifying the decision to other people. Blair has frequently shown evidence of this flawed mode of thought with its over-reliance on intuition.

Tony Blair valued the UK's special relationship with the US, centred on friendship first with Democrat Bill Clinton and then, surprisingly, with Republican George W. Bush. Blair bonded with Bush at their very first meeting after the latter's stolen election victory, and the friendship deepened with many subsequent encounters and exchanges. Blair's heart-felt expression of support immediately after 9/11 was greatly appreciated, as was his visit to New York nine days later.[33] In April 2002 Blair visited Bush at his ranch at Crawford, Texas.[34] Plans were under discussion for the invasion of Iraq in the spring of 2003 in order to bring about a regime change and install a democratic government, which was supposed to bring stability to the Middle East. Any suggestion that the US was intent on securing an interest in Iraqi oil was dismissed as 'utter nonsense'; much later it was admitted that this was a major motivating factor, reinforced by the announcement that American forces would remain in Iraq for the long term.[35-37] Having listened to US intelligence which chimed with his own concerns regarding Saddam's weapons of mass destruction (WMD), Blair agreed to support the US policy on Iraq. He believed passionately that the overthrow of a bloody tyrant who had used WMD against his own people was the right thing to do, and he was committed to join forces with the US in doing it. But UK support would not be unconditional: the use of force had to be sanctioned by the UN, and there had to be progress in the Middle East peace process. Although these were worthy aims, Blair's negotiating position to achieve them was already compromised by his 9/11 declaration of 'shoulder to shoulder' support for the US in its war on terror. In now showing his fervour for the invasion of Iraq and the overthrow of Saddam, Blair had revealed his hand. His support could now be taken for granted; the conditions, almost an afterthought, were passed over.[38]

As the date set by the military for the invasion of Iraq grew closer, Blair was anxious to persuade parliament and the country of the need to go to war. His methods conformed closely to the social intuitionist model: using his well-honed skills as a barrister, he presented the rationalisation of his emotionally based intuitive decision, persuading his audience, and himself, of its reasonableness. Bolstered by the notorious 'dodgy dossier', he argued that if there was a chance, however small, that WMD should fall into terrorist hands, it was his duty as prime minister to act so that that would not happen. Under the gaze of TV cameras he engaged with the public as few politicians have ever done, presenting the case for war with passion, confident that his cause was morally right. Many who had genuine reservations about the course of action on which he had set his mind were not so convinced: his debating technique was to insist on his rectitude rather than deal effectively with the counter arguments.[39] So strong was his prayerful intuition that this was a just war, he did not change his mind when contradicted both by the Archbishop of Canterbury and the Pope, heading respectively the church to which he belonged, and the church that he would later join.[40,41] Right up to the time of his demission as prime minister he justified his decision to go to war by the 'conversation stopper' that 'hand on heart, I did what I thought was right', claiming also that God would be his judge.[42]

We may surmise, then, that Blair's intuition that it was morally right to go to war was emotionally based and derived from three sources: his close friendship with Bush, with whom he shared Christian beliefs, and to whom he had repeatedly made a promise of support;[43] his revulsion for Saddam's regime, and his sympathy with the Iraqi people; and his fear of WMD getting into terrorist hands.

Whereas there is little doubt that Blair saw the decision to go to war as a moral one, members of the Bush administration, if not Bush himself, had a hidden agenda not confined to the control of Iraqi oil. Neocons, including Vice-President Cheney and Secretary of Defense Rumsfeld, had close links to oil, armaments, construction and security industries, and had many conflicts of interest, particularly when the Iraq debacle entered the so-called reconstruction phase, when huge profits were made.[44] By allying himself with the bellicose project of a duplicitous administration, Blair's own integrity was tainted, but had he not done so, he would have reneged on his promise to Bush, and relinquished his part in bringing Saddam to justice.

What is to be learned about decision making from this momentous episode in our recent history? From the tangle of relevant moral, legal and military factors, no great generalisable moral principle, no categorical imperative, stands out as having primacy over all other considerations. And with due respect to Kant, Blair's decision to go to war was not good simply because it was done from a sense of duty and was well meant. The predictable consequences of a decision have to be taken into account, and as a result of the war, 2 million refugees have fled the country, 2 million persons are displaced within Iraq, nearly 100,000 Iraqi civilians have been killed, and there have been several thousand deaths of coalition forces as well as Iraqi military.[45-47] In addition there has been widespread destruction to the physical infrastructure, and much of what was not destroyed was looted, including the country's rich cultural heritage in museums, libraries and galleries. This devastation could have been foreseen, and if foreseen, avoided, or at least, minimised.

Rather than relying so heavily on Blair's moral intuition, a better outcome is likely to have been achieved by an approach focussing on the desired end result and the best ethical and legal means of achieving it. Because everyone puts the best gloss on their own favoured scheme, it is important that the means of attaining an agreed result should be discussed by a group comprising a wide spectrum of opinion. Blair's cabinet, however, came to consist of people who shared his views or, at least, did not openly oppose them. Decisions regarding the war were made, not by the full cabinet, but by a 'War

Cabinet' including military and intelligence representatives. But finding this group too unwieldy, Blair met in his office with a few of his closest advisors immediately beforehand to decide the direction that the full meeting of the war cabinet should take.[48] His small office was known as the 'den' and the ruling clique became known as the 'denocracy'.[49] Blair thus made the classic leader's error of surrounding himself with people who only told him what he wanted to hear.

The consequences of Tony Blair's decision to go to war in Iraq provide a spectacular illustration that intuitions, particularly of a moral or religious nature, are unreliable as a guide to achieving the best outcome possible.

***Belief Without Evidence:*** The third type of thought error in our bestiary is belief without or contrary to the evidence. This error was shown in Blair's reaction to an unacceptable level of drunk and disorderly behaviour in city centres at closing time. He believed that by deregulating the opening hours of pubs and bars the British attitude of drinking to get drunk would change into a more civilised café culture, as seen on the continent.[50] There was no evidence for this belief, which was little more than wishful thinking. However, the policy of 24-hour drinking was pursued against the advice of the police, who said it would not reduce street crime, and the doctors, who, concerned with an epidemic of alcohol related disease, stressed that alcohol should be made less rather than more readily available, and also more expensive. Two years on, and antisocial behaviour had not lessened, but violent alcohol related crime had extended into the small hours of the night, where it was more expensive to police.[51] And the epidemic of cirrhosis of the liver, particularly in young women, was unabated.[52] The only likely beneficiary of deregulation was the drinks industry.

The suggestion has been made that Blair was influenced by lobbying from the drinks industry, a charge he would certainly deny. But even if he was sincere in his belief that his policy was the correct one, and that he had not been influenced by a lobby group or donations to party funds, he could never fully know the influences which gave rise to his baseless belief. As described in Chapter 6, the mechanisms of insight are as invisible as the mechanisms of sight, and the reasons adduced for holding a belief are often no more than rationalisations. It therefore behoves every politician to submit their pet policies to rigorous independent evaluation of the likely consequences, and only proceed if the benefits are worth the financial, social and political costs and do not involve the violation of human rights. Some hope.

## The End of History

Besides the fallible modes of thought described and illustrated above, there is a frame of mind, an attitude, essentially religious, which also contributes significantly to our human predicament. It is the belief that in the past there was a blissful harmonious state of grace from which we have fallen, and to which we can hope sometime to return, if not in this world, then in the next. Paradoxically, this optimistic belief that somehow, somewhere, there is a utopian state where all our problems will be solved, conspires massively to worsen them.

In *Black Mass: Apocalyptic Religion and the Death of Utopia*, the philosopher John Gray asserts that 'modern politics is a chapter in the history of religion'.[55] He argues that the book of Revelation, with its prophecy of a millennium and an apocalyptic day of judgement, introduced the idea of history having an end, in both senses of the word: as an abrupt termination and also as a purpose. Christianity has given us the notion of history progressing towards a utopian destination, progress encompassing both gradual improvement, as in the millennium, and sudden revolutionary transformation as in the apocalypse. The utopia towards which Christians are progressing is a never-never-land of harmony, peace and love. This notion harks back to Plato and the idealistic world in which Truth, Beauty and Goodness combine in a harmonious unity, the Essence of Essences, an idea which was later subsumed into the Christian deity. In utopia all human needs and desires are satisfied, and there is no conflict but perfect accord.

The first American colonists endeavoured to establish a godly utopian society in the New World, but they soon came into conflict with native American Indians; but even when they had been forcibly pacified the harmony did not last. There have been many other utopian projects, religious and secular, in which groups of like-minded people have endeavoured to live together harmoniously: New Harmony in Indiana US, the Israeli kibbutzim, and Auroville in India are examples. New Harmony was established by William Owen in 1825 and dissolved four years later due to constant quarrels; the kibbutzim are in decline, and have abandoned their egalitarian principles, communal child-rearing in particular. Auroville, renowned for its golden golf ball meditation centre, was established in 1968, and its utopian nature is indicated by its charter which speaks of 'constant progress, and a youth that never ages... a living embodiment of an actual Human Unity'.[56] The community of Auroville has recently been implicated in the sexual abuse of children.

Utopia (which means nowhere) has not proved to be durable on earth, nor will it ever be. For human needs and desires are incompatible: we want tranquillity and excitement, freedom and security, constancy and change. Moral values are in conflict, and in the world of ideas, truth may prove to be neither good nor beautiful, and beauty neither good nor true. Utopia, the final solution to our problems, is a human concept projected into the remote past before the Fall, or into a future paradise when our nature will have been redeemed.

Philosophers of the enlightenment mostly abandoned the concept of a deity involved in human affairs, but clung to the essentially Christian idea of progress towards a state of utopia. This was to be attained, not by obedience to religious prescriptions, but by the application of reason. We recall how Descartes considered reason to be transcendent and universal, and how Kant thought that a consistent moral system could be constructed by means of it. In such a system moral conflict could not occur since reason admits no contradiction. Science is the apotheosis of reason, and with advance of scientific knowledge there would be progress also in the social sciences of economics, ethics and politics, and in the governance of society. Human nature would improve in such a way that discord and strife would become a thing of the past; the possibilities for human improvement were boundless.

Enlightenment thinking was one of the inspirations behind the French Revolution, in which the Ancien Régime was overthrown with the object of establishing a utopian society. The Jacobins, a radical and ruthless political group, systematically used terror to achieve their aims. The use of terror and violence to achieve a desirable end was not considered contradictory; on the contrary: 'pity is treason' said Robespierre; to give way to sentiment would be against reason. The prospect of an everlasting utopian society is so enticing that anybody resisting its launch must be out of their mind; for their own good they must be coerced into compliance or else eliminated. The utopian end amply justifies the violent means.

The use of violence against people ostensibly for their own good was nothing new. The Inquisition tortured and punished apostates and heretics in order to return them to the true faith, enabling them to escape the torments of hell. But the Jacobins were the first to use terror as an instrument, not for correcting individuals, but for perfecting humanity. The French Revolution was the first of many to be inspired by an ideology.[57] The Jacobins use of terror became the model for subsequent revolutions which had the aim of reshaping society.

Lenin thought that the Jacobins had been defeated because they had not guillotined enough people, and following Marx, he advocated the liquidation of all remnants of the old regime, and the ruthless use of force against internal and external enemies of the new. In Russia after the revolution, the enemies within included many intellectuals, who were deported or interred in the Gulag. More numerous than intellectuals and bourgeoisie were peasants who resisted change and remained loyal to the former regime; a great many were evicted from their land and held in concentration camps in the North, and many millions died of starvation or were executed. The Soviet regime was totalitarian in that it had a centralised dictatorial government and required complete subservience to the state. The utopian objective of this repressive regime was to remake society and to realise human potential to the full. In a similar vein, the Cultural Revolution in China represented the total destruction of the old order to make way for a new, improved version of society.

Gray suggests that Nazism too had utopian aspirations.[58] But whereas the communist utopia was meant to be inclusive and universal, that of Nazism was exclusively for those of the Aryan race. In Hitler's Third Reich the evil obstructing its attainment was racial impurity, for which genocide was the final solution.

351

Thus, in these various totalitarian regimes the slaughter of millions was justified by reason and pseudo-science in the hope of eventually creating a utopian society. After the apocalypse of revolution would come the millennium.

*

The end of the cold war was famously hailed as the end of history: in the defeat of communism, which left the way clear for liberal democracy to become the universal system of government, history had finally reached its destination. The cold war, however, was not so much a battle of ideologies, but a contest between two different economic systems, free market capitalism and a centralised command economy.[59] Capitalism, pandering to people's wants, was the hands down winner against a system in which the government decided what people should have. But if communism is not very receptive to people's needs, neither is democracy, where the wishes of the majority outweigh those of minorities. On the other hand, free market capitalism thrives on the production of an immense variety of goods and services to satisfy every taste. Capitalism has its roots in Western Christianity, in the same soil which gave rise to the democratic ideal. Until recently capitalism and democracy have been closely associated with each other, indeed, some would say too closely, capitalism having permeated state institutions and subverted democracy to its own ends. It could perhaps be argued that democracy owes its success as a method of government, not to its inherent merits, but to the benefits of capitalism with which it has been associated – employment, prosperity and a wide range of consumer goods. While the extent to which democracy owes its success to capitalism is debatable, it is clear that capitalism does not depend for its success on democracy, as evidenced by the way it is flourishing in non democratic states: communist China, autocratic Russia and theocracies in the Middle East being outstanding examples.

The collapse of communism bolstered confidence in the West to such an extent that it became possible to think of forcibly introducing democratic government into countries under repressive illiberal regimes, expediting the fulfilment of the utopian vision of freedom and democracy. The liberation of Iraq, and the replacement of Saddam Hussein's tyranny by a democratic government advanced this worthy aspiration. In his advocacy of the war on Iraq, President Bush frequently spoke of freedom. He believed that:

> The United States is *the* beacon for freedom in the world... We have a duty to free people. I would hope we wouldn't have to do it militarily, but we have a duty.'[60]

Asked whether this conviction would not seem dangerously paternalistic, he replied that it probably looked that way to some elites, but it was not paternalistic to those whom they freed. He was mistaken, however, for the coalition forces invading Iraq were only very briefly welcomed as liberators, and soon became persona non grata.

## The Ends of Men

Amongst the elite whose views would have been opposed to those of George Bush is the late Isaiah Berlin, from whose essay 'Two Concepts of Liberty' the epigraph for this chapter is taken. Paternalism comes in for harsh words from Berlin:

> Paternalism is despotic...because it is an insult to my conception of myself as a human being, determined to make my own life in accordance with my own (not necessarily rational or benevolent) purposes, and, above all, entitled to be recognised as such by others.[61]

What is true of individuals is true also of groups, whether social, racial, religious, political or national, each having its own identity and its particular needs and purposes. Paternalism is a 'monstrous impersonation' in which a choice is made on behalf of a group, making assumptions about what it would choose if it was not the group it is, but the group whom we believe it should be. To presume to impose on a people a form of government, or an economic system, that it would not have chosen itself is monstrous.

Berlin was writing in the 1950s when the memories of World War II were fresh, and when Stalin's atrocities were becoming known at the start of the cold war. He warned of the dangers of imposing an ideology on a people 'for its own good'.

> One belief, more than any other, is responsible for the slaughter of individuals on the altars of the great historical ideals – justice or progress or the happiness of future generations, or the sacred mission or emancipation of a nation or race or class, or even liberty itself, which demands the sacrifice of individuals for the freedom of society. This is the belief that somewhere, in the past or in the future, in divine revelation or in the mind of an individual thinker, in the pronouncements of history or science, or in the simple heart of an uncorrupted good man, there is a final solution.[62]

In Berlin's view paternalism carries the terrible risk of tyranny, with 'the slaughter of millions on the altar of ideals'. Postwar memories of an ideology which offered a 'final solution' strongly underlined his message, and there were many other ideologically inspired movements as far back as the French revolution which illustrated his thesis.

*

Using the words 'freedom' and 'liberty' interchangeably, Berlin describes freedom as being 'negative' or 'positive'. Negative freedom is liberation from all constraints on one's actions; being allowed to do what one wants without interference from anybody. On the other hand, positive freedom is liberty to lead a life that is fulfilling, living life to the full, being the best that one can be, being freed from the slavery of one's passions to live a life ruled by reason. Berlin is at pains to show that these two varieties of freedom, each highly desirable and worth striving for, are fundamentally irreconcilable one with the other.

Berlin's argument, paraphrased in the following paragraphs, is eloquent and subtle, and on his own admission some of the steps are logically dubious. Negative freedom is doing what I want in my own way. But, he says, my freedom has to be curtailed because it encroaches on that of other people. My freedom can be restored, however, by contraction of my wants: what I cannot have I do not want; desire eliminated equals desire satisfied. This is none other than an attitude of sour grapes, and the reductio ad absurdum of this move is for me to commit suicide, for where there are no desires there is perfect freedom.

This version of negative freedom, where I renounce my desires, will not do says Berlin. Neither is self-fulfilment to be found in isolation because a large part of my identity depends on the recognition of my unique qualities by other people. Like most people, I would not find self-realisation on a desert island. I must therefore seek it in the company of other people, where my autonomy is limited by their desires. But since they, like me, are reasonable people, I have no grounds to resist their pressure on me to conform to their wishes. If the universe is governed by reason, all true solutions to genuine problems must be compatible. The rational ends of our true natures, theirs and mine, must coincide. Freedom is not freedom to do what is irrational, stupid or wrong. A life ruled by reason has no choices, hence the service of reason is perfect freedom. Thus, in submitting to the authority of other people's rational opinions and institutions, I become free.

A variant of this argument applies particularly to groups, whatever their basis. I would much prefer to be governed harshly by my own group with whom I identify, rather than be governed benignly by a superior group who do not recognise me as one of themselves. In this way I would willingly trade liberty for fraternity or equality, and a sense of belonging.

But, says Berlin, make no mistake about it, submission to authority, whether benevolent and distant, or harsh but of one's own kind, even if freely consented, is loss of liberty. And an argument which leads to the conclusion that despotism, however mild, is the same thing as freedom must have faulty premises.

The mistake is to believe that the universe is controlled by reason, and that the many worthy ends of men may be reconciled in a final solution. Rather, it is a brute fact that the fulfilment of some ideals makes the fulfilment of others impossible: we cannot have complete freedom to do what we want in our own way, *and* belong in a society of like-minded people governing themselves; autonomy is incompatible with authority; negative and positive freedoms are irreconcilable, as are various other positive values.

In choosing between types of liberty, Berlin favours the negative variety in a compromised version where the individual has limited but absolute rights – such as those incorporated into the UN Declaration of Human Rights – which protect core personal values from encroachment. Correspondingly, the authority of the state would be curtailed so that it would not have absolute power so as to treat people inhumanely, using torture, for example. He recognises that the barrier separating the area of personal freedom from that containing the authority of the state would be arbitrary to an extent, and would be likely to change over time. Nevertheless, principles are no less sacred because their duration cannot be guaranteed.

Isaiah Berlin concludes that choosing between incompatible absolute claims is an inescapable feature of the human condition, and with characteristic British understatement he suggests that it is not impossible that this pluralism of human ends might lead to conflict and tragedy.

# Summing Up

Human reason is just that: human and fallible, not transcendent and unerring. Moreover, the errors of our reasoning adversely affect our behaviour and that of our leaders. Perhaps the greatest flaw in human thinking is the tendency to project our own concepts outside of ourselves onto the universe at large. Wars are waged, atrocities are committed, sacrifices are made, and also countless courageous acts are performed, all in the name of our reified notions, which are taken to be absolute truths.

Another flaw, which leads to the utopian conviction that there exists a final solution to our problems, is the inspired but unwarranted belief that 'Nature binds truth, happiness and virtue together by an indissoluble chain'.[63] But positive values do not combine in a coherent whole, and many virtues are incompatible one with another, so that we are forced to choose between them. It is this necessity to choose the ends to which we strive that gives freedom its value to us. And it is our choosing of different and incompatible ends which leads to conflict and tragedy.

It is probable that our faulty ways of thinking are irremediable, but even if they were to be corrected, life would not then be trouble free because some human problems have their origins elsewhere, as will be recounted in the next chapter.

# Notes

## Chapter 9: The Matter with Us

1   Isaiah Berlin. 'Two Concepts of Liberty'. In *The Proper Study of Mankind: An Anthology of Essays*. Henry Hardy, Roger Hausher (eds). London: Pimlico, 1998: p239.
2   Karen Armstrong. *A History of God*. London: Vintage, 1999.
3   Ibn Warraq. 'The Koran'. In Christopher Hitchens (ed). *The Portable Atheist: Essential Readings for the Nonbeliever*. London: Da Capa Press, 2007: p384-444.
4   *The Koran*, Sura 56:15. Translated by NJ Dawood, 4th revised edition. Harmondsworth: Penguin Books, 1974: p110.
5   Ibid, p21.
6   Ibn Warraq. 'Virgins? What Virgins?' *The Guardian* 12 January, 2002.
7   www.bbc.co.uk/religion/programmes/beliefs/scripts/jonathansacks.shtml
8   *Exodus* 3:8.
9   *Deuteronomy* 20:16-17.
10  Michael Northcott. *An Angel Directs the Storm: Apocalyptic Religion and American Empire*. London: IB Taurus, 2004: p15.
11  *I Thessalonians* 4: 16-17.
12  Bill Moyers. 'Welcome to Doomsday'. *New York Review of Books*. 24 March 2005.
13  Michael Northcott. *An Angel Directs the Storm: Apocalyptic Religion and American Empire*. London: IB Taurus, 2004: p59.
14  Ibid, p61.
15  George Monbiot. 'Waiting for the Apocalypse'. *The Guardian* 21 April, 2004.
16  John Mearsheimer, Stephen Walt. 'The Israel Lobby'. *London Review of Books* 23 March 2006.
17  Nicholas Guyatt. *Have a Nice Doomsday: Why Millions of Americans are Looking Forward to the End of the*

*World.* London: Ebury Press, 2007: p64.

18   George Lakoff. *Moral Politics: How Liberals and Conservatives Think.* 2nd ed. Chicago & London: University of Chicago Press, 2002.

19   Jonathan Baron. *Judgment Misguided: Intuition and Error in Public Decision Making.* Oxford University Press, 1998, p179.

20   'Mbeki Urged to Sack Ally Over HIV Views.' *The Guardian* 7 September 2006.

21   Anthony Seldon. *Blair Unbound.* London: Pocket Books, 2008.

22   Anthony Seldon. *Blair.* London: The Free Press, 2005.

23   Ibid, p528.

24   'Tony Blair Finally Becomes a Catholic.' *The Sunday Times* 23 December 2007.

25   Anthony Seldon. *Blair.* London: The Free Press, 2005: p488.

26   John Gray. *Black Mass: Apocalyptic Religion and the Death of Utopia.* London: Allen Lane, 2007: p33.

27   Noam Chomsky. *Hegemony or Survival: America's Quest for Global Dominance.* London: Hamish Hamilton, 2003: p188.

28   John Gray. *Black Mass: Apocalyptic Religion and the Death of Utopia.* London: Allen Lane, 2007: p177.

29   'Bin Laden: Palestinian Cause Prompted 9/11.' *CBS News* 16 May 2008. Report of an audiotape released by Osama Bin Laden on 60th anniversary of the creation of the State of Israel.

30   Bob Woodward. *Plan of Attack.* London: Pocket Books, 2004: p1-3.

31   Anthony Seldon. *Blair.* London: The Free Press, 2005: p488.

32   Ibid, p491.

33   Ibid, p496.

34   Ibid, p573.

35   'Interview with Donald Rumsfeld.' *The Times* 10 February 2003.

36   Jim Holt. 'It's the Oil'. *London Review of Books* 18 October 2007.

37  'We could be in Iraq for 50 years says US defence chief.' *The Times* 1 June 2007.

38  Anthony Seldon. *Blair*. London: The Free Press, 2005: p574.

39  Ibid, p531.

40  Ibid, p525.

41  Ibid, p522.

42  Anthony Seldon. *Blair Unbound*. London: Pocket Books, 2008: p553.

43  Bob Woodward. *Plan of Attack*. London: Pocket Books, 2004: p178,338.

44  Naomi Klein. *The Shock Doctrine: The Rise of Disaster Capitalism*. London: Allen Lane, 2007: p311-16.

45  *Iraq Body Count*: 85-93 thousand documented civilian deaths since 2003. www.iraqbodycount.org/

46  *Iraq Coalition Casualties*. 4433 deaths since 2003. http://icasualties.org/oif/

47  According to the UN Refugee Agency and the International Organization for Migration in 2007, almost 5 million Iraqis had been displaced by violence in their country, the vast majority of which had fled since 2003. Over 2.4 million vacated their homes for safer areas within Iraq, up to 1.5 million were living in Syria, and over 1 million refugees were inhabiting Jordan, Iran, Egypt, Lebanon, Turkey and Gulf States.
www.refugeesinternational.org/content/article/detail/9679

48  Anthony Seldon. *Blair*. London: The Free Press, 2005: p580.

49  Ibid, p696.

50  'Under the Influence.' *The Guardian* 20 November 2004.

51  'All Day Drinking a Failure.' *The Independent on Sunday* 24 February 2008.

52  Bosetti C. Levi F. Lucchini F. Zatonski WA. Negri E. La Vecchia C. Worldwide mortality from cirrhosis: an update to 2002. *Journal of Hepatology*. 46:827-39, 2007.

53  John Gray. *Black Mass: Apocalyptic Religion and the Death of Utopia*. London: Allen Lane, 2007: p1.

54  Greetings from Auroville, a universal city in the making

in South India. www.auroville.org

55  John Gray. *Black Mass: Apocalyptic Religion and the Death of Utopia*. London: Allen Lane, 2007: p26.
56  Ibid, p55-69.
57  Ibid, p30.
58  Bob Woodward. *Plan of Attack*. London: Pocket Books, 2004: p88-89.
59  Isaiah Berlin. 'Two concepts of liberty'. In *The Proper Study of Mankind: An Anthology of Essays*. Henry Hardy, Roger Hausher (eds). London: Pimlico, 1998: p228.
60  Ibid, p237.
61  Condorcet, cited in Ibid, p238.

# Chapter 9

# The Matter with Matter

'Human creativity and innovation can be understood as the amplification of laws of nature already present in physics and chemistry.' *Ilya Prigogine*[1]

The supposition in the previous chapter was that since many of the difficulties we face are man-made, then they must be due in some measure to deficiencies in our knowledge, and faults in the way we think, and hence, the way we behave. How various fallacious modes of thought may exacerbate our problems was then discussed and illustrated for us by Tony Blair. But besides arising from faulty ways of thinking at the level of individuals, some human problems have their origins at a higher level, when as individuals we interact with each other in a group or in society – as components of a system.

In the preceding chapters, in step with the main account of our epic human history, the theme of dynamic, non-linear, complex and chaotic systems has been developed in the boxes. Such systems abound at all levels, from the subatomic to the whole universe, from microbes to man, and from man to mammon. The unpredictable emergent properties of systems – whether physical, chemical, biological, ecological, societal, financial or organisational – are a source of wonder and, often, of delight. But emergent properties of complex systems, especially those that are man-made, also contribute importantly to our parlous predicament. On the other hand, if there is any hope of our extricating ourselves from the predicament we are in, it too is to be found possibly in the emergent properties of systems consisting of humans, not acting in isolation, but interacting with each other.

There are three important properties common to complex, non-linear systems: connectivity, unpredictability, and creativity. These dynamic properties of matter, in all the many ways in which it is organised into systems – including, of course, ourselves and our institutions – will now be examined more closely.

## The Properties of Matter: Connectivity

In Box 1 (p4) was described how every atom in the universe is connected to every other by means of gravity, which may be thought of as acting instantaneously at a distance, and being transmitted as a wave. Atoms are also extensively interconnected by electro-magnetic waves, some of which are visible to us as light. Matter, even in its most elemental form, is thus hugely inter-active and lively, with many remarkable emergent properties – new properties that are not present in the components of a system, but derive from, and can be explained in terms of, interactions between the components. Not the least of these is the passage of day and night, and of the seasons of the year, a consequence of the interactions of matter by means of both gravity and light. We have learned to exploit the communicative properties of matter to enhance human connectivity: even a closed room is permeated through and through with a rainbow of electromagnetism of every hue, carrying a Babel of internet, radio, television and telephone conversations, all available to us at the tip of an antenna.

The variety of ways in which we humans are connected to each other is described by the sociologist Duncan Watts in *Six Degrees: The Science of a Connected Age*.[2] The title refers

364

to a study, now apocryphal, which purports to show that in a world viewed as an enormous network of social acquaintances, any two people may be connected by a short chain which, on average, has only six links, 'six degrees of separation'. It is, as we say when we meet a stranger and discover that we have a mutual acquaintance, 'a small world'.

Our connectedness with each other has many consequences, both good and bad. Close physical proximity of individuals to each other makes it possible for epidemics of disease to spread throughout a population, as happened in Europe with the plague in the 14th century. At that time very few people travelled long distances, so the epidemic spread relatively slowly through neighbouring communities, taking three years to reach Northern Europe from its origin in Southern Italy.[3] Nowadays, high-speed long distance travel means that communities distant from each other can become infected almost simultaneously, and epidemics may spread with alarming rapidity mediated by just a few travellers carrying the infection. An epidemic typically has a slow initial phase, then the number of cases increases explosively, to be followed by a burn-out phase when the disease is no longer propagated because there are too few susceptible people remaining in the population. Either they will have been infected and developed resistance to a second infection, or they will have died. Epidemics recur periodically, the interval between recurrences depending on the infectivity of the agent and the speed at which the proportion of susceptible subjects in the population returns to a critical level. This is illustrated by measles, a highly infectious childhood disease, in which an attack confers life-long immunity against reinfection. An epidemic of measles comes to an end because the proportion of susceptible people in the population falls below the critical level as a result of immunity conferred by infection in the current or a previous epidemic. Only after a sufficient number of uninfected infants have been born can another epidemic occur. Thus, epidemics of measles used to be seen every two years, but immunisation of infants has put a stop to that, though epidemic measles could return if the uptake of immunisation were to fall too low.

In a previous chapter there was mention of memes, a word coined by Richard Dawkins to characterise self-replicating agents analogous to genes. Memes are tunes, ideas, fads or fashions, which spread through society like an infection. One example cited by Dawkins was the habit of wearing a base-ball cap back to front,[4] while Malcolm Gladwell in *The Tipping Point* described the fashion of sporting Hush Puppies, and also the sinister epidemic of copycat suicides of young men in Micronesia.[5] The particular behaviours in these three examples confer no special advantages on those who adopt them, in the sad case of the Micronesians, quite the contrary. But the feature which marks these memes, and which ensures their propagation, is their propensity to be mimicked: the behaviours are self-replicating.

A parallel may also be drawn between memes and infectious agents. A virus, such as that causing measles or influenza, consists of little more than a packet of DNA or RNA which carries instructions for its own replication. The influenza virus invades the mucous membranes of the host's respiratory system where it hijacks the mechanisms normally used for cell replication to produce instead more copies of itself, which are then disseminated in droplets of mucous. Spread of an epidemic of influenza results from person to person transmission of the virus through the same network of social relations that may be used for the spread of memes. Transmission both of viruses and memes may occur locally amongst members of a group, such as those who work in the same office, while transmission further afield occurs between groups which have members in common. An influenzal office worker may thus pass on the virus to fellow passengers in the tube, who in turn transmit it to colleagues in their places of work. Nowadays, besides direct person to person transmission, memes have many indirect modes of propagation not available to viruses, including mass media and the internet. Nevertheless, the principles underlying the transmission of both infectious diseases and infectious ideas by means of a network are very similar.

An important difference between infectious agents and memes concerns susceptibility, the propensity of the host to be overcome by the invading agent, whether an infectious bug or an infectious idea. In the case of a bug, an individual's susceptibility is not affected by the susceptibility of others. Whether or not others have succumbed to smallpox affects neither my resistance to, nor the virulence of, the organism, and my susceptibility, which is the balance between these two forces, is unchanged. But when it comes to ideas, fads and fashions, whether others have adopted them does alter the way I behave. If most of my peers are wearing their baseball caps back to front, or sporting Hush Puppies, then I am likely to be swayed to do the same. The acceptance of a fashion by other people increases the likelihood that I will join them. And my joining them increases the likelihood that my acquaintances will in turn jump on the bandwagon. This positive feedback behaviour is the explanation for tipping points where, all of a sudden, everybody seems to be behaving the same way, wearing the same colour or style, or expressing the same opinion. But in contrast to infectious diseases, where the virulence of the organism largely determines its spread, the epidemic spread of an infectious idea may depend much more on who adopts it and how well they are connected than on any quality of the idea itself.[6] People like to be cool, trendy, and on the winning side, so a swing voter may vote for whichever party is predicted by a pollster to win. Or a book may be purchased because its cover describes it as a best-seller. Or we may fly BA because it describes itself as the world's favourite airline. The peculiar nature of human connectivity thus makes us prone to adopt an idea or a practice that may have little virtue in itself, its main merit being that many people of our acquaintance have adopted it.

*

In Chapter 7, Box 19 (p284) dealt with the association between institutional Christianity and the emergence of capitalism. That account illustrates how individuals are not only components of a network of contemporaries, but they are also connected with a myriad others across the centuries: connectivity applies to events which are distant in time as well as space.

Popes Gregory I and Gregory VII, separated by 500 years but linked by virtue of their holding the same ecclesiastical position, both sought to augment their political power in order that the Church should maintain its monopoly and suppress the competition in the market for spiritual goods. In pursuit of the power of wealth, Gregory I prohibited close marriages, including that of a man to his brother's widow, and discouraged widows from remarrying.[7] This ruling had the desired effect of increasing bequests to the Church, but a thousand years later it rebounded on Henry VIII's plans to marry Catherine of Aragon, his brother's widow. Meanwhile, Pope Gregory VII had assumed to the Church the power to make or depose heads of state, and sanction royal marriages. Thus Henry's marriage to Catherine could only be sanctified by a special papal dispensation. Fourteen years later, when Henry wanted a divorce, the best argument available to him was that his marriage had been null and void in the first place. But the then pope could not assent to this as it would have contradicted the decision of his predecessor to permit Henry's marriage to his brother's widow. In retrospect it is seen that by proceeding with the divorce, accepting excommunication and setting himself up as the Supreme Head of the Church of England, Henry played a pivotal role in the protestant revolution. However, the consequences for Protestantism, let alone for the emergence of capitalism, were not recognised at the time since apart from rejecting papal supremacy Henry retained his Catholic beliefs. If Henry had had a male heir, then England might have remained a Catholic country, and it is anyone's guess what effect that might have had on protestants, their work ethic, the burgeoning capitalism of the industrial revolution and the subsequent economic dominance of the West. Henry played an important role in promoting Protestantism, and thus advancing capitalism, but he was cast in that role by chance and not by choice, retrospectively but not prospectively.

In fact, Catherine of Aragon had six pregnancies from which there were two live births, Henry, Prince of Wales, who died at two months, and Mary, later queen of England. As well as having another daughter, the future Elizabeth I, Henry sired an illegitimate son as well as the future Edward VI. He therefore amply proved his fertility and his capability to produce male children. His failure to father a male heir with Catherine of Aragon, a non-event with a cascade of consequences down the centuries, was therefore a matter of contingency, or chance. The word 'contingency' is preferable to 'chance' because although chance means something that happens without obvious intention or cause, it carries a suggestion of being uncaused; we do not usually think of what caused a dice to come up with a six. But contingency, as used in philosophy, is more narrowly defined as being the opposite of necessity: there is no necessity, no logical reason, why a contingent event should not be different from the way it is. There is no

.

logical reason why a sperm carrying a Y rather than an X chromosome should not have fertilised the ovum that became the surviving child of Catherine of Aragon and Henry VIII; history would then have been very different.

\*

For two centuries the West has dominated the rest of the world economically, a fact for which historians seek an explanation. As we have just seen, for some it is that capitalism's infrastructure was laid down by the Roman Church whose excesses provoked the protestant reaction which included a serious minded industriousness leading to worldly success. In this history, the contingent actions of some individuals had significant and unforeseen consequences for the development of capitalism centuries later. A completely different account of the economic dominance of the West, and one which illustrates connectivity of a different sort, is given by Alfred Crosby in *Ecological Imperialism: The Biological Expansion of Europe 900-1900*. Crosby records that between 1820 and 1930 more than 50 million Europeans emigrated to the temperate zones in North and South America, Australia and New Zealand, regions which now produce the bulk of the world's exported foodstuffs and dominate the global economy.[8] The origins of this remarkable Caucasian propagation and proliferation go back 180 million years to the break up of the single land mass of Pangaea into separate continents, and the evolution there of different flora and fauna. Neither humans nor anthropoids were native to the Americas or to Australasia. The arrival of the first wave of humans in these continents thousands of years ago coincided with the disappearance there of many species of large animal, presumably hunted to extinction. Examples are large marsupials and reptiles in Australia, and mammoths and mastodons in North America. In the Old World of Eurasia, humans co-evolved with large animals

370

which learned to be wary of small bipedal predators, or were tamed and bred by them. At the same time, native grasses were selected and cultivated for the size and abundance of their nutritious grain. Agriculture and animal husbandry came to support a huge population expansion in Europe, though survival became increasingly precarious, and famine was never far away. In the 19th century, the availability of steam ships enabled emigration from an overcrowded Europe on a massive scale. In the Americas, Australia and New Zealand, the horses, cattle, sheep and goats, and the wheat, barley, rye and oats which the Europeans took with them flourished in the relative ecological emptiness prepared for them by the indigenes descended from the first waves of settlers thousands of years previously. The economic dominance of the West thus has what Crosby calls a biogeographical explanation.

*

The same author has written another, different, account of European imperialism in *The Measure of Reality: Quantification and Western Society 1250-1600*.[9] In considering the causation of European dominance, Crosby makes the conventional philosophical distinction between necessary and sufficient causes, using the metaphor **Causation as lighting a fire**: necessary causes of the flames are paper, wood and oxygen in the air, while the sufficient cause is the striking of a match. According to Crosby, necessary preliminary causes of Europe's blazing progress towards the end of the second millennium include the use of the alphabet to make knowledge more accessible when filed alphabetically in dictionaries and encyclopaedias; the adoption of Arabic numerals, greatly simplifying arithmetical procedures; the invention of the clock and the measurement of short intervals of time; and the Copernican revolution leading to a better understanding of the nature and magnitude of space. In brief, there was a shift from a qualitative to a quantitative attitude to the world.

The sufficient cause, the match that started Europe's blaze, consisted of a number of separate inventions which had the effect of making knowledge of time, space and mathematics more accessible and easier to understand by being visual. Sight, and insight, as described in Chapter 1, are closely bound up with understanding. Thus, the invention of printing by Gutenberg made the spoken word visible, and made silent reading possible, a more convenient, rapid and efficient method of understanding than is reading aloud, the main way in which information in books was propagated when they were hand-written and scarce. The passage of time, which could now be measured with a clock, was beginning to be represented graphically, by a sequence of marks on paper, most obviously, as bar lines and as notes of different durations on newly invented musical scores. Three dimensional space was now accurately represented in pictures in linear perspective by Florentine masters such as Brunelleschi, renowned also as the architect of Florence cathedral with its magnificent dome. The compass bearing to be followed to reach a destination across the ocean could now be read from a chart drawn using Mercator's projection, a way of representing the surface of the globe in two dimensions so that a ship's curved course following a compass bearing is shown as a straight line. And not the least important, a merchant could now tell whether he was making a profit or a loss by examining his accounts following Pacioli's double-entry method of bookkeeping. Europeans' expansionist success was owed to their being the first people in the world to think quantitatively, and to represent their thoughts visually.

In these three disparate accounts of European expansion and economic and political dominance – due to the Church, biogeography and thinking quantitatively – plausible causal connections between events and people have been traced by historians using their professional judgement of what was important. But the distinction between necessary and sufficient causes is surely redundant since it depends on what is being emphasised, and a sufficient cause at one point in history becomes a necessary cause at a later time. In the complex web that is history, the classification of influences as necessary or sufficient, or their ranking in order of importance, is a matter of judgement on which there can be little agreement. The immediate consequences of an action may be disproportionate to its scale, and the distant repercussions quite unforeseen. The significance of events cannot therefore be fully realised at the time, but only in retrospect, and then only in the light of sequelae yet revealed. None of the actions, events, inventions and discoveries that made up these three accounts of capitalism was logically necessary, they might all have happened differently, or at a different time, or not at all; all were contingent. But all three historical accounts are true insofar as they identify the happenstance by which people, and events, differing in time and place and disparate in nature, are connected.

Just as our solar system is an outcome of the connectivity of matter, the emergence of capitalism has resulted from connections across time and space between a multitude of distant luminaries, amongst whom were Copernicus, Gregorian Popes, Luther, Henry VIII, Gutenberg, Brunelleschi, Pacioli and Mercator. They are only visible to us today because they burned so brightly in their own time. A galaxy of lesser lights and a great cloud of plebeians have also contributed to capitalism's emergence, but in most cases their influence was not recognised in their time, or has since been forgotten. Capitalism was not the brainchild of an individual, nor of a committee nor of a corporation nor of a government; it arose over the course of centuries from the interconnectedness of Western society. Capitalism just happened.

373

The emergence of capitalism illustrates that every historical event or movement, however banal or momentous, is connected through a network of causal links to innumerable previous events and personalities; everything is linked to everything else. The links, better described as influences, may be simultaneous or they may span centuries. All events necessarily take place in a material context of time, place and environmental conditions which may themselves be more or less relevant and influential. No event occurs without context, in a causal vacuum. All events are determined, and given the immediate antecedents, could not happen otherwise. Yet no event is predetermined, no event is predestined to happen; history is contingent and unpredictable.

## The Properties of Matter: Unpredictability

In Chapter 1, mention was made of Newton's law of universal gravitation, which states that the gravitational attraction between two bodies is proportional to the product of their masses divided by the square of the distance between them ($F=Gm_1m_2/d^2$). He was led to this formulation after learning of Kepler's laws of planetary motion, which described planetary orbits as ellipses rather than as circles as previously supposed. Ever since Plato, astronomer-philosophers had considered that an orbit with the perfect form of a circle was the only one that was fitting for a heavenly body. Kepler had based his pragmatic laws of motion on the careful measurements of planetary movements made by the astronomer Tycho Brahe, evidence here trumping intuition. From Kepler's description of planetary motion in elliptical orbits, Newton deduced that the force which prevented planets from shooting off into space at a tangent – like stones thrown from a sling – was gravity, acting in accordance with the inverse square law described above.

The scope of the law of gravity is vast, explaining and unifying the fall of an apple, the trajectory of a cannon ball, the twice daily occurrence of tides and the course of comets, as well as the elliptical orbits of planets. For each of the planets in our solar system, its orbit is calculable given its mass and that of the sun, the latter being very much greater than the mass of all the planets combined. The gravitational attraction between planets is tiny compared with that between each of the planets and the sun, so inter-planetary attraction only causes small perturbations of the orbit calculated for each planet considered singly. It was a perturbation of the orbit of Uranus which led astronomers to infer the existence of the planet Neptune, whose discovery in the predicted place was a triumphant vindication of Newton's account of the laws of gravity and of motion.

The scope and predictive power of the law of gravity gave support to a deterministic, mechanical view of the universe where everything works like clockwork. This attitude was expressed by the French mathematician, Pierre-Simon Laplace (1749-1827), who worked out from Newtonian law the combined effects of the perturbations of all the planets on one another, concluding that the solar system was a stable, perpetual motion machine. In *A Philosophical Essay on Probability* he wrote:

> We may regard the present state of the universe as the effect of its past and the cause of its future. An intellect which at a certain moment would know all forces that set nature in motion, and all positions of all items of which nature is composed, if this intellect were also vast enough to submit these data to analysis, it would embrace in a single formula the movements of the greatest bodies of the universe and those of the tiniest atom; for such an intellect nothing would be uncertain and the future just like the past would be

present before its eyes.[10]

This view of the universe as a system in which the future is predetermined and, in principle, predictable, is gainsaid by what is known as the 'three-body problem', the simplest version of the more general '$n$-body problem'. In the simplest of physical systems, consisting merely of two bodies revolving in space around a common centre of mass, the motion of the bodies relative to each other may be completely described by a solvable equation. But in a system in which three or more bodies of comparable mass move in three dimensions in accordance with the universal law of gravitation, there is no general solution to the problem of calculating their movements given their initial masses, positions and velocities.[11] There is no 'single formula' as proposed by Laplace, but a set of differential equations which are insoluble. In a system with three bodies, the sun, the earth and the moon for example, their respective orbits may only be calculated by means of an approximation in which the moon is considered to be weightless, effectively reducing three bodies to two. In a similar way the estimated orbits of the many planets in the solar system are calculated by considering each planet in turn to be part of a two-body system together with the sun. The effect of the interactions of the planets on each other's orbits is then calculated in a further approximation in which the effect of planetary movements on the sun is ignored, planetary mass in relation to that of the sun being minute. By such means quite accurate predictions of planetary movements may be made, but they are valid for only a limited time period.

At the other end of the measurement scale, the $n$-body problem presents itself in predicting the behaviour resulting from the movements of a large number of interacting molecules in a gas or a liquid. Individual trajectories are too numerous and too complicated to be known, but the problem yields to an approach known as statistical mechanics, in which estimates are made of the uncertain but probable behaviour of the mo-

376

lecular ensemble.

When Laplace surmised that the future could be accurately predicted by the application of Newton's laws to 'the movements of the greatest bodies of the universe and those of the tiniest atom', the existence of atoms had not yet been proved, nor was anything known of their size or properties. He would have been surprised to learn how very small atoms are, that they are mostly empty space, and that they have constituents to which Newton's laws do not apply. The nucleus occupies only about one billionth of the volume of an atom, and it is surrounded by electrons which obey the strange laws of quantum mechanics. Electrons have mass and an electrical charge and sometimes behave as waves and sometimes as particles, a property known as complementarity which, stated simply, means that electrons travel as waves, but arrive as particles. Another aspect of this central feature of quantum theory is the uncertainty principle, the impossibility, in principle, of knowing both the momentum and the position of a quantum object such as an electron or a photon. If the location of an electron is known, its speed and direction of travel is not; if where it is going is known, then its location is unknown. The impossibility of knowing precisely both the momentum and the position of a quantum object is another block to the prediction of future events.

Laplace laid the foundations of probability theory, and while asserting that a superhuman intelligence could predict the future, he conceded that humans would have to make do with probabilities. But the implication of the $n$-body problem and the uncertainty principle is that not even a superhuman intelligence can predict the future with certitude. In the real physical world, consisting of a great many bodies more than two, related in complicated ways, and of which it is impossible to have complete knowledge, future events are unpredictable *in principle*. The present is being clinched only now, and the

377

future is open.

*

When Galileo declared that 'The book of nature is written in mathematical characters', he was surely hypnotised by the regular to and fro of the pendulum and the planets he was studying. For in nature such orderly behaviour is exceptional, and irregular and seemingly arbitrary behaviour is the norm, the capricious conduct of the weather providing an obvious example.

In spite of the strict adherence of atmospheric gases to well-known, simple, physical laws, unpredictability is a notorious feature of weather forecasting. Meteorology is associated with the 'butterfly effect', a phenomenon also known as 'sensitive dependence on initial conditions', in which a minute localised change in a complex system can have large effects elsewhere: 'The notion that a butterfly stirring the air today in Peking can transform storm systems next month in New York.' This description of the butterfly effect is taken from a classic of popular science, James Gleick's *Chaos*.[12] As the book makes clear, chaos, also known as complexity, is the science of everyday things, of dripping taps, pendulums, wild animal populations, heart rhythms and economics, as well as the weather. Chaos theory originated in an attempt to model the behaviour of a weather system mathematically, using a small number of equations which describe the way in which the atmosphere behaves with changing pressure, temperature and convective air movement, where these and other factors are all interrelated. The iterative computation in the model mimicked nature in that the result of one calculation became the starting value for the next, just as changes arising from the initial conditions become the starting conditions for the next spell of weather evolution. The computer output also

378

mimicked nature in that it varied chaotically, never settling into a steady state, nor into a regular, repeated pattern. Moreover, it was found that the behaviour of the model was exquisitely sensitive to the initial conditions: varying the input values by a single decimal place could change completely the subsequent course of events. This was likened to remote and important consequences arising from the flurry of the apocryphal butterfly, which, incidentally, first flapped its wings in Brazil, setting off a tornado in Texas.[13]

The implication of the butterfly effect – sensitive dependence on initial conditions – is that in a chaotic system we can never know the initial conditions in sufficient detail, nor with sufficient accuracy, to enable the immediate future of the system to be predicted. But there is a paradox here, for although the medium-term behaviour of the system is unpredictable, the system may be stable in the long term, its behaviour remaining within fairly well defined bounds. Thus, although we cannot predict exactly what the weather will do tomorrow, we can say with some confidence that a frost is unlikely in July, or a heatwave in January. Weather forecasts are probabilistic.

In these two examples, of planetary movements and weather forecasting, the relationships between components of the systems are well understood and can be fully expressed mathematically, as the law of gravity and the gas laws respectively. The advantages of a mathematical description of a phenomenon are that the underlying assumptions about its mechanisms are explicit, and the logic of a mathematical argument is irrefutable. However, because of the $n$-body problem and the butterfly effect, and at atomic level the uncertainty principle, mathematics cannot do any better than to provide us with probability estimates of future events.

If the particular behaviour of relatively simple physical systems is unpredictable both in principle and in practice, how much more so will be that of a system involving living creatures where their relationships to each other are not fully amenable to mathematical treatment? Classical economics is just such a system, where the assumption is made that every player is *Homo economicus,* always acting in such a way as to maximise his own interest. It is then that 'the invisible hand of the market' comes into play, matching supply with demand and determining the price of goods in the market place. But in reality, we may act in a way which, to the economist, is irrational, paying well over the odds for our purchase. There may be several explanations for this bizarre behaviour: we may be ill-informed, and not know that the goods are being sold more cheaply elsewhere, or, feeling charitable, we may deliberately pay more than we need to, for Fair Trade produce, for instance. Or, in the case of Hush Puppies, we may buy them because everybody, but everybody, is wearing them these days. The economist's mathematical model does not cope well with such irrational acts, which are dismissed as 'decision externalities'.[14] Externalities contribute substantially to the uncertainty of economic forecasting and to the appearance from time to time of bubbles of speculation – 'irrational exuberance' – which burst almost as quickly as they form.

Individual human behaviour arises from neurochemical activity in the brain, itself the most complicated structure in the universe. Although knowledge of the brain's physical and dynamic structures is accruing fast, neurocomputational scientists have scarcely begun to construct a model of the brain as a whole which might explain why we behave the way we do. As it is, our behaviour often appears as capricious and as unpredictable as that of the weather, perhaps for similar reasons: our brains are non-linear physico-chemical systems with a sensitive dependence on initial conditions. We are, after all, made of the same stuff as the winds which make the weather.

## The Properties of Matter: Creativity

The theme of the unpredictability of nature is elaborated by Nobel laureate chemist Ilya Prigogine in *The End of Certainty: Time, Chaos and the New Laws of Nature*.[15] He distinguishes between dynamic systems which are at or near equilibrium, and those which are far from being in equilibrium with their surroundings. The latter are maintained in an unstable state by a substantial throughput of energy obtained by the system and then dissipated, returning to the surroundings it came from. The behaviour of systems close to equilibrium, if not completely predictable in principle, is largely predictable in practice. By contrast, the behaviour of dissipative systems far from equilibrium is predictable neither in principle nor in practice; such dissipative systems are creative, giving origin to emergent properties.

An example of unpredictable behaviour far from equilibrium was given in Box 4 on page 34, describing a smoothly flowing mountain stream which falls over a cliff. To begin with there is a stable throughput of energy through this system as gravity accelerates the flow of water in the gently inclining stream bed until the water attains a steady speed. At this point the energy imparted to the water by gravity is equal to the amount of energy dissipated in friction between water molecules, and between the water and the stream bed. This equilibrium is violently disrupted when the stream goes over the edge of the precipice, when gravity, now unconstrained, imparts more and more kinetic energy to the column of water, which fragments into a kaleidoscopic turmoil. Because of the ever-varying lumpiness of the falling water, the moment-to-moment flow rate (litres per second) is quite unpredictable, though the statistically averaged flow rate will be the same as in the steady stream at the top of the cliff. At the foot of the cliff, the kinetic energy of the free-falling water is dissipated as it chisels into the rocks below, sculpting them into organic forms worthy of Henry Moore.

Another watery example of the transformation of a stable into an unstable dissipative system with emergent properties was given in Box 7 on page 78. A pan of water (or porridge) is allowed to stand until it attains room temperature. It is then at equilibrium with its environment with which there is no net transfer of thermal energy. The water molecules within the pan have an erratic random motion, but the overall behaviour of the water is predictably uneventful. When the equilibrium is disrupted by· the application of heat to the bottom of the pan, Bénard convection cells begin to form, and the astonishing pattern they create is not foreseen, nor in its detail is it foreseeable. Prigogine emphasises the remarkable nature of this phenomenon in which the random motion of water molecules at equilibrium is transformed into the coherent, coordinated movement of trillions of molecules in convection cells: order arises from chaos. The creation of order out of chaos is also seen, on a very much larger scale, in a hurricane, where the energy maintaining the dynamic structure of the vortex comes from the latent heat of moisture-laden tropical air.

In his own specialty of chemistry, Prigogine describes a surprising chemical reaction in which a solution of different inorganic compounds changes colour with clockwork regularity from red to blue, and from blue to red, due to the coherent behaviour of a huge number of molecules acting together, the energy driving this reaction being supplied by the substrate chemicals.[16] Under other conditions the solution will show a novel spatial pattern of different colours. Besides originating patterns in time and space, the system in its state of disequilibrium demonstrates creative behaviour in another sense: many ephemeral intermediate compounds are formed whose occurrence would not be anticipated from a knowledge of the initial ingredients and the compounds present at the end of the reaction. This is very different behaviour from a chemical system at equilibrium, where, due to random molecular motion, a coloured end product of a chemical reaction becomes uniformly diffused throughout the solution, which then undergoes no further changes.

Two conditions are necessary for the occurrence in a chemical system of a state of creativity such as described above: being far from equilibrium, and non-linearity.[17] In a chemical reaction at equilibrium, the rate of the reaction in the forward direction is the same as the rate in the reverse direction, and there is a steady ratio of starting ingredient to end product. But if the starting ingredient is supplied continuously, and the ratio of starting ingredient to end product is forcibly increased above a critical value, new and unpredictable phenomena occur in the resulting state of disequilibrium. Non-linearity is a disproportion between cause and effect, for example, where doubling the concentration of the starting ingredient causes a quadrupling of the rate of formation of the end product. In a chemical system non-linearity may result from autocatalysis: the acceleration of a chemical reaction by its own end-products. Thus the presence of an end-product, $X$, stimulates the production of more $X$, in a positive feedback loop. Another non-linear chemical mechanism at work is autoinhibition, where the presence of an end-product inhibits its production. Both autocatalysis and autoinhibition may be working at the same time but at different rates, resulting in an oscillation of the amount of an end-product as first one and then the other process predominates.

The behaviour of chemical systems may be modelled mathematically, enabling the circumstances necessary for the emergence of new phenomena to be defined. The concepts derived from the study of relatively simple physical and chemical systems may then be applied to more complex systems which are not so amenable to mathematical analysis. Thus autocatalysis in a chemical system, where the presence of an end product catalyses its own production, is analogous to the spread of Hush Puppies, where the more they are worn, the more people start wearing them. 'Nothing succeeds like success' epitomises an autocatalytic process. One can imagine that autoinhibition might also apply to the wearing of Hush Puppies as they come to be associated with last season's fashion. Autoinhibition in this general sense applies also to the transmission of measles, where, because of induced immunity, the higher the proportion of infected subjects, the lower the incidence of new cases; before the practice of immunisation, autoinhibition was responsible for the two-yearly cycle of epidemics, itself analogous to the cyclical behaviour of the chemical reaction described by Prigogine.

Non-linearity and being far from equilibrium, as conditions necessary for new properties to emerge in chemical systems, are always present in living things, which are never completely at equilibrium with their surroundings; and autocatalytic and autoinhibitory biochemical mechanisms are ubiquitous. Consequently, at a cellular level, examples of ordered structure, often in aesthetically pleasing patterns, abound. Ordered function is represented by the maintenance of an internal biochemical milieu in which, amongst other things, acidity and degree of hydration are closely regulated. These are examples of self-organised dynamic structures and states which are created and maintained by the flux of energy and matter passing through and dissipated by the living biochemical system. Besides the maintenance of conditions within the cell which differ from those without, the disequilibrium between an organism and its environment is represented also by a concentration of chemical energy locked into proteins, lipids, polysaccharides and other structural materials. On the death and decomposition of a creature this energy is yielded up, often to another organism in the food chain of which it constituted a link. In a warm-blooded animal, the disequilibrium is marked also by the maintenance of a body temperature that differs from that of its surroundings.

Some vertebrates, including *Homo sapiens*, are endowed with a biochemical system which exhibits a quite remarkable degree of creativity, being able to synthesise entirely new molecules to order.[18] This is the humoral immune system, evolved to protect us against invasion and attack by micro-organisms such as viruses and bacteria. A major component of the immune system consists of millions of white cells called lymphocytes, which circulate continuously in the blood stream. On the surface of invading microbes are molecules known as antigens which, when recognised as 'foreign', provoke lymphocytes to produce antibodies. Antigens have a complicated three-dimensional structure which meshes with that of its corresponding antibody, rather like a key fitting a lock. The antigens of micro-organisms are continuously evolving in a perpetual arms race against their opponents' immune systems. The binding of the antigen of an invader with the closest matching antibody is the signal for the lymphocyte producing that antibody to go into mass production by cloning itself. Within a few days, there is a massive increase in the supply of antibody, which binds with the antigen of the attacking microbe, marking it for destruction by phagocytes, another type of white blood cell; with luck, the invaders will be repelled and the infection overcome. The augmented number of lymphocytes producing that specific antibody often confers a long lasting immunity against reinfection with the same organism, such as we saw with measles.

A remarkable refinement comes into play when cloning of a

lymphocyte is triggered by binding of antigen and antibody. A process called somatic hypermutation induces random mutations of the lymphocyte's antibody gene, resulting in variations of the fine structure of the antibody that best fits the antigen of the invading microbe. Some of these variants will result in a more specific binding of antibody to antigen, stimulating that cell to reproduce itself more often. In the whole population of lymphocytes there is an increase in the frequency of the gene for the antibody that most closely binds with the antigen. This is a classical Darwinian process of mutation, genetic variation, selection and differential reproduction with increase in gene frequency, but one which is proceeding at the level of the cell rather than the species.

*

The mechanism just described, in which antibodies are ingeniously adapted to bind closely with the antigens of pathogens, scaled up, becomes evolution, the creative force of nature. Darwin's theory of evolution by natural selection, without postulating a creator or a designer, explains the generation of complexity, diversity, and adaptation of organisms to their environment, the latter being of such subtlety that it has the appearance of design. Furthermore, Darwinism is a universal theory in that the explanation is independent of the nature of either the structural or the hereditary material. If life exists elsewhere in the universe, it is likely that some version of evolution by natural selection will underlie it even though it may well not be based on biochemistry as we know it, in which the code for the assembly of structural proteins is written in DNA.

Some aspects of human creativity may be explained by a variant of Darwinism in which memes are the hereditary entities. Without pressing this metaphor too far, one can see how

386

phrases, themes, melodies, forms and colours may be combined in a myriad acts of inventiveness, which may be likened to the formation of novel antibodies from new combinations of antibody fragments. The obvious difference between these two processes is the involvement of consciousness in one but not the other, though the part that consciousness plays in human creativity is not clear since many artists, writers and scientists report eureka moments when whole concepts come to them in a flash of inspiration.

What is clear is that matter is creative at all the many levels of its organisation, from the simplest of atoms to the immensely complex human brain, and from populations of blood cells to human societies. At every level, the interaction and recombination of system components leads to new properties or new varieties of matter, which in turn become incorporated into a higher system with emergent properties of its own. In the simplest physical or chemical systems a fairly complete description may be made of its operation, and the conditions – far from equilibrium – in which new properties emerge may be defined.

Complex systems, particularly those which involve people, do not readily lend themselves to mathematical descriptions, and verbal accounts, where the assumptions are less explicit and the logic less rigorous, have to suffice. Nevertheless, the insights gained from the analysis of simple systems carry over into complex ones: for better or for worse, unpredictable and novel phenomena occur when conditions are far from equilibrium. Moreover, novelty arises, not just from the components of a system but from their interactions. In a system whose components are people, novelty arises, not only from individuals, but from their interactions with each other, whether the system is demographic, economic or political. Thus, a group considered simply demographically has very different properties depending on its age structure. If more than half are under 20 years old, the group is almost ungovernable.[19] Or a country with a very high proportion of young people may be in a state of demographic entrapment, where the growth of the population exceeds that of the economy, perpetuating the conditions of poverty and illiteracy which contribute to population growth.[20] On the other hand, urbanisation and affluence in some Western European countries has resulted in an ageing population with a birth rate less than replacement, and in which there is a strain on people of working age to support the large number of pensioners. These are examples of emergent properties which are not willed by individuals nor by governments, but which arise, quite literally in these cases, from relationships between individuals. These things happen.

The economic system with its three tiers has the dynamic properties of matter as just related – connectivity, unpredictability and creativity. In the upper tier, capitalism, people relate to each other in market pricing mode, on their own accounts or on behalf of institutions such as corporations or banks. Capitalism's unplanned birth, exponential growth and symbiotic relationship with government were recounted in Chapter 7. The unpredicted and unprecedented near collapse of this tier of the economy in 2008 is characteristic of a complex, non-linear system far from equilibrium, where the unexpected is only to be expected. These things happen.

As for political systems, mention of the unheralded collapse of the Soviet Union is sufficient to make the point that there too, arising from the behaviour of people in groups, novel and unpredictable things just happen. Systems far from equilibrium are creative of new prodigies.

## Is Consciousness a Property of Matter?

We have been considering the dynamic properties of matter:

its connectivity, unpredictability and creativity. Of these three properties, it is the last which is most difficult to accept. For how can complexity arise from simplicity, order from chaos, man from dust, mind from matter? Creativity appears to be a breach of logic, the generation of something from nothing, the spontaneous occurrence of design without designer.

In the preceding chapters it has been argued that complexity does indeed arise from simplicity, the combination and interaction of the components of a system resulting in the emergence of new species of matter and new properties not possessed by the constituents. We reviewed the growth of the universe after its origin in the Big Bang, the development of our solar system, the origin of life from matter, the long prokaryote prelude before nucleated cells evolved, the evolution of vertebrates and the colonisation of the land, where *Homo sapiens* continues to walk upright, with a big brain. It was argued too that consciousness is an emergent property of the brain, a necessary prerequisite for the evolution of moral behaviour needed for living together in large groups. This epic progression has a 'bottom up' explanation, and although many questions remain, the success of such an approach, and the grandeur and coherence of the vision so far achieved, give us confidence that it is the correct one. In any case, as discussed in Chapter 2, a 'top down' account of creation has little explanatory power and leads to an infinite regress – what caused the First Cause, and what caused that?

But there are those who, while accepting this materialistic account of 'life, the universe and everything', baulk at the last stage, that of the emergence of consciousness from the stuff of which our big brains are made. One of those who cannot be reconciled to the material and evolutionary origin of consciousness is the physician-philosopher Raymond Tallis. According to him:

The fundamental problem [with consciousness] is that there seems nothing in neural activity, understood as events in the world, and subject to the latter's laws, to explain what it is like to be a creature with conscious experiences.[21]

In his book *The Explicit Animal: A Defence of Human Consciousness*, Tallis devotes a chapter to the celebration of man's uniqueness, above all as a rational, economic and moral animal.[22] Human morality is qualitatively different from the constraints which regulate other animals' dealings with each other, and, as an example of what he calls 'the great mystery of human morality', he contrasts 'the reading or writing of a treatise on comparative morality' with the instinctive inhibition against killing a member of one's own species which prevails in many animals. Man is also the maker of tools, enabling him to escape from the slow evolutionary process of adaptation to the environment by adapting the environment to himself. Above all, he is man the talking animal, who makes sense of himself. Tallis sums up the unique quality of human consciousness in one sentence 'Man knows what he is doing.'[23] He summarises the dilemma he is in:

There are two ways of bridging the gap between consciousness and unconscious matter: materialising consciousness, and mentalising matter. Both types of ploy lead to difficulties because, by closing the gap, they leave unexplained the very fact that explanation began with: the special nature of conscious beings, their difference from all else. If conscious beings are like everything else, how is it that they have the distinctive property of consciousness; if matter contains the essential elements of consciousness, how is it that matter is not universally conscious?[24]

He plumps for the second option, of mentalising matter, in a version known as 'neutral monism'. There is only one sort of stuff, of which consciousness and matter are two properties, and he drums up support for this position by an appeal to quantum theory, where:

> It is no longer acceptable to ignore the fact that modern particle physics now recognises the crucial influence of the consciousness of the observer on the very observations upon which physical theories depend... The ghost that modern neuroscience has evicted even from the human brain has re-entered the world at the sub-atomic level.[25]

Unfortunately for Tallis, the validity of quantum wave mechanics as a tool of unprecedented power for dealing with the atomic structure of matter is not dependent on any particular philosophical interpretation, least of all one which depends on the involvement of mind. The entanglement of matter, with its 'spooky action at a distance', is an empirical finding explicable by quantum theory. But the entanglement of mind in quantum affairs is supported neither by theory nor by experiment but was an unfortunate misunderstanding which arose from Schrödinger's intuition that Max Born was wrong, and to prove it, his devising a thought experiment concerning a cat.

Having seen off all alternatives to neutral monism as an explanation for human consciousness, Tallis acknowledges that he has replaced one mystery with another, and admits that he cannot conceive of any kind of research programme to characterise the stuff from which both mind and matter are made.[26]

Box 21

Schrödinger's Cat

In 1925 the Austrian physicist Erwin Schrödinger devised a mathematical equation which perfectly captured the strange dual nature of electrons, which
travel as waves and arrive as particles. The equation
accurately predicts the behaviour of electrons and
other quantum objects, and has been used successfully by quantum physicists ever since. Part of the
equation characterises the electron as a wave, and
this part 'collapses' when the electron's position is
known. One of the situations causing 'collapse of the
wave function' is recording the arrival of an electron
with an instrument, at which time it ceases to behave
as a wave and acts as a particle. Schrödinger was
uncertain as to what the mathematical wave function
represented physically. Max Born considered that it
did not have a physical equivalent but represented
the statistical probability of finding an electron in any
particular location. On this interpretation, the wave
function represents all of the potential positions of the
electron superposed on each other; with the act of
observation the wide range of possibilities condenses
into one actuality. The collected ideas of complementarity, uncertainty, probability and disturbance of the
system by the act of observation became known as
the Copenhagen interpretation of quantum theory.
Einstein disliked this interpretation declaring that 'God
does not play dice', and Schrödinger devised his famous thought experiment to show that the superposition of probability states had ridiculous implications
and was not acceptable.

Imagine a closed box containing a cat, a vial of cyanide,
a hammer, an electron detector and an electrongun.
There is a 50% chance that the gun will emit an

electron sometime during the course of one hour. The electron detector is connected to the hammer in such a way that should an electron be present the hammer will fall, the vial containing the cyanide will be broken, and the cat will die. At the end of one hour there are two possible electron states within the box, which, in the absence of an observer, will be superposed: electron present and electron absent. Corresponding to these two superposed electron states will be two superposed feline states: cat alive and cat dead. When an observer opens the box and peeps in at the end of an hour, the wave function collapses and one or other of the superposed states of the electron, and the cat, become reality. A physicist called Wigner suggested that the factor in making an observation which causes collapse of the wave function is the involvement of conscious mind. Extrapolation of this idea leads to the notion that all possible states of the universe are superposed, and a particular state is only realised when somebody is observing it. Born's account of the meaning of the wave function is now generally accepted; the idea of the involvement of mind with quantum events has been seized on by science fiction writers and philosophers, and ignored by working physicists. What Schrödinger and others seem to have overlooked is that every time an electron arrives at a destination there is collapse of its wave function, whether or not mind is involved; observation is not necessary for this to occur. The general lesson to be learned is that a scientist, or a philosopher for that matter, may look rather silly if he has too strong an emotional attachment to an intuition.

An alternative interpretation of quantum theory which does not involve mind is described in Chapter 1, Box 3.

Another philosopher who cannot accept that consciousness has a physical basis is Galen Strawson, who expounds his position in *Consciousness and its Place in Nature: Does Physicalism Entail Panpsychism?*[27] The book also contains the responses to his paper of some of his many critics. Strawson asserts that consciousness undeniably exists, being what we know best. Also, that there is only one sort of stuff, of which familiar everyday things, and ourselves, are made. But, contentiously, he insists that consciousness, being so very different from anything material, cannot possibly emerge from matter which has none of it. Therefore, he reasons, consciousness must be one of the universal properties of matter, inhering in everyday objects right down to their smallest constituent parts; panpsychism is the name for this belief, also described by Strawson as realistic monism.

Strawson's panpsychism has a great many problems which are explored in all their technical detail by his critics. Many of the arguments are beyond a lay reader, including this one, and no attempt will be made to summarise them here. But if consciousness is inherent in the ultimate constituents of matter, what does it mean for an atom to be conscious? And what sort of consciousness would be enjoyed by an electron when it is in full flight, as a superposition of probabilities? What's more, the so-called hard problem has not gone away. For if all my constituent parts each has its own conscious experience, how does that account for *my* being conscious?[28] Why do I have a unified conscious experience rather than being a conglomeration of the separate conscious experiences of my kidneys, liver and lights, let alone my innumerable quarks?

At the end of his book Strawson indicates that he would be satisfied with a neurophysiological or particle-physics explanation of the mind-body problem providing it did not show that 'the mental was epiphenomenal or causally inefficacious'.[29]

So there we have it. Strawson and Tallis are respectively prepared to go to any intellectual lengths in order to cling on to an intuition of free will, and 'to refute any materialist account of what it is to be a human being.'[30]

The fact that matter, the stuff of which we are made, has the potential to be conscious is self-evident. The way in which it is so organised that consciousness emerges and becomes explicit – the neural correlates of consciousness – given time, will surely be revealed. But the gulf between the neurophysiological explanation of consciousness and its experience will probably never be bridged. Because of the poverty of our imagination or the weakness of our intellect, or both, it will remain a mystery just how objective neurological events cross over into subjective experience. But the chasm is no wider than the gap between the explanation of other properties of matter and their experience. Armed with Newton's law of universal gravitation, or Einstein's theory of relativity, do we really *understand* the weightiness of an apple and the earth, and how they are mutually attracted? Informed by a Theory of Everything will we *know* how sunshine is made and how it travels to us? Explanation is metaphor, but ultimate things have no parallels, and they can only be explained in their own terms, or not at all.

## The Place of Consciousness in the World

There is no evidence whatsoever that consciousness is a fundamental property of matter, widespread in the universe. Quite the contrary: the only direct evidence we have for consciousness comes from one species which populates a small portion of the animal kingdom on planet Earth. As members of that species, we have the hubristic belief that ours is the most highly developed consciousness on the planet, and some would say, the universe. We may be right, but we must take account of our tendency to project our categories and concepts onto the world, to then take them to be universal. It could be that certain species, primates, and also whales, dolphins and elephants, have as rich a mental life as we do but cannot communicate it to us because we do not share the same concepts – our worlds are incommensurable. In a similar way, in the search for intelligence in other parts of the universe it would be a mistake to think that all aliens will be like-minded with us. Although Pythagoras' theorem may be true everywhere, two-dimensional geometry is less likely to be developed by inhabitants of a three dimensional world of water or air than by those living on a plane land surface. Our categories and concepts, and the ways in which we think, including the metaphors we use, are fundamentally determined by the way in which our bodies are constructed and function. If intelligent life has developed elsewhere in the universe, it will have taken a very different evolutionary course from our own, and be as estranged from us as we are from denizens of the deep on earth.

A corollary of the belief that consciousness is an emergent property of a complex living brain, is that it has no independent existence apart from a brain of some sort. It follows that there was no consciousness anywhere in the universe until complex life had evolved. Its earliest appearance on earth might have been about 500 million years ago, when the first vertebrates emerged. By this time life had already existed here for three or 4 billion years, and had had a profound effect on the planet. Microscopic photosynthesising organisms, unconsciously doing their own thing, completely transformed the world's atmosphere along with its climate, replacing carbon dioxide with oxygen. Some time later, plants colonised the land and increased further the concentration of oxygen in the air. Other creatures combined calcium with carbon dioxide dissolved in sea water to make themselves shells. In the course of aeons their mortal remains amassed on the sea bed and became compressed into limestone. The accumulated decomposed bodies of sea creatures became reserves of oil, and on land, dead forests were fossilised into seams of coal. The transformation of the planet, creating the preconditions for the emergence of land animals, was wrought by micro-organisms and plants in total oblivion of what they were doing and what would be the consequences of their various ways of life.

To begin with, the emergence of big-brained animals had much less effect on the planet than had the life forms which preceded them. Planetary conditions were altered to a much greater extent by purely geological events, most notably at the end of the Permian period 250 MYA, when 90% of all species became extinct. This was the most devastating of five recognised mass extinctions, and is thought to have resulted from massive volcanic eruptions with emission of acid greenhouse gases, a rapid rise of global temperature, and depletion of the oxygen of the oceans, all of which may be seen as a moral for our times.[31] A further mass extinction occurred at the end of the Cretaceous period 65 MYA, when 65% of species became extinct following a collision with a meteorite which crashed to earth at Chicxulub at the tip of the Yucatan peninsula in Mexico.[32] The dinosaurs were amongst the many species wiped out in this catastrophe, and their disappearance provided ecological openings for mammals to exploit. Another contingent event which may have altered the course of our evolutionary history was the flooding of the Rift Valley 7 million years ago.[33] This is thought by some to have provided the impetus for our ancestors to adopt an upright gait, a seemingly necessary precondition for the development of the big brain that so defines our species. By this point in evolutionary history we can be fairly confident that our ancestors had a consciousness not unlike our own, which now began to influence the direction which evolution would take.

The big human brain is a feature which seems to be more trouble than it's worth, conferring insufficient benefit to justify its heavy cost. Metabolically speaking, it is expensive to run, and, fully grown in its bony box it would make birthing impossible. Thus, a baby's brain at birth is only one third of its final size, entailing a long period of vulnerable dependency during infancy while the brain completes its growth. As recounted in Chapter 3, the most satisfactory explanation for the brain's size is that a large brain is associated with reproductive rather than survival advantages, in accordance with Darwin's theory of sexual selection. A large brain, or rather, a manner of behaving which requires the support of a large brain, is the human equivalent of the peacock's tail. Choosing a mate for his or her artistry, craftsmanship or winning way with words resulted in the genes for these features increasing in frequency. In this way human nature changed, and in a direction which was found desirable by the opposite sex. Since brain size is similar in males and females, sexual selection may be presumed to have been in both directions. Thus, the conscious appreciation of the mental qualities of others unwittingly gave direction to evolution, so that we are now the way we are because that is the way we like each other to be.

*

The emergence of human consciousness, as well as giving direction to the evolution of human nature, also contributed to the development and direction of culture, of which the basis is agriculture. In *The History of the World*, J M Roberts writes:

> Man increasingly chooses for himself and even in prehistory the story of change is therefore increasingly one of conscious adaptation. So the story will continue into historical times, more intensively still. This is why the most important part of the story of Man is

the story of consciousness; when, long ago, it broke the genetic slow march, it made everything else possible.[34]

The momentous leap which prepared the way for civilisation was the invention of agriculture in the 'Neolithic revolution' 10,000 years ago. The essentials of agriculture are the growing of crops and the practice of animal husbandry, increasing the amount of food that a given area of land can supply. A better supply of food allowed the population to increase and gave time for people to specialise in other tasks than procuring food. From the enlarged and settled communities emerged leaders with vision who would strive to make sense of the world and man's place within it. Humankind's accelerated progress was now assured. However, as we have seen, things turned out rather differently.

## The Great War

The First World War is a perfect example of connectivity, unpredictability and creativity, those dynamic properties of organised matter which are manifested especially under conditions of disequilibrium. It is also an outstanding example of something bad that happened, rather than something which was caused, or for which somebody or something was to blame. As the historian AJP Taylor wrote in 1969:

> It is the fashion nowadays to seek profound causes for great events. But perhaps the war which broke out in 1914 had no profound causes... In July 1914 things went wrong. The only safe explanation in history is that things happen because they happen.[35]

Certainly, as historian Barbara Tuchman describes, the socio-politico-economic system in the run up to the 1914-18 war was far from equilibrium.

Since...the Napoleonic wars, the industrial and scientific revolutions had transformed the world. Man had entered the 19th century using only his own and animal power, supplemented by that of wind and water, much as he had entered the thirteenth, or, for that matter, the first. He entered the twentieth with his capacities in transportation, communication, production, manufacture and weaponry multiplied a thousandfold by the energy of machines. Industrial society gave man new powers and new scope while at the same time building up new pressures in prosperity and poverty, in growth of population and crowding in cities, in antagonisms of classes and groups, in separation from nature and from satisfaction in individual work. Science gave man new welfare and new horizons while it took away belief in God and certainty in a scheme of things he knew... Although *fin de siècle* usually connotes decadence, in fact society at the turn of the century was not so much decaying as bursting with new tensions and accumulated energies.[36]

After 40 years' peace in Europe it seemed to writers at the time that there was a build-up of energy in society which needed a violent release. Young men, and some of their elders too, welcomed the prospect of war as a therapeutic blood letting, a rejuvenating experience which would sharpen intelligence and give a new savour to life.[37]

Another prevalent meme was that of social Darwinism, and the notion of there being superior and inferior races and nations. For progress to occur, survival of the fittest had to be allowed full reign, which meant also the subjugation of weak and inferior peoples. How else could this occur but in bloody combat? War was social hygiene, a biological necessity.[38] In Britain, the only major European power not to have conscription in 1914, the outcome of this heady, jingoistic mix of ideas was the recruitment of nearly 2 million volunteers into the army within a year of Britain declaring war on Germany on 4 August 1914.[39] This was an autocatalytic process with rather more serious consequences than the sporting of Hush Puppies, and it went ahead in spite of fervent appeals by socialist leaders for a rising of the workers of the world to forestall the war.[40]

While connectivity at community level helped recruitment into the army, at government level it ensured that any conflict involving a Great Power was likely to draw in other nations, all being tangled in a web of treaties, understandings, loyalties and interests. Thus, Austria-Hungary, at odds with Serbia, was supported by Germany, while Serbia was backed by Russia, putting Germany and Russia into opposite camps although they had no real quarrel directly with each other. France had an unsettled account with Germany which meant that France and Russia were allies on the basis that my enemy's enemy is my friend. Britain, after centuries of conflict with France, had recently signed the Entente Cordiale which settled outstanding grievances but carried no formal obligations. Britain's preference was to remain neutral and not get embroiled in European conflicts. Belgium was neutral with respect to her neighbours, a position reinforced by a long-standing treaty of which Britain was an architect and signatory. A possible stabilising factor in the relations between the Great Powers, but one which proved to be ineffective, was that King George, Kaiser Wilhelm and Tsar Nicholas were kinsmen. This, then, was the delicately balanced system which was in place in the summer of 1914, a system with a sensitive dependence on initial conditions.

The butterfly that touched off the storm was a nationalist Serbian student who shot dead Archduke Franz Ferdinand of Austria when he visited Sarajevo in spite of advice that anti-Austrian feelings there were running high. Earlier on the day of his death on 28 June, Franz Ferdinand and his wife had survived a bomb attack which wounded one of his attendant officers. That afternoon, the driver taking the archduke on an unscheduled visit to see the injured man in hospital took a wrong turn. While the car was reversing, the assassin, sitting in a café, spotted his hapless victim in the open car, and ran out and shot him and his wife. The killer, though Serbian, had no connection with the Serbian or any other government.[41] If ever there was a contingent event, this was it. But with most European countries having monarchies, assassination of minor royalty, while not an everyday occurrence, was not infrequent and, except for those immediately involved, was usually of little moment.

During the month following this flutter, it was mostly business as usual in Europe, where a major event was the naval regatta at Kiel, attended by Kaiser Wilhelm of Germany. As the ships of the British naval squadron sailed away from Kiel, where they had been honoured guests – the battleship *King George V* was visited by the Kaiser himself – messages of everlasting friendship were exchanged with the German fleet. And on July 6, Kaiser Wilhelm set off on his annual summer cruise.[42]

The outbreak of a general war that summer was totally unexpected and neither intended nor desired by any of the protagonists. The sequence of events was that, encouraged by Germany, Austria-Hungary declared war on Serbia even though Serbia had agreed to almost all of Austria's demands that followed the Archduke's assassination. As a token of support for Serbia, and as a warning to Austria, limited Russian forces were put on a war footing, to which Germany replied with a full declaration of war, declaring also against France three days later on 3 August. Then began the invasion of France through neutral Belgium, which resisted fiercely. The German infringement of Belgian neutrality provided the legal and moral grounds for Britain to declare war on Germany in defence of France and Belgium.

Austria, whose initial intention was to humiliate Serbia and provoke a response which would legitimate an incursion into Slav territory, found herself involved in a European war rather than a local skirmish. Russia under the Tsar was threatened internally with revolution, and was ill prepared for war being backward socially, economically and militarily, with a war minister who believed in the superiority of the bayonet to firepower. Partial mobilisation of its forces on the Austria-Hungarian border was a gesture of support to the Slavs, but was misinterpreted as preparation for war. Full Russian mobilisation, intended to deter, instead provoked the German war machine. The German war plan, first drawn up by General Schlieffen in 1899, was of a lightning strike through Belgium into France which would be knocked out in a matter of weeks and before Russian forces could be mobilised, thus avoiding a fight on two fronts. Germany, however, needed a provocation from France so as to not appear to be the aggressor, which would trigger a reaction from Russia under the Franco-Russian Alliance, and probably also bring Britain into the war. But France, while having an offensive military strategy, expressly withdrew her forces from the border with Germany to avoid giving Germany any such excuse, which the Germans therefore had to invent, deceiving nobody. Belgium, due respect being given to her neutrality, was requested to give free passage to German forces. But this ingenuous demand was rejected and Germany's invasion of Belgium, as well as delaying the German advance, brought Britain into the war which was soon being fought on two fronts, not at all according to the German plan. Britain, reluctant to fight to fulfil an obligation to France which had never been formalised nor even fully discussed in the country, entered into the war against the wishes of a majority of the cabinet, and without a parliamentary vote. In all the protagonists there had been a tendency for political decisions to be driven by military timetables.

Thus, the Great War resulted from bluff, counter bluff, multiple misunderstandings and a massive failure of diplomacy. It was a titanic cock-up rather than a Teutonic conspiracy. As historian Eric Hobsbawn describes:

> Even those who found themselves pressing the button of destruction did so, not because they wanted to but because they could not help it, like Emperor William, asking his generals at the very last moment whether the war could not after all be localised in eastern Europe by refraining from attacking France as well as Russia – and being told that unfortunately this was quite impracticable. Those who had constructed the mills of war and turned the switches found themselves watching their wheels beginning to grind in a sort of stunned disbelief.[43]

In 1914, no one took the dangers of war seriously except at a military level. Few foresaw the war of attrition which it would prove to be, a trial of strength of economies as much as a contest of arms. Lord Grey, Britain's foreign secretary, cautiously presenting the case for war in the house of commons on 3 August, said that Britain would suffer little more by engaging in war than if she stood aside; by suffering he meant loss of trade.[44] He anticipated that Britain's involvement would be limited to a naval presence in defence of her own shores and the French channel ports. When it did start, the war, though unexpected, was not predicted to be long in finishing. The Kaiser, sending off his troops in August told them that they would be back before the leaves had fallen from the trees, a matter of weeks, or at the most, a few months, an opinion widely shared by all the protagonists.[45]

The year 1914 marks a rupture in history, being the beginning of a period of creative destruction without precedent, changing everything it touched. The 1914-18 war was on a far vaster scale than any war previously experienced. Whole generations of men in the prime of life were wiped out, some ten million in all. It was the first global war, involving countries of every continent, in which fighting occurred in far flung colonies, deploying armies taken across the world to fight in foreign lands far from home. It was the most mechanised war to date, the machine gun and heavy artillery making killing possible on an industrial scale. It was the first war involving civilians in such huge numbers, as victims of military violence, and also as workers contributing to a war economy, participating in 'total' war.

The First World War saw the overthrow of many political regimes, most notably that of the Romanov dynasty in the Russian revolution of 1917; it also resulted in the break-up of the Habsburg and Ottoman Empires. In 1918 the map of Europe was redrawn with the creation of an independent Finland and the Baltic states of Estonia, Latvia and Lithuania. The former south Slavic provinces of the old Austria-Hungarian empire formed the future Yugoslavia, the northern provinces becoming Czechoslovakia. Poland regained its independence and Alsace-Lorraine was restored to France. Germany lost some of its European territory, and was deprived of its colonies. Harsh reparations intended to curb its economic recovery were imposed, but these provided conditions conducive to the emergence of fascism and the Second World War, which culminated in Hiroshima and Nagasaki. Many historians view World War II as a continuation of the 1914-18 war, the war which was meant to end all wars.

Entry of America into the Great War marked a suspension of its isolationist policy and the start of its role as the major international power. The 1914-18 war saw a reversal of the economic positions of Britain and the US, and the shift of capitalism's epicentre from London to New York.

Diplomacy between the Great Powers having utterly failed to prevent the 1914-18 war, the post-war mechanism for settling disputes was to be the League of Nations. Unfortunately this, too, proved to be ultimately ineffective, an important reason being that the US refused to join, partly for internal political reasons, and partly to avoid further involvement in European affairs.

Total war necessitated mass production of materiel, requiring reorganisation of industry along the lines pioneered in America. The pursuit of victory at any cost meant also that the entire economy needed to be organised and managed while maintaining as far as possible social justice and equity of sacrifice. In Britain, the bargaining power of organised labour was transformed, and a greatly expanded trade union movement negotiated improved working conditions and a better standard of living for its members. The wartime recruitment of women to work in factories and on the land accelerated their post-war emancipation; women over 30 who were ratepayers or married to a ratepayer obtained the vote in 1918, when the franchise was extended to all men over 21.

The Great War, whose onset was unexpected and outcome unforeseen, touched the lives of every family in Europe, and had global repercussions at all levels of human society. In all of recorded human history this was the most powerful force for change and innovation to have yet emerged from the interactive behaviour of this extraordinary species of matter, *Homo sapiens*.

# Summing Up

Connectivity, unpredictability and creativity are dynamic properties of matter which are manifested simultaneously at many levels. Connectivity is present at every level upwards from the fundamental constituents of atoms. The entanglement of matter ensures that every thing is linked to everything else. Every event is influenced, and held in place, by a multitude of links to other events. An event is a knot at a crossing of threads in a multidimensional net. By this metaphor, to seek the cause of an event is to attempt to tease out and give primacy to just one of many connections passing through a tangled skein: causation is a human conceit. Events are not caused, but happen as a result of the coming together of many influences. Historical happenings include the abolition of slavery (good), the Great War (bad), the industrial revolution (good and bad), and the evolution of capitalism (jury's out, but looking bad).

Matter is fundamentally unpredictable. The future is not predestined to happen in a certain way, it is open, unknown and unknowable, a superposition of possibilities at every level, from the atomic to the universal. At an intermediate and human level, the complexity of human society, and the ecosystem in which it is embedded, together with their present states of disequilibrium, means that unpredictable and unprecedented events which cannot now be imagined are only to be expected. These future happenings – revolutionary new technologies, popular mass movements, new ideologies – could result in our salvation or our damnation, but what cannot be imagined cannot be brought about intentionally. But because of the connectivity of matter, we can influence future events, and we can, and should, strive to bring about desirable outcomes and avert disaster; our actions, however, will often be ineffective or have unforeseen and unintended consequences.

407

Thus, matter is intensely lively stuff, interacting with itself in a huge variety of ways which lead to the emergence of new structures and properties, amongst which may be counted life and consciousness. Human consciousness is a very recent arrival in the universe, and in the short time it has existed it has indulged in self aggrandisement on a colossal scale. From being a thin scum of epiphenomenal froth at the edge of the universe, it has sometimes considered itself to be the very *fons et origo* of the cosmos. The reality, as far as we can understand it, is very different, and much more astonishing. Creativity resides in every atom of the universe. All around us the matter of the universe is engaged in a continuous process of innovation and renewal, from the alchemy of the sun to the birth of children. The fecundity and the power of human imagination, whose imaginings cause us so much trouble, also are owed to the creativity of the material of which we are made. Our inventiveness, together with our consciousness, arise from the formative matter of our bodies, the fertile stuff of stars.

# Notes

## Chapter 9: The Matter with Matter

1   Ilya Prigogine. *The End of Certainty: Time, Chaos and the New Laws of Nature*. New York: The Free Press, 1997: p71.
2   Duncan J Watts. *Six Degrees: The Science of a Connected Age*. London: Vintage, 2004: p37-42.
3   Ibid, p178.
4   Richard Dawkins. *Viruses of the Mind*. In Bo Dahlbom (ed). *Dennett and his critics*. Oxford: Blackwell Publishers Ltd, 1995: p19.
5   Malcolm Gladwell. *The Tipping Point: How Little Things Can Make a Big Difference*. London: Little, Brown and Company, 2000: p3-5, 216-220.
6   Duncan J Watts. *Six Degrees: The Science of a Connected Age*. London: Vintage, 2004: p243-4.
7   Deepak Lal. *Unintended Consequences: The Impact of Factor Endowments, Culture, and Politics on Long-run Economic Performance*. Cambridge, Mass.: The MIT Press, 1998: p83-6.
8   Alfred W Crosby. *Ecological Imperialism: The Biological Expansion of Europe 900-1900*. Cambridge University Press, 1986: p5.
9   Alfred W Crosby. *The Measure of Reality: Quantification and Western Society 1250-1600*. Cambridge University Press, 1997: p49-74.
10  Pierre-Simon Laplace. *Essai Philosophique sur les Probabilités*. www.en.wikipedia.org/wiki/Pierre-Simon_Laplace#Laplace.27s_demon
11  "Three body problem." Britannica CD 99 Multimedia Edition © 1994-1999 Encyclopædia Britannica, Inc.
12  James Gleick. *Chaos: Making a New Science*. London, Sphere Books Ltd, 1987: p8.
13  Ibid, p322.
14  Duncan J Watts. *Six degrees: The Science of a Connected Age*. London: Vintage, 2004: p211.

15 Ilya Prigogine. *The End of Certainty: Time, Chaos and the New Laws of Nature*. New York: The Free Press, 1997.

16 Ilya Prigogine, Isabelle Stengers. *Order out of Chaos: Man's New Dialogue with Nature*. London: Fontana Paperbacks, 1985: p146-53.

17 Ilya Prigogine. *The End of Certainty: Time, Chaos and the New Laws of Nature*. New York: The Free Press, 1997: p66.

18 Niall Shanks. *God, the Devil, and Darwin: A Critique of Intelligent Design Theory*. Oxford University Press, 2004: p120-23.

19 Monique Canto-Sperber, Jean-Christophe Rufin. Où va le monde? Désordres, organisation et valeurs. *Banquet: Revue du CERAP* 2005; 22: 37-41.
www.leeds.ac.uk/demographic_entrapment/index.htm

20 Interview with Tallis, The ardent atheist. *The Guardian* 29 April 2006.

21 Raymond Tallis. *The Explicit Animal: A Defence of Human Consciousness*. Basingstoke: Macmillan Press Ltd, 1999: p161-209.

22 Ibid, p197.

23 Ibid, p245-6.

24 Ibid, p244. ·

25 Ibid, p247.

26 Galen Strawson et al. Edited by Anthony Freeman. *Consciousness and its Place in Nature*: *Does Physicalism Entail Panpsychism?* Exeter: Imprint-academic.com, 2006.

27 Jerry Fodor. Headaches have themselves. *London Review of Books* 29(1) 24 May 2007.

28 Galen Strawson et al. Edited by Anthony Freeman. *Consciousness and its Place in Nature*: *Does Physicalism Entail Panpsychism?* Exeter: Imprint-academic.com, 2006: p275.

29 Raymond Tallis. *The Explicit Animal: A Defence of Human Consciousness*. Basingstoke: Macmillan Press Ltd, 1999: p3.

30 Marcia Bjornerud. *Reading the Rocks: The Autobiogra-*

*phy of the Earth.* New York: Basic Books, 2005: p139-44.

31  Richard Dawkins. *The Ancestor's Tale: A Pilgrimage to the Dawn of Life.* London: Phoenix, 2005: p176-80.

32  Elaine Morgan. *The Scars of Evolution: What our Bodies Tell us About Human Origins.* London: Souvenir Press, 1990: p51.

33  J M Roberts. *The History of the World.* Revised edition. Oxford: Helicon Publishing Ltd, 1992: p29.

34  AJP Taylor. *The First World War and its Aftermath.* London: The Folio Society, 1998: p26.

35  Barbara W Tuchman. *The Proud Tower.* London: The Folio Society, 1995: p xii.

36  Eric Hobsbawm. *The Age of Empire: 1875 –1914.* London: Weidenfeld & Nicolson, 1987: p190.

37  Barbara W Tuchman. *The Proud Tower.* London: The Folio Society, 1995: p232.

38  Eric Hobsbawm. *The Age of Empire: 1875 –1914.* London: Weidenfeld & Nicolson, 1987: p326.

39  Barbara W Tuchman. *The Proud Tower.* London: The Folio Society, 1995: p379-434.

40  AJP Taylor. *The First World War and its Aftermath.* London: The Folio Society, 1998: p27-34.

41  Martin Gilbert. *A History of the Twentieth Century. Volume One: 1900 – 1933.* London: HarperCollins*Publishers,* 1997: p310-11.

42  Eric Hobsbawm. *The Age of Empire: 1875 –1914.* London: Weidenfeld & Nicolson, 1987: p304.

43  AJP Taylor. *The Struggle for Mastery in Europe II.* London: The Folio Society, 1998: p570.

44  Barbara W Tuchman. *The Proud Tower.* London: The Folio Society, 1995: p110.

# Chapter 10

# Materialism and Meaning

'Shit happens'. *Anon*

## In Defence of Materialism

The previous chapter extolled the virtues of matter, the stuff of which the universe is made. In all respects, matter has every desirable property. Its connectivity means that we are not alienated from the universe, quite the contrary: we are a constituent part of it, and its matter is our matter. In a myriad ways the matter comprising our bodies is in communication with the whole universe, transcending space and time, though only time past and not time future. Our evolutionary history means also that we are intimately related to every other living thing, with which we share the same basic biochemistry represented by DNA.

Our own species, like those most closely related to us, is intensely social, and, as with other primates, we are capable of fellow feeling, of sharing each other's emotions, of joy or grief which bring us together, or anger and hatred which come between us. We share, too, as do chimps, basic notions of right and wrong. Our behaviour in the society of our fellows arises from our interactions with them, and we rely on our connectivity with others, and their appreciation of us, for our self-fulfilment.

The inherent unpredictability of matter means that the future – including our individual destinies – is open and undetermined. Within this material system, our selves, that is to say, our bodies in their entirety, have a considerable degree of freedom to act in different ways. The connectivity of matter and events ensures that we then affect the future, though not in an entirely predictable direction.

Matter is prodigiously creative, continually producing new varieties, novel properties and singular events, which are mostly unimaginable until they happen. The scale of the universe, and the complexity of the stuff of which it is made, is awesome. Most marvellous of all is that, as creatures of matter, we have the capacity to understand a little of the epic succession of material processes by which we came to be here, and how it is that we are able to contemplate our own contemplation.

Notwithstanding matter's many laudable emergent properties, including life and consciousness, over the centuries materialism has had a rather sinister reputation. As the word is used here, signifying the belief that nothing exists except matter, materialism is tainted by association with its other meaning – as a way of life in which satisfaction is sought in material possessions and physical pleasures. There is, perhaps, a supposed link also with the Marxist theory of dialectical materialism. But philosophical materialism does not entail any particular way of life or political affiliation, and those who accept materialism can be as ascetic or as sybaritic as they come, and may hold any political opinion or none; the charge against philosophical materialism, of guilt by association, is unwarranted.

Another reason for materialism's bad odour is its association with determinism, with its implied threat to our individual freedom of action. Laplace's espousal of Newtonian mechanics must bear much of the blame for this. For as recounted in the last chapter, Laplace was mistaken when he claimed that a superior intellect, knowing the position and momentum of every particle, would be able to predict the future. In principle, and in practice, the future is unknown and unknowable, making possible the notion and the experience of choice. Although it is difficult for us to conceptualise causation that has a physical basis but which is indeterminate, yet that is the way it is: very seldom is the outcome of a causal process 100% certain.

A third element contributing to materialism's bad reputation derives from the soul/body split of Christianity, which in turn had its origins with Plato and the Neoplatonic philosopher, Plotinus. He claimed that the universe originated in the One, which was also the ultimate Good. Emanating from the One were the Platonic forms, or essences, which moulded matter into its many varieties. Matter, being at the furthest remove from the ultimate Good, is therefore evil, though only in the negative sense of lacking good. But according to the second century heresy of Gnosticism, the world is positively evil, having been created by the lesser divinity of the demiurge antagonistic to the spiritual world created by the Ultimate Good. These antiquated ideas of good spiritual forces struggling to overcome evil material powers linger on, and to be 'other-worldly' is considered good even today, while those reprobates who believe that the universe is all and only made of matter are thought by some to leave a sulphurous scent in the air when they pass...

The vision of materialism presented in the previous chapter turns the spiritualist world view on its head. For rather than being dumb, passive stuff, which only comes to life when breathed upon by some ethereal spirit, matter is the origin of all creatures and all creation, including the spiritual world dreamed up by matter walking on two legs.

414

# Does Life Have a Meaning?

For many people, a world from which all things spiritual are banished would be incomprehensible and very alarming. The disquiet experienced at the very idea of a Godless universe is well expressed by a creationist, Nancy Piercey:

> If our life on earth is a product of blind, purposeless natural causes, then our own lives are cosmic accidents. There's no source of transcendent moral guidelines, no unique dignity for human life. On the other hand, if life is the product of foresight and design, then you and I were meant to be here. In God's revelation we have a solid basis for morality, purpose and dignity.[1]

Her unease has its source in contingency – the succession of cosmic accidents that led to the appearance of the universe, our solar system, life on earth and the origin of our species. For her peace of mind she has to believe that these things were not accidental, but meant to be. For Christians such as her, it is God's purpose that we should exist, and the universe is said to be grounded in His Being; God is the First Cause, First Mover or Prime Necessary Being, the buffer at the end of the explanatory line. God is also the author of the final cause of creation – the end for which all creatures were created. Unless the universe is *for* something, that something being to do with ourselves, Piercy claims that as well as there being no basis for morality, our individual lives are meaningless, lacking both purpose and dignity.

In a book ambitiously entitled *The Meaning of Life*, lapsed Catholic writer Terry Eagleton describes this as a false antithesis: in several senses life may have a meaning even for non-believers.[2] But Eagleton points out that even if the belief is held that existence is grounded in God, ironically, this does not get the believer off the hook of contingency.[3] For if there is a Reason for our existence, that is to say, if it was logically necessary that there should be something rather than nothing, this would have been a constraint on God's omnipotence and freedom. The medieval theologians therefore argued that our creation must have been contingent rather than necessary. But neither did our creation answer a need that God may have had – for company, perhaps, or for something to do. Almighty God does not have needs. So creation was the result of a whim, a capricious act of unreason that renders life hardly more meaningful for the believer than it is for the non-believer: whatever one's belief, there is an awareness that we might never have come into existence, and that we are going to die. Whether or not the premise of God's existence is true, the same conclusion is reached: our existence is accidental, and our life may come to an inadvertent end at any moment. We are playthings, either of God or the gods – the latter being a metaphor for the mischievousness of matter.

Eagleton puts it rather differently: 'the world is like a work of art, [which] God created...out of love rather than need.' However, the assumption that God is good, and that His creation of the universe was an act of love, turns out not to be the missing piece of a puzzle which, snapped into place, makes the whole picture meaningful. Quite the reverse: there now has to be an explanation for the existence of evil. Although we cannot understand the mysterious ways in which God moves, some evil is apparently necessary for there to be a greater amount of good. Where does evil come from? God does not cause it but allows it to happen. And it happens because He has given us the freedom to act autonomously according to our essential natures. In His goodness and wisdom, and having considered all the possibilities, God created a world in which the sum of good is as great as it could possibly be, and the sum of evil is as small as it could possibly be. Ours is the best of all possible worlds, being the solution to an infinitely complex cost/benefit calculation. Tell that to a mother whose children are starving. She is more likely to conclude that God is either not loving, or is not all-powerful, or both; perhaps he does not exist.

*

There are several different senses of the words 'to mean', but when thinking about the meaning of life the two which are most relevant are 'to intend' or 'to purpose', and 'to have a significant pattern'. The first of these meanings is seen in the random movements of a young baby's limbs, from which we may infer the intention to grasp the pretty object dangled in front of him. Although they are uncoordinated and as yet ineffective, the baby's movements may be correctly interpreted teleologically – as being purposeful. The second sense, of a significant pattern without intention, is exhibited by the planet Venus moving through the night sky on successive evenings; although purposeless, its stately progression is far from meaningless, its movements relative to the stars having a pattern full of significance for those who can understand it.

In former times, the appearance of design in nature was taken to be evidence of intention on the part of a Designer who meant nature to be the way it is. Darwinism provides a better explanation, the appearance of design now signifying the operation of natural selection acting on genetic mutations, and resulting in adaptation to whatever ecological niche is occupied by the organism. Although evolution is not directed purposefully to a goal, it has left a significant pattern on the natural world, which required the genius of Darwin to recognise. Thus, rejection of spiritual and teleological explanations of natural phenomena has not resulted in an outbreak of meaninglessness, quite the contrary. The many discoveries in cosmology, physics, chemistry and biology constitute a coherent world view where previously there was confusion, ignorance and superstition.

The two senses of 'meaning' – 'having purpose' and 'having a significant pattern' – correspond to two ways of interpreting causation: active or passive; as having been caused or as having happened; purposeful or aimless. Because we are teleologically promiscuous, predisposed to see purpose even when there is none, we incline to the former of these two ways of thinking about events; and where there is purpose there is agency. These contrasting modes of thought correspond to spiritualistic and materialistic attitudes, and for most people the former is the natural way of interpreting the world and our place within it. Thinking materialistically, that events happen rather than that they are caused, and considering the system in which they happen rather than trying to identify individual influences, does not come readily.

The scientific method of acquiring knowledge of the natural world consists essentially of trying to disprove hypotheses rather than finding additional evidence in support of them. As such, it too is a very unnatural activity which goes against the human grain. Moreover, scientific knowledge is considered by some to detract from our appreciation of the natural world. The poet Keats berated science – known as philosophy in his time – for removing nature's mysteries:

> Philosophy will clip an Angel's wings,
> Conquer all mysteries by rule and line,
> Empty the haunted air, and gnomed mine –
> Unweave a rainbow...[4]

Keats' target was Isaac Newton, who had split white light by means of a prism into its constituent rainbow colours – from which he then reconstituted white light using another prism.

418

From these and other observations he deduced that light travels as a wave. In *Unweaving the rainbow*, Richard Dawkins, formerly Professor of the Public Understanding of Science at Oxford University, roundly repudiates Keats' attitude towards science. Dawkins relates how Newton's experiments with light resulted in the science of spectroscopy, and our knowledge of the composition of stars. Then came the detection of the red shift of starlight – the vital clue that showed that the universe is expanding consequent on the Big Bang, fourteen billion years ago. Teasing the rainbow apart has revealed it to be part of an even greater tapestry, before which few remain unmoved. Some unweaving!

\*

A few fundamentalists apart, most people could not care less about their accidental cosmic and evolutionary origins, while the casuistical reasoning of theologians and philosophers is of interest only to themselves. For most of us, what gives meaning to life is having loving relationships with a partner, and with children, and having things we want to do. The meaning of life is not a top-down given, but a bottom-up construct, centred on the family. It is what is most important to us, what we strive for daily. It might be power, money, or fame, or physical fitness, or beauty. But these, like being warm, well-fed, safe and sound, are enabling conditions rather than ends in themselves. A more fundamental aim is to find happiness, something that requires no justification, but which by common consent is a legitimate end in itself.

Happiness is to be distinguished from pleasure, particularly the hedonistic, drowning of one's sorrows sort, which is a denial of life, a token dying. Happiness is self-fulfilment, making the best of one's abilities, living life to the full. As such it is not a state of mind, but an ongoing long-term endeavour. Neither is it rampant individualism, where one person's success is achieved at the expense of another's failure. Rather, the happiness which derives from self-fulfilment requires other people, and does not occur in isolation; our well-being is dependent upon other people's appreciation, and they need ours. While pursuing our own interests, we have to create the space in which other people can pursue theirs, an accomplishment which requires virtuoso social skills developed by lifelong practice.

Terry Eagleton comes to the conclusion that what gives the greatest meaning to life is *agape*, Christian love. Agape is non-erotic reciprocal love, in which we pursue other peoples' interests as if they were our own. In so doing, we do not sacrifice our own happiness, but rather, we find it more abundantly, while our own lives are enriched by others' concern for us. Agape goes beyond Aristotle's concept of living virtuously, which was essentially a political system and had little to do with either love or happiness.

Eagleton claims that love is the stuff of stars, and loving puts us in touch with God, eternity, and the very ground of existence. But loving one's neighbour as oneself is a human concept, which, even if it is not applied globally, has global appeal. It is the highest ideal yet to emerge from the troubled experience of human beings living together. Eagleton defines God as 'the condition of possibility of any entity whatsoever, including ourselves...the answer to why there is something rather than nothing.'[5] But that is a definition which applies equally well to matter, of which love is an emergent property. God's love is not at the origin of matter; rather, it is matter which is the source of love, life, consciousness and everything else that we value.

# Positive Pessimism

After progressing from the Big Bang to the war in Iraq and the future of capitalism, with many detours and digressions on the way, we return again to consider our human predicament. We are facing nine serious problems – population growth, economic growth, the end of oil, climate change, environmental degradation, armed conflict, nuclear catastrophe, subversion of democracy and societal collapse – which are related to each other in many complicated ways (frontisepiece). Each is ultimately of human origin, though none occurs solely at the level of the individual. These problems, together with their inter-relationships, which often include unstable positive feedback loops, may be considered as a system whose elemental components are humans: the problems are emergent properties arising from the many ways in which we relate to each other. As such, they are all unintended consequences of our activities, and for the most part they are problems which were also unforeseen until they forced themselves on our attention. Furthermore, the system as a whole is so complex, and is in such a state of disequilibrium, that new problematic properties are likely to emerge at any time to exacerbate the already grievous situation. What is so disturbing about this system is the absence of any higher centre from which control can be exercised. Our disentanglement from this ensnaring net is dependent on the spontaneous emergence of solutions out of the actions of a mass of individuals acting primarily in their own interests.

A parallel may be drawn between the human situation and the first attempts of bees to live together in colonies. How long did it take them to evolve colonies of optimum size – small enough to survive the winter on the available stores of honey, and big enough to huddle together and defeat the cold? How many failures were there before the best division

421

of labour emerged, with the optimum ratio of drones to workers? How many colonies collapsed from in-fighting before reliable mechanisms were developed for distinguishing friend from foe, us from them? The human situation, where planet Earth is our one and only hive, is so very complicated compared with a hive of bees; it seems to me unlikely that we will get the numbers, the social structures and the energy balance right first time.

The answer to the question of how we humans got ourselves into this predicament is succinctly summarised by the epigraph to this chapter. To be sure, flaws in the way we think contribute significantly to our problems, but they do not provide a sufficient explanation. Problems happen. In shovelfuls.

However, just as we may expect additional new and unforeseen problems to emerge, by the same token, we may hope for propitious new developments, in technology, and in social organisation, and in mass movements. But like other emergent properties, these are mostly unimaginable until they occur, and for that reason cannot be brought about intentionally. Like Micawber we are living beyond our means, and like him we can hope that something will turn up.

Although no remedies for our human predicament were promised in the Introduction, any readers who have come this far will feel that these conclusions are a very poor reward for their perseverance. Surely, readers have a right to expect the author to propose some positive programme, some scheme for extricating ourselves from our parlous situation? But the nine problems listed above, to which others could be added, are nine obdurate grounds for pessimism. Population growth – to increase and multiply – is at the very core of our biological nature; armed conflict has existed ever since humankind became a toolmaker; other problems are more recent in our history, but no less intractable. In the face of these facts a pessimistic outlook is not inappropriate.

\*

Doom-and-gloom mongers may perhaps have a better grasp of reality than optimists: psychologists have shown that people who are clinically depressed may sometimes have a more realistic assessment of their life situation than those who are not.[6] But pessimism does not have to be a disposition to be gloomy and look on the black side, and it is not a contradiction to be a happy pessimist. Nor is pessimism to be confused with scepticism, cynicism or nihilism. According to the political philosopher Joshua Foa Dienstag, pessimism is a philosophical position which has a diverse and creditable, though somewhat covert, tradition, going back to the presocratic philosophers in ancient Greece.[7] Pessimism as a philosophy tends not to be taken very seriously today, partly perhaps because Arthur Schopenhauer (1788-1860), its grimmest modern exponent – 'human life must be some sort of mistake' – has become something of a figure of fun.[8] Another reason is that Friedrich Nietzsche (1844-1900), doyen of pessimism, wrote in an aphoristic style, which while appropriate for an account of a chaotic and incomprehensible universe, does not make for a coherent message.

In *Pessimism: Philosophy, Ethic, Spirit*, Dienstag describes three strands of pessimism: the burden of time, the irony of history and the absurdity of life.[9] In contrast with animals, which live in the present and have no hopes for the future or regrets for the past, we are ever conscious of the passage of time and the transience of life and happiness. We pass our lives in suffering under the shadow of death which will de-

423

stroy all that we love most dearly. Time is our great enemy, laying waste to everything we build, and eroding all certainties; moral values come and go, and even the most secure knowledge gained by science is provisional. Our inability to live in the present and to enjoy simply *existing* is shown by our propensity for boredom: we are not content unless we are striving after some future satisfaction which, no sooner achieved, is only a memory.

Optimists believe that reason will enable us to exercise control over our circumstances, solve our problems, ameliorate our lives, and make us happy. The irony of history is that reason has destroyed the illusions that gave us solace, such as those of a benevolent deity overseeing an anthropocentric universe, or of an autonomous self in control of its own destiny. Moreover, many of our actions have had consequences which were the opposite of what was intended. Although there has been undoubted progress in some fields, in technology for instance, it often comes at a cost which nullifies the benefit. It would be an extreme irony if catastrophic climate change were to wipe out the gains of the industrial revolution – but that is a distinct possibility. Or, one evil may be eliminated, only to be replaced by another: wage or sex slavery replacing the previous indentured version.

The word 'absurd', applied to existence, was first used by the French writer, Albert Camus (1913-60).[10] Absurdity here is the mismatch between our desires and our means of achieving them; the cosmic joke of our seeking incompatible ends; the fatuity of life-long striving culminating in annihilation.

Pessimism, then, is not the opposite of optimism, but its negation. Things are not necessarily getting worse, but the enlightenment claim of indefinite progress is certainly false.

Nothing endures. Expect nothing, and you will not be disappointed.

The response to this pessimistic account of the human condition varies, from a paralytic resignation to an invigorating liberation. While some pessimists declare that it would be better not to have been born than endure a life of suffering, no pessimist actually recommends suicide.[11] Schopenhauer, however, advocates something similar in a solitary life of asceticism and self-denial.

By contrast, Nietzsche's particular variety of pessimism has been characterised as the 'art of living', and is strongly life affirming, though only for those strong enough to tolerate life's ultimate meaninglessness.[12] Pessimism need not lead to resignation but may give rise to spirited self-realisation and the finding of meaning, albeit temporary, in whatever materials life presents us with.

Camus, too, is life-affirming, asserting that a life in retreat, and suicide even more so, is not a judgement on life but an abdication of judgement, an evasion of the challenges presented by existence.[13] Another evasion, dismissed by Camus as a 'betrayal', is offered by hope in a utopian future, either in this life or in the next. As for making the leap of faith necessary for belief in God, he describes this as philosophical suicide and the sacrifice of the intellect.[14]

Camus' heroic and absurd ideal is the mythical figure of Sisyphus.[15] A mortal with a passion for life, Sisyphus mocked the gods and tricked death, for which he was punished by everlastingly having to push a great rock to the top of a mountain, only to see it roll to the bottom where he had to start the onerous task all over again. Sisyphus gladly accepted this never-ending hell of pointless toil as the price for a life lived to the full in defiance of the fates. This philosophy was further developed by Camus in fictional form in *The Plague*, written during the Nazi occupation of France.[16] The central, heroic, character, Dr Rieux, alongside other responsible citizens, unsparingly does what he can to alleviate the suffering of the occupants of the besieged plague city – an allegory for France under fascism. During the occupation, Camus was a member of the resistance, and the editor of a clandestine journal, *Combat*. Regardless of what it achieved, involvement in the resistance movement was its own justification as an appropriate response to oppression. Camus' life history thus exemplifies his philosophy of personal defiance and political engagement in the face of absurdity. His is the philosophy we need to adopt to bring about the conditions conducive to the emergence of new solutions to age-old human problems. Micawber was content to wait for relief, but for us, so much more is at stake that we cannot afford to leave it to chance. It is crucial that we work together to produce the conditions in which new solutions are more likely to emerge.

Another figure who personifies the positive pessimistic approach to life is Cervantes' Don Quixote.[17] Inspired by stories of chivalry, he sets off, taking whatever road his horse chooses, not to change the world according to some ideology, but seeking 'grievances to redress, wrongs to right, injuries to amend, abuses to correct, and debts to discharge'.[18] By the experience of his life, and by his interactions with the people he encounters, he and they are changed, and the Knight of the Sad Countenance leaves the world a better place than he found it. Unconsciously following Aristotle's dictum that to become virtuous you have to live virtuously, Don Quixote, through the narrative of his absurd life, provides an example for us to follow.

# Summing Up

Dualism, a belief in the coexistence in the universe of both matter and spirit, is widespread. In particular, the creation of the universe is widely thought to have had a spiritual explanation, variously named God or First Cause. Belief in the spiritual is unfounded, and incapable of being confirmed or refuted. Belief in materialism – that the universe is all and only made of matter – in no way diminishes or limits the splendour of creation, but it makes for a more economical and coherent account of it. Acceptance of materialism also calls for a reassessment of our place within the universe.

Human nature reflects the properties of the matter of which we are made, and which is the source of all that we value. Hence, the human body is not the despised and unworthy receptacle of the eternal soul, but body and soul are one and the same, comprised of the same material. Since we are not responsible for our evolved nature, we need not castigate ourselves for being sinful and for having fallen from a state of grace – there never was such a state. But neither should we assume a privileged position in creation; our presence on Earth is contingent and serves no supernatural purpose.

Love and consciousness, being emergent properties of the living matter of which we are composed, are extinguished with life itself. This certitude makes our own and other's lives all the more precious: it is the only life we have, and like a shooting star it is preceded and followed by an infinitude of oblivion.

Given the basic necessities, life offers much to enjoy. The greatest satisfaction is to be found in loving relationships with others, and the highest human ideal is mutual love between all members of the extended human family. However, a great many people on Earth lack the basic necessities, and for most people life is far from being ideal. The gulf between the possibility of human happiness and the reality is so great, and the difficulty of bridging the gap so immense, that pessimism for the future of humanity is only realistic. An authentic response to the human predicament is a pragmatic engagement with whatever problems come immediately to hand.

# Notes

## Chapter 10: Materialism and Meaning

1  Nancy Pearcey of the Discovery Institute (the home base for intelligent design theory), *cited in* Niall Shanks. *God, the Devil, and Darwin: A Critique of Intelligent Design Theory.* Oxford University Press, 2004: p230.

2  Terry Eagleton. *The Meaning of Life.* Oxford University Press, 2007: p77.

3  'Does the donkey have to bray?' Terry Eagleton. *London Review of Books* 25 September 2008.

4  John Keats. 'Lamia' *cited in* Richard Dawkins. *Unweaving the Rainbow: Science, Delusion and the Appetite for Wonder.* London: Penguin Books, 1998: p39.

5  'Does the donkey have to bray?' Terry Eagleton. *London Review of Books* 25 September 2008.

6  Katharine J Mair. 'Depression and the Facts of Life'. *Changes* 1989; 7: 112-16.

7  Joshua Foa Dienstag. *Pessimism: Philosophy, Ethic, Spirit.* Princeton University Press, 2006.

8  Terry Eagleton. *The Meaning of Life.* Oxford University Press, 2007: p82.

9  Joshua Foa Dienstag. *Pessimism: Philosophy, Ethic, Spirit.* Princeton University Press, 2006: p19-36.

10  Albert Camus. *Le Mythe de Sisyphe: Essai sur l'absurde.* Paris: Editions Gallimard, 1942.

11  Joshua Foa Dienstag. *Pessimism: Philosophy, Ethic, Spirit.* Princeton University Press, 2006: p37.

12  Ibid, p164.

13  Ibid, p130.

14  Albert Camus. *Le Mythe de Sisyphe: Essai sur l'absurde.* Paris: Editions Gallimard, 1942: p48-74.

15  Ibid, p163-68.

16  Albert Camus. *La Peste.* Paris: Editions Gallimard, 1947.

17  Joshua Foa Dienstag. *Pessimism: Philosophy, Ethic, Spirit.* Princeton University Press, 2006: p201-25.

18  Miguel de Cervantes Saavedra. Translated by JM Cohen. *The Adventures of Don Quixote*. Harmondsworth: Penguin Books Ltd, 1950: p35.

# Epilogue – or New Chapter?

'Today I say to you that the challenges we face are real. They are serious and they are many. They will not be met easily or in a short span of time. But know this, [America] – they will be met.' *Barack Obama*

Legend has it that at his accession to the throne of the city of Gordium, King Midas tied up his chariot using an intricate knot which defeated all attempts at its undoing, and of which it was prophesied that whoever undid it would rule Asia. When Alexander heard of the reward for meeting this challenge he tried his hand at untying the knot, but finding no loose end, lost patience and slashed it through with his sword. His flatterers then declared that the prophecy applied to him, Alexander the Great; and so it proved.[1]

Unfortunately, with regard to the nine great challenges which face us, there is nobody with Alexander's chutzpah to impose radical solutions. Alexander had only one knot to unravel, but we have many, which are tied in with each other in complicated ways. Our only recourse is to worry away at our knotty problems thread by thread, hoping for some slackening of the tensions, but not expecting a complete disentanglement.

We are in a deep trouble, and it is by no means sure that we will be able to extricate ourselves in time to avert disaster, or indeed, that the problems we face are soluble. Nevertheless, inspired like Don Quixote with the highest human ideals, and ever respectful of core human rights, we must focus on the outcomes we need to achieve, and engage energetically with whatever means of achieving them come to hand.

# Nine Gordian Knots

## 1. Population Growth

The fundamental problem of our species is that, having out-witted our predators, including those responsible for infectious diseases, there are <u>too many of us</u> for the planet to support in the manner to which we in the developed countries have become accustomed, and to which those in the developing countries aspire. For us all to have a European standard of living would require three additional planets, or five for living as North Americans do. This is not a problem the market will solve since however great the demand for new planets, the market cannot begin to satisfy it. The radical solution is a <u>diminution of human numbers,</u> which will either come about voluntarily, or will be brought about by famine, disease and war.

The limit to the number of people the earth will support sustainably is set by global biocapacity, the total area of biologically productive land. The number of people supported by each hectare (1 hectare = 2.47 acres) is determined by their consumption of renewable resources, described as a footprint. A person's ecological footprint is the area required to produce the resources he or she consumes, and to absorb the waste he or she generates. This area is expressed in global hectares per person (gha/p), that is, hectares with world-average biological productivity. In 2003 the average ecological footprint of the 6.3 billion inhabitants of the world was 2.23 gha/p. The range of footprint size is huge, from over 9 gha/p in North America, about 5 gha/p in European Union (EU) countries, to 1 gha/p in Asia and the Pacific, and in Africa.[2]

By comparison with the footprints of high-income countries, the global average of 2.23 gha/p is very modest. Nevertheless, it exceeds the available biocapacity of 1.8 gha per person, so according to the Optimum Population Trust the sustainable population for the 2003 footprint is 5.1 billion, a contraction of 1.2 billion from the total then of 6.3 billion.[3]

The inequitable distribution of resource consumption between high and low-income countries is morally repugnant. If the footprint of developing countries were to be raised to 3.3 gha/p (30% less than that currently enjoyed in the EU), and the developed countries' footprint, including that of North America, were to be reduced to the same level, and if predicted loss of global biocapacity due to climate change, deforestation and loss of biodiversity is factored in, then the sustainable population is estimated to be 2.7 billion.

This estimate, which assumes a 60% reduction of carbon emissions in high income countries, has to be viewed against a world population which has more than doubled since it was last at a sustainable level in 1950, and is projected to be more than 9 billion by 2050.

*

The freedom to start a family is a core human right which only a totalitarian regime would consider infringing. We have reason, though, to be grateful to the Chinese government for its imposition of a 'one child' policy on its people, without which, world population would now be 400 million greater than it is.[4] However, with an increased standard of living and better education, couples voluntarily choose to have smaller families. Without imposing a strict limitation on family size, governments could nudge us towards having even fewer children by the withdrawal of family allowances and other financial inducements which are in place in many countries, especially in Europe. It is important, too, that the fundamen-

433

tal problem of over-population should be acknowledged and given greater publicity, and that there should be a change in our attitude towards having children, with approval for those who unselfishly decide to have none, and strong disapproval of those who do not heed the motto of the Optimum Population Trust, to 'stop at two'.

Key factors for reducing human fertility are education of girls, empowerment of women, and the availability of a full range of family planning services, including termination of unwanted pregnancies. Unfortunately, there are religious objections to contraception and, especially, to abortion, on the grounds that these vitally important matters of life and death are for God (in absentia) and not man to decide. Thus, under the Bush administration, American aid to charitable organisations providing family planning services in developing countries was denied if termination was offered for unwanted pregnancies, or even discussed as an option.[5] The upshot of this 'Gag' rule was that contraceptive services had to contract, with an increase in the number of unwanted pregnancies and illicit abortions, endangering the lives and health of the women involved, and contributing to the foremost human problem of overpopulation.

---

## Three Quixotic Things to do Today Concerning Population Growth

- ❖ Unless it's already too late, resolve to 'stop at two' or preferably fewer

- ❖ Send a donation to the International Planned Parenthood Federation

- ❖ Send a donation to Oxfam to support a programme for the empowerment of women

---

## 2. Economic Growth

Population growth is probably the simplest of the problems we have to solve, being directly dependent on individual decisions, and entailing a shift of attitude in favour of small families which is already underway in developed countries. Economic growth, on the other hand, is perhaps the greatest challenge to overcome because it concerns institutions and multinational corporations several removes from the actions of individuals, largely beyond the control of governments, and whose very purpose is growth.

For all but the last few hundred years of human history, global economic activity has closely tracked global population. But with the industrial revolution and the emergence of capitalism, average wealth per person has increased, and total economic activity has grown much faster than has the population. Economic activity in both manufacturing and service industries is now a problem for us because it impacts on planet Earth by its demand for energy and raw materials, and its production of waste. Whatever the means by which wealth is created, it is ultimately translated into *stuff*: gated mansions and private jets for the super rich, houses, cars, HD televisions and bottled water for the moderately rich, or subsistence food, fuel and shelter for the poor. Environmental impact is related to overall economic activity, expressed as gross domestic product (GDP). Global GDP increased nearly 15-fold during the last century, equivalent to an annual increase of 2.7%, apportioned roughly half and half between population growth and economic growth per person.[6] In this century, the average percentage increase in GDP per person in the five years up to 2007 was 3.4% per year, higher than in any period on record.[7] If global population were to remain as at present, this rate of growth by itself would result in a fourfold increase in the global economy by 2050, and a 22-fold increase by 2100.

Compounded with a projected world population of 9 billion, this growth in income per person, if maintained, would result in a sixfold expansion of the economy by 2050.

Because of its environmental impact, this rate of economic growth is not sustainable beyond the next decade or so unless it is decoupled from its consumption of resources and its production of waste. But while industry is capable of much greater efficiency in its use of energy and raw materials, and a much higher proportion of waste could be recycled, the environmental impact of a growing economy cannot be eliminated. A growth rate of only 1% per annum is equivalent to a 2.7-fold increase in a century, and even zero growth in the use of raw material in short supply cannot be considered truly sustainable; at a constant rate of consumption, a limited supply of a non-renewable resource will eventually run out. In order to halt the loss of Earth's biocapacity there needs to be a drastic contraction of the economy and an axing of consumption, something which unregulated free market capitalism is quite unable to bring about.

In *Capitalism as if the World Matters*, Jonathon Porritt presents a comprehensive exposé of free market capitalism, and presents a framework for a supposedly sustainable capitalism based on natural, human, social, manufactured and financial capital.[8] By 'capital' is meant any stock that yields valuable goods and services. Natural capital consists of material resources, sinks that absorb, neutralise or recycle waste, and services such as climate regulation. Each of the varieties of capital must be sustainable in its own right, and there can only be a very limited trade off between them. We are currently living off our capital in this enlarged sense since financial and manufactured capital are growing at the expense of natural, human and social capital: the whole system is headed for disaster.

436

Porritt notes that in an affluent industrial country, to preserve 'natural capital' and to achieve environmental sustainability, a reduction of about 90% in the environmental impact of consumption is required; this is to be achieved mainly by 'resource efficiency'.[9] He notes with approval that the UK's 'total material requirement' grew by 12% between 1970 and 1999, while GDP increased by 88%, a significant 'decoupling' of economic growth from its environmental impact. However, much of this decoupling resulted from a shift from manufacturing to services, and some of the environmental impact of the UK's consumption is simply relocated to countries such as China, which are now producing our consumer goods.

Without further growth of either population or economy, we are already eating into our natural capital and destroying Earth's capacity to support life, including our own. The urgent need is therefore to reduce global consumption while alternative renewable sources of energy and material are developed, and measures to increase resource efficiency are put in place. While he recognises this point of view, and lambasts greed-driven consumer society, Porritt argues against a reduction of consumption because it would lead to lower economic growth, reduced tax revenues, and inability to deal with poverty, either national or global.[10] Such ambivalence to the core problem of excessive consumption leads to the anomaly that Friends of the Earth, the green movement of which Porritt was one-time director, sends out an 82 page glossy catalogue of goods for sale, which includes a stainless steel solar-powered garden light, complete with rechargeable Ni-Mh battery. The promotion of consumption in this way is contributing to the very problems that the green movement was set up to combat. Porritt's reluctance to advocate a reduction of consumption is also partly explained by his not wanting to give the project of 'sustainable development' a negative image, there being no public, corporate or government appetite for a 'consume less' policy.

Because of its environmental impact, in particular its associated carbon emissions, exponential growth in the production and consumption of goods must be stemmed before the tipping point for runaway climate change is reached. If not by design, a slow-down may occur inadvertently as a result of the collapse of the financial and economic system taking place as this section is being written in October 2008. The widespread take-over of the banking system by government is also an opportunity to rectify some of the worst faults of unregulated capitalism.[11] Perhaps Micawberism will be vindicated.

Governments are judged on the economic growth that occurs during their term. But above a level of GDP which has long been surpassed in developed countries, neither the happiness, nor the quality of life, nor the longevity of the electorate is related to further growth in the economy. Many activities, which reflect societal malaise, such as expenditure on policing and construction of prisons, contribute to the calculation of GDP, as does defence spending. There is therefore a lot to be said for replacing GDP with a measure which more closely reflects peoples' contentment.[12] The aim of government would then be not perpetual growth of the economy, but 'the pursuit of happiness'. Such a change is likely to be strongly resisted by businesses whose shareholders look for year on year increases in share values and profits, and who look to government to encourage and assist economic growth whatever its basis.

Another factor militating against a reduction of economic activity is the link to employment. A person's job serves a dual purpose, to provide him with money for subsistence, and to give him a role in society. Now an industry, such as the manufacture of armaments, even though it may not make a positive contribution to the sum total of human happiness, and has a large negative impact on the environment through its carbon emissions and consumption of raw materials, may be difficult to close down because it will result in loss of jobs. If, as proposed by the Green Party, there were to be a 'citizens' income' whereby everybody unconditionally received an allowance for the provision of basic necessities, then many people would find meaningful occupation in pursuits that have a lower environmental impact and enhance civil society.[13] The creative and public spirited activities of many pensioners who are fortunate enough to receive a pension adequate for their subsistence illustrate this point. Attractive as it is, such a radical restructuring of society is as unlikely as pigs learning to fly. But good things do sometimes happen.

## Six Quixotic Things to do Concerning Economic Growth

❖ Resolve to work less, earn less and spend less

❖ Be less acquisitive of consumer goods; make-do and mend rather than buy new

❖ Live within your means: pay off your credit card every month

❖ Use your vote for whichever party seems most likely to curb capitalism's excesses

❖ Support the New Economic Foundation, and its attempt to find alternatives to GDP for measuring social and economic progress

❖ By all means take part in demonstrations to 'make poverty history' – but don't fly to get there

Box 22

Fossil Fuels – Coal, Oil and Gas

Coal consists of the buried and fossilised remains of the forests which covered the earth in the Carboniferous period 345-280 million years ago. Although coal reserves are finite, and coal was the first of the fossil fuels to be exploited as an energy source, the global endowment of coal is immense and there is no immediate prospect of its exhaustion.[14]

Oil (petroleum = rock oil) and gas were formed in two main geological periods 150 and 90 million years ago when there were giant blooms of plankton in the world's oceans. Plankton consists of a mass of small organisms drifting in the sea which, like the forests on land, ultimately obtain their energy from the sun by means of photosynthesis. Dead plankton fell into the sediment on the seabed where the high pressure at great depths turned the sediment into rock. In the absence of oxygen, high temperature caused the organic matter trapped in the 'source rock' to break down into compounds of carbon and hydrogen of varying length. The deeper the source rock the higher the temperature, the higher the temperature the shorter the hydrocarbon compounds and the lighter the oil. At greater depths still, a flammable gas of hydrocarbons was formed of which the principal constituent is methane, $CH_4$. Oil and gas then percolated upwards, gas rising above oil, both being trapped in the pores of permeable 'reservoir rock', today's oilfields. Another geological feature necessary for the accumulation of oil and gas in appreciable quantities is a dome shaped cap of impermeable rock over the porous reservoir rock. Without this cap, oil and gas eventually find their way to the surface and disperse. After it has been extracted, crude oil is refined into various fractions including diesel, kerosene and petrol.

Because of the very long timescale and the particular geological circumstances required for its formation and accumulation, oil is a limited and relatively scarce commodity, globally speaking: the oil we burn in one year took 100,000 years to make. Geologists now understand the precise conditions under which oil was formed and trapped underground, and have explored the whole world looking for locations where it might be profitable to drill. It is now very unlikely that there are any large undiscovered oilfields, the last significant finds being in the 1970s in Alaska and the North Sea.

Natural gas, besides being found in association with oil, also occurs on its own as a result of similar geological processes to those that created oil, though at a higher temperature. Like the reserves of oil, those of gas are limited, but since it was not tapped as an important source of energy until the 1970s, the reserves should last well into the 21st century.[15]

Of the hydrocarbon fossil fuels, gas has the highest ratio of hydrogen to carbon, while coal has the least, oil being intermediate. Combustion of gas therefore results in the lowest emission of carbon dioxide per unit of heat energy liberated, making gas the preferred fossil fuel for generation of electricity.

There are other fossil fuels which are being considered as eventual replacements for conventional crude oil, these include heavy oil, oil-shale, tar-sands and bitumen. The yield from these sources is small, however, and the extraction processes are very expensive in terms of energy and damage to the environment.[16]

## 3. The End of Oil

The fossil fuels – coal, oil and gas – are currently the primary source of 90% of the world's commercial energy.[17] The continued functioning of industrial economies, and the prospects for economic growth in developing countries, are predicated on an uninterrupted and ever-increasing supply of energy. However, planet Earth's endowment of fossil fuels is finite and, sooner or later, will be exhausted. Each year the quantity of fossil fuels consumed globally represents 3 million years of past production.

Oil is the most convenient of the fossil fuels, being the most compact and the easiest to transport, and it is all but irreplaceable, not only as the principal means of fuelling transport, but as a source of hydrocarbons used in the manufacture of a huge range of chemicals and plastics. But as recounted in *The End of Oil* by Paul Roberts, and *Half Gone* by Jeremy Leggett, the supply of oil is about to run out. Both writers have insider knowledge of the oil industry (Leggett was a geologist working for the oil industry before becoming Chief Scientist at Greenpeace UK), and tell of the deception and misinformation resorted to by the industry to conceal the fact of the impending shortage – an event for which we are almost completely unprepared.[18,19]

The first oil was drilled in 1859, and oil production and consumption have been increasing ever since. In 2000, world production of crude oil was 3.5 billion tonnes (1 billion tonnes = 1,000,000,000 tonnes = 1 gigatonne or 1Gt) and this had increased to 3.9Gt by 2006.[20] Global demand is expected to rise by about 2% per year to reach 5.8Gt by 2025.[21]

Earth's total endowment of recoverable oil is a matter of debate, but the fact of its being limited is generally accepted.

The total amount of oil already extracted is known with reasonable certainty and was put at 124Gt in 2003.[22] The reserves of oil yet to be extracted comprise the oil in fields already known, and that in small fields yet to be discovered. In 2004 the chairman of Shell admitted that the company had over-estimated its reserves in known oilfields by 20%, a practice which is now considered to have been widespread in the industry. A cautious estimate of known reserves is 105Gt, some 40Gt less than previously declared. There is a discrepancy too between the realistic and optimistic estimates of reserves yet to be discovered. The peak of oil discovery was 1965, and the last year in which more oil was discovered than consumed was 1980. Only some 20Gt of oil is thought likely to be extracted from fields yet to be discovered. Thus the total reserves of readily recoverable oil amount to about 125Gt, sufficient for little more than 30 years at present rates of consumption, less if consumption increases as predicted.

As oil becomes increasingly scarce its price will rise, and demand is expected to fall. It is presumed that the same market mechanism will act as an incentive for the development of alternatives to oil. This makes the date when the reserves of oil run out speculative. A date preferable to that of the end of oil, with all its uncertainties, is that for the beginning of the end of oil: the year in which production reaches its all-time maximum, after which it will inexorably decline. This maximum is likely to be a plateau over a number of years rather than a peak in a single year. The least optimistic opinion is that the plateau in production is occurring now, in the years 2005-2010. The most optimistic estimate, by the US Energy (mis)Information Administration, is of peak oil production in 2037, not declining to exhaustion until the end of the century or beyond.[23]

Once production of oil has passed its peak, output will fall, while demand will continue to rise. Leggett writes, in upper case for emphasis:

> THE SHORTFALL BETWEEN CURRENT EX-PECTATION OF OIL SUPPLY AND ACTUAL AVAILABILITY WILL BE SUCH THAT NEI-THER GAS, NOR RENEWABLES, NOR LIQ-UIDS FROM GAS AND COAL, NOR NUCLE-AR – NOR ANY COMBINATION THEREOF – WILL BE ABLE TO PLUG THE GAP IN TIME TO HEAD OFF ECONOMIC TRAUMA AS A RESULT OF THE OIL TOPPING POINT.[24]

The appropriate reaction to this dire prediction is, surely, outrage. Outrage that the industry should conspire to conceal from us the fact of the imminent end of oil, which will have such a devastating effect on all our lives. Take transport, which is almost 100% dependent on the internal combustion engine fuelled by petroleum. Within a few decades the global stock of vehicles, together with the infrastructure of oilwells, refineries and distribution network, will be obsolete and will need to be replaced or adapted for a different fuel. We need as much notice as possible to prepare for this eventuality. As it is, the expansion of oil production and consumption right up to the peak means that the decline in production when it comes will be all the steeper, and all the more disruptive.

The biggest user of oil on Earth is the US (and in the US, the military), whose own plentiful endowment of oil peaked, after a century's exploitation, in 1970.[25] The country was soon importing oil, and in 1980 President Carter declared that America had a strategic interest in the Persian Gulf to ensure continued access to Middle East oil reserves, an interest intensified by subsequent administrations.[26] Notwithstanding this predatory foreign policy, Carter urged greater restraint on domestic consumption, a stance that contributed to his failure to be re-elected for a second term. He was succeeded by Ronald Reagan, an oilman who, amongst other encouragements to consumption and consumerism, froze the legislation on fuel economy of automobiles.[27]

The close association between US government and the oil industry reached its apogee with the administration of G.W Bush.[28] In his second term, he admitted to a serious problem: 'America is addicted to oil, which is often imported from unstable parts of the world. The best way to break this addiction is through technology.' Fuel economy did not feature in the proposals for curing America's addiction, nor was mention made that supplies were failing, nor that climate change was looming.

In talking up future supplies, the oil industry was only doing what big business is supposed to do, but by colluding with industry in opposing all measures to reduce the consumption of fossil fuels, the US government has been shockingly shortsighted and irresponsible. In its self-appointed leadership position as the world's economic and military superpower, it has not only failed to face up to an immense global problem, but it has contributed massively to it. The US government has also failed its own people, who are quite unprepared for the hardships that will follow the end of oil.

Another fitting reaction to the bombshell of the impending end of oil is shame. It is shameful that we should have squandered, in a 200 year binge, an irreplaceable vintage organic product, fermented from the rare harvest of countless summers, and matured in Earth's cellars for millions of years – leaving none for future generations to enjoy. As a bountiful source of hydrocarbon compounds, oil is a raw material much too valuable to be simply burned for its heat, or used for the propulsion of SUVs. What will our great-grandchildren think of us? (Read Michael Moore to find out) [29]

---

## Four Quixotic Things to do About the End of Oil

❖ Resolve never again to fly

❖ Get rid of your car and use your bike for short journeys

❖ Use public transport for longer journeys

❖ Buy locally grown produce – shun air-freighted flowers and apples from across the globe

---

## 4. Climate Change

Climate change is an unintended and unpredicted consequence of the industrial revolution and our use of fossil fuels as an energy source, a practice which releases greenhouse gases into the atmosphere. Another important contribution to greenhouse gas emission is deforestation, which has greatly accelerated in the past 50 years. The most important greenhouse gas (GHG) is carbon dioxide ($CO_2$), whose pre-industrial concentration in the atmosphere was 280 parts per million (ppm); in 2007 it was 383 ppm and rising by 2 ppm per year.[30]

Greenhouse gases are so named because they act like a greenhouse – allowing heat from the sun to enter the atmosphere and warm the Earth, but reducing the loss of heat from Earth into space. About half of all GHG resulting from human activity is absorbed by land and ocean 'sinks' consisting principally of photosynthesising forests and plankton respectively.[31] But this is a slow process, and a large fraction of fossil fuel emissions stays in the air a long time, one-quarter remaining airborne for several centuries.[32]

The greenhouse effect is rapid in that a measurable increase in surface temperature quickly follows a rise in GHG concentration such as we are now experiencing. The effects are all too obvious: heatwaves, droughts, melting glaciers, disappearance of Arctic Sea ice, destruction of ecosystems and loss of species, amongst others. The rise of temperature is hastened by two fast-acting positive feedbacks, involving the atmosphere, and sea ice. Warmer air temperatures over the oceans result in more evaporation, water vapour itself then acting as a greenhouse gas. At the poles, white summer sea ice reflects back the heat from the sun, but as it melts more heat is absorbed by the dark sea, further hastening the melt.

While some consequences of a rise in GHG are quickly seen, it takes centuries for the Earth to reach a higher equilibrium temperature where it is once more in heat balance, radiating as much heat as it absorbs. This thermal inertia is due to the slow warming of the great mass of deep ocean water, and the slow melting of the polar ice caps. Here, too, these processes are hastened and augmented by positive feedbacks. As the ocean warms it gives up dissolved $CO_2$, and in polar regions the disappearance of reflective ice, and the growth of vegetation, increase heat absorption. Should the permafrost of the tundra melt, huge quantities of methane would be released, a GHG 23 times more potent than $CO_2$. At temperatures only a little higher than we are now experiencing, the important $CO_2$ sinks of tropical forests and ocean plankton will die back and become net $CO_2$ producers.

The rise in temperature attributed to anthropogenic global warming amounts to 0.6°C since the beginning of the last century, and there is estimated to be a further 2°C 'in the pipeline' but not yet apparent because of the thermal inertia of the global climate system.[33]

According to the 2007 report of the Intergovernmental Panel on Climate Change (IPCC), global mean temperature changes of up to 2°C above 1990-2000 levels would have widespread adverse repercussions on food supply, infrastructure, health, water resources, coastal and ecosystems.[34]

Temperature increases of 2 to 4°C would result in extensive loss of biodiversity, decreased global agricultural productivity and inevitable melting of glaciers and ice sheets, with a significant rise in sea level.

Increases greater than 4°C would lead to 'major increases in vulnerability, exceeding the adaptive capacity of many systems'. In other words, it would be disastrous. George Monbiot in *Heat: How to Stop the Planet Burning*, draws a parallel with the mass extinction at the end of the Permian period 250 million years ago, when 90% of species disappeared from the fossil record.[35] Volcanic eruptions belched huge quantities of greenhouse gases into the atmosphere, and the temperature rose by 6-8°C. Earth took many thousands of years to recover.

At one time an upper limit of $CO_2$ of 550 ppm, twice the pre-industrial level, was considered to be adequate to limit the damage from global warming. But it is now estimated that such a level would result in a global temperature rise of about 6°C and an almost ice free Earth. Additionally, the global climate system is chaotic: far from equilibrium, as it would be with such an extreme rise of temperature, it is liable to behave unpredictably, producing rapid, extreme and irreversible climate changes against which we would be powerless.[36]

A lower target $CO_2$ level of 450 ppm, if long maintained, would still propel Earth towards an ice-free state, though the rate of climate change might be slower.

Because of its inertia, the climate system has not yet fully responded to the current $CO_2$ concentration of 385 ppm. Yet climate impacts are already occurring that point to the conclusion that today's level is deleterious. Furthermore, the eventual sea level rise for this concentration of $CO_2$ is judged to be at least several metres.

For all these reasons, James Hansen and other climate scientists are now urging an immediate and initial target $CO_2$ level of 350 ppm, 35 ppm *lower* than the current value. This might have to be revised downwards when more information becomes available about the thermal inertia of oceans and ice sheets. A level of 300-325 ppm may be needed to restore sea ice to its area of 25 years ago. Their first recommendation is that the use of coal should be rapidly phased out, and that exploration for new sources of oil and gas should cease forthwith; the bulk of the reserves of all fossil fuels should remain underground and unused for ever. No wonder that the fossil fuel industries have strenuously attempted to deny global warming! Hansen and others conclude that:

> Present policies, with continued construction of coal-fired power plants without $CO_2$ capture, suggest that decision-makers do not appreciate the gravity of the situation. We must begin to move now toward the era beyond fossil fuels. Continued growth of greenhouse gas emissions, for just another decade, practically eliminates the possibility of near-term return of atmospheric composition beneath the tipping level for catastrophic effects.[37]

The first sentence of this quotation is particularly apposite to the UK, where the government has given the go-ahead for a new coal-fired power station without carbon capture, and is planning for a threefold growth in aviation. At the same time, the government has made a commitment to an 80% cut in emissions by 2050; it cannot have it both ways.[38, 39]

*

In 2007, total anthropogenic emissions of carbon were 10 Gt (1 Gt = 1 billion tonnes), 8.5 Gt from fossil fuels, and 1.5 Gt from deforestation.[40] For atmospheric $CO_2$ not to rise above its present level, emissions would have to be cut so as to be no more than the amount absorbed by the land and ocean sinks, equivalent to 4.9 Gt of carbon. Assuming that the emissions from deforestation are unchanged, this would require an immediate 60% reduction in fossil fuel emissions worldwide. But because of global warming already underway, the combined capacity of the sinks will be reduced by one third by the year 2030.[41] To avoid a rise in atmospheric $CO_2$, fossil fuel emissions would then need to be reduced by about 80% compared with 2007 values.

The difficulty in achieving such a drastic reduction in global emissions from fossil fuels is illustrated by the extent of their recent *increase*: by 0.9% per year 1990-1999, and by 3.5% per year 2000-2007, an overall increase of 38% from the Kyoto reference year of 1990.[42]

At the 1997 Climate Convention in Kyoto, a 20% reduction of $CO_2$ emissions from their 1990 base by 2012 was proposed, and an average 5.2% cut was agreed by the signatories. The Convention was eventually ratified by 132 countries, with the US and Australia being the notable exceptions amongst advanced industrial nations. The modest reduction in emissions achieved in fulfilment of the Kyoto protocol will be more than exceeded by the increase in emissions by non-Kyoto countries, particularly the US and China. These countries had increases respectively of 120% and 231% between 1990-2005, compared with -4% for the UK in the same period.[43]

450

The long-term strategy for reduction of GHG emissions is substitution of renewable energy for that derived from fossil fuels. In the short-term there must be stringent economies in the use of fossil fuels, and a switch from coal to gas. Carbon capture, in which emitted carbon dioxide is captured, compressed and stored underground, perhaps in exhausted oil reservoirs, is a technique which is currently in its infancy. It would add considerably to the cost of energy, and millions of plants would have to be constructed worldwide to have any significant impact.[44]

If reduction of emissions to stop the rise of atmospheric $CO_2$ is exceedingly difficult, reducing $CO_2$ to the 1988 level of 350 ppm is impossible at this time. Various techniques of withdrawing $CO_2$ from the atmosphere are being contemplated, including the adoption of agricultural and forestry practices that sequester carbon,[45] but the task of retrieving even a fraction of the 488 billion tonnes of carbon that has been emitted into the atmosphere since the beginning of the industrial revolution would be gargantuan.[46]

---

## Five Quixotic Things to do About Climate Change

❖ Resolve to never again burn coal

❖ Insulate your house and heat it using renewable energy or non-fossil fuels

❖ Wear more clothing indoors and turn down the heat

❖ Reduce your carbon footprint by becoming vegetarian

❖ Reaffirm your resolution not to fly

---

# 5. Environmental Degradation

The problem of environmental degradation may be largely summed up as 'the tragedy of the commons', a phrase coined by an environmentalist, Garrett Hardin.[47] Where there is a natural resource, such as grazing on common land, freely available to all but for which nobody is responsible, it is over-exploited and becomes degraded. It would be in the common interest for every user to exercise restraint, but as long as there is no effective legislation concerning access it is rational for everybody to use as much of the resource as possible before it becomes exhausted.

The tragedy of the commons applies to habitats such as forest, wetland, coral reefs, and the ocean floor, to resources such as oil and gas, to wild foods such as fish and game, and even to such essentials as water and air, not only as basic needs but as repositories for our waste. Only now, at the 11th hour, are we considering restraining our freedom to dump our carbon emissions into the atmosphere.

Various ways in which communities have averted or succumbed to the tragedy of the commons are explored in depth by Jared Diamond in *Collapse: How Societies Choose to Fail or Survive*.[48] This is a wide-ranging account of the dependency of human societies on the environment, and how communities deal with the challenge of minimising their environmental impact and living sustainably.

In a telling parable for our times, Diamond describes the collapse of the isolated Pacific society living on Easter Island, renowned for its gigantic stone statues. Palm trees were fundamental to their fishing and farming way of life, providing material for constructing deep sea fishing rafts, fuel for cooking, heating and cremation, as well as timbers and rope for hauling and erecting the statues. Under pressure of a population which grew to several thousand, and due to rivalry between different groups to erect bigger and better statues, the big palms necessary for survival were felled faster than they were allowed to regenerate, until there were none for making rafts. Forced to turn from the sea to the land for food, the hungry islanders drove all nesting birds to extinction. Chickens were the only remaining source of animal protein, while deforestation led to erosion and loss of soil fertility. The final stages of collapse were marked by conflict and cannibalism. Deprived of access to its main source of food, with no means of escape, and no assistance from outside, the community and its advanced culture were doomed. When first visited by Europeans on Easter day 1722, the island was barren, almost treeless, and home to only a few hundred people supported by subsistence farming.

Jared Diamond describes many other varieties of environmental degradation, ranging from destruction of unique ecosystems and extinction of the species that constitute them, to the world-wide dissemination of harmful chemicals such as the banned insecticide DDT, or phthalates used in plastics, which subtly alter the endocrine system of many animals, and may be responsible for the increasing prevalence of infertility. Here though, there is space to deal with only one example of environmental degradation, though one of the most pressing, and one which illustrates many of the difficulties to be encountered in tackling the others. As on Easter Island, it concerns deforestation, but with global rather than local consequences.

About 10 000 years ago, when humans first started to practice agriculture, forests covered about half of the Earth's land area; the proportion now is about one third, and declining rapidly, especially in tropical regions; the greatest losses are in Africa and monsoon Asia.[49]

Standing forests and their soils represent a huge store of carbon, twice as much as is present in the atmosphere.[50] As a forest grows, more $CO_2$ is captured from the air and stored in the biomass 'sink'. In many cases, almost all of the biomass is above the surface, and the soil beneath is very poor in organic matter. However, some tropical forests, especially in Indonesia, grow on a thick bed of peat which constitutes an even greater store of carbon than the biomass above.

Forests have evolved over thousands of years, and comprise immensely rich and intricate ecosystems which, once destroyed, cannot be reconstructed. About 50% of all living things may be represented there, and it is thought that there are many more species yet to be identified than the number that have already been recognised. About 1.6 billion people also live in and on Earth's forests.

Forest trees draw up water from the earth and release it into the atmosphere from where it will fall as rain, sometimes thousands of miles distant. Five times as much water is pumped into the air from forest trees than is evaporated from an equivalent area of ocean. The energy expended by vegetation in this way results in the forest being much cooler than would be a similarly located area of desert. Falling on forest, rain is trapped by the undergrowth and the root systems, to be recycled by transpiration and evaporation.

Thus, forests, especially in the tropics, provide services of global importance, by being an important carbon dioxide sink and carbon store, and by harnessing and mitigating the heat of the sun, promoting rainfall, and ameliorating the climate. If not over-exploited, forests are also a durable source of timber and other valuable biological produce. But the most important service provided by forests is to act as a reservoir for life itself. The genetic information stored in a living forest, and reflected in its biodiversity, constitutes the cumulative record of 4 billion years of evolutionary history. It is the source of the variations on which natural selection will work to enable a multitude of species from all kingdoms of living organisms to adapt to a changing future environment. It is life's future-proofing. It is priceless.

Forests providing these vital global services are a common good from which we all benefit. But that is not how they are seen by the peoples and governments of countries where the forests grow. Quite reasonably, forests are seen by the owners and those who live in them as a natural asset with which they can do what they like. Pristine forest, freely providing vital global services, brings in no revenue, while there may be substantial immediate gains from its destruction for farming, logging or development.

Slash-and-burn is commonly used to clear the land ready for farming, the ash being used to fertilise the poor soil, which is liable to erosion and is soon leached of nutrients. Poor subsistence farmers may then be forced to move on and make another clearing elsewhere. On a larger scale, extensive rainforest clearances are being made for farming beef, for export to Europe, soya, for feeding to China's chickens and pigs, and palm oil, of which 75% comes from Indonesia. Palm oil is in great demand as a biofuel, even though when grown on cleared peatland its life cycle $CO_2$ emissions are five times as high as for diesel, for which it is a substitute.[51] The governments of some countries endowed with tropical forests are attempting to control forest destruction, but much logging is carried on illegally, there being a lucrative market for tropical hardwood. Population growth, necessitating the expansion of cities and the motorways to connect them, constitutes another destructive force eating into forested areas.

The global impact of deforestation occurring on this massive scale is considerable, it being responsible for 18% of all greenhouse gas (GHG) emissions, second only to those resulting from electricity generation. Because of the use of fire to clear its peat forests, Indonesia is the third biggest GHG emitter after China and the US, with Brazil not far behind.[52]

Interest in the contribution of deforestation to climate change has recently come to the fore because of two reports which identify stopping deforestation as a means of slowing the rise of GHG.[53,54] Such a move would require no new technology, would have an immediate and substantial effect, and, importantly, would be achieved at a lower cost than that of a comparable reduction of emissions from energy efficiency and transport.

Conservation of forest is important not only for limiting GHG, but also for the beneficial effects on climate, soil stability, and the preservation of biodiversity. Globally, the financial value of the services provided by all ecosystems, including those of rainforests, has been estimated at $33 trillion per annum.[55] Although this figure has a wide margin of error, and is somewhat academic, it does illustrate the great importance of preserving natural capital which gives such a high rate of return. Ecosystem services, however, do not feature in any market, and payment for them does not appear in any set of accounts. It is difficult to see how any system of payment for services that hitherto have been free, and which benefit everybody, could be introduced and enforced.

*

Thus, the previously-mentioned problems of over-population, economic growth, the end of oil and climate change, all come together in deforestation, a form of environmental degradation which clearly illustrates the connectedness of the problems we face.

Concerning environmental degradation, a fundamental point is that the generation of wealth derives, not from inaction and preservation of a state of nature, but from working on raw materials which in their natural state are economically valueless. Left alone they do not increase in value except through increasing rarity and the prospect of eventual exploitation. Applied to ecosystems, of which forests are a good example, the problem is that the economic incentives to destroy them are greater than the incentives to conserve them or, often, even to manage them sustainably. When the whole world is the commons, the tragedy is that there is no authority powerful enough to ensure that no country exploits more than its fair share, and that cheats never prosper.

---

## Four Quixotic Things to do About Environmental Degradation

❖ Donate £50 to World Land Trust to preserve an acre of rainforest in perpetuity

❖ Contribute to the Bhopal medical appeal for the victims of the Union Carbide disaster of 1984

❖ Don't buy goods made of tropical hardwood

❖ Buy accredited organic produce. Better still, grow your own

---

# 6. Armed Conflict

Conflict between humans has always existed.[56] A perennial source of strife is competition for resources such as food, or the land on which to grow it, or energy, and the forests, coal or oilfields which supply it. Also, conflicts of interest and differences of opinion and belief are part of the human condition, and they occur between sexes, siblings, generations, in-groups and out-groups and between Us and Them. A relatively new problem, however, is the ready availability of weaponry which greatly increases the deadliness of disputes and the distance over which they may be conducted. Thus a simple disagreement may become a fatal gunfight, and a dispute over resources may now involve weapons of mass destruction.

It is estimated that around the world there are at least 640 million firearms in circulation, one for every ten people on the planet; every year enough bullets are made to kill every man woman and child twice over; one person every minute is killed by armed violence.[57] One of the most successful guns of all time is the AK-47 Kalashnikov rifle, which can fire up to ten bullets every second and may kill at a distance of 1km. With its light weight and ease of operation even a child as young as eight can use it, as they commonly do in such countries as Liberia, Angola and the Democratic Republic of Congo.

Africa, Asia, the Middle East and Latin America spend $22bn on arms every year, money that could otherwise be used to support basic rights such as education and health care.[58] Over 80% of these arms purchases are from the five permanent members of the UN Security Council: the US, UK, France, Russia and China, listed in decreasing order of the value of their arms trade. From 1998 to 2001, the US, the UK, and

France earned more income from arms sales to developing countries than they gave in aid.[59] The UN is 'dedicated...to the maintenance of international peace and security and the solution of economic, social and political problems through international cooperation.' But in pursuing the lucrative arms trade these countries, far from promoting peace and security, contribute substantially to the social and political problems of the world, particularly the developing part of it.

The UK is the second largest arms exporter after the US, and its export trade is supposed to be 'responsible' and 'properly regulated'. Mark Curtis in *Web of Deceit* reveals how, in violation of its own and EU export guidelines, the UK supplies arms to countries known for their abuse of human rights; to countries on both sides of a conflict, thus promoting an arms race; to those that others have embargoed; and even to the very poorest African countries, adding to their debt burden.[60]

In such countries arms may be used arbitrarily and indiscriminately to kill or injure, to threaten people and drive them from their homes, to deny them access to humanitarian aid or education, and to commit gross abuses of international human rights and humanitarian law. In the long term this has the effect of increasing poverty and derailing development.

For several years Amnesty International, International Action Network on Small Arms (IANSA) and Oxfam have been working to establish an international arms trade treaty to limit and control the export of arms, with the aim of reducing armed violence, particularly in the developing world. Exports of arms would be prohibited if they were likely to be used for violations of human rights, would undermine sustainable development, exacerbate armed conflict, contribute to violent crime, or risk being used for terrorist acts. A UN resolution to work towards a legally binding treaty has been approved by

147 countries. The only countries to vote against the resolution were the US and Zimbabwe.[61]

Concerning armed conflict, the US poses a singular problem. With no more than 5% of the world's population, the US accounts for almost 50% of global military expenditure, nearly equal to that of the rest of the world combined. At over $700bn per year, US military expenditure is 350 times the annual disbursement of the UN, to which it owes dues of $846 million.[62] Military expenditure represents 4% of its GDP, the highest proportion of any of the developed countries.[63]

The US achieved its dominant military position in World War II when its industrial might, still recovering from the 30s' recession, was directed to produce war machines; the US government became industry's most important client. At the end of the war the US was dominant not only militarily, but also economically, and the close relationship between government and industry was perpetuated into the subsequent cold war period and beyond. The armaments industry now had a vested interest in war, and could influence the allocation of the military budget by warning of dangerous gaps in the nation's defences. This manipulation of the perception by the public and by politicians of the threats facing the country led President Eisenhower to warn the American people that:

> We must guard against the acquisition of unwarranted influence, whether sought or unsought, by the military-industrial complex. The potential for the disastrous rise of misplaced power exists and will persist.[64]

This warning has not been heeded, and under the last US administration, and especially since 9/11, the influence of the military-industrial complex has mushroomed. There has been a steep rise in US military spending, and a marked increase in weapons exports, justified at home by the provision of jobs and the support of the defence industrial base. Factories producing military equipment are distributed in as many different states as possible in order to maximise political influence. The industry donates thousands of dollars to congressional and presidential campaigns, ensuring that their lobbyists have access to members of the house and senate at the very highest levels. In addition, arms industry executives sit on federal advisory commissions dealing with arms export policy.

In commissioning new weapon systems the government bears the cost of research and development, so that arms manufacturers in effect receive subsidies for their products. In addition, recipient countries may be offered US government loans to enable them to purchase weapons from the US.[65] While free trade and investment agreements with other countries normally prohibit subsidies, government programmes and policies deemed vital for national security are exempted, and US corporations receive large hidden subsidies through defence contracts.

As new weapons become available they are often offered to foreign customers, each overseas sale of new combat equipment then representing a decrease in US military superiority. This decline in relative military strength prompts the defence industry and the military to lobby politicians for higher military spending to procure increasingly sophisticated equipment to counter the weapons shipped overseas. In this way, weapons exports, and new weapons procurement, come to drive each other in a US arms race against itself.[66]

As detailed in a report by the World Policy Institute, the United States' role as the world's leading arms exporting nation has many unintended consequences.

> All too often, US arms transfers end up fuelling conflict, arming human rights abusers, or falling into the

hands of US adversaries. As in the case of recent decisions to provide new F-16 fighter planes to Pakistan, while pledging comparable high-tech military hardware to its rival India, US arms sometimes go to both sides in long brewing conflicts, ratcheting up tensions and giving both sides better firepower with which to threaten each other. Far from serving as a force for security and stability, US weapons sales frequently serve to empower unstable, undemocratic regimes to the detriment of US and global security.[67]

Among the key findings of this report were that since 9/11, of the top 25 recipients of US arms transfers in the developing world, 20 (80%) were either undemocratic regimes or governments with records of major human rights abuses (Israel featured amongst the latter). Thus the US military aid programme in support of the 'war on terror' is detrimental to the image, credibility and security of the United States. It is an example of what the CIA calls 'blowback', where a policy has the opposite result of what is intended, rebounding on its originator. Other examples of blowback include CIA support of the Mujahidin for confronting the Soviet Union in Afghanistan, and support for Saddam Hussein during the Iran-Iraq war. Both operations would later lead to confrontation with the United States.

Arguably, another example of blowback results from the United States' unwavering support for Israel, a policy which is considered by some to be against America's interests, having inflamed Arab and Islamic opinion and jeopardised not only US security but that of much of the rest of the world.[68] Israel has been the largest recipient of US foreign assistance for almost 30 years, and since 1985 has received about $3 billion in military and economic aid each year.[69] On top of regular military aid, Israel has also received supplementary funding for anti-terrorism including the purchase of counter-terrorism

462

equipment. Israel is one of the United States' largest arms importers, and has more F-16 fighter-bomber aircraft than any other country besides the US, possessing 260 of them with another 102 on order from Lockheed Martin.[70]

Since the onset of the War on Terror, the Israeli economy has burgeoned, the result of the military-industrial complex there evolving in a new direction. Since the second intifada and the collapse of the Palestinian peace process, Israel has pursued a policy of enclosure, controlling the movement of Palestinians by means of the Apartheid Wall and numerous checkpoints in order to protect themselves against suicide bombers. After the dotcom collapse, the government encouraged the high-tech industry to move from information and communications into security and surveillance. Thus it was that after 9/11 Israel was perfectly placed to meet the huge demand for homeland security equipment and services, all of which had been battle-tested in their dealings with Palestinians. In addition, Israel had decades of experience of gathering intelligence in the Arab world, expertise which was also now in great demand. In 2006 Israel's exports in counter-terrorism related products and services increased by 15% and were projected to grow by 20% in 2007.[71]

Naomi Klein in *The Shock Doctrine* sees the Israeli experience as an example of what she calls 'disaster capitalism'. Formerly, wars and rumours of wars, or social and political turmoil, resulted in loss of confidence in investments, and a falling stock market. But for free market capitalists, disasters, whether natural, like hurricane Katrina or the tsunami in Southeast Asia, or man-made, like 9/11 or the ongoing Palestinian conflict, offer opportunities for high-yielding investments. Klein records that the Israeli war with Lebanon in 2006 was associated with a rise on the Tel Aviv stock exchange, and that Israel's economy grew by 8% following the election of Hamas.[72]

In Israel…an entire country has turned itself into a fortified gated community, surrounded by locked-out people living in permanently excluded red zones. This is what a society looks like when it has lost its economic incentive for peace and is heavily invested in fighting and profiting from an endless and unwinnable War on Terror. One part looks like Israel; the other part looks like Gaza.[73]

All five permanent members of the UN Security Council have a vested interest in perpetual, global, armed conflict.

---

## Something Quixotic to do About Armed Conflict

❖ Sign up to support the Arms Control Treaty campaign at armscontrol.org

---

## 7. Nuclear Catastrophe

Humans have always been at war with each other, and for most of our long history the root cause of conflict has been population pressure and competition for food. In prehistoric times, warfare with a neighbouring tribe potentially benefited the whole community, and all members participated on an equal footing, as fighters and as victims of fighting. With the development of complex societies warfare came to serve the political and ideological ambitions of its rulers rather than the needs of their subjects, and it was carried out by armies of soldiers rather than the populace. With this development, and with the invention of powerful armaments, there gradually came the conviction that non-combatants should be protected from attack, this view being expressed formally in the Hague Conventions of 1907. In keeping with this enlightened view the Convention specifically prohibited the launching of projectiles or explosives from balloons because it did not discriminate between military and civilian targets. However, the prohibition was only for a trial period of five years, and had conveniently lapsed by the start of the Great War, in which airships were used quite legitimately for this purpose.[77]

In 1937 the German air attack on the Spanish town of Guernica caused widespread condemnation and moral outrage. But in the Second World War, 'strategic' bombing of cities in order to terrorise and demoralise civilians was practised by axis and allied forces alike, as at Coventry and Dresden. The heaviest bombing raids of the war were carried out by the US airforce on Japanese cities, and 180,000 civilians died in a firestorm in Tokyo in a single night; in all, 15 million Japanese civilians were made homeless in the raids.[78] The war with Japan was brought to an end with the dropping of atomic bombs on Hiroshima and Nagasaki, immediately killing 70,000 and 40,000 civilians, with many additional delayed deaths due to exposure to radiation.[79] By this time there was little outrage at the scale of civilian slaughter, which was justified by the claim that the dropping of atom bombs had brought the war to an end, thus saving the lives of many American servicemen who would have been killed if an invasion of Japan had been necessary. *Readers Digest* declared that 'Never in all the long history of human slaughter have lives been lost to greater purpose.' Never in the history of utilitarianism has there been a better example of its deficiency as a moral principle. Hiroshima was a catastrophic moral free fall, and the strategic bombing earlier in the war was the slippery slope leading to it. Slippery slopes are difficult to climb, and whatever moral high ground there may have been previously in the conduct of war, it has never been reclaimed by the US, which has not renounced its policy of strategic bombing of civilian targets; carpet bombing with conventional explosives, cluster bombs, napalm and Agent Orange was extensively used in Vietnam and Cambodia.[80]

Box 23

The Development of Nuclear Weapons

The possibility of a bomb of unprecedented power was conceived by atomic physicists in the 1930s and taken up by the US government in 1942 as a means of winning the war with Germany. Physicists of many nationalities were recruited into the top-secret Manhattan project centred in New Mexico, where the first test bomb was exploded in 1945 just as the war in Europe had come to an end. The first deployment of the new weapons was in Hiroshima and Nagasaki, bringing the war with Japan to a close. The two atomic bombs dropped on Japan, of different designs and using different fuels, were a spectacular vindication of the theory and technology of nuclear physics.

As World War II ended, so the cold war began, and the US became jealous of the military superiority it had by virtue of its possession of nuclear weapons. Although British scientists had been involved in the Manhattan project, the US government decided that nuclear technology would not be shared with its allies, but would be kept secret as a 'sacred trust' for the nation.[74]

The British government, not wanting to be left behind as a world power in an emerging arms race, then embarked on a programme to build its own atomic bomb as quickly as possible. In spite of the dire state of Britain's post-war economy, an expensive nuclear weapons programme was commenced in secret, directed by a committee of the newly elected labour government; it was never discussed in parliament.[75] The project entailed the construction of reactors for the production of plutonium at Windscale in Cumbria. The first announcement to the British people that Britain had become a nuclear power was made by

Churchill shortly before the first bomb was exploded in 1952; Britain's first hydrogen bomb was detonated five years later. In 1956 the queen opened two dual-purpose reactors at Calder Hall at Windscale, 'the first in the world to produce electricity from atomic energy on a full industrial scale.' The public was not told that the electricity was a by-product of the production of plutonium for nuclear weapons.

France, humiliated by its wartime defeat, was also determined to gain a position at the top table by becoming a nuclear power. This ambition was achieved in 1960 with the explosion in the Sahara desert of its first atomic bomb, fuelled by French plutonium. As in Britain, the French atomic weapons programme had been covert until it could no longer be kept secret.

Meanwhile, the detection of fallout from the first Soviet atomic bomb in 1949 increased the fear of the US administration that it might be falling behind in the arms race. Strategic bombing with nuclear weapons had become the cornerstone of military and foreign policy, but while some politicians and atomic scientists were back-pedalling on moral grounds, others were keen to proceed with the development of a hydrogen bomb, a fusion device a thousand times more powerful than the fission bombs dropped on Japan. In 1950 President Truman authorised the making of a hydrogen bomb and the construction of five new nuclear reactors for the production of fissile material.[76]

The pace of the nuclear arms race quickened in 1964 when China exploded its first atom bomb, having previously had a good deal of technical assistance from Russia. There were now five nuclear armed powers, all of whom were also the only permanent members of the UN Security Council and possessing the power of veto.

In the aftermath of World War II, the Geneva Convention of 1949 outlawed the direct targeting of civilians. This treaty now has the status of customary international law, and is thus binding on all countries whether or not they have ratified it.[81] Under international humanitarian law the use of weapons that cause superfluous injury or unnecessary suffering is also prohibited, including dum-dum explosive bullets, booby traps, blinding laser weapons and cluster bombs. Nuclear weapons are not specifically prohibited but their use would breach international law by causing suffering disproportionate to military gain, and also by targeting civilians indiscriminately. Moreover, the upgrading by the nuclear powers of their nuclear weapons, and indeed, their continued possession of them, may be a breach of the Nuclear Non Proliferation Treaty, in which the signatories undertook to negotiate in good faith towards nuclear disarmament. There are other arguments against nuclear warfare: radiation induced genetic damage affecting unborn generations; delayed deaths and malignancies, many involving children; radioactive fallout causing contamination far beyond the theatre of war; nuclear winter following a major exchange. But the heart of the case against nuclear weapons is not that their possession or use violates international law, but rather, it is that wholesale killing of civilians is wrong. A century of escalating military violence has numbed our sensibility to the moral fact that killing people is wrong. Sixty years after Hiroshima, and a century after the indiscriminate slaughter of civilians was declared unacceptable by the Hague Convention, nuclear weapons are still in our possession and have a central role in military strategy: both the US and the UK declared their willingness to use nuclear weapons in the second Iraq war.[82] Hiroshima represented a moral threshold; once passed, there was no turning back. A nuclear catastrophe has already happened, and it has made us morally blind and crippled.

The opportunities to renounce nuclear weapons, immediately after World War II, and at the end of the cold war, were not grasped, and it is now extremely unlikely that they will ever be relinquished since, in addition to the five original countries, nuclear weapons are now also held by Israel, India, Pakistan and possibly North Korea, with other countries such as Iran keen to join the nuclear club.

There are some 27 thousand nuclear warheads in the world, which is fewer than the 50 thousand at the peak of the cold war. But 70 tonnes of plutonium has been accrued by the US and Russia from dismantling their nuclear weapons, and hundreds of tonnes remain in nuclear arsenals.[83] Reprocessing of spent fuel from nuclear reactors has yielded a further stockpile of 200 tonnes of plutonium, which is enough for 40,000 bombs. It is now impossible to ensure that none of the colossal stock of plutonium and uranium-235 is diverted for illicit weapons production by terrorists or rogue states. As the number of weapons in a hair trigger state of readiness increases, together with the number of countries and organisations possessing them, the likelihood of their deployment by accident or by design will increase inexorably. Given sufficient time, likelihood becomes near certainty.

*

When Eisenhower was elected President in 1953 he was embarrassed to discover that, unbeknown to the American public, the US had embarked on a nuclear arms race and had amassed enough weapons and material to annihilate every city in the world. To soften this news he announced an 'Atoms for Peace' initiative in which atomic energy would be used to produce electricity. In Britain also an Atomic Energy Authority was set up to generate electricity which would be 'too cheap to meter'. France, too, embarked on its atomic energy programme, promoted on the grounds of energy independence. In all of the five original nuclear powers, the use of nuclear technology to produce electricity was an afterthought: the primary purpose was to produce weapons of mass destruction. 'Atoms for Peace' was a sweetener to enable the public to swallow the bitter pill that without their knowledge or consent, scientists, politicians and the military had devised a means of bringing about their extinction. Neither was the public informed of the fact that the technology, in the hands of the military-industrial complex, was out of control.

The International Atomic Energy Agency (IAEA) was established in 1957 with the contradictory aims of promoting the peaceful uses of atomic energy, while at the same time acting as the world's inspectorate to verify that nuclear material and plant were not used for military purposes. These objectives are contradictory because nuclear reactors may be used to produce weapons grade nuclear material as well as to generate electricity. The best way to prevent the proliferation of nuclear weapons is to decommission the reactors that produce weapons material, not to construct new ones. Carried away by its 'Atoms for Peace' rhetoric, the IAEA was committed to assist developing countries to acquire nuclear energy which was promoted as the key to future prosperity. It was not a coincidence that this policy was very profitable for US construction companies, which had benefited since the beginning of the Manhattan project by the government's paying the research and development costs of this advanced technology. Developing countries such as India and Bangladesh were beguiled into embarking on prestigious nuclear projects providing energy in excess of their needs, at a time when the energy infrastructure was inadequate, and conventional energy plants would have been much cheaper.[84] Such projects paved the way for the later acquisition of nuclear weapons. To date, the US Department of Energy and the IAEA have involved over 25 countries in a programme which has disseminated nuclear technology, expertise and materials.[89] Apart from au-

470

thorised nuclear technology transfer, there is also a vigorous black market in nuclear material and know-how.[90]

The present precarious situation, where nuclear weapons and the wherewithal to make them abound, was unintended though not unforeseen. Amongst the first nuclear scientists there were some who saw the dangers of an arms race and the proliferation of nuclear weapons. They did what they could to prevent matters coming to the present pass, but their counsel was not heeded.[91] National pride, in bed with the military-industrial complex, spawned the nuclear behemoth which is quite likely to destroy us utterly.

*

Nuclear energy turned out not to be 'too cheap to meter': it has production costs quoted by the industry which appear to make it competitive with fossil fuels. However, the price paid for nuclear power would be very much higher if the industry were not in receipt of huge state subsidies, of which the most obvious is accident indemnity.[92]

Serious accidents involving nuclear reactors are not that un-common: Windscale, Three Mile Island and Chernobyl are no-torious examples. Since the Chernobyl disaster in 1986 there have been 22 major accidents of which 15 involved radiologi-cal release, and two came close to meltdown.[93] After Chernobyl no private company was able to provide insurance cover, and states possessing nuclear installations became obliged to in-demnify them against accidents, this representing a substantial state subsidy. In France, 80% of generated electricity is nucle-ar, and it would be three times more expensive if Electricité de France had to insure itself against the full cost of a meltdown.[94] Also, the cost of decommissioning nuclear reactors at the end of their 50 year life is usually left off the balance sheet, as is the expense of long term management of nuclear waste.

Box 24

Nuclear Energy

Weight for weight, nuclear fission gives millions of times as much energy as burning a fossil fuel, without releasing any greenhouse gases. The nuclear fuels most commonly used are the heavy elements uranium (U) and plutonium (Pu). Splitting the atoms of these elements releases a huge quantity of energy which, if controlled in a nuclear reactor, may be used to drive a steam turbine and generate electricity. Uncontrolled, the explosive power of nuclear fission is highly destructive, as seen at Hiroshima and Nagasaki.

Naturally occurring uranium consists mostly of the U-238 isotope, with a small and variable percentage of U-235; both isotopes are radioactive with half-lives of 704 million and 4.5 billion years respectively. The ore is mined, milled and then enriched, increasing the proportion of U-235. All these processes are highly energy intensive, and use fossil fuels. A concentration of 3% is necessary for the uranium to be used in a nuclear reactor; weapons grade uranium has a U-235 concentration of 50%.

Plutonium is a highly toxic and radioactive element which occurs only in trace amounts in nature, but which may be created in a nuclear reactor fuelled by uranium. One-millionth of a gram of plutonium is a carcinogenic dose, and its half-life is 24,400 years.[85] Part of the Manhattan project was the construction of nuclear reactors specifically for the manufacture of plutonium for nuclear weapons; less than 5kg is sufficient to make a bomb. The bombs dropped at Hiroshima and Nagasaki used uranium and plutonium respectively, requiring different techniques for their detonation; that they both exploded was proof that nuclear theory and technology had been mastered.

While it is true that greenhouse gases are not produced during fission of uranium-235 in a reactor, that process depends on a vast energy-intensive infrastructure which uses fossil fuels and produces large quantities of carbon dioxide and other greenhouse gases. A complete lifecycle analysis of all the processes involved in producing nuclear energy – the construction and later decommissioning of reactors, mining, milling, enrichment and transport of uranium, transport and storage of waste, etc – shows that carbon dioxide production is 20-40% of that of a gas fired power plant. Other powerful greenhouse gases are also released in unknown quantities.[86] The reserves of high grade uranium ore are limited, however, and with the proposed expansion of the industry, lower grade ore would have to be used, with a greater production of greenhouse gases relative to electricity generated. Below a certain grade of ore, more energy is expended in the nuclear lifecycle than is generated from fission of the uranium produced. Thus, for the same production of electricity, less $CO_2$ would be emitted by burning fossil fuels directly in a conventional power plant than by using them to produce uranium to fuel a nuclear plant.

To place nuclear power in its global context, its share of the world energy supply is presently about 2%, which is the most it would mitigate the increase in greenhouse gases if it were free of emissions – which it is not.[87] Globally, production of electricity, which is the only thing nuclear energy is good for, is responsible for only about 15% of all greenhouse gases. Replacing all fossil fuel plants with nuclear, which would require the construction of 75 nuclear reactors each year for 100 years, would have no effect on 85% of emissions.[88]

After Chernobyl, plans for construction of new reactors were cancelled, and it looked as if the nuclear energy industry was finished. But with the recent awareness of climate change there has been a renaissance of the nuclear industry, which is claiming to be part of the solution to global warming since, to quote President Bush, 'Nuclear power plants produce electricity without producing a single pound of air pollution or greenhouse gases.'[95] In the light of the history of nuclear power outlined above, and the warning given by President Eisenhower concerning the influence of the military-industrial complex, one would be naive to accept this claim at face value. It is surely not a coincidence that the UK government has given the go-ahead for a replacement of the Trident nuclear missile defence system at about the same time as the decision was made to build new nuclear reactors. The nuclear energy industry has always been an appendage of the military-industrial complex, whose business is the manufacture of weapons of mass destruction and the systems needed to deliver them. The provision and maintenance of nuclear weapons requires the services of an industry capable of processing nuclear fuels. An industry by-product is heat, which may be used to run steam turbines and generate electricity. The claim that nuclear energy is part of the solution to climate change is pure greenwash intended to camouflage the primary purpose of an immoral industry.

Nuclear fission thus has no part to play in a sustainable solution to our energy crisis. Investment in nuclear energy diverts funds from energy efficiency measures and renewable energy technologies which could bring about a greater reduction of emissions than nuclear, and at an earlier date. Moreover, none of the arguments for not going down the nuclear road have lost their force: supplies of uranium are dwindling; the technology is very dangerous; it is extremely expensive and not commercially viable without government (taxpayer) subsidies; it provides material for nuclear weapons; it is vulnerable to terrorism; and it produces volumes of toxic waste with no satisfactory storage solution.[96],[97] Let's have none of it.

---

## Something Quixotic to do That Might Avert Further Nuclear Disasters

❖ Join CND and support every anti-nuclear campaign you can

---

## 8. Subversion of Democracy

Democracy – government of the people, by the people, for the people – has been subverted by industry and big business. The UK government, in promoting nuclear power as being green, is manipulating public opinion, engineering our consent for this nuclear policy of which the beneficiaries are the industry tycoons and not the people, who, by their taxes, are footing the bill, and with their lives are taking the risk.

The phrase 'engineering of consent' was coined by Edward Bernays, nephew of Sigmund Freud, and known as the 'father of public relations'. In his classic and influential book, *Propaganda* (1928), he wrote that:

> The conscious and intelligent manipulation of the organised habits and opinions of the masses is an important element in democratic society. Those who manipulate this unseen mechanism of society constitute an invisible government which is the true ruling power of our country. We are governed, our minds moulded, our tastes formed, our ideas suggested, largely by men we have never heard of... They govern us by their qualities of natural leadership, their ability to supply

needed ideas and by their key positions in the social structure.[98]

'They' are a ruling elite who, while recognising that government is only possible by virtue of public acquiescence, consider that we, the people, should not be participants in decision making, but merely give our consent. Democracy has been subverted, not only by industry and big business, but also by the elite who govern in the name of the people.

In *Manufacturing Consent* (1988), Edward Herman and Noam Chomsky analyse the mechanisms by which public opinion is fashioned to suit the needs of the elite: by control of the mass media, by patronage of the media by advertisers, by the sourcing of the news broadcast by the media, by its critical monitoring, and by propaganda campaigns.[99]

Amongst the ruling elite who mould our opinions is the media tycoon Rupert Murdoch, who owns newspapers ranging from *The Sun* to *The Times,* and television channels including *BSkyB* and *Fox News.* Murdoch takes a close interest in right wing politics: 'It's *The Sun* wot won it' was the claim made after the surprise election victory of the Tories in 1992; and in the run up to the Iraq war, all of Murdoch's 175 newspapers supported the invasion of Iraq.[100]

Commercial television channels are supported by the corporations that advertise on them, and the production costs of newspapers are similarly subsidised by advertising. The mass media are thus constrained in the content they carry: to be critical of the activities of industry or big business would be to risk the loss of advertising revenue. In addition, the advertisements placed in the media cultivate consumerism by creating in us the demand for industry's products.

476

A third mechanism of controlling what we think is to restrict the number of sources of information to a few which are manageable. In a recent study of four quality papers, 60% of their home news stories were wholly from agencies or from public relations material, and just 12% were generated by reporters. The Press Association, the agency from which most stories originate, simply relays the reports it is given and has no time to check whether or not they are true; many of them are government press releases. On websites reporting news, more than half of all stories emanate from just two agencies, Associated Press and Reuters.[101]

The media are continuously monitored by the elite, and the BBC is particularly vulnerable to pressure from the government because it is dependent on it for its funding, indeed, for its very existence. A notorious episode in the feud between Alistair Campbell, Tony Blair's press secretary, and the BBC, was reporter Andrew Gilligan's apposite but indiscreet use of the term 'sexed-up' to describe the 'dodgy' dossier on Sadam Hussein's weapons of mass destruction. It resulted in his and the Director General's resignation. Once the war in Iraq was underway, criticism by the media of the government's reasons for going to war was restrained for fear of the charge of being disloyal to the troops. The American press in particular has been criticised for its pack mentality and its unwillingness to diverge too sharply from the official White House line.[102]

In these various ways, the information on which we, the people, form our opinions is controlled and manipulated so as to lead us to assent to the policies of the elite. In the case of the Iraq war, this thought control was not entirely effective, but the very occurrence of mass protests against the war was contorted into a justification for the war: the people of Baghdad must be given the same freedom to protest that we enjoy.[103]

*

George Monbiot, in *Captive State: The Corporate Take-over of Britain*, documents the close relationship between corporations and local as well as national government.[104] The book is replete with examples of deals being struck between planners and corporations which are kept secret, but which lead to outcomes which are contrary to the interests and wishes of the people most involved. One of these was construction of the toll bridge to the Isle of Skye, the most expensive crossing in Europe, reaping huge profits for the American bank which financed the deal. Other examples are Private Finance Initiatives (PFI) involving hospitals, prisons and infrastructure projects where the preferences of local people are of no account, and public accountability is denied 'for reasons of commercial confidentiality'. Because of the huge financial clout of corporations such as the supermarket giants Tesco and Asda, their repeated planning applications eventually succeed as the funds of local protest groups, and the energies of their volunteer representatives, are exhausted.

*

The image of itself which the United States likes to project is of a principled and benevolent nation desirous of bringing freedom and democracy to less fortunate countries oppressed by dictatorships or other undemocratic forms of government. The reality is shockingly different, as the following examples show.

In 1944 in Guatemala a popular uprising toppled the military leader, and a reformist party was elected to power with a programme of economic and social reform, including granting the vote to women. Under a land reform programme, extensive tracts of unused United Fruit Company land were expro-

478

priated, but this was portrayed as 'a threat to US interests' by Edward Bernays, author of *Propaganda*, who was conducting public relations on behalf of the multinational company. US Secretary of State, John Foster Dulles, doubling as company lawyer and shareholder, condemned the reforms, and the director of the CIA, who was also a former president of the company, organised an invasion. The land was restored to its previous owners, reforming President Arbenz was overthrown, and two decades of military rule followed.[105]

In Chile, Salvador Allende won the 1970 election, and proceeded with land reform and nationalisation of strategic industries and banks. The traditional elite conspired with the Pentagon, the CIA and multinational corporations to overthrow the government in a coup which was led by General Pinochet; the presidential palace was bombed and President Allende died. Pinochet's military dictatorship lasted until 1988, and at the time of his death in 2006 around 300 criminal charges of human rights abuses were still pending against him.[106]

In 1980 in Nicaragua, after decades of murderous rule by the Samoza dictatorship, the Sandinista National Liberation Front came to power in a popular uprising. Lands and industries were nationalised, and a literacy campaign was implemented together with a policy of political pluralism and respect for individual rights. But in 1981 President Reagan announced his aim of destroying the Sandinistas, and troops supported by the US invaded from Honduras. With funds from illegal arms sales to Iran, Reagan supported covert CIA operations and counter-revolutionary forces known as contras, and later imposed a trade embargo. In 1989 President Bush senior granted $40 million 'humanitarian aid' to the contras, and in elections in the following year the Sandinistas had to accept defeat, attributing it to the state of the economy and the Nicaraguan people's desire for peace after a decade of guerrilla warfare sponsored by the US.[107]

There are many other examples of more or less violent suppression of popular governments which menaced US *economic* interests, but the idea of them being a serious threat to US national security is laughable. Grenada, with a population of 100,000, and famed for its nutmegs, is a case in point, yet it was invaded by 5000 US marines in 1983. Under military supervision a new national government was established which subsequently reached an agreement with the International Monetary Fund which included a wage-freeze and incentives to private enterprise.[108]

Noam Chomsky sums up US policy with respect to the developing world in the title of his book, *Deterring Democracy*.[109] He documents in great detail how popular socialist governments wishing to nationalise their natural resources in order to finance social welfare programmes found themselves up against the economic and military might of the US whose corporations were desirous of exploiting the same resources for themselves. During the cold war the ostensible reason for intervening in the internal affairs of sovereign nations was the fight against communism. This was the pretext for selling perpetual war to the American people, and the justification for the expansion of the military-industrial complex.

After the cold war a different ploy was required, which in the Iraq war was the noble campaign to overthrow the tyrant Saddam Hussein in order to give freedom and democracy to the Iraqi people. But the underlying motivation was the same as ever – to gain control of a strategically important resource (oil), and enable US corporations to invest in the country's infrastructure. An unintended consequence of installing democracy in Iraq was that it empowered the Shiites, closely linked to Iran, a designated 'axis of evil' country. Washington considered rigging the 2005 election result to prevent the Shiites from getting an absolute majority, but it is not certain whether this plan was carried out.[110]

A recent anti-democratic action of the US, which has had very serious consequences, was to refuse to accept the result of the Palestinian elections in 2006, in which Hamas, a designated terrorist organisation, had a large majority in an election judged by EU observers to have been properly run.

Democracy may be the least bad system of government, but it has been hijacked by other interests than those of the people it is supposed to serve. The US, far from promoting democracy, has a long history of using the export of 'freedom and democracy' as a cover for extending its economic empire.

---

**Two Quixotic Things to do to Counter the Subversion of Democracy**

❖ Use your vote, and use it wisely; it's the least you can do

❖ Get engaged in local, national and international politics

---

## 9. Societal Collapse

Society is the sum total of the individuals who comprise it, plus the web of the relationships based on love, friendship, trust, common interests, power and money that unite them. The structures, institutions, networks and relationships that enable humans to fulfil their potential in partnership with others are known as 'social capital'.[111] Societal collapse comes

481

about through depletion of social capital by weakening and destruction of the bonds that link people together. The antithesis of society is an anarchic collection of autonomous individuals intent on satisfying their own interests. Both a strong society and individual autonomy are desirable ends, but they are in some measure in conflict one with the other.

We live in a capitalist democracy, which is also a system with inherent contradictions which threaten social cohesion. Democracy nominally entails equity: at the very least the right of all to vote, and also to be treated equally by the law. In addition, democratic societies aspire to provide equal opportunity for self-fulfilment through education and employment. By contrast, capitalism is about inequity; it presupposes a society which is divided into a relatively small number of capitalists who live off the profits from their investments, and a large number of workers who live off their wages from employment in capitalist enterprises. The interests of the capitalists are considered paramount because if their profits are insufficient there is no investment; if there is no investment there is no employment; without employment the workers, whose principal resource is their capacity to produce goods and services, go hungry.[112] Although there is mutual dependency between workers and capitalists, there is also conflict between them in the matter of wages and profits. There is, too, a marked imbalance in favour of capitalists in the extent of their wealth, information and influence.

Although we all now have a vested interest in the capitalist enterprise – as workers, consumers and investors – the structural inequities inherent in the democratic capitalist system give rise to serious tensions which render the system fragile and liable to sudden collapse. In order for the system to work there needs to be mutual trust between all parties.

Workers need to believe that their employers are not asset stripping but are investing a share of the profits in keeping the company up to date and competitive, so protecting the future of their jobs. The capitalists need to be able to trust their employees to maintain their productivity by keeping to their agreements with the company which employs them. There also needs to be a sense of fairness: that the salaries, bonuses, stock options and other perks of directors and money market traders are not disproportionately high in relation to their responsibilities and performance, or relative to the wages of the workers.

At the time of writing this section, at the beginning of the recession in 2009, none of these conditions for the smooth working of the economy is being met. The public, with good reason, has lost confidence in the banking system, and a number of banks have collapsed. The banks themselves no longer trust each other, so that inter-bank loans of capital have dried up. Lack of capital is causing a slowdown of industry and commerce with multiple job losses. British workers, threatened with unemployment, are suspicious that their employers are using the occasion to bring in foreign workers at cheaper rates. The workers' distrust of management is expressed in wildcat strikes, disrupting production and deterring investment. The assurances of politicians that they are doing all they can to help the victims of the recession are not believed. Meanwhile financial traders are still making millions by short selling on a falling market. Trust has been eaten away.

At the same time there is mounting anger at the unfairness of the system, where CEO pay is a hundred or more times greater than the average wage of full-time workers, and financiers are paid million pound bonuses.[113] Besides widespread tax avoidance by the wealthiest individuals and the largest corporations, there is corruption and malpractice in business and government, with members of the House of Lords accused of being willing to accept bribes to alter legislation, and members of parliament fiddling their expenses.[114-116] The sudden loss of trust, with the fear of unemployment and social unrest, is an indication of the fragility of a society founded on the conflicting principles of democracy and capitalism.

In the capitalist system money breeds money, and without regulation unequal economic growth in different sectors of society is inevitable. The increase in income inequality was steepest in the Thatcher years, but has continued to rise under the Labour government and it is now at an all time high.[117] In the US, income differences are the widest of any of the developed capitalist democracies.

Many studies have shown that inequality is associated with a decline in social relationships, which become less caring and more conflictual. Less egalitarian societies have more violent crime, less trust, less involvement in community life, and more racism, so that the quality of life for all members of society is reduced.[118] Not only is the quality of life diminished by inequality, but also the quantity of life: the expectation of life is shorter and the mortality rate is higher in the less well off, and this seems to be due to relative rather than absolute poverty.[119]

In estimating the stock of social capital, important factors are the level of trust between people, the membership of clubs and civic organisations, the degree of participation in politics, the extent of volunteering and charitable giving, and the amount of informal socialising.[120] On these and other measures the stock of social capital has declined markedly in the last half century, and the percentage of people agreeing that most people can be trusted almost halved between 1959 and 1999.[121]

Symptomatic of loss of trust at an inter-personal level is an incident in which a two year old girl was seen walking along on her own, having left her day-care centre unnoticed.[122] A man seeing her did not intervene for fear of being taken as a child abductor; she fell into a garden pond and drowned. In another incident, a boy fell over in a school playground and was in pain with what was thought to be a broken leg. A young male teacher comforted the boy by putting his arm around him, for which he received a written reprimand. Adults are inhibited from following their natural inclination to help children in need, and conversely, children are taught not to turn to strangers when help is needed. Parents drive their children to school rather than let them walk unaccompanied, for fear that they might be abducted or abused. In this climate of distrust, in which a Criminal Record Bureau vetting is required before a lollipop lady is allowed to help children cross the road, it is increasingly difficult to recruit leaders for scouts and other youth groups. Furthermore, risk aversion has become institutionalised, so that nurses and carehome workers are instructed never to touch a patient except when required for the performance of a clinical task. The fear of scandal overcomes our natural kindness, and much human misery goes uncomforted. We are all the losers from this loss of trust in one another.

The decline in social capital has been attributed to the growth of individualism, defined as the belief that the prime duty of an individual is to make the most of his or her own life, rather than contribute to the good of others.[123] Other factors are changed patterns of working, suburban living, and television, all of which reduce involvement in the communities in which people live.

Jonathon Porritt, citing a UK government review, advocates trying to rebuild social capital for its instrumental value in promoting primarily economic growth, but also educational attainment, reduction of crime and better health.[124] But Richard Wilkinson in *The Impact of Inequality*, argues persuasively that this is to mistake the direction of causality: dysfunction in society is a symptom of poverty, not its cause. The origin of low social capital is due in large measure to inequality and relative poverty.[125] In a consumerist society, where people identify themselves by what they consume rather than by what they do, the consequence of relative poverty is exclusion from the society of consumers, with an adverse impact on psychological and physical health, especially in young people.

The future of society rests with our children, and recent evidence suggests that all is not well with them. In a UNICEF study of the children of 21 OECD countries, the UK had the lowest overall rank for child well-being.[126] This was measured under six different headings: material well-being, health and safety, education, peer and family relationships, behaviours and risks, and young people's own sense of well-being. The UK was in the lowest third under all six headings, and was bottom in the last three. It is no coincidence that the UK and the US shared between them the bottom two places in both overall well-being and relative income poverty.

In order to rebuild social capital relative poverty must be tackled. Of the measures available to government to overcome social exclusion and strengthen society, redistributive taxation is the one that is most readily available; it is also the measure which is most vehemently attacked.

## Five Quixotic Things to do to Help Forestall Societal Collapse

❖ If only for your children's sake, make a commitment to your partner, and keep it

❖ Cherish your neighbours, friends and community

❖ Volunteer – to help children, the elderly, homeless or disabled

❖ Vote for whichever party most favours redistributive taxation

❖ Pay your taxes with pride and pleasure

# Summing Up

This book was commenced in 2004 at the time of the re-election of G.W Bush as President of the United States of America. At that time hope of a better future faded, and never had the problems ahead seemed so intractable. Nobody then could imagine such a turn of events as we have recently witnessed – a slump in the global economy, and the election of President Barack Obama.

The economic recession may give us a little more time to avert catastrophic climate change, as well as providing an opportunity to redress some of the excesses of unregulated capitalism. The election of President Obama has shown that in spite of the many imperfections of the democratic system of government, including its vulnerability to subversion by interests other than the electorate's, it is possible for a person of integrity to rise to the top through the system, bearing the hopes and aspirations not only of Americans, but of the peoples of the world.

But neither one man, nor even one nation, can carry such an enormous burden of hope. It is up to all of us to set our sights on what sort of world we want, and steadfastly work towards that vision, seeking 'grievances to redress, wrongs to right, injuries to amend, abuses to correct, and debts to discharge'. We should not be modest about our efforts, but loudly proclaim what we want to do, and how we mean do it, in the hope that we can be instrumental in bringing about an epidemic of change for a better world. We should strive to become trendsetters and role models. We need to become political, and join with other people in signing petitions and making protests for worthy causes. We must be forever hopeful that something will turn up – but not rely on it, but work to make it more likely to happen. Let's start a New Chapter.

# Notes

## Epilogue, or New Chapter?

1   Robin Lane Fox. *Alexander the Great*. London: The Folio Society, 1997: p137-39.
2   World Wildlife Fund. *Living planet report, 2006*. http://assets.panda.org/downloads/living_planet_report.pdf
3   Optimum Population Trust: http://www.optimumpopulation.org/opt.optimum.html
4   Ibid. http://www.optimumpopulation.org/opt.earth.html
5   International Planned Parenthood Federation: http://www.ippf.org/en/What-we-do/Advocacy/Global+gag+rule.htm
6   John McNeill. *Something New Under the Sun: An Environmental History of the Twentieth Century*. London: Allen Lane, The Penguin Press, 2000: p6-7.
7   'Grossly Distorted Picture.' *The Economist*, 13 March 2008.
8   Jonathon Porritt. *Capitalism as if the World Matters*. London: Earthscan, 2006.
9   Ibid, p226-27.
10  Ibid, p271.
11  'This Terrifying Moment is our One Chance of a New World.' Will Hutton. *The Observer*, 5 October 2008.
12  Jonathon Porritt. *Capitalism as if the World Matters*. London: Earthscan, 2006: p222-39.
13  Ibid, p191-92.
14  Christian Ngô. *L'énergie: Ressources, Technologies et Environnement*. 3ᵉ édition. Paris: Dunod, 2008: p36.
15  Ibid, p33.
16  Ibid, p32-33.
17  Ibid, p38
18  Paul Roberts *The End of Oil: The Decline of the Petroleum Economy and the Rise of a New Energy Order*. London: Bloomsbury, 2004.
19  Jeremy Leggett. *Half Gone: Oil, Gas, Hot Air and the Global Energy Crisis*. London: Portobello Books Ltd, 2005.

20  Christian Ngô. *L'énergie: Ressources, Technologies et Environnement*. 3ᵉ édition. Paris: Dunod, 2008: p25, 29.

21  Jeremy Leggett. *Half Gone: Oil, Gas, Hot Air and the Global Energy Crisis*. London: Portobello Books Ltd, 2005: p21.

22  Ibid, p44-80.

23  Christian Ngô. *L'énergie: Ressources, Technologies et Environnement*. 3ᵉ édition. Paris: Dunod, 2008: p38.

24  Jeremy Leggett. *Half Gone: Oil, Gas, Hot Air and the Global Energy Crisis*. London: Portobello Books Ltd, 2005: p219.

25  Ibid, p54.

26  Ibid, p22.

27  Paul Roberts *The End of Oil: The Decline of the Petroleum Economy and the Rise of a New Energy Order*. London: Bloomsbury, 2004: p219.

28  Michael Moore. *Stupid White Men*. London: Penguin Books, 2002: p16-25.

29  For the answer to this question *see* Michael Moore. *Dude, Where's my Country?* London: Allen Lane, 2003: p86-94.

30  Dr. Pieter Tans, NOAA/ESR
    L www.esrl.noaa.gov/gmd/ccgg/trends

31  Global Carbon Project (2008) Carbon budget and trends 2007. www.globalcarbonproject.org

32  James Hansen, Makiko Sato, Pushker Kharecha, David Beerling, Robert Berner, Valerie Masson-Delmotte, Mark Pagani, Maureen Raymo, Dana L Royer and James C Zachos. Target Atmospheric CO2: Where Should Humanity Aim? http://www.citebase.org/abstract?id=oai:arXiv.org:0804.1126

33  Ibid.

34  Schneider SH, S Semenov, A Patwardhan, I Burton, CHD Magadza, M Oppenheimer, AB Pittock, A Rahman, JB Smith, A Suarez and F Yamin, 2007: *Assessing Key Vulnerabilities and the Risk From Climate Change. Climate Change 2007: Impacts, Adaptation and Vulnerability. Contribution of Working Group II to the Fourth*

*Assessment Report of the Intergovernmental Panel on Climate Change*, ML Parry, OF Canziani, JP Palutikof, P. van der Linden and CE Hanson, Eds, Cambridge University Press, Cambridge, UK, p779-810.

35  George Monbiot. *Heat: How to Stop the Planet Burning*. London: Allen Lane, 2006: p13.
36  James Hansen et al. Op cit.
37  James Hansen et al. Op cit, p17.
38  'Fight the Power'. Joss Garman. *The Guardian* October 8 2007.
39  'The Climate Change Disconnect.' Michael Meacher *The Guardian* October 17 2008.
40  Global Carbon Project (2008) Carbon Budget and Trends 2007. www.globalcarbonproject.org
41  George Monbiot. *Heat: How to Stop the Planet Burning*. London: Allen Lane, 2006: p16.
42  Global Carbon Project (2008) Carbon Budget and Trends 2007. www.globalcarbonproject.org
43  Carbon Dioxide Information Analysis Centre. http://cdiac.ornl.gov/
44  Christian Ngô. *L'énergie: Ressources, Technologies et Environnement*. 3ᵉ édition. Paris: Dunod, 2008: p146-7.
45  Freeman Dyson. 'The Question of Global Warming.' *The New York Review of Books* June 12, 2008.
46  100 Months. Technical note: http://www.neweconomics.org/gen/uploads/sbfxot55p-5k3kd454n14zvyy01082008141045.pdf
47  Hardin G. 'The Tragedy of the Commons'. *Science* 162 (1968): 1243-48.
48  Jared Diamond. *Collapse: How Societies Choose to Fail or Survive*. London: Allen Lane, 2005: p79-119.
49  John McNeill. *Something New Under the Sun: An Environmental History of the Twentieth Century*. London: Allen Lane, 2000: p229.
50  Mitchell, A. W., Secoy, K. and Mardas N. (2007). *Forests First in the Fight Against Climate Change*. Global Canopy Programme. http://www.globalcanopy.org/
51  Ibid.
52  Ibid.

53 Stern N. *The Stern Review on the Economics of Climate Change*. Cambridge University Press, 2006.

54 Enkvist PA, et al. 'A Cost Curve for Greenhouse Gas Reduction.' *McKinsey Quarterly* 2007; No 1.

55 Jonathon Porritt. *Capitalism as if the World Matters*. London: Earthscan, 2006: p131.

56 Steven A LeBlanc with Katherine E Register. *Constant Battles: Why We Fight*. New York: St Martin's Griffin, 2003.

57 Amnesty International: http://www.controlarms.org/en/documents%20and%20files/killer-facts2

58 'Shattered Lives: The Case for Tough International Arms Control'. Amnesty International and Oxfam International, 2003. www.controlarms.org

59 Arms Control Campaign. www.controlarms.org

60 Mark Curtis. *Web of Deceit: Britain's Real Role in the World*. London: Vintage, 2003: p180-206.

61 Arms Control Campaign. http://www.controlarms.org/en

62 UN Finance. http://www.globalpolicy.org/finance/

63 CIA World Factbook. https://www.cia.gov/library/publications/the-world-factbook/fields/2034.html

64 JW Smith. *World's Wasted Wealth II*. Institute for Economic Democracy, 1994: p225.

65 Federation of American Scientists: http://fas.org/asmp/campaigns/subsidy.html

66 'US in Arms Race with Itself.' Council for a Livable World, *Arms Trade Insider* August 9, 2001.

16 A World Policy Institute Special Report. 'US Weapons at War 2005: Promoting Freedom or Fueling Conflict?' http://worldpolicy.org/projects/arms/reports/wawjune2005.html

68 John Mearsheimer, Stephen Walt. 'The Israel Lobby.' *London Review of Books* 23 March 2006.

69 A World Policy Institute Special Report. Ibid. http://www.f-16.net/f-16_users_article7.html

70 Naomi Klein. *The Shock Doctrine: The Rise of Disaster Capitalism*. London: Allen Lane, 2007: p436.

71 Ibid, p440.

72 Ibid, p441.

73 Peter Pringle, James Spigelman. *The Nuclear Barons: The Inside Story of How They Created Our Nuclear Nightmare*. London: Sphere Books Limited, 1983: p42.

74 Ibid, p74.

75 Ibid, p100.

76 Barbara W Tuchman. *The Proud Tower*. London: The Folio Society, 1995: p268.

77 Stan Winer. *Between the Lies: Rise of the Media-military-industrial Complex*. London: Southern Universities Press, 20004: p91.

78 Ibid, p92.

79 Noam Chomsky. *For Reasons of State*. Introduction by Arundhati Roy. New York: The New Press, 2003.

80 Michael Byers. War law: *International Law and Armed Conflict*. London: Atlantic Books, 2005: p116.

81 Ibid, p125.

82 Helen Caldicott. *Nuclear Power is Not the Answer*. New York: The New Press, 2006: p132.

83 Peter Pringle, James Spigelman. *The Nuclear Barons: The Inside Story of How They Created Our Nuclear Nightmare*. London: Sphere Books Limited, 1983: p389-91.

84 Helen Caldicott. *Nuclear Power is Not the Answer*. New York: The New Press, 2006: p133.

85 Jan Willem Storm van Leeuwen. *Nuclear Power – the Energy Balance*. February 2008. Update of *Nuclear Power – the Energy Balance*. Jan Willem Storm van Leeuwen and Philip Smith, August 2005. www.storm-smith.nl/

86 Ibid, Part A.

87 'Nuclear is the New Black'. *New Internationalist* September 2005: p2-6

88 Helen Caldicott. *Nuclear Power is Not the Answer*. New York: The New Press, 2006: p131.

89 Ibid, p158.

90 Niels Bohr for one. Peter Pringle, James Spigelman. *The Nuclear Barons: The Inside Story of How they Created*

*Our Nuclear Nightmare*. London: Sphere Books Limited, 1983: p39-40.

91 Helen Caldicott. *Nuclear Power is Not the Answer*. New York: The New Press, 2006: p19-37.

92 'Nuclear facts'. *New Internationalist* September 2005: p12.

93 Helen Caldicott. *Nuclear Power is Not the Answer*. New York: The New Press, 2006: p32.

94 Ibid, p vii.

95 Frank Barnaby, James Kemp (eds). *Secure Energy? Civil Nuclear Power, Security and Global Warming*. Oxford Research Group, 2007. www.oxfordresearchgroup.org.uk

96 Paul Brown. 'Voodoo Economics and the Doomed Nuclear Renaissance: A Research Paper: www.foe.co.uk/resource/reports/voodoo_economics.pdf

97 Edward Bernays. *Propaganda*. New York: Ig Publishing, 2005: p37.

98 Edward S Herman, Noam Chomsky. *Manufacturing Consent: The Political Economy of the Mass Media*. London: Vintage Books, 1994: p3-35.

99 'Their Master's Voice'. The Guardian, 17 February 2003.

100 Nick Davies. *Flat Earth News: An Award Winning Reporter Exposes Falsehood, Distortion and Propaganda in the Global Media*. London: Vintage Books, 2009: p52-53.

101 Michael Massing. 'Now They Tell Us.' *The New York Review of Books*. 26 February 2004.

102 'Protest has Rattled Number 10 Say March Organisers'. *The Daily Telegraph* 16 Feb 2003.

103 George Monbiot. *Captive State: The Corporate Takeover of Britain*. London: Pan Books, 2000.

104 Instituto del Tercer Mundo. *The World Guide: An Alternative Reference to the Countries of our Planet*. Oxford: New Internationalist Publications Ltd, 2003: p274.

105 Ibid, p177.

106 Ibid, p416-17.

107 Ibid, p270.

108 Noam Chomsky. *Deterring Democracy*. London: Vintage, 1992.

109 Seymour M. Hersh. 'Get Out the Vote: Did Washington Try to Manipulate Iraq's Election?' *The New Yorker* 25 July 2005.

110 Jonathon Porritt. *Capitalism as if the World Matters*. London: Earthscan, 2005: p113.

111 Joshua Cohen, Joel Rogers. *On Democracy: Towards a Transformation of American Society*. London: Penguin Books, 1983: p53.

112 'Unions Attack Executive Pay as Board Pay Soars.' *The Independent* 6 November 2006.

113 'Firms' Secret Tax Avoidance Schemes Cost UK billions'. *The Guardian* 2 February 2009.

114 'BAE Accused of 100m Secret Payments to Seal South Africa Arms Deal.' *The Guardian* 6 September 2008.

115 George Monbiot. 'This Lobbying Scandal Confirms It. The Dying Days of Labour are Upon Us.' *The Guardian* 27 January 2009.

116 Institute for fiscal studies. IFS Commentary C109. *Poverty and Inequality in Britain: 2009*: http://www.ifs.org.uk/comms/c109.pdf

117 Richard Wilkinson. *The Impact of Inequality: How to Make Sick Societies Healthier*. New York: The New Press, 2005: p40-56.

118 Ibid, p101-43.

119 Jonathon Porritt. *Capitalism as if the World Matters*. London: Earthscan, 2005: p154.

120 Richard Layard. *Happiness: Lessons from a New Science*. London: Allen Lane, 2005: p81.

121 Julia Neuberger. 'Unkind, Risk Averse and Untrusting: if This is Today's Society, Can We Change It?' www.jrf.org.uk/sites/jrf/2280.pdf

122 Richard Layard, Judy Dunn. *A Good Childhood: Searching for Values in a Competitive Age*. London: Penguin Books, 2009: p6.

123 Jonathon Porritt. *Capitalism as if the World Matters*. London: Earthscan, 2005: p156-9.

124 Richard Wilkinson. *The Impact of Inequality: How to Make Sick Societies Healthier*. New York: The New Press, 2005: p33-56.
125 UNICEF, *Child Poverty in Perspective: An Overview of Child Well-being in Rich Countries*. Innocenti Report Card 7, 2007. UNICEF Innocenti Research Centre, Florence.

# Index

Cambrian explosion 128-132,152
Campbell, Alistair 477
Camus, Albert 424-6
capitalism 41,352,388,406,407,421,435,436,438,439,463,482,484,487
       evolution of 268-317
       origins 51,284-7,368-73
capital 272,275,277-80,282,289-91,294,296-8,302,308,309,312,483
       social 311,481-2,484-6
       varieties of 282,311,436-7,456,482
Capras' delusion 219
carbon, creation in stars 2
carbon dioxide 58-9,62-3,80,82-3,92-3,155,213,396
       atmospheric concentration of 446,451
       emissions 441,473,
       sinks 63,454
Carroll, Sean 151-2,156,158
catastrophe, cretaceous 101,112,397
categorical imperative 210-16,222,244,245,346
category 45,47,52-4,56,68,183,215
Catherine of Aragon 286,368-70
causation/causality 43-5,47,61,70,98,168-9,176,180,190,197-8,327,339,
340,371,407,414,418,486
       Aristotle on 56-7,61,168,215
cell, nucleated 86,88,94,95,97,112,113,122,151,389
Cervantes, Miguel de 426
chalk 62,80,92
chance 31,111,112,130,269,369,392,426
chaos ii,11,34,84-5,378,381-2,389
Cheney, Dick 345
children 23,43-4,51,142,145,147,149,171,174,175,177,178-9,201,211,
214,221,224,232,236,245,257, 260,268,270,281,284,336,337,338,349,
369,408,417,419,433-4,468
       welfare of 485-87
Chile, coup led by General Pinochet 479
chimpanzee 101,102,104,124,151-3,226,230-2,234
China 351,352,437,450,455,456,458,467
Chomsky, Noam 476,480
Christianity 40,49,54,55,60,414
       institutionalisation of 49,250,332
       role in origin of capitalism 287,368
       millennialism 348,352
chromosome 86,94,96,122,151,155,370

Greek philosophy 6,10,17,43,54,55,266
Grey, Lord Edward 404
Gribbin, John 13,20
Guatemala, invasion of 478
Guernica 465
Gutenberg, Johannes 372-3
Hague Convention 1907 464,468
Haidt, Jonathan 241,242-3,343
Hamas 330,463,481
Hansen, James 449,
happiness i,210,210,241,247,248,311,317,318,337,354,357,419,420,423,
428,438-9
        principal 220-1,222,
        pursuit of 251,258,309-10,428
Hardin, Garrett 452
helium 2,4-5,14
Henry VIII 285-6,368-70,373
Heraclitus 56
heritability 170-1
Herman, Edward 476
Herrnstein, Richard J 175-6
Hick, John 39-40
Hiroshima 405,465,466,468,472
history, end of 332,348,352
Hitler 351
HIV/Aids 339,340
Hobsbawn, Eric 404
Hominidae 101
Homo 101,104
        economicus 316,380
        sapiens i,3,52,77,97,104,108,134,150,153,230,328,385,389,406
Hubble, Edwin 7,11,14,15,17
human nature 61,137,143,145,151,160,167,168,170,172,176,177,180,
182,202,209,217,226,340,350, 398, 427
Human Rights 251,256-7,299,348,431,459,461,462,479
        Universal Declaration of 256,356
Hume, David 36,60,61,168,177,193,210,217-8,220,224
hurricane 16,38,84-5,90,382,463
Hussain, Saddam 344,345,346,353,462,480
hydrogen i,2,4-5,15,78,80,81,440-1
Hymenoptera 138
IAEA International Atomic Energy Agency 470

Midas, King of Gordium 431
Middle East 329-30,334,343-4,352,444,458
Midgley, Mary 127,142
Milgram, Stanley 199-200
military-industrial complex 460,463,470,474,480
Milky Way 3,7,11,16
millennialism 332,332-4
Miller, Geoffrey 107-9
Mill, John Stuart 210,221,244
mind 22,45-6,48,53-7,60-1,65-6,69,70,111,119,159,194-5,197,199,219,
391,393
        embodiment of 47,69,197,327
        evolution of 167,389
        theory of 183,240
mirror neurone 185
Mithen, Steven 43
mitochondria 87-8,113,156
Monbiot, George 306,448,478
monkeys 101,146,184,185,231
morality 41,42,48,65,126,159,177,217,221,223,231-2,232,240,260,268,
279,329,390,415
        as natural law 210-6
        evolution of 203,208-10,225-7,236-8,248-50
        intuitive 240-8
        metaphors for 222
        progress in 250-7,257-60
moral
        family 248-252,258,269,328
        goods 233,256
        judgement 213,223,229,240-3
        perception 237-241
        progress 250-6
        responsibility 200
        sense 208,232,236-8
Morgan, Elaine 102-3,164
Moses 330
Murdoch, Rupert 476
Murray, Charles 175-6
NAFTA North American Free Trade Agreement 298
Nagasaki 405,465,466,472
Nagel, Thomas 184
Napoleon 253,254

unpredictability i,34-35,84,197,281,363,364,374,374-80,381-3,387,388,
399,407,412,448
uranium 121,469,472-3,474
USAID United States' Agency for International Development 295
utilitarianism 220-2,465
utopia 342,348-53,357,425
UN United Nations Organisation 137,256-7,344,356,361,458-60,464
US United States of America 130,294-5,307-9,321,333,342-4,349,406,
443-5,450,456,458-9,460-3,465, 466-7,468-70,478-81,484,486
          antidemocratic activities 462,478-81
Virgin Mary 39,50,55,132
virus 366-7,385
vision 15,39,67,77,106,187,238
Voltaire 16,60
Waal, Frans de 226,230-2,240
walking, upright i,102-3,110-1,113,118,130,144,146,167,171,212-3,269,
389,397
Wallace, Alfred Russel 106,126,167,183,208,209,239
Wallerstein, Immanuel 314
Washington consensus 297
water 78-9,82-3
Watts, Duncan 364
wave function, collapse of 392-3
war 231,234-5,254,283,288,313,432,462,463,480
          American Civil 252,304
          Korean 294
          cold 352,354,469,480
          Iraq 344-7,353,468,477,480
          on terror 341-2,462,463,464
          World War I 291,292,318,399-406,407,465
          World War II 256,293,297,460,465,466-7,468,469
weather 34-5,84,146,190,378-9,380
Weber, Max 41
White, Harry Dexter 294-5
Wilberforce, William 254-5
Wilhelm II, Kaiser 292,401,402
Wilkinson, Richard 310-1,486
Wilson, Edward O 134,136-9,142,145-50,175
WMD weapons of mass destruction 344-5
World Bank 295,297
WTO World Trade Organisation 274,296-9
yeast 83,99,151